Managing My Life: My Autobiography

MANAGING MY LIFE

MY AUTOBIOGRAPHY

ALEX FERGUSON

with Hugh McIlvanney

CORONET BOOKS
Hodder and Stoughton

First published in Great Britain in 1999 by Hodder and Stoughton
First published in paperback in 2000 by Hodder and Stoughton
A division of Hodder Headline PLC

A Coronet Paperback

7 9 10 8

ISBN: 0 340 72856 6

Typeset by Rowland Phototypesetting Ltd,
Bury St Edmunds, Suffolk
Printed and bound in Great Britain by
Clays Ltd, St Ives plc

Hodder and Stoughton Ltd
A division of Hodder Headline PLC
338 Euston Road
London NW1 3BH

Dedication

It is a simple fact that in every phase of your life there are constant reminders of those who have helped you, guided you, loved you. I can thank the Lord for such a happy childhood and can still feel the warmth of my mother and father and the surrounding support of both sides of the family. Basically you are what your parents are; experiences may help to shape personality but the essence of the person is determined by the make-up of the parents and that is very much the case with me.

My brother Martin has travelled the same road as me and, although different in nature, he is nonetheless a product of our parents. No one could have a better brother.

My wife Cathy is the mainstay of our family. It is she who has carried the main burden of bringing up our three sons, Mark, Jason and Darren. This is more than I could have asked for and they have turned out to be fantastic sons and fantastic people. We have all got to thank her for being such a great wife and mother. It has always been Cathy's way to stay in the background, but now it is time for her to accept some limelight. I gratefully acknowledge her role in any success I have had. Without her down-to-earth attitude to life and her unstinting support none of it would have been possible.

1995 is a summer I cannot forget. Cathy and I decided to go to Canada to visit my dad's sister Isobel and her husband Sonny because I had a feeling during a telephone conversation that my Uncle Sonny was failing. Martin and I owe a lot to Sonny; he was a teacher and in our school days he tutored us privately in his own time in the quest to improve us academically, so I could not ignore the opportunity to visit him. During our many conversations I mentioned the possibility of writing my autobiography at some point. I asked him if I could include one of his poems as a mark of respect and he immediately agreed. Sadly he died four months later. Here are three verses from the poem he sent me after my mother Liz died, which celebrate her happy and caring nature and are very special to me.

> Growing up in the thirties was really quite bad
> When money was scarce and most people were sad.
> Yet during those dark days of despair
> Liz still found time to help and to care.
>
> Count all your blessings, Liz used to say
> Add them all up at the end of the day.
> Never mind if you only have one or two
> Remember some people are worse off than you.
>
> I can still see Liz clearly in my mind's eye
> Because fond memories of her will never die.
> It is then I thank God for the things that be
> For having met and known such a person as she.

That same holiday brought the tragic death of our nephew, Stephen, at the early age of nineteen. Even, or perhaps particularly, whilst I am celebrating the successes of 1999, it is difficult not to think back to those earlier times.

Alex Ferguson

CONTENTS

Acknowledgements

Once the decision to go ahead with this book was taken it was simply a matter of getting the best sports journalist of our time to write it – step forward Mr McIlvanney. I asked my good friend Mike Dillon to sound out the great man because I knew how busy he was with *The Sunday Times*. Luckily the response was favourable. That was in January 1998 and over the next three months our trips to Glasgow together brought a flavour of the people who have played a part in my life. In the summer of 1998, Hugh and I continued to meet regularly whilst I started to write in longhand every fact I could remember of my life; this finally amounted to some two hundred and fifty thousand words – quite a bit of work. Then it was Hugh's turn to make some sense of it and, in his words, 'machine gun it'. But, my goodness, he has done a fantastic job; only he has the style to transform all those meanderings and bring such definition and order to the story of my life. Well done, Hugh – you are a genius. All those phone calls at ungodly hours – 'Do you spell McLean with a small "c" and a capital "L" or is "mac"?' It has been a pleasure to witness his professionalism.

Hugh's niece Patricia Murphy also played a key role in the production of this book. Every time a wad of my handwritten accounts was ready, it was sent to Patricia to decipher, type out and send on to Hugh pronto. It is with great thanks that I acknowledge her work on behalf of both of us.

Similarly, I must thank my secretary Lyn, who made sure my

handwritten script reached its destination safely, liaised constantly with the publishers and happily is always just a telephone call away.

I have been fortunate throughout my career at Aberdeen and Manchester United to have had wonderful people working for me – players, office and ground staff. I wish to acknowledge my debt to them.

Others whom I would also like to thank include Roddy Bloomfield, my publisher, and his assistant Nicola Lintern. Roddy met me regularly at the Cliff to offer help and encouragement. He worked closely with Hugh and stage managed the team of specialists (all eleven of them!) who played a significant part in the production of the book. My old friend Glenn Gibbons checked the early Scottish section of the manuscript and my long-time friend and colleague David Meek did the same for the Manchester United section. Others in the team who deserve credit are Alastair Macdonald and Cliff Butler who compiled the statistics, picture researcher Gabrielle Allen, copy editor Marion Paull, map designer Rodney Paull, book designer Bob Vickers, indexer Jill Ford, Hodder and Stoughton production director Sandie Steward and the *Independent* football writer Phil Shaw who read everything through as a final check and raised some most important points.

INTRODUCTION

WHEN he signed a contract in 1998 to produce this book, Alex Ferguson already had a remarkable story to tell. What he had achieved in eight-and-a-half years with Aberdeen and eleven Manchester United had assured him of a place on any list of the most successful managers in the history of British football. Yet there was a danger that the story would lack a natural climax, that it would have to conclude with the ache of one great unfulfilled aspiration. So Ferguson, the hater of loose ends, put that right by leading United through a season of unprecedented triumph. The European Cup that they and he had coveted for so long was brought back to Old Trafford and the Premiership title and the FA Cup were added along the way to complete the kind of treble that would seem outrageous in a dream. It was a pretty fancy way of keeping his promise to do everything possible to ensure that his autobiography was worth publishing.

I became involved with the writing of the book because I knew that Alex's commitment to the project was sure to be unstinting. He had made it clear to me that he felt an obligation to be honest and comprehensive, to avoid the hypocrisy and bland fudges that are often found in an account of a career delivered by somebody who is still at work in it. I knew, too, that his memory was as prodigious as his energy. The combination was to enable him to unload an avalanche of detailed recollections spanning more than fifty years, much of the material set down at breakneck pace in his own hand within whatever gaps he could contrive in a daily schedule that would constitute a tough week for the average work-aholic. It was typical that during the fortnight or so in which the championship was clinched and the two cups were won, he churned out about fifteen thousand words of that stream-of-consciousness testimony, never taking time to break the flow into anything as orthodox as paragraphs.

The riches contained in Alex's tireless scribbling somehow became mountains of typescript at the hands of my wonderful niece, Patricia Murphy. In addition to those heroic endeavours, she devoted many weekends to helping me with the painstaking process of turning Alex's splendidly voluminous notes (two hundred and fifty thousand words can fairly be called voluminous) and the fruits of countless conversations into the finished text. For all of that labour, and the warmth with which it was performed, I am forever in Patricia's debt.

In trying to assist Alex to present himself accurately to the reader, I have been heavily influenced by his dislike of over-simplification. He readily confronts the complexities of his world and other people's and his enthusiasm for language encourages him to reach out for means of expression that allow no truck with over-the-moonery. He prefers thought-out answers to stock responses, and English to jargon. If the odd touch of the lyrical occurs in the following pages, it originated in something Alex said or wrote down. As was to be expected, he was most expansive when dealing with his family and the Clydeside background that shaped his values. For my part, I was delighted to accept that this should not be simply a football book but rather the story of a life in which a great game has been the vehicle for expressing a passionate and fascinating personality.

Amid all the hard work, there has been plenty of fun. For those who know him mainly through television glimpses of him on the touchline, the familiar image of Ferguson is the one created by his addiction to winning: a man whose face is clenched with tension and who appears to be spitting blood. In fact, laughter is never far away when he is around, and there is no better company once relaxation has been earned, especially when his wife Cathy and their three sons are also on the scene. It must be said, however, that it pays to have a pair of spiked shoes handy if he decides to organise one of his notorious quizzes. They brim with so much controversy that they could have made a brawler out of Gandhi.

At every stage of my work on the book, I have received priceless support from many sources. As publisher, Roddy Bloomfield has been a model of kindness, intelligence and, when necessary, tolerance. Roddy's assistant, Nicola Lintern, has been a bright and reassuring presence, and no doubt endeared herself as much to the courier companies as she did to me. Between Nicola and Lyn Laffin, Alex's marvellous secretary at Old Trafford, the delivery organisations were kept busy. It was a further indication of how agreeable working with Hodder and Stoughton was that even discussion of the legal implications of certain passages in the book proved much less fraught than it might have been. Jane Phillips, the distinguished barrister acting as the firm's consultant, was positive, practical and friendly.

Phil Shaw, David Meek and my old punting partner from Glasgow, Glenn Gibbons, rendered invaluable service with some thorough checking. Another stalwart when it came to steering me clear of pitfalls was John Watt, who didn't know when we began out friendship forty years ago that he was going to be so ruthlessly exploited eventually as an archivist. Ken Jones, too, was roped in at times but if you are as knowledgeably immersed in football as the doyen of the *Independent*'s sportswriters is, pals will always make use of you. Both Alex and I are lucky enough to have Mike Dillon as a friend, so there was no escape for him. We have both lost count of the favours Mike has done for us. In my case, much the same could be said of Alex Butler, the Sports Editor of *The Sunday Times*. I could not have asked for a more helpful boss. And in the middle of the whole operation, I had the steadying influence of my agent and friend, Geoffrey Irvine. No wonder my mother regards Geoff as the anchor of my professional existence.

There were occasions when the pressures of doing justice to the Ferguson assignment made me less than a bargain socially and Jae Moore has my warmest thanks for putting up with my glooms.

All the members of my family were, as always, immensely supportive throughout the long period of fevered behaviour that the writing of such a sizeable book was bound to involve for me. Apart from Patricia, there must be special mention of the backing I was given by those two great stars of my team, my son and daughter, Conn and Elizabeth. No father ever had more reason to be thankful than I have.

Nobody, of course, deserves more thanks from me than the new knight himself. He is an unmitigated marvel. If Alex Ferguson had never done anything extraordinary in football, it would still be one of the major privileges of my life to know him.

Hugh McIlvanney

MIRACLE AT THE NOU CAMP

Among all my bright memories of the most dramatic climax ever produced by a European Cup final, there is an equally vivid recollection of a quiet moment a few hours before the Nou Camp exploded into delirium. I was making my way to the team coach at Manchester United's hotel in the coastal resort of Sitges, about to begin the short journey into Barcelona for the biggest night of my professional life, when my son Jason said to me, 'Dad, if you don't win tonight it won't change things. You will still be a great manager and we all love you.' Who could fear anything after hearing words like those? I have been blessed in having a wonderful wife for more than thirty years and Cathy and I could not have had three better sons than Mark, Darren and Jason. It meant a lot to me that Cathy and the boys were in Barcelona, along with my brother and her sister and other close members of our family. I was glad to have so much supportive warmth around me on a day like Wednesday, 26 May 1999, which had as much potential for pain as for celebration.

I had gone to Spain convinced that, in spite of having to field a team seriously weakened by the suspension of Roy Keane and Paul Scholes, we could beat Bayern Munich and take the greatest prize in club football, the trophy United and I coveted above all others. We had just won the English Premiership for the fifth time in the seven years of its existence and had added the FA Cup to set up a glorious and unprecedented treble. But the European Cup had proved so cruelly elusive that I had to steel myself against the possibility of yet another disappointment. In each of the two previous seasons we had seemed good enough to win it, only to have our hopes crushed in the late stages of the tournament by a combination of injury problems and our own lack of the absolute conviction needed to finish off the highest calibre of opponents when we had them at our mercy.

After giving the last of my preparatory team-talks for the 1999 final at lunchtime on the Wednesday, I found myself sitting on the verandah of my hotel room in Sitges, looking out over the sea and wondering if perhaps this was one piece of silver destined to stay forever beyond my reach. If it did, I said to myself, I would still have reason to be satisfied with a career in management that had begun twenty-five years earlier at East Stirlingshire, where I learned when I took over that we didn't have sufficient players to put a team on the park. I had won ten major trophies in Scotland and eleven with United, having taken the European Cup Winners' Cup to both Pittodrie and Old Trafford (I have never included extras like the Charity Shield and the European Super Cup, because they are won with a single victory). Yet I knew I would be branded as falling short of the ultimate standard as a manager if I did not stretch that list to take in the European Cup. This was my eighth bid for it, three with Aberdeen and five with United, and at the age of fifty-seven I could not be presumptuous about my chances of going all the way to the final again.

Watching some of our supporters frolicking around in the hotel pool, there was a part of me that wanted to be as light-hearted as they were. They were relying on the players and my staff and me to deliver happiness to them. But I knew it would be dishonest to envy them their carefree mood. I had always craved the pressure of responsibility, of being asked to make things happen on the football field. All my working life had been a preparation for the challenge that was awaiting Manchester United a few miles away in the magnificent arena of the Nou Camp. My mind was so firmly fixed on what had to be done there that I may have been too brusque with the fans who were crowding the hotel lobby on the Monday before the match. They were mobbing the players and me and, dreading the distracting effects if those scenes continued over the ensuing two days, I enlisted the security people to clear the place. Several of the groups of supporters included children and I felt sorry afterwards about disappointing them. I cherish my affinity with the followers of United – they have made ours the greatest football club in the world – and I can only hope those who were ushered out of that lobby understand that, when I am focused on winning, everything is secondary to the welfare of my players.

When at last the waiting was over and we had travelled to the stadium and were in the dressing-room, I looked, as I always do, for signs of how the players were coping with the demands that were facing them. I found them utterly quiet but it was a healthy silence, the silence of concentrated minds. There was a strong sense of purpose in that room and by then there was little to do but wish them well. Once the game was under way, Bayern played exactly as I thought they would, relying heavily on long balls slung up to their front men, Carsten Jancker and Alex Zickler. What I could not foresee was that one such unsubtle attack would have disastrous consequences for us as early as the sixth minute. When Bayern were awarded a free kick on the edge of our box, they used Markus Babbel to block out Nicky Butt on the end of our defensive wall. Mario Basler side-footed his shot into the corner of the net and we were plunged into the nightmare of chasing the game against opponents who could emphasise their strengths and hide their limitations by applying a policy of unambitious containment. After that blow, it took us fifteen minutes to settle and even when we did our football did not approach the levels of fluency and penetration that had distinguished our best performances during the season. But at least we were the only team with a positive attitude. If we had taken the lead, we would have tried to kill off the opposition. The Germans were concerned with killing the game. With such a barren philosophy, they did not deserve to win but, as the minutes ebbed away, it looked increasingly likely that they would thwart us. I had always intended to bring on Teddy Sheringham and when he replaced Jesper Blomqvist with twenty-four minutes left we began to have more success in opening up the Bayern defence. Of course, the eager pursuit of an equaliser stretched us at times to the point of vulnerability and we might have been buried if the occasional German counter-attacks had brought a second goal for them instead of sending the ball against the woodwork twice. Those escapes apparently strengthened our players' belief that all was not lost and, with Ole Gunnar Solskjaer on as a substitute for Andy Cole, we subjected Bayern to a late pummelling. However, when the stadium clock showed that the full forty-five minutes of the second half had expired, I began to prepare myself to handle defeat with dignity.

The Bayern colours had already been tied on to the Cup in readiness for the presentation to the winners and Lennart Johansson, president of UEFA, was making his way under the stands to perform the ceremony. Then, as the world knows, something almost miraculous occurred. Put starkly, what happened was that two David Beckham corners from the left led to two goals by Teddy Sheringham and Ole Gunnar Solskjaer but, as somebody suggested to me, such a description is about as adequate as saying that the Battle of Hastings was settled on a cut-eye decision. The magical transformation crowded into less than two minutes of stoppage time at the Nou Camp deserves more expansive treatment, and I will try to provide it when the Barcelona experience takes it natural place in the story I am setting out to tell. Surely nowhere in football's past was there ever such an improbable or electrifying finish to one of the great occasions of the game. Bayern, who were totally gone after Sheringham scored and couldn't have hoped to live with us if the match had carried into extra time, were like corpses when the amazing speed of Solskjaer's reactions enabled him to jut out a leg and turn the ball forcefully into the roof of their net. We were like dervishes, and so were our supporters. The European Cup was coming to Old Trafford for the second time, after a gap of thirty-one years, and on what would have been Sir Matt Busby's ninetieth birthday. For me, the result meant arriving at a peak of aspiration that had sometimes seemed unreachable. In the turmoil of celebration, there was a private corner of my mind that was recalling some of the key stages of the climb. I remembered . . . but perhaps I had better begin at the beginning.

derelict yards that came to litter the banks of the river, cannot possibly imagine the clamour and vitality they, and all the engineering works that were crowded supportively around them, brought to the streets of my boyhood. At the end of a shift, those streets would be filled with thousands of hurrying men, nearly all of them wearing the cloth caps they called 'bunnets'. It was an unforgettable sight, that tide of bunnets. I remember waiting at the gates of the yard where my father worked, eager to recognise him among the mass of grimy, heavy-booted figures clattering towards me, or looking from the back window of our tenement on to the main artery of the Govan Road to pick out his distinctive walk so that my mother could put his food on the table. I was never employed in the yards but my younger brother Martin joined Dad there and, like everybody else in the area, I grew up accepting that shipbuilding was part of the fabric of my existence. In a community that relies heavily on a single industry, there is an intensity of shared experience that draws people together and tends to make them appreciate the need to support one another. It has been said that the values great managers like Jock Stein, Sir Matt Busby, Bill Shankly and Bob Paisley brought to their jobs in football were rooted in their mining background. I have no doubt it is true and I am sure, too, that any success I have had in handling men, and especially in creating a culture of loyalty and commitment in teams I have managed, owes much to my upbringing among the working men of Clydeside. Strangers are liable to think our house in Wilmslow is called 'Fairfields' to strike a rustic note in suburban Cheshire. But it was at the Fairfield shipyard that Dad and Martin worked and I had the same reason for choosing the name as I did for registering my first racehorse as Queensland Star, which was a ship my father helped to build. I like plenty of echoes of Govan around me.

I am always slightly baffled by people who are quite happy to lose contact with their roots. Friendships forged in my earliest days remain as strong as ever for me. Two of my closest pals, Duncan Petersen and Jim McMillan, were with me in the local nursery when we were four. Duncan remembers being in the bed next to me when we were put down for a wee sleep in the afternoons. All three of us are still in regular touch with other mates, including Tommy Hendry, who played with us in Life Boys football. Tommy ranks as a latecomer because we didn't know him until he was five and a half. It seems natural to us that connections made back then have lasted more than fifty years.

Most of my childhood memories are centred on the tenement we lived in. The address was 667 Govan Road, which meant it was on the corner with Neptune Street, a more than lively thoroughfare sometimes known, for obvious reasons, as the Irish Channel. Neptune Street was one of many reminders of how much of a magnet Glasgow had been for Irish people who crossed the water in search of work, and the Protestant–Catholic mix produced by that immigration was as volatile in Govan as anywhere else. But a glance at my family tree suggests why bigotry never had a chance of spreading its pollution among the Fergusons. Through all its branches, and for as far back as we can trace, there have been mixed marriages. That is a common pattern in the West of Scotland. Perhaps it doesn't always breed religious intolerance out of the later generations but it certainly did so in our case. I am a Protestant married to a Catholic and my father's circumstances were exactly the same, whereas his father was a Catholic married to a Protestant. The children of all three marriages were raised as Protestants but with a natural abhorrence of sectarian bitterness. My brother Martin and I grew up as passionate Rangers fans and Dad had no problem with that, although (typically scorning the obvious religious affiliations) he was a Celtic supporter. But Dad was so against the provocative flaunting of club colours that Martin had to hide his Rangers scarf behind the lavatory cistern. Since my mother's Catholic faith was strong and my father never held any serious religious convictions, it is interesting that they chose to baptise their two sons Protestant (in my case at St Mary's Church, near Govan Cross). No doubt the decision was related to their concern about our prospects when we reached working age. In those days it was standard for anyone applying for a job in our part of the world to be asked: 'What school did you go to?' If the answer was a Catholic school, the chances of being hired were instantly diminished, often obliterated. That kind of prejudice was especially prevalent in shipbuilding until the last two decades of its existence on the Clyde.

My Catholic Grandfather Ferguson, who was employed in building boats rather than ships, and in Dunbartonshire rather than Glasgow, was presumably spared the worst effects of discrimination. He was certainly no stranger to religious tension. In marrying my granny, Janet (Jenny) Beaton, he gained a father-in-law who was not only a staunch Protestant but so deeply involved in Freemasonry that he was a Provincial Grand Master. Old Beaton, who was a formidable character, was apparently placated by the fact that the couple had a Church of Scotland wedding and brought up their children, my father and his brother John and sister Isobel, in that faith. But trouble erupted when my granny discovered that on the quiet Grandad Ferguson had been taking my dad, who was then about four, to the Catholic church. She put a stop to that and from then on it was Church of Scotland and only Church of Scotland. The truth is, however, that in later life my father had little time for religion in any shape or form and found expression for his strong sense of principle in a devotion to humanitarian socialism. His independence showed when Great-grandad Beaton died and made him a bequest of his Masonic regalia. For moral reasons, Dad refused to accept it or to become a Freemason and the Past Master's apron passed to my Uncle John. I have always been proud of that demonstration of integrity.

My father, Alexander Beaton Ferguson, was born in Renton, Dunbartonshire, in 1912. After his father was gassed in the First World War and invalided out of the army to a temporary hospital in Bellahouston Park, near Ibrox, the family moved to Glasgow to be closer to my dying grandad. They settled in Hamiltonhill, on the borders of the Maryhill and Possilpark districts of the city, and at fourteen Dad left school to help support his mother and younger brother and sister by working in various factories. My granny often told me of his bravery when he almost lost an arm that was caught in a machine. His left wrist was a terrible mess of scars and his right thumb had been removed by another factory accident, all of which meant that he was unfit for service when the Second World War came around.

The passion for football he developed in his teens made him instrumental in persuading Glasgow City Council to provide a social club for youngsters growing up on the north side of Glasgow where he lived, and later Hamiltonhill won the Scottish Boys' Club Cup. Their left-winger, Jimmy Caskie, went on to considerable fame with Rangers and Scotland. Dad spoke proudly of those days. His own football career reached its high point in Belfast when he played for Glentoran alongside the man he said was the finest player he ever saw, the great Peter Doherty. By that time Grandad Ferguson had died, my granny had remarried a man named Johnny Miller and the family had moved to Northern Ireland, where Dad worked in the Harland and Wolff shipyard. By his mid-twenties he was back on the mainland, with a job in the BSA factory in Birmingham, and soon afterwards the entire Miller household was re-established in Scotland.

Their council house was at 357 Shieldhall Road in Drumoyne, which is really an extension of Govan. That is a particularly important address for me. I was born there. But first, to state the obvious, my father and mother had to meet. Dad's sister, my Aunt Isobel, was employed in a factory known as Christies' Wire Works in Broomloan Road, just round the corner from Ibrox Park. The premises have since been renamed Ferguson House and accommodate a job-creation programme run by Govan Initiative. They served as a marriage agency in 1940 when two attractive workmates, Aunt Isobel and her best friend Elizabeth Hardie, were discussing the opposite sex and Isobel suggested that Lizzie should meet her 'big, handsome brother'. Dad was ten years older than the teenaged Lizzie but they fell for each other and were soon married. Just how soon had always been shrouded in vagueness but, being an inquisitive bugger, I was determined to find out the details. So on a recent visit to Aunt Isobel's home in Oshawa, Canada, I confronted her about the circumstances of the marriage

and got a decidedly shirty response. She was in no mood to tolerate any slights on her big brother, even from his son. 'Your Dad
was a great man,' was her simple declaration. My willingness to
agree with that claim was unlikely to be lessened by learning
that Mum had become pregnant while they were courting. They
married in June 1941, and I arrived on the last day of December.
Being born on that date might seem a wonderful privilege for a
Scot, considering how much celebratory enthusiasm the nation
brings to Hogmanay, but, when I was a boy, it struck me as rotten
luck. Its proximity to Christmas meant that the same present
could cover the two occasions. Eleven months and twenty-one
days after my arrival, our family was completed by the birth of
Martin, so he was no better off than I was as far as presents were
concerned. To be truthful, with the parents we had, neither of us
was in danger of going short.

Our first home was in Broomloan Road but before long we
were in the tenement two-bedrooms-and-kitchen at 667 Govan
Road and it was there that all the upbringing I remember took
place. We were very fortunate to have an inside toilet. Most resi-
dents of the Govan tenements had to share lavatories located in
the stairwells of the buildings, an arrangement that would, for a
start, have made it difficult for Martin to hide his Rangers scarf.
Our facilities did not stretch to a bath, other than the big zinc
one which was kept under the recess bed in the kitchen (where
Mum and Dad slept). The term applied to that room may be
misleading. In fact, it doubled as kitchen and living-room and
was the hub of family life, as in most Glasgow homes. We had
the original fire range, where a lot of the cooking was done, and
a bunker for storing coal. Space was tight but there seemed to be
enough for everything we needed. Martin and I shared a bedroom
looking on to the Govan Road and, between the rattle of the
tramcars and the hammering in the nearby Harland and Wolff
shipyard, sleeping at night was seldom easy. There is a story in
our family that the Fergusons once owned the land occupied by
Harland and Wolff but all I know for sure is that their activities
gave my eardrums some serious abuse. When we were kids, the

other bedroom was rented out to an Irish couple, Frank and Madge McKeever, and they stayed with us for a number of years until they got their own house.

The average tenement was three storeys high and once you went through the entrance passageway, known as a close, you found three, and very occasionally four, flats on each landing. Our building housed the usual total of nine families and some of the numbers crowded into those small apartments were astonishing. Among our neighbours, the Law family had about sixteen living in a kitchen and one bedroom. When one of the sons, Joe, came home from fighting with the army in Korea, the entire clan turned out at the street corner to welcome him. With grannies, aunties, uncles, nephews, cousins and the rest, they must have numbered nearly a hundred. If the North Koreans had realised how much backing he had, they might have packed in early.

Govan in those days was a vibrant place, with a population which, by the end of the Second World War, had risen well beyond 100,000. In addition to Fairfield and Harland and Wolff, there was the third great shipbuilding company of Alexander Stephen and Sons to provide employment. There were also many jobs to be had at the huge dry dock, where major ship repairs were carried out. To me as a child, life around the tenements had all the buzz and variety conveyed in films showing streets in the poorer areas of New York earlier this century (like 'Godfather II'). On Saturday mornings, our neighbourhood was alive with noise and movement as organ grinders, fruit sellers, backcourt singers and bookies' runners competed for whatever few shillings people had to spare. There would be a beer delivery at the pub directly beneath our first-floor flat, Dick Welsh's, and Martin and I would watch in fascination as the barrels were dumped off the lorries on to a sawdust sack and rolled down a hatch into the cellars. The coal merchant, Fletcher, could be heard streets away as he advertised his prices. He had a horse-drawn cart and that poor animal had to put up with all sorts of pranks while old Fletcher was lugging sacks of coal up the tenement stairs. Maybe I was easily enthralled, but at times I felt I was in the midst of a carnival.

Nobody could say it was the gentlest environment. My first school, Broomloan Road Primary, was not noted for blazers and badges. Elizabeth Thomson – a teacher there who earned my lifelong gratitude and with whom I keep in touch through regular correspondence and occasional meetings – says that when she took up her appointment it was rated the worst school in Glasgow, with the highest ratio of boys on probation. Nor were the adults in the area consistently law-abiding. One of the last men to be hanged in Scotland was convicted of a stabbing murder committed in Neptune Street and the victim was the uncle of a lad who played football with me at Harmony Row Boys' Club. But there was never a shadow of menace over my boyhood. I was relaxed and generally carefree, although straying out of my own immediate locality had its risks unless I was visiting friends. Dunky Petersen, Jim McMillan and Tommy Hendry lived only about 300 yards from me, nearer to Ibrox Park, but I might not have ventured up there if I hadn't been going to see them. Before emigrating to Canada, Aunt Isobel and Uncle Sonny were in a really tough quarter called Wanlock Street. Once, when my cousin Christopher, who suffered from polio, was being systematically bullied by a couple of lads, my auntie called me in to deal with them. I did the necessary but you can be sure I didn't hang around in Wanlock Street.

Being able to take care of yourself, refusing to stand for liberties, was obligatory. One Saturday when I was about ten or eleven, and no doubt should have been engaged in more childish pursuits, I looked in on Docherty's snooker hall in Broomloan Road. I thought my luck was in when a pair of youths in their late teens offered me a drink from a limeade bottle. After taking an eager swig, I almost vomited. The green liquid I was spitting and spluttering out of my mouth was urine. As the jokers dissolved in laughter, I went off to plot revenge. I seem to have been concerned with forward planning even then and my first priority was to find a piece of wood that would fit neatly into the loops of metal that formed the outside handles on the snooker hall door. Having set that aside, I went back in and unobtrusively picked up two balls from an unoccupied table. I waited until my tormentors were on the far side of their table before firing my missiles at them with all the violence I could muster. I scored two hits, catching one of the targets somewhere around the jaw. Then I darted outside, jammed the door shut with the wood and made my escape. Weeks later I was walking along the Govan Road when I saw the character I had hit on the jaw. He was with his girlfriend and he had a huge sticking plaster on the side of his face. I dived into a close in case he recognised me. Maybe he learned to think twice about taking the piss out of, or putting it into, wee boys.

There were no repercussions for me from that escapade but another that occurred shortly afterwards came back to haunt me at later stages of my life. The initial incident was simply one of those little playground scraps, of which I had my share. I had much the better of the skirmish but as the years went by I was unlikely to mention that juvenile victory, since the loser became one of the most notorious hard-men in Govan, somebody whose adult reputation was enough to loosen the bowels of an ordinary citizen like me. Willie Bennett, nicknamed 'The Devil' and once described in a courtroom as having 'taken men's faces off for a few pounds', died as violently as he lived. My first post-schooldays encounter with him came while I was playing for St Johnstone. I was on my way to training at Petershill Juniors' ground when he suddenly shouted at me from the doorway of a newsagent's shop at Govan Cross. It was a summons.

'Hey you! Ferguson!'

He was with his younger brother, Malky, who was another you wouldn't regard as the ideal companion for a cocktail of an evening, and the group was completed by a well-known tearaway from Partick. Rapidly realising that my insides weren't to be trusted, I tried to give Willie the hail-fellow-well-met treatment but he wasn't listening.

'I hear you're playing for St Johnstone,' he growled at me. 'Well, I want a game.'

There was no question of, 'Can you get me a trial?' His next line was: 'Fucking get me a game.' Blathering some nonsense about talking to the manager that night, I managed to extricate myself and was at full gallop by the time I had turned the corner.

Fortunately, he did not follow up on his demand to turn out for St Johnstone and the next time our paths crossed was more than twenty years on, in the early Eighties, when I was manager of Aberdeen. I had agreed to a request from the Governor of Peterhead Prison to conduct a quiz for the inmates. It was one of those horribly cold, dirty nights when Peterhead is at its bleakest, and that is saying something. When the Governor told me on my arrival that he had been plagued by a problem all day I knew it had nothing to do with escapees. Anybody who had escaped in that weather into the surrounding desolation would have pleaded to get back into his cell. The actual nature of the Governor's problem shook me slightly.

'I've had one of your old pals from school giving me all sorts of trouble,' he said.

Then he explained that Willie Bennett had been an absolute pest, thrusting himself forward as some kind of advance publicist for the quiz.

'He's been telling everybody what a great guy you are and he says he's your best pal.' As it happens, The Devil had not been a fellow pupil at Broomloan Road Primary. He attended another Govan school (one which, in spite of what Elizabeth Thomson says, was probably worse) but he and his schoolmates sometimes used our facilities. However, it was healthier to have him claiming me as a pal than recalling the distant day when I gave him a doing.

The Governor had arranged to hold the quiz in a large room that I imagine was a dining hall and it had been filled with rows of folding chairs. Some time before we were due to start, he called me over to look through a little window into the room and there, in that otherwise empty expanse of seating, was Willie Bennett. He was planted in the middle of the front row, with his arms folded and a concentrated expression on his face. There wasn't another soul in the hall. I'm sure by then he had gone doolally, a bit stir-crazy. When the other prisoners had assembled, I walked in to start the proceedings and I greeted him straightaway.

'Hi, Willie.' He was on his feet immediately.

'Alex!' he shouted. 'Tell them! You're my mate, aren't you? We were at school together in Govan. Tell them!'

'Aye,' I said. 'And, by the way, he played for Glasgow Schoolboys.'

It was true and the mention of it had him preening like a peacock. There was no danger that he was going to be nasty but he went the other way and started acting like the master of ceremonies, running the show: 'Hey, hey, out of order there! Just shut up now. One question per questioner.' The prison staff were happy to let him carry on. Normally he didn't give them a moment's peace. Probably that day at the quiz was about as happy as Bennett was likely to be in what was left of his life. His murderous ways had caused him to spend most of his adult years in prison and he was no sooner out, at the age of fifty, than he was fatally stabbed in a brawl outside a Govan pub in 1991.

Many of the boys from Govan who were brought up with me ended up in jail or took to drink. The temptation to slide into that dead-end existence was all around us but most families had a working-class ethic founded on the parents' determination to give their kids a chance. A majority of my friends responded to the encouragement they were given but, inevitably, there were others who did not have the strength to resist the influences that were always threatening to drag them down. And, of course, if the parents were weak, the children had little hope of making a success of themselves. Elizabeth Thomson says she could read sad stories of a troubled home life in the condition of pupils turning up for her class. Nobody could have had a better home than I had. Martin and I were never without the precious reassurance that came from knowing our mother and father invariably put our interests ahead of theirs, that they felt nothing was too good for us. We benefited, too, from the support that flowed in from the wider reaches of the family on both sides.

Unlike Dad, Ma came from a background with no religious complications. Her people were a hundred per cent Irish Catholic. Her mother, Susie Mansell, was born in Newry, Northen Ireland,

and when Susie married Thomas Hardie it meant the merging of two large Catholic families. For some reason, Grandad Hardie went missing and later my granny remarried, a man called Sam Irwin, but the Hardies have remained a strong presence in my life and they have always shown a protective interest in my progress. My mother loved singing and dancing and was a superb birler on the floor. She and my dad's sister Isobel went dancing two or three nights a week in their teens, often returning jam jars to secure the admission money. That recreation was curtailed when I arrived but she took it up again once I was toddling. She had a marvellous spirit and a deep, quiet courage.

There was an unmistakable strength about my father. Aunt Isobel was justified in orginally describing him to my mother as 'big', if only because, at about five-ten, he was taller than most Scots of his generation. He could certainly be imposing, especially when his features were set in a characteristically stubborn expression under his full head of dark hair. He was the opposite of extrovert, and one of my persistent memories is of him sitting by the fire for hours, silently reading, but when his temper blew it could be like a volcano. I usually contrived to be out of the way of the consequences, leaving Martin, who had a much more lackadaisical disposition, to take the brunt of Dad's anger. At the first sign of danger, I would be under the recess bed, hiding behind the zinc bath, keeking out at Martin taking the licks. The fact that I had probably instigated the mischief that caused the outburst was neither here nor there. If I needed to take refuge outside the house, such as when we were caught smoking cinnamon sticks in the backcourt, I sprinted round to Granny Irwin's. I was her favourite and she wouldn't let Dad lay a finger on me. One of the worst scrapes ever produced by Martin's doziness was the result of our secret decision to ignore Dad's warning that we must stay away from Rangers–Celtic matches. When bottle-throwing violence broke out at a game we attended in the early fifties, I wasted no time in getting over the boundary wall and on to the park. Martin hung around dreamily and next day there was a photograph on the front page of the *Sunday Express* showing him standing there with the bottles flying over his head. His face was circled in the picture and the words referred to 'the boy who stayed behind'. Dad made breakfast for everybody on a Sunday morning and when he brought ours into the bedroom that day he had the *Sunday Express* in his other hand. Martin was almost wishing one of those bottles had hit him. When Dad turned on me, I lied through my teeth. 'I was playing football,' I assured him. Fortunately, he just about believed me.

Though there was less than a year between Martin and me, I was much the more active and dominant brother and, to be honest, I was not above bullying him. I would have died rather than let any outsider hurt him but, as boys do, I felt seniority gave me a right to give him a hard time. My mother used to warn me that at some point he would turn and make me pay but I laughed at the thought. That was a mistake, as I discovered when at last I pushed him too far. There was usually a poker thrust into our grate, to let air into the burning coals, and in his rage Martin pulled that red-hot poker out and hit me across the left thigh with it. I still have the livid scar that was left after I was treated at the Southern General Hospital.

As a boy, I had the feeling that I was never out of the Southern General. I had two hernia operations, then I was in with a kidney problem diagnosed when I started peeing blood. The odd accident added to the list, such as the gash to my arm that was the reward for trying to break through the glass-and-mesh window of the school gym to 'borrow' a ball for a game of football. Absences from class for medical reasons took their toll of my studies and contributed to the horrible disappointment of failing the qualifying examination I had to pass to move from Broomloan Road to Govan High School. At that stage Elizabeth Thomson, after a plea from my parents, took a personal interest in my case and became a heroine of my childhood. She was a stunningly attractive young woman and, like nearly all my schoolmates, I had a crush on her. On her wedding day, Martin and I rode a ferry across the Clyde and hiked further miles to Hillhead, in the west end of Glasgow, so that we could be on the steps of the church to greet her as she emerged after the ceremony. There is a photograph of the scene, with us looking like urchins in the little jerseys that were our standard schoolwear.

Elizabeth did a tremendous job of helping me to do myself justice at primary school and my continuing friendship with her is a wonderful, warming legacy of my childhood. When I passed the 'qually' (our version of the eleven-plus) it was with excellent marks that put me in the top stream at Govan High. But I arrived there a year later than I should have done, and then had to wait six months for the start of an academic year before I could be properly settled in a class. That meant I was thirteen and a half, and being pitched into a much younger group had a traumatic effect on me. The embarrassment I felt, especially in relation to the girls, was so deep that I never overcame it and the rest of my time at school was torture, at least as far as the lessons were concerned. My confidence took a hammering to an extent that I experienced in only one other phase of my life, when my spell as a player with Rangers ended in rejection. Both periods were so miserable that they might have done me permanent damage. Ultimately I was able to use those bad times to fuel the drive that carried me forward in later years but that didn't seem likely while I was going through them. Sometimes the feeling of vulnerability I had then can come back to remind me that nobody is ever totally safe from the demons of insecurity. But I have learned a lot in my fifty-seven years about how to beat them down. At Govan High the positive attitude I had always shown previously gave way to a fear of failure. I was among high-achievers and the depressing fact that they were all nearly a couple of years younger than I was discouraged me from channelling my energies into trying to keep up with them. The course was demanding, with French and German added to the usual subjects, and I took the easy way out by cribbing from a few of my brightest classmates. Some were glad to assist because, in contrast to the sense of inferiority I had as a student, I was a minor hero to them as a result of my involvement with Govan High's successful football teams. Football was my constant consolation in that period but I recognise that its influence was probably double-edged. If I had not been able to escape into the reassuring world available to me on the park, I might have been forced to cope better in the classroom. Obviously, any benefit I gained from copying other people's work was purely cosmetic and the inadequacy of my own efforts was bound to be exposed in exams. At the age of sixteen, when I should have been preparing to sit for my Higher Leaving Certificate (the equivalent of A-levels), the headmaster told me something I already knew – that I had not performed solidly enough in the preceding four years to give me a realistic chance of doing well. The sensible alternative was to leave school and begin an apprenticeship in a skilled trade. My parents must have been disappointed but they were as supportive as ever, and there were no recriminations. The trade I was to enter was toolmaking but privately I was convinced that my future would be in football. It had dominated my dreams for as long as I could remember.

My first taste of it in an organised form came when one of the neighbours, Mr Boyd, took it upon himself to turn out a team from our block of tenements, which included about four closes. Rather grandly, he called the team Govan Rovers and opted for the Arsenal strip. There were two obstacles to my participation: firstly, I was seven and the Rovers were in an Under-12 league and, secondly, I had no football boots. I was precocious, so age was less of a problem than footwear and when another neighbour, Tommy Gemmell, earned my undying gratitude by presenting me with a pair of hand-me-down boots, I graduated from mascot to player. My biggest disappointment in those days was that Broomloan Road Primary did not have a teacher willing to take charge of a football team. We boys compensated by arranging friendly matches with nearby schools, St Saviour's and Copeland Road. The Catholic St Saviour's were making a habit of winning cups and leagues in the Govan area and two of their best players were pals of mine, Des Heron and Bernard McNally. Des came from the top end of Neptune Street and Bernard lived in a place known as the Wine Alley, which was as tough as it sounds. Bernard emigrated to the States and became a writer. Des made it as a professional footballer with Aberdeen and we are still friends. Cathy and I are godparents to his daughter. I can still kid him about Broomloan's ability to beat St Saviour's comfortably most of the time. We had a number of excellent players and it was frustrating that we could not play in a league. The Life Boys provided our outlet. Once it had been decided that Martin and I would be raised as Protestants, my mother made sure we had a Christian upbringing and at six or seven we were attending the local Bible school, the Shiloh Hall. I still have my first Bible from there, presented for perfect attendance. From the Bible school, it was on to the 129th Company of the Life Boys. Being in the Life Boys meant church twice on a Sunday. It also meant football and most of the good players from Broomloan joined the 129th.

The highlight of my football with the Life Boys was winning the Glasgow and District Cup, beating Polmadie Company in the two-legged final. We won the first game on our territory, the Fifty Pitches, a famous public layout in the Cardonald area, which adjoins Govan. There were once as many pitches as the name indicates but by the time I was growing up much of the ground had been claimed by the Hillington Industrial Estate. The journey across the south side of Glasgow to Polmadie for the second leg may only have been seven or eight miles but it was the furthest we had ever travelled for an away game and it was like being in another country. Only the playing conditions were familiar. Ash surfaces were standard on the public parks of the city and, in the dry conditions of summer, dust was forever swirling into your face. Wiping it away left big rings round your eyes and mouth and we were a strange sight at the end of that match. But that was the least of our concerns. We had finished 4–2 winners and what we felt was more than pleasure. It was joy. Our team manager, Johnny Boreland, bought us all ice creams with double nougat wafers and eating them walking down the Polmadie Road, with our boots tied at the laces and dangling round our necks, was the most exhilarating experience of my young life.

There was never enough football for me and my pals and as soon as the local boys' club, Harmony Row, spread word that new players would be welcomed, the Four Musketeers – Duncan Petersen, Tommy Hendry, Jim McMillan and myself – were queueing up to enrol as members. The leader of the club was a man named Bob Innes and in many ways Bob was Harmony Row. It was his creation and he had given his life to it. The football team for our age group came under the control of a wonderful obsessive, Mick McGowan. I was already growing accustomed to adults who were as besotted with football as I was. Johnny Boreland, my mentor at the Life Boys, was and still is a delightful fanatic about the game. When I visited him not long ago, I found he had a miniature goal set up in his back garden and, in spite of being old enough to have survived years in a prison camp during the Second World War, he let me know it was not for decoration.

Mick McGowan, who was in his thirties when I encountered him, not only had a passionate enthusiasm for football but a fanatical, one-eyed, all-consuming commitment to Harmony Row. Nothing and nobody came before the interests of the club. He was an impossible man. We all loved him but at one time or another fell out with him. My very first memory of anything that could be described as coaching is associated with Mick. He had taken a bunch of us from Harmony Row, which is a street right in the heart of Govan, to a nearby pitch called Polar Engine Park. We called it 'the puggy' because it was beside the main railway goods line running into the shipyards. Having gathered us around him, Mick started to explain the values of team play. At the age of ten or eleven, we weren't too keen on enlightenment. We just wanted to get the ball out and play. But he kept on about passing and movement. Then he turned to me and said: 'Alex, you dribble far too much. You will have to learn to distribute the ball.' I was quite bright at school but I have to confess that I didn't know what distribute meant, so I could not wait to get home and ask my dad for the definition. He knew every word in the dictionary, or so I believed. Dad did have an excellent vocabulary, and could help me with meanings much less obvious than the one I needed that day. But as the years rolled on, if I taxed him with an unfamiliar word, particularly a technological term, he delivered arbitrary judgements. 'Spell it,' he would say. When I did so, there would be a dismissal: 'No such word.' I would persist, passing him the book or newspaper I had been reading. After a few seconds' perusal, he would give his final pronouncement: 'No such word, never heard of it.' He had his own ideas about how far the English language could stretch.

Harmony Row's football was played in the Glasgow Boys' Club league and our fixtures were scattered over a wide area. Our fiercest rivals were Bridgeton Boys' Club and trips to their home ground on Glasgow Green, the renowned park located on the south bank of the Clyde in the city centre, were never relaxed excursions. As usual, the pitches were all black ash, so gravel rash was the one certain memento of any engagement, but there could be more serious hazards. During one cup game against Bridgeton BC the atmosphere was more than usually intense, with the field completely ringed by their supporters. We were winning 3–0 at half-time when my Uncle Andrew approached me and suggested that a quick getaway at the end of the match would be advisable. Uncle Andrew, who lived in Oatlands, on the same side of the river as the Green, had overheard a gang of about thirty young lads mouthing dire threats. News of the danger spread with amazing speed through the rest of the team. Mick McGowan told us that he would collect our clothes and that as soon as the referee blew to finish the game we should make a dash for Ballater Street, the main road that carried the trams for Govan. Despite our nervousness, we cruised to a 4–1 victory in the second half. The sprint to Ballater Street was rather more hectic and I kept imagining what would happen if no tram came when we reached the stop. Luckily one did, and the potential lynch mob were left trailing about thirty yards behind it. I suppose I could say I had an early introduction to the dramas of cup football.

I did a lot of growing up at the Harmony Row Club, as did most of my pals from that era. Quite a few of them married girls they met at the club. Duncan Petersen met Janette there and was the first to go to the altar. Bob Innes used to organise dance nights and he insisted that we all braved the floor. All the aggression we showed on the field evaporated then and many of us were paralysed by shyness. So Bob used to put the lights out to spare us the embarrassment of having our mates watch us tread on our partners' feet and we would float around that little hall in Harmony Row as the sound of the Platters drifted over our heads – great days.

Playing football for the club was combined with playing for school and Boys' Brigade teams. When I moved from the Life Boys to the Boys' Brigade, I passed from the care of Johnny Boreland to that of his brother, Jim, and by the age of thirteen I held a regular place with the 129th Company of the BB, although theirs was an Under-18 team. School football in Glasgow in those days was of remarkable quality. At Govan High we had the McKinnon twins, Ronnie and Donnie. Both had notable success at centre-half in the senior ranks, Donnie with Partick Thistle and, more memorably, Ronnie with Rangers and Scotland. Ronnie, in fact, started as an outside-right and regularly amazed us by disdaining boots and playing in his stockinged feet. Of others who were at Govan High in my time, Craig Watson had some years at Rangers before going to Falkirk and Morton, Jimmy Morrison played for Clyde and Dumbarton, and my brother Martin had spells at Partick Thistle, Barnsley, Doncaster, Dunfermline and Morton. Martin then took on the player-manager's job at Waterford in Ireland. He won the league title for them and reached the final of the Irish Cup.

Govan High's main rivals, St Gerard's, had Joe McBride, who lived in the close next to ours and, being a little older, was always something of a hero to me. Joe had a great career with Motherwell, Wolves, Kilmarnock, Celtic and Scotland and his goalscoring achievements would surely have been truly historic but for the bad knee injury he suffered in 1966, during the season of Celtic's European Cup triumph. Incredibly, he had scored thirty-five goals in that season before the injury cut him down around Christmastime. Jim Craig, who would win a European Cup medal with Celtic, was also at St Gerard's around that time.

Emerging in these years from the wider reservoir of Glasgow and district (Dunbartonshire was a particularly strong breeding ground) were schoolboys who were to have notable careers as professionals in England and gain plenty of caps with Scotland: Eddie McCreadie, Andy Lochhead, Bobby Hope and Asa Hartford. The high standard meant that there was tough competition for team places at the major football schools, of which Govan High was one, and I was surprised soon after my arrival there to see on the noticeboard that I was to report to play trials for the Under-13 eleven. Apparently my buddy from Broomloan Road Primary, Tommy Hendry, had recommended me to the teacher in charge of the team. George Symington was his name. He looked a fearsome figure and his looks were not deceiving. Nobody trifled with Mr Symington. He achieved extraordinary success with the team and we went more than a year without losing a game.

In my first season the pinnacle was our Whitefield Cup encounter with St Gerard's, the Catholic secondary school we were always striving to beat at every age level. I don't recall any religious bitterness between the schools but the division in loyalties was always clear. Our boys supported the local heroes, Rangers, and the lads from St Gerard's were Celtic fans, which ensured that when we met there was an extra edge. The first attempt to settle our Whitefield Cup tie ended in a 1–1 draw on the big ash pitch at Pirie Park, the ground we shared with St Gerard's. It was a day of high winds and the ash gusting into the players' faces made the game a bit of a farce. We were rather fortunate to survive with a draw, although I didn't feel especially lucky when a few parents of St Gerard's players made me the target of some severe heckling. I had been attracting quite a lot of coverage in the local paper, the *Govan Press*, and the fact that I performed badly that day gave those adults an opportunity to hound me. I was taken aback by this hostility from grown men but my dad was completely unmoved afterwards and merely said that the only appropriate answer was to play well in the replay, preferably with a hat trick thrown in. That second game took place on a perfect Saturday morning, I played a blinder and did score a hat trick and we won 6–3. After striking one of my goals in at the junction of upright and crossbar from twenty yards, I could not resist celebrating in front of the

St Gerard's supporters. Dad was right about the best way to shut them up.

That season we won our league, the Whitefield Cup (beating Bellahouston Academy 7–1 in the final) and the Castle Cup. In the Castle Cup our final victims, Adelphi Secondary from the Gorbals, were pulverised 6–0. We maintained our form into the following season, again capturing the league title and reaching the final of the Scottish Shield at Hampden, where we faced St Pat's of Dumbarton, who were so powerful that they had six players in the Scottish Schools team. The scoreline for that match shows that we lost 4–0 but it totally misrepresents the truth about the action. There was nothing between the two sides until our goal-keeper, Angus Birnie, broke his finger with ten minutes to go and had to go off. We went to pieces after that and lost the four goals, making it look like a slaughter. Mr Symington was devastated. He couldn't believe we had lost. It was not in his make-up to contemplate defeat and he had instilled his will to win in all of us. At times we found him terrifying and yet the attitude of our parents, who all thought him wonderful, indicates that he had many qualities other than his driving competitiveness. My dad, who was never prone to overpraise anyone, defined Mr Symington as 'a good man' and to me that meant more than a royal seal of approval.

During that season, the trials to find the boys who would represent Glasgow Schools were held at Scotstoun Showground and Tommy Hendry and myself were chosen to take part. We arranged to meet at Govan Cross and travel together, but, as the time for leaving approached, Tommy's stepfather, Mr Gibson, came to say that Tommy didn't want to go. He was too nervous, too unsure of himself, and all the hours Mr Gibson had spent trying to talk him round had failed to bridge the confidence gap. Everyone who has made it in football has a story to tell of at least one contemporary who could have been a great player but for some element of his personality that created an insurmountable obstacle. Right through my career, as a player and a manager, I have been saddened by such cases. Tommy's problem was one of self-belief. It was a pity because he was an extremely talented right-half, but his ambitions did not stretch beyond playing for Govan High and Harmony Row. He remains as modest today as he was then and even forty years on I would not dream of broaching the subject of those trials with him.

My own experience of the occasion was mixed but came out well in the end. The man in charge of Glasgow Schools was David Letham, who had enjoyed a good career with Queen's Park and would figure in my life later when I joined that great amateur club. As we stripped for the trials, he told me that I was to play outside-left. I had not been in that position since I was about eight and my lack of familiarity with it showed in the first half. I hardly got a kick of the ball. As I have mentioned, my father's quiet nature could be transformed by explosions of temper and, having watched his son's prospects of selection withering away on the wing, he went marching round the pitch to deliver his views to David Letham. The result was a switch in the second half to my normal inside-left role and the improvement in performance was highlighted by one exceptional through pass that allowed the outside-right to score. My place in the Glasgow team to play Lanarkshire was secured.

As further evidence that my career was on the upswing, I received an offer to join Drumchapel Amateurs, the most successful Scottish team of the day in that grade of football. Initially I wasn't interested, being content to carry on with Harmony Row, but after a visit from the indefatigable Douglas Smith, who ran Drumchapel, I started to waver. Then my dad had a decisive conversation with our neighbour, Joe McBride, who was playing for Drumchapel's chief rivals in amateur football, Kilmarnock Boys' Club.

'He's got to go to Drumchapel,' Joe said unequivocally. Such certainty from someone Dad always respected eradicated any doubts in his mind and he quickly persuaded me out of my own reservations. It was the best move I could have made, one that forced me to challenge myself to an extent that couldn't have occurred if I had stayed with the Row.

Drumchapel operated with five teams – Under-14, Under-15, Under-16, Under-17 and Under-18 – and the scale of their success was fully demonstrated when, in one year, thirty players graduated from their ranks to senior football. That was quite phenomenal even in an era when Scotland was rich in youthful talent. One of Douglas Smith's great assets was that he made us think big time. If you played for the school on a Saturday morning he spared you the need to make a hectic dash home and then head for the Drumchapel game. Instead you went to Reid's restaurant in Gordon Street, Glasgow, and had your lunch at Douglas's expense. It made you feel a cut above the boys you played against and, however foolish that may have been, it did not hurt your confidence on the pitch. My team-mates at Govan High and Harmony Row could hardly believe I was being given such grand treatment. Some of them probably thought when I mentioned it that I was a big-head but I knew their basic reaction was envy. Such was the quality of the team I played in with the Drum that we won one of our early games against Mosspark Amateurs 35–0. I managed to score nine that day but our centre-forward, Bobby Stark, scored twelve and was dropped the next week to make way for our regular centre, David McBeth. How's that for competition?

If amateur football was providing the highest standard available to me at that stage, it was never a let-down to play for the school. In the 1956–57 season, Govan High were once more chasing all honours and we relinquished our interest in the Scottish Cup only after being beaten 2–1 in a semi-final replay by West Calder High School. That December I was chosen to turn out for Glasgow Schools in the traditional derby against Edinburgh at Cathkin Park, home of the now-defunct Third Lanark. There had not been a bigger game in my short football life and I was as nervous as a kitten going into it. It is quite amazing how swiftly reputations can build in football and all the talk in the days before we lined up at Cathkin was of the young inside-right of Edinburgh Schools, John Greig. In that phase of my career I was playing as a left-half (left midfield in modern parlance), so I was set to be directly opposed to this prodigy. When we went out on to a field covered with about three inches of snow, I was surprised by how small Greig was and said to myself, 'He'll need to be good to do much on this pitch.' Fortunately, he did find difficulty in trudging through the snow for ninety minutes and little was seen of his abilities as Glasgow swept to a comfortable 4–0 victory. I played well and scored with a penalty. For John, more distinguished days were ahead and during them he did not forget to chide me about bullying a wee boy from Edinburgh. How could that little angel-faced lad turn out the way he did!

My last year of schoolboy football was in the Govan High Under-18 team, although I was still only fifteen when I joined them. We didn't have a bad side in that older age group and our league challenge went all the way to the last game, when we needed to beat Holyrood at Pirie Park but could only draw. However, there was plenty of personal compensation for that disappointment when I was chosen for the Scottish Schools party that travelled to meet England at Dulwich Hamlet's ground. I didn't make the team but was just delighted to wear the jersey as a substitute, even though we lost 4–3.

At Drumchapel, our Under-15 team proved good enough to be entered in the Under-16 league, which meant the club had two sides in the same competition and Douglas Smith loved it when we came second to the older team. We were never overawed by them, although they included several players who would go on to good professional careers, and indeed were so far from being intimidated that every meeting with them was littered with feuds. The Under-15s set a pattern by beating our Drumchapel elders in the final of the league cup competition, and it was felt that Douglas was not too happy, having decided that the Under-16s should make their success in the league a springboard for claiming all the major trophies. We put a further dent in his assumptions by defeating the Under-16s 1–0 in the semi-final of the Scottish Amateur Cup after a real battle at Kilbowie Park, Clydebank. By the time the final came round we were no longer suffering the depletions caused by the demands of schools, county and international football and were at last able to field our strongest team. When that happened, I was put back to left-half to accommodate our brilliant first-choice inside-left, Davie Thomson. In a period remarkable for the volume of Scottish schoolboy talent, Davie Thomson ranked as utterly outstanding along with Bobby Hope, Billy Bremner and Willie Henderson. He was really tremendous but, like a lot of schoolboys, did not realise his potential as a professional. After a spell with Clyde, he gave up the game and emigrated to Canada to become a songwriter. In the Scottish Amateur Cup final we beat Dundee Butterburn 3–2 in Dundee, and the depth of satisfaction that dramatic match gave me is still one of the most vivid memories of my youth.

The next year, the familiar principle was applied and we were pitched into the Under-17 league. We did quite well but had to endure the horrible disappointment of losing the final of the Scottish Amateur Cup 1–0 to Calder. I missed a penalty and at the end of the game Douglas Smith demanded to know why I had taken it. This annoyed me, as I had been a regular taker of penalties and, in fact, in the semi-final I had scored in the last minute against Ayr Albion to give us a 2–2 draw, setting up a replay that we won 1–0 on a difficult pitch directly behind Rabbie Burns's cottage in Alloway. The true source of Douglas's annoyance was the decision I had taken to leave Drumchapel for the most famous amateur club of all, Queen's Park. He had tried to talk me out of the move but my mind was made up. It had been an ambition cherished by my dad since I first showed aptitude for football.

My involvement with Drumchapel had naturally changed Mick McGowan's attitude to me at Harmony Row. He was inclined to leave me out of the team, and in a way I saw the justification for that, but nevertheless I was angry. There was nobody around who had been a member of the club longer and I still attended every week. Proof that the circumstances created a dilemma for Mick came when Harmony Row faced a cup final against the dreaded Bridgeton BC at the ground of St Anthony's Juniors, Moore Park. The previous week they had lost 6–1 to Bridgeton in another cup final. Mick had declined to pick me for that match but when the

Moore Park fixture loomed he decided to recall me. We won that final 7–0 and I scored four. But the real excitement started after the game as we headed back towards Harmony Row. To reach the club premises, we had to walk down Helen Street and past the Polar Engine Park, where Harmony Row normally played. The park was being used as a fairground and as we approached the rides and stalls all feelings of jubilation were suddenly driven out of us. A local gang, known as the Bingo, attacked Tommy McDonald, a brother of one of our players, Hugh McDonald. The gang had become notorious in the area and were not loath to use all sorts of weapons. Razors, bicycle chains and knives were common in their armoury, so it was a serious matter when they set upon Tommy. At that moment all the parents, my dad included, went for the gang and a battle ensued. Most of the team made off for Harmony Row. There, all the neighbours were waiting for our arrival and when told of the attack they raced the 300 yards or so to the scene. One well-known family of McDonalds (no relation to the victim of the original assault) stopped their game of street football to go to the rescue and I can tell you that when they went into action they were about evens with the Red Army. The next day the front pages of the *Daily Record* ran the story of the gang who ruined the night for the victorious Harmony Row team. That was my last game of the summer before I joined Queen's Park. The decorous traditions associated with that great amateur institution would be a far cry from the donnybrook that had been my farewell to Harmony Row.

— 2 —
APPRENTICED IN
TWO TRADES

Not everything that happened to me at sixteen was sweet but most of it was exciting and I had a sense of life beginning to open up for me. New and sometimes daunting experiences came in a rush in the few months after I left school. First I started my apprenticeship as a toolmaker and then I made a significant move towards senior football by joining Queen's Park, one of the greatest amateur clubs in the game.

Most people nowadays will be unaware of the important part played by Queen's Park in establishing football as a major sport in the nineteenth century. For them the club will be just a name that occurs around the lower fringes of the weekly football results on radio or television. I don't claim that Queen's Park's historical associations meant a lot to my adolescent mind but the fact that their home ground was Hampden Park was enough to guarantee feelings of awe. I don't know how many times in my schooldays I had fought my way through the stampede to board a bus at Govan Cross for the journey across the south side of Glasgow to Hampden for internationals, Scottish Cup semi-finals and finals and other momentous matches played in the huge old stadium. Now I was carrying training kit when I caught the 25 bus from Hillington Industrial Estate – where I was employed by Wickman, a company specialising in the manufacture of carbon-tipped tools – and then changed in Cardonald to a 4A for trips to Hampden that were rather quieter than those big-match journeys.

The pre-season training was done at the shrine itself and once involved I was too busy fighting off exhaustion to be awe-struck by the surroundings. An easy jog of four laps was the misleading preparation for a breathless slog up and down every terracing stairway. I think there were forty-two around that massive bowl. If the idea was to put us off football, they were having a good go at it. It was agony, but I managed to keep up with the leading pack quite well without challenging a little slip of a lad called Kelly, who had emerged as the resident hare, a species encountered at every football club I have known. He bounded up and down those endless steps as if he had found masochist heaven. As I panted behind him, with my lungs protesting against the scale of the place, I found it easier to understand how the record attendance at Hampden came to be more than 149,000.

Queen's Park in those days operated four teams. The First XI were called exactly that, with capital letters; the reserves were known as the Strollers; the proper name for the third team was the Hampden XI and the fourth string took the plainer title of the Queen's Park Youth Team. As that list of names suggests, the old school tie was not without influence at the club and quite a number of players arrived there because doors had been opened by family or friends. But connections never helped in gaining a first-team place. You had to earn that and there were some feisty lads around to ensure that competition was lively. Being amateur did not prevent the men in charge from taking the game seriously and, as I soon discovered, if the exchanges became physical out on the field, Queen's Park players were expected to stand up for themselves. There was a wonderful spirit in the club, a camaraderie that extended from the senior players down to the rawest teenagers, and I think back to my time there not only with pleasure but with the realisation that I should have stayed longer than I did.

I had gone to Queen's Park at much the same time as two of my closest pals from Govan, Duncan Petersen and John Grant. They, too, had decided to leave Harmony Row to try to better themselves. (Mick McGowan's reaction must have been high on the Richter scale.) The three of us were soon regulars in the youth team, playing alongside quite a few promising lads. I knew about

the goalkeeper, Jim Cruickshank, who was a year older than I
was and had, like myself, come from Drumchapel Amateurs. Jim
quickly convinced me that he had one of the prerequisites of a
goalie in that he was a bit crazy. On one of my first nights of
going to Hampden I saw him ahead of me, sprawling around on
a hill leading down to the ground. He was practising his diving,
lunging dramatically after an invisible ball. He practised all the
way to an outstanding professional career with Hearts and
Scotland.

Queen's Park Youth Team matches were played at Lesser
Hampden, adjacent to the main stadium, and the pitch there
was always excellent, something that could not be said for the
conditions we were liable to endure on our travels. After a few
games, I was promoted into the Hampden XI, who competed in
an open-age league where the line about men against boys had a
literal application. One fixture took us to Eaglesham. It is an
extremely attractive hamlet a few miles south of Glasgow but my
memories of it are dominated by the paddy field that passed for
a pitch and an opposing team that suggested the village had eleven
blacksmiths. Eaglesham were among the most successful amateur
teams in the country in that era, making a habit of reaching the
final of the Amateur Cup at Hampden, but it was the size of them
that impressed me. Although I was tall for my age, I was still
just skin and bone, and, with the gluepot surface neutralising my
quickness, I got battered about a bit. On the three-bus journey
back to Govan, I made the mistake of mentioning the hardness
of the opposition to my dad. 'It will do you the world of good,'
I was told. 'If you can't take it, don't play it.' The sermon lasted
most of the way home. Fortunately, Eaglesham and its giants only
flitted briefly into my life. I was picked out for rapid promotion
and by mid-October I was a reserve-team player with the Strollers.
Although I was glad to keep my place with the reserves, it was
always a pleasure to be drafted back into the youth team for
important games. The players at that level were of my age and I
had forged friendships with most of them. Another attraction was
that I liked the official responsible for the youth team, Willie

Burgess. He had a good way with young players and always made you feel special. Remembering how much that meant to me then, I have tried hard to convey warmth and reassurance to youngsters I have dealt with as a manager.

Those characteristics do not jump instantly to mind when I think of David Nimmo, who was my foreman in that first year of my apprenticeship with Wickman. It didn't bother me that I was the butt of all the hoary jokes inflicted on boys learning a trade – being sent for a bottle of blue gas, for a long stand and so on – but Mr Nimmo was a different proposition. I wasn't scared of him. I was terrified. One of his favourite tricks was hitting you on the back of the head with small nuts that he carried in his dust-coat pockets. If he came across you talking while operating the turning machines, you found one of those nuts cracking into your skull. I didn't even feel safe from him when I was outside the factory gates. One night, having met a pleasant girl at the dancing and been allowed to walk her home to Cardonald, I asked her about her job.

'I work in an office at the Hillington Estate,' she said. 'What about you?' I told her I was an apprentice toolmaker, also at Hillington.

'Where?'

'Wickman.'

'Wickman! My dad is a foreman in there,' she said, delighted at the coincidence. Less delighted, I nervously asked for the family name and almost wet myself when my worst fears were confirmed. I made my excuses and left at the gallop, grateful that I hadn't even attempted to kiss David Nimmo's daughter. Innocence did not save me from paralysing fear every time he approached me over the next week. He might have called upon something heavier than his pocket armoury if he had thought I was taking liberties on the doorstep.

My first year as a wage-earner passed quite swiftly as I set about learning the variety of skills a toolmaker had to acquire. One month I would be on the lathes, learning to use different turning machines, then in the grinding department, then the milling. The section that gave me most trouble was the electrical department. I was useless in there and rejoiced when I moved on before I could electrocute myself. A more general concern was the doubt hanging over the future of the factory. Redundancies were prevalent and, as a recent recruit, I had cause to be gloomy. Then I was told to report to the general manager's office. Normally that would not have worried me since the manager, Jimmy Malcolm, was a distant relation on my dad's side and friendly with our family; but with so much uncertainty in the air, I headed for the appointment with foreboding. Sitting outside his office waiting for the call, I reflected on how I had turned down the chance of jobs with Thermotank and Polar Engines, solid engineering firms, to land myself with what looked like being a lame duck company. There had also been an opportunity to become a Customs and Excise officer but I passed that up because it necessitated working on a Saturday and I always had plenty to do on a Saturday. With so many grim possibilities in my head, I was actually shaking slightly when I sat down in front of Jimmy Malcolm but he turned out to be one of those people who have had a vitally helpful influence on my life. A transfer to the main Wickman factory in Coventry was on offer but he had rightly dismissed that as an option which, in view of my football aspirations, would suit neither me nor my parents. So he had concentrated on the alternative of continuing with my trade as a second-year apprentice with Remington Rand and had already spoken to the personnel officer of that firm. Jimmy was terrific and within weeks I had started at Remington Rand, who were also located on the Hillington Estate, which is about three miles from Glasgow airport. That means it is on the western or (to give a more significant geographical marker) the Govan side of the city.

It is difficult to imagine what would have happened had I moved to Coventry. I could not have contemplated an existence without football, and, although I could obviously have found an outlet for my enthusiasm in the Midlands, transplanting all the threads and connections of a budding career would have been impossible.

Most of my days were taken up with dreams of football glory and those dreams had a Scottish setting. It became specific on the odd occasion when (because one of the veteran officials at Queen's Park had a soft spot for me) I was permitted to take a ball on to the otherwise deserted expanse of Hampden Park. I was fantasising more than practising as I ran from one penalty box to the other and shot the ball into the empty net. The nets at Hampden swept away deep behind the goal and you had to go down on your haunches to retrieve the ball, and repeating that ritual gave me a profound thrill. As I pounded up and down the empty field, I heard more than a hundred thousand voices roaring me on to the winning goal in the Cup final or against England. Now and again, admittedly, I visualised actual Hampden experiences: that missed penalty against Calder the previous season and the Scottish Shield final in which Govan High had been drawing 0–0 with St Pat's Dumbarton ten minutes from the end and yet finished 4–0 losers; but the dreams usually held those painful recollections at bay.

I certainly had no reason to hide from the realities of life at Queen's Park, for they were increasingly agreeable. Help and encouragement were plentiful and one particular source of support for me was Willie 'Junior' Omand, a senior player and respected figure around the club. Most nights Willie would walk with Duncan Petersen, John Grant and myself to the bus stop, giving us good advice and making sure we got on our bus before he departed in the opposite direction. It was a considerate attitude that said a lot about the man and a great deal, too, about the spirit that ran through Queen's Park. My fondness for the club dramatically increased when in late November, still more than a month short of my seventeenth birthday, I received a surprise call-up into the First XI. There was tremendous excitement in the Ferguson household until my dad made the point that if I played in the game I would never be able to take part in junior football. The relevance of that intervention will probably be lost on anybody from outside Scotland, where 'the juniors' constitute a football world of their own. A substantial network of leagues spread across the country accommodates an extraordinary variety of players (young and old, paid and unpaid, crude and skilful) and sometimes the competitiveness reaches a level of ferocity worthy of the Hong Kong Triads. If a player registered with a junior club then tried the senior grade and didn't make it there, he could be 'reinstated' as a junior and so salvage something from his career. Dad was insisting that I should cover myself by being registered with our local juniors, Benburb, and then transferred to Queen's Park. I was having none of it and the fall-out between us was so serious that we didn't speak for months. There was no way I was going into junior football. I was with a senior club and I was determined to be successful.

My debut in the first team was an away match with Stranraer (see map on page 478) and we travelled down to that seaport in the south-western corner of Scotland by train from Central Station. I just sat in that train and absorbed everything that was said by my older team-mates, Willie Hastie, Bert Cromar, Ian Harnett, Willie Omand and, an absolute original, Charlie Church. They were all true Queen's Park players, brought up in the traditions and happy to wear the black-and-white hoops throughout their footballing lives. Two of the other lads went on to play for their country. David Holt, the hardy left-back, was from a working-class background and after a good professional career, mainly with Hearts, he is now driving a taxi in Glasgow. Willie Bell, who did well with Leeds United, subsequently became a lay preacher in the United States. In later years, I used to wonder why that Queen's Park team did not achieve more, because to my eyes they were brilliant, but maybe I was still dreaming. However, that debut confrontation with Stranraer was closer to nightmare. My troubles began with the decision to play me at outside-right, which didn't suit me at all – nor did their left-back, a little tank by the name of McKnight. After a collision had put the two of us on the ground, the bastard bit me. At half-time the official in charge of our team, Jackie Gardiner, roasted me for not being combative enough.

'You don't sidestep players at this club,' he shouted. 'You go through them. You've come into this team with a big reputation. What's the matter with you?'

'The left-back bit me,' I said pitifully.

'Bit you?' Gardiner screamed. 'Then bite him back.'

Any suspicion that Scotland's leading amateur team would be too Corinthian to go to war was soon dispelled from Stranraer minds and the second half was warfare. Our boys waded into them and Willie Hastie went across to right-back to get a kick at McKnight. There was no doubting the all-for-one-and-one-for-all team spirit and, considering that nobody on our side was earning a penny for his exertions, their commitment elevated them above most team-mates I have had. Charlie Church's involvement outstripped the referee's tolerance and Charlie and their centre-half, Simpson, were ordered off for fighting. On his way into the tunnel, the Stranraer man engaged in an argument with a Queen's Park supporter. He must have been a real warrior that centre-half. His opponent this time was a member of the official blind party attending the match. All in all, it was quite an introduction to the senior grade. The next week I scored with a header in a 4–2 win over Alloa at Hampden and I went on to play quite a few matches for the first team that season.

Away from the pitch, too, my horizons were widening. I had my first steady girlfriend, Doreen Carling. Like Ann Nimmo, she came from Cardonald, a residential district just along the road from Govan, but she did not carry the hazard of being a foreman's daughter. My relationship with Doreen lasted for about a year and a half before it suffered the fate of most first romances and petered out. We got back together from time to time until the connection was severed permanently when she emigrated to America and got married. As much as Doreen's prettiness, I remember how well I was treated by her mother, a strong Irish Catholic. I have pleasant memories of that generous woman's hospitality.

That summer of 1959 I had my first holiday away from the regular Boys' Brigade camps. With two pals, John Donachie and Jim Connell, I went to stay with Jim's aunt and uncle on the Walkinstown housing estate in Dublin. We all had a marvellous time and I really savoured the sense of personal freedom the trip gave me. One of my earliest impressions of the great city of Dublin, which has since become one of my favourite places to visit, was of the number of cycles. Everybody seemed to have a bike and crossing the road in the vicinity of the bridge at the end of O'Connell Street could be quite an adventure. Of course, the lads from Glasgow took pride in their alertness. At least we did until we had dealings with a street photographer who demonstrated how he could produce instant prints. We chipped in a pound each and the happy snapper went to work. He took our pictures, dipped the negatives in a solution he had to hand, and Bob's your uncle, we had the prints. We crossed the Liffey marvelling at the progress photography was making, but by the time we reached the other side of the river the photographs had faded to a brownish blur. Fifty yards further on, the images were gone altogether. We sprinted back over the bridge to attack the photographer, but should have known better. Fading was his speciality. Once the anger had subsided, we had a good laugh at ourselves. That holiday was full of laughs and even now when John and I meet up another story of Dublin is sure to come out.

Our favoured hunting ground for dates was a dance hall called the Four Provinces in Harcourt Street. We went there most nights and on one occasion we bumped into a lad from Govan, Rab Donnachie, who had played in the Govan High School team at the same time as I did. He was on his own and we had no hesitation about inviting him to join us, as I had always thought of him as decent enough. However, at the end of the night, when the Irish national anthem was being played, Rab refused to stand and became belligerent towards the stewards. The three of us quietly stepped out of the way as he was escorted into the street. Almost every night afterwards we would meet him and invariably he would go through that silly procedure of not standing for the national anthem. He was a strange lad and it transpired that he had gathered a bit of a reputation while working in the Fairfield shipyard, where his dodgy characteristics had earned him the nickname Barabbas. When I learned some years later that he had died a young man, somehow I was not greatly shocked. I had sensed a deep self-destructiveness in Rab.

It was a severe shock, though, when Jim Connell died in his early forties. Jim and I went our separate ways after that Dublin holiday but I would bump into him now and again at football matches. He was a nice, quiet lad and I was always glad to see him. Apparently, after his wife died suddenly, he could not come to terms with the loss. He had no heart for life afterwards. When John Donachie and I share our reminiscences of those carefree days in Ireland long ago, there is now a shadow over the memories.

Back in Glasgow during the summer of the Dublin expedition, my mates and I used to hang around the Cardonald stretch of Paisley Road West. Our favourite haunt was Bill's Café, where we could listen to the latest records and chat up the girls while drinking our Cokes. Then we would saunter along Paisley Road West having a bit of a carry-on among ourselves, providing proof of just how irrationally amusing teenagers find their own wit. Usually the low-calibre jokes were aimed at each other but on one Saturday afternoon we were unexpectedly provided with an outside target. It came in the shape of a wedding we happened to be passing. It wasn't just any old wedding. The blushing groom was none other than McKnight, the Stranraer cannibal. Once I had told the rest of our group about the biting incident, the stick was merciless, and he could do nothing but stand there in the church doorway with his bride and keep a fixed grin on his face. 'Away, ya mug, who would marry you?' was about as close as we came to wishing him well. It didn't end until an old woman chastised us and sent us on our way. Being a laughing avenger was great fun but I had to hope that I never met the new husband again, on the field or off it.

My second year at Queen's Park brought more first-team games but not sufficient to satisfy me and thoughts about turning pro began to harden in my mind, especially as one or two options had already been presented to me. After a youth international at St James' Park, Newcastle United had approached me, and, although a move to England was improbable because of my apprenticeship, I was flattered by their interest. The funny thing about Newcastle's reaction to that game was that I didn't think

I had played well in it. I was happier with other performances in the five youth internationals I played for Scotland, none of which we lost. In that drawn match at St James', England's team contained some memorable players, not least a midfielder called Venables. Terry laughs when I remind him that he had one of those Bobby Darin haircuts with the bob at the front. He stood out as he always does. Martin Peters was in midfield and the centre-half was Alan Bloor, who went on to play regularly for Stoke City. The goalkeeper was Gordon West of Everton and the centre-forward was Frank Saul of Spurs. We were lucky we didn't have to face Geoff Hurst, Nobby Stiles and Alan Ball, who were also figuring in English youth football at the time. Scotland weren't too bad themselves. Our right-winger in Newcastle was Willie Henderson, who had a brilliant career with Rangers, and most of the others made it to the senior ranks. Some had good careers, like George Murray of Motherwell and Aberdeen and Eric Stevenson of Hibs. In that period Scotland was constantly producing outstanding footballers. Without giving a long list of names, Billy Bremner, Bobby Moncur and Andy Penman all came through schools or youth football about that same time. What would be the odds against such talent emerging in Britain from a single crop these days?

Perhaps it was natural that my growing desire to make a move should lessen my chances of making the right one. Willie Neil, the St Johnstone scout, had been badgering away at me, never leaving me alone, forever waxing lyrical about the benefits of going to Muirton Park. His principal sales pitch was, wait for it, the promise of a first-team place in the First Division. Why do young players listen to that stuff? Any time I try to sign a young footballer I emphasise the facts of life. Nobody but yourself can guarantee you a first-team place. Whatever you do on the field determines whether you are in the team or not. Any bullshit promises from scouts or managers should be ignored. In fact, if I were a young player I would not sign for a club that dangled guarantees of first-team football. There is never any point in looking back and regretting decisions but I soon knew that leaving Queen's Park was a big mistake and that an even bigger mistake was failing to confide in Willie Omand. Many years later, in conversation with Willie, I could feel that my lack of trust had been a terrible disappointment to him. You live and learn, sometimes too slowly. I was going to miss that wonderful team spirit Queen's Park engendered. But, like most young men, I was in a hurry and I decided to join St Johnstone as an amateur. I didn't know whether good times or bad awaited me in Perth but the attraction of the First Division was not to be resisted.

— 3 —
UNPAMPERED PROS

I SIGNED for St Johnstone simply because I failed to see where loyalty ended and stupidity took over. The Saints' Glasgow scout, Willie Neil, was the trainer at my local junior club, Benburb, when I trained there as a schoolboy and my gratitude for the help given me by the Bens produced a mistaken sense of obligation that made me vulnerable to Willie's blandishments. Going to St Johnstone (initially on a one-year arrangement as an amateur) was a blunder that led to a nightmare. I cannot say I ever got to the point where I was in despair but I went close enough to make me remember my time in Perth with a shudder. Obviously I had to be a fool to believe half the assurances Willie poured out to me but, even allowing for my naivety, I think I was entitled to be shocked by the gulf between his promises and the reality. Having to fight for a first-team place was natural. Having to fight for basic travelling expenses was not.

As I was required to travel two evenings a week by train from Glasgow to Perth, the cost in hard cash (not to mention time and energy) was never going to be negligible. For me, a training night started at four o'clock when I left the Remington Rand factory on the Hillington Estate. I took a bus to the suburban station, a train to Glasgow Central, then a taxi to the other mainline station, Buchanan Street, leaving there before five o'clock for the two-hour journey to Perth, where another taxi got me to Muirton Park to begin training at 7.30 p.m. Coming back was no better. The train out of Perth was London-bound, so it travelled considerably faster than the one which took me north, but unfortunately not to Glasgow. The most convenient stop for me was Coatbridge. I would arrive in Coatbridge an hour before midnight, catch a bus or train to Glasgow and a bus from the city centre to Govan. Having collapsed into bed around 1 a.m., I had to be up at 6 a.m. for work in the factory. Just writing down that schedule leaves me exhausted. But still ahead of me was the struggle to be reimbursed. According to a set procedure, every Saturday the part-time players would hand in their expenses to the secretary but we knew that was just the start of a complicated game. The next week there would be no sign of repayment, which meant going to knock on the door of the manager, Bobby Brown, who was later to be in charge of Scotland. Of course, Bobby Brown never lied to us, but he did come up with an amazing variety of excuses for denying us the few bob that we were due. If it wasn't the fault of the secretary or the banker or the accountant, a motley cast of local tradesmen might be roped into the story. Prompt payment of expenses from Mr Brown? There was more chance of a blood transfusion in a quarry.

Maybe he felt it was right that I should pay the fares for those train journeys, considering how entertaining the company of older players often made them. John Docherty, a tough little wing-half from Glasgow, was the instigator of much of the amusement, although his appearance did not suggest that his former existence in the rough-and-tumble of junior football had been a barrel of laughs. John, who had won a Scottish Junior Cup medal with Petershill, had a face that looked as if it had seen too much of life or had felt the back of too many opponents' skulls. He had a regular double-act on the train with Matt McVittie, a winger who had come from Celtic, and it paid to stay out of the line of fire when the Glaswegian barbs were flying between them. With seasoned pros like Charlie McFadyen, Ron McKinven, Jim Ferguson (no relation), Jim Walker and Jim Little also in the group, men who had plied their trade at clubs all over Scotland and ate upstarts for breakfast, an eighteen-year-old had to tread warily. But if any of them had a go at you, you either took it lying down or you stood up to them. I preferred to stand up.

I appreciated the crack of the senior players on those train rides but, naturally, I was closer to lads nearer my own age and two of them became good friends of mine: Joe Henderson, a flying machine of an outside-left, and John Bell, a clever midfielder. John emigrated to Australia and when he returned it was to prove rather a significant day in my life. That, however, was some years in front of us. For the moment it was enough that we enjoyed each other's company and shared the pleasure of being young and doing something we loved. In memory, every day of pre-season preparation in that summer of 1960 seems to have been sunny and the lush expanse of Muirton Park, perhaps the finest pitch in Scotland, would have struck any aspiring footballer as a field of dreams.

The start of the season was quickly upon us and with it came word of a new signing. 'Never heard of him,' I said to myself. 'Jimmy Gauld. Who the hell has he played for?' Anyway, it was definitely bad news for me. It meant I got the old pat on the back from the manager: 'Your time will come.' By the time the new player turned up for the first match I had heard plenty about him from my dad, who let me know that Gauld had, in fact, been an excellent performer for Everton. However, a glance told me that it was going to be a mammoth task for Jimmy to excel for us. He must have been a stone overweight and when you are in your thirties that's a lot. Gauld showed outstanding ability early on but once the autumn leaves began to fall his form withered rapidly. Soon he was returning south, just in time to prepare himself for a different challenge – in a courtroom. He had been charged with match-fixing along with several more famous players: Tony Kay and Peter Swan, who had both played for England, and Bronco Layne. Gauld was named as the ringleader of the plot, a distinction that earned him the severest jail sentence when the guilty verdicts came in. Our brush with a notorious conspirator was the subject of conversation for weeks in the Muirton dressing-room as everyone tried to come to terms with the implications of the scandal. Without ever being certain, I had the uneasy feeling that there were games played in Scotland at the beginning of the Sixties which were at least in the doubtful category. Nothing could ever justify the corruption the Gauld case uncovered but there is no doubt that the greed and callous indifference of those who ran major football had created a climate in which dishonesty was liable to take root. In the ten to fifteen years after the Second World War, when many grounds (in England especially) were packed to capacity, there was not the slightest attempt to improve the rewards of players in keeping with the vast revenue that was flooding in; nor was any thought given to rescuing the fans from the squalid spectating conditions they had endured for generations. Where did all that money go? Its misuse represented a graver scandal than the grubby machinations of a few unscrupulous players.

Given that during my first season at St Johnstone I was allowed to play only about ten minutes in the first team, it can be assumed that I was not glowing with contentment. I was rapidly convincing myself that it would make sense to exploit the privilege of my amateur status by getting the hell out of the place at the end of the season. Yet, in spite of my frustration, for a while I enjoyed playing for the reserves. Sometimes, admittedly, it could be hairy and never more so than when we met the Celtic reserves of that era, who often fielded a half-back line capable of chilling the blood: the three Big Bad Johns, Cushley, McNamee and Kurilla. The most legendary of these three frighteners was McNamee and it may have been unwise of me to become so warlike with him in one game that team-mates had to drag us apart. John, whose habit of speaking through his nose somehow added to his menace, said, 'I'm going to fucking kill you at the end of the game.' Presumably heartened by the proximity of so many players and the referee, I answered with a defiant oath or two of my own and told him I would be around at the end. The match ended without further mayhem and my mind was on other matters when, as I combed my hair after coming out of the bath, one of the groundstaff told me there was somebody waiting for me. Assuming it was a friend or a relative, I stuck my head out of the door and looked up the long corridor that ran past the dressing-rooms at Muirton Park.

I nearly fainted when I saw McNamee standing there. Now I wasn't a coward by any means, and I could look after myself, but this was a monster I was dealing with and a little common sense was in order. So I went back to combing my hair and waited for the noise of the Celtic coach pulling out. A few weeks later I was in Joe McGeachie's tailor's shop in Glasgow, having a fitting, when Big John came in. Fortunately, his wife was with him, which put him on his best behaviour, and he even said hello. God, I was relieved.

In the 1960–61 season, our second team had a successful campaign, culminating in an appearance against Falkirk in the two-legged final of the Reserve Cup. An exciting 3–3 draw in the first game at Falkirk set us up perfectly for the second leg in Perth the following week. That decider was on a Saturday, so my father was able to be there, and we travelled up from Glasgow together on the train. During the journey he started to complain about stomach pains and kept going to the lavatory, and his complexion was worryingly grey. He dismissed my concerns and eventually I accepted that the problem was nothing worse than a bout of diarrhoea. We managed to win the game and the Cup, beating Falkirk 2–0, so it was a good finish to the season and I was sure I would have no difficulty improving my lot with a new club. But the truth about my father's illness changed everything. The stomach pains turned out to be symptoms of bowel cancer and he was rushed to the Southern General Hospital in Glasgow for immediate surgery. The operation known as a colostomy was not nearly as common in 1961 as it is now and there was much dread at 667 Govan Road, with my mother conducting prayers every day. When I went to see my dad on the eve of the operation he was so apprehensive that he told me to be sure to take good care of my mother if he didn't pull through. To be honest, I was terrified and didn't know what to say to my father but I assured him, as people do, that everything would be OK. The next day I rushed out at lunchtime from my work at Remington Rand to a phone box and called the hospital but the only information I was given was that Mr Ferguson had come out of theatre and was comfortable. I couldn't concentrate on my job that afternoon and spent my time in the canteen office, which was my usual hideaway when I was in need of refuge. It was run by one of the great characters in the factory, Clare Park, who looked after me as if I were her own son. The news, when it came at last, was basically good in that the operation was a success. Of course, my dad had to wear a bag for the rest of his life. Since our tenement home did not have a bathroom, bathing and changing the bag involved great indignity for him, but I never once heard him complain.

Having recognised that my father would never again be able to cope with the hard work inseparable from the job he had been doing in the shipyard, and that his earning power would be drastically reduced, I had decided that it was time for me to become a professional in football. So when Bobby Brown made me an offer to turn pro I snatched at it far too eagerly. My dad seethed when he heard what I had done and, although I had acted for the best of reasons, he was dead right. My signing-on fee was £300 tax free. What a mug I was. Still, once the decision was made, I had to press on.

Over the next season my appearances in the first team became more frequent and I succeeded in notching a few important goals. In truth, any goal was bound to be important to St Johnstone, who were deep in relegation trouble. As the final weeks of the season loomed, Stirling Albion were already doomed and we were in a dog-fight for survival with four other clubs – Falkirk, Raith Rovers, Airdrie and St Mirren. The drama stretched into the very last day of the season, when our home match with Dundee was not just crucial for our survival but a championship decider for our opponents. Dundee needed only one point to take the title but their pursuers, Rangers, were at home to Kilmarnock, so the leaders were obviously not going to play for a draw. Escaping relegation in those days could come down to decimal calculations, since teams finishing level on points were separated not by goal difference but by goal average, which was established by dividing goals-for by goals-against. We were optimistic that we wouldn't put a strain on the mathematicians, since all four of our fellow strugglers had to win to put us in danger and their fixtures (Airdrie v Partick Thistle; Falkirk v Third Lanark; Raith Rovers v Hibernian; St Mirren v Dunfermline) gave all of them opposition from the top half of the League. Our chances of matching Dundee were slight and they shrank spectacularly when Bobby Brown displayed suicidal eccentricity by opting to switch our centre-forward, Laurie Thomson, to left-back to face the great Gordon Smith. Gordon, a right-winger of dazzling grace and skill, was in the twilight of his career after herculean service with Hibs and later Hearts but he was in terrific physical condition and we feared the worst. Dundee at that time were a team without a conspicuous weakness, an amalgam of all the attributes needed to win a championship. Even now, almost forty years on, their team list stirs admiration: Slater, Hamilton, Cox, Seith, Ure, Wishart, Smith, Penman, Gilzean, Cousins and Robertson.

On an afternoon of bright sunshine, Muirton Park was bursting at the seams, with fans on the roof of the stand and sitting all the way round the track. The setting and the atmosphere were ideal for one of the most memorable exhibitions of wing play I have witnessed. Poor Laurie Thomson was reduced to such a state of demoralised confusion that at one point in the second half, when Smith played the ball inside him and then swerved outside on to the track to go past, the big man was thrust into a situation where he ignored the ball altogether and charged over the touchline to go chasing after his tormentor with boots swinging wildly. A jail sentence for grievous bodily harm might have been more appropriate than a booking.

In the dying minutes, with us 3–0 down, I climbed above Ian Ure to score with a header but the goal was chalked off. Then the final whistle sounded and the field was invaded by celebrating Dundee supporters. When we reached the dressing-room, we learned to our horror how important that disallowed goal had been. Unbelievably, every one of the four other matches that mattered had gone against us: Falkirk 3 Third Lanark 0; St Mirren 4 Dunfermline 1; Raith Rovers 3 Hibs 1; Airdrie 1 Partick Thistle 0. Yet, even with those results, we were being relegated only because our goal average was the worst by a margin of 0.0471.

When I reported for work at Remington Rand on the Monday morning, I was still very low and not at all in the mood to tolerate the banter of one of my tradesmen, Dick Montgomery, who was giving me a rough passage about being thrashed on the Saturday and denying his team, Rangers, the chance to win the League. I snapped and gave him a barrage of abuse. He was totally shocked and just walked away. Some time afterwards he approached my bench and whispered in my ear.

'I know you are disappointed about Saturday,' he said, 'and maybe I should not have joked about it, but if you ever talk to me like that again, I'll ram your head in that machine.' It was the kind of whisper I was likely to remember.

Descent into the Second Division was a bitter blow to everyone at St Johnstone but obviously the full-time players with families suffered most. As a single man whose football wage was supplemented by my apprentice's pay packet, I was reasonably well fixed. Nonetheless, I was as determined as the others to bounce straight back and when we did I made a creditable contribution to the championship success, scoring nine goals. My form was helped by the fact that I had stopped travelling to Perth in midweek for training, a blessing brought about by the spirited intervention of my superintendent in the tool room, Jim Cameron, who was fed up seeing me coming to work tired and listless after my cross-country tours. But Bobby Brown was clearly not happy about having to let me train in the Glasgow area and for a while I was frozen out of favour.

For a spell I trained with Third Lanark at Cathkin Park but their mixture of full-time and part-time players meant that on some nights there would be as few as six of us working out. So I changed to Airdrie, which was a few miles outside Glasgow but easily reached by train. Airdrie's players were all part-time and the training was the kind of hard routine I appreciated. The trainer of the time, Bobby Morrison, delighted in giving us fast-walking sessions, making us rattle round the track with that ugly action you are forced to adopt if you are forbidden to break into a trot.

Anybody who ever tried it will know it is bloody murder but nobody complained, least of all Airdrie's most experienced player, Tommy Duncan. Nobody ever beat him and Tommy's proficiency in that peculiar contest was his pride and joy. There are some strange people going around.

Promotion for St Johnstone brought happiness to the Fair City, as Perth is called, but it signalled a decline in my fortunes. The manager recruited fresh players to guard against a yo-yo return to the lower division and I was not looking forward to another season in the reserves. There was something bizarre about our reserve team. Whether or not the manager was to blame, there was undeniably a fetish about outside-lefts. In one season I played with nineteen of them. Being a feeder for a further succession of would-be Gentos was not a prospect I relished. I had been reading with interest a lot of speculation about my future and eventually Bobby Brown said he had agreed a deal with Doug Cowie, the manager of Raith Rovers. I told him vehemently that it was a non-starter. Before long that was a term that could be applied to me, for I was put out of action by a rather serious facial injury. It occurred in early October during a reserve game at home against Airdrie, whose reputation for toughness I had been able to confirm at first hand on the training ground. Predictably, the exchanges in this particular match had been fairly physical and I got involved with one of their old guard, Jackie Stewart. There was rugged give-and-take throughout the game until I went to head a bouncing ball. Good night Vienna! The next thing I knew I was in the dressing-room waiting for an ambulance to take me to hospital. Stewart had caught me a real one with his head. Most of my team-mates reckoned it was deliberate and that was my feeling, too, but my own play could be described as robust and I suppose if you live by the sword you must be ready to die by the sledge-hammer. The surgeon who turned up at my bedside was in his dinner suit and he said I had done him a favour as the dinner he had left was lousy. Glad to be of service!

I had a fractured cheekbone and a broken nose and the bone above my eyebrow was also fractured. The hospital staff were superb and contacted my parents to let them know what had happened and that I was comfortable after an operation. For the next two days I lay in pain and isolation. I remember that I sought occasional solace in listening to the 'Hello Mother, Hello Father' record of Alan Sherman, which was a hoot at the time. No one from the club came to see me. I felt neglected and got depressed, but I imagine my team-mates thought I had been released. On the Tuesday, Bobby Brown did come to pick me up and drive me to Perth station to catch my train home to Glasgow. The journey was enough to give me a complex. My face was encased in plaster and each time someone passed there would be an exaggerated double-take.

The plaster stayed on for six weeks, making it difficult to watch football, let alone play it. But there was plenty going on in my other job. The factory was in turmoil, with one strike meeting after another. I always took trade union activity seriously but I must admit that at one of those militant gatherings I found it hard to give the speakers my undivided attention. One of the senior women workers, who was a good friend of mine and used to give me the odd scouting report about interesting new girls on the premises, had told me of one recently arrived after working in a hotel in Jersey. When she was pointed out to me I was impressed. She was pretty and had a lovely walk and a nice bum and I made it my business to find out that she was Cathy Holding from Toryglen, near Hampden. That was as much as I knew when I found myself standing not far from her at that strike meeting. I couldn't take my eyes off her. It seemed that I was having the same effect on her but, considering that I had plaster where my face should have been, it would be rash to assume that her curiosity was romantic. Mine was, and Cathy Holding's name was top of my attack list.

Once the plaster was removed in early December, there was trepidation about my first taste of action. That reserve match with Celtic produced psychological rather than physical pain. We lost 10–1 and on my second outing after the injury, Kilmarnock reserves beat us 11–2. Those were results to harden the depressing conclusion that my football career was grinding to a halt, and it was about then that I began to contemplate emigration to Canada. Privately, as I surveyed my lack of progress in the game, I had to admit that I was by no means blameless. If you want to make it as a player you have to be fully committed and willing to make sacrifices and in both respects I was coming up short. I wasn't in love with toolmaking but having to serve my apprenticeship meant that I couldn't really get my teeth into football, which I did love. My attitudes were in a mess and the notion of crossing the Atlantic grew increasingly attractive. Toolmakers were in demand in Canada and I knew quite a few who had gone there and were earning far more than they had in Scotland. Of course, what I was really doing in that winter of 1963 was looking for an easy way out of my troubles, and with St Johnstone's hapless reserve team due to take on Rangers reserves in Perth on Saturday, 21 December maybe I could be excused for wanting to flee the country. While I thought about emigration, I made a less ambitious escape to my granny's in Neptune Street, round the corner from Govan Road. The atmosphere at the parental home had been desperately soured by the relations, or lack of them, between Dad and me. With confidence in my football future badly shaken by the St Johnstone experience, I had begun to enjoy myself overmuch socially and a terrible bust-up was inevitable when Dad smelled drink on me one Saturday night. Looking back, I can understand what a let-down my behaviour must have been for my father, who had invested so much hope and energy in encouraging Martin and me to be footballers. Back then, the most comforting antidote to continual rows and being branded the black sheep was some of Granny Irwin's doting indulgence. Selfishly, I went for it. For the family, it was a bad situation and it would get worse before it got better but when the improvement came it was so sudden, so dramatic and on such a scale that it transformed my life. Making sense of what happened is not easy. All I can do is set down the facts as they unfolded.

By Friday, 20 December I had decided that I didn't want to play for the St Johnstone reserves again, and certainly not the next day against Rangers. I felt I couldn't handle another drubbing. So I persuaded my brother's girlfriend, Joan Parker, to phone Bobby Brown and pretend to be my mother and say I had the flu. The absence of a bathroom in our house made me a regular at the local swimming baths, where I could have a steam bath as well as a swim, and while there after work on that Friday I began to have regrets about the gutless way I had used Joan. I wasn't proud of myself but was still unprepared for the reception at home. That Dad was in his worst Old Thunder Face mode did not surprise me. What did was the way my mother let rip in front of Martin and Joan. I cannot think of another occasion in my lifetime when she gave me such a public dressing down. She preferred to deal with you quietly on your own, whereas Dad (and I know I have inherited this characteristic from him) would never let anything pass without having his say there and then. While I was absorbing all the hostility, reinforced by deadly looks from Martin, my mother shoved a telegram in front of my face. It was from Bobby Brown, and said simply: 'Phone me immediately.'

'What will I do?' I addressed the question to my mother but it was my father who answered.

'What will you do? I'll tell you exactly what you're going to do. You'll get along to that phone box and speak to that manager and apologise or you will never get in this house again!'

Now that was serious, so without even the slightest mention of my dinner I made my way along the Govan Road towards the dry dock to the nearest phone box. I can still remember the number to this day: Stanley 267. Stanley, a small village on the outskirts of Perth, was where Bobby Brown lived. By the time I had put my money in and dialled, my stomach was churning.

'Stanley 267.'

'Boss,' and I put on the big gravel voice, 'it's Alex.'

'Oh, it's you. How dare you get someone to phone me up on a Friday and tell me you are not well, and I know it wasn't your mother. I have five first-team players down with real flu, so you make sure you report at the Buchanan Hotel at twelve o'clock tomorrow or you are in deep trouble.' End of conversation.

As I walked back to the house I was quite relieved. No fine, no suspension and – given the reference to the Buchanan Hotel in Glasgow – I might be playing in the first team. Relief lasted as far as our front door, where the interrogation began.

'What did he say?' my dad barked.

'I've got to report for the first team tomorrow. I might be playing.' If I imagined that news would soften him, I was instantly corrected.

'I know what I'd do with you, and I won't be going to the game . . .' and on and on he went, so it was a mercy when I was able to slip off to my bed.

The next morning I went along to the Glasgow Savings Bank at Paisley Road Toll to withdraw £80 to pay for a smart Crombie coat I'd had made by the well-known tailor Joe McGeachie of Duke Street in the east end of Glasgow (I had developed a fondness for good clothes in quality materials – maybe they made me feel less like a reserve). Then it was off to meet the team at the hotel in Buchanan Street, where I was to learn almost immediately through the trainer that I was definitely playing. Two complimentary tickets came with my status. As we disembarked from the coach outside the main entrance of Ibrox I was astonished to see Dad waiting for me along with another man. The stranger proved to be the manager of the bank I had visited earlier. One of his tellers had made a mistake during the morning and he was having to trace every customer who had withdrawn money, which must have been a rip-roaring way to spend his Saturday. Once he was satisfied about the details of my transaction, he went off and I was left standing alone with my father, neither of us saying a word. I broke the silence and asked him if he wanted a ticket. After a little hesitation, he said, 'I might as well, I've nothing else to do.' I was delighted, and I am sure in retrospect there is nowhere else in the world my father would rather have been that afternoon.

What happened to me on the field at Ibrox that day can only come under the category of miracles. I scored a hat trick, the first player ever to do so against Rangers at Ibrox. It was the first time St Johnstone had ever won there. A local boy, born and brought up within 200 yards of the ground, scoring three goals to beat the mighty Rangers, the team he had supported all his life – it was just too crazy for words. I do honestly believe that some power somewhere gave me a break and that it was a signal for me to grasp this opportunity and not ever to forget the responsibilities that came with it. Time and again my thoughts wander back to that day. My efforts to rationalise the events leave me none the wiser but since then I have never been sceptical about the existence of influences beyond ourselves.

The game itself I recall quite clearly. There was nothing in the first half to hint at a shock on the horizon. Rangers were leading 1–0 at the interval, thanks to a goal from George McLean. At half-time in those days the managers said very little and it was usually left to the senior players to inject enthusiasm or give advice. In our dressing-room Ron McKinven, Jim Little and Jimmy Walker were urging the others to keep going, telling them all was not lost. I had no problem believing that. I was feeling great. Early in the second half I was starting to give big Ronnie McKinnon, the Rangers centre-half, serious difficulties and he showed his discomfort by pulling me back by the jersey as I was going through for a shot. I felt other chances would soon arrive, and I was right. Ally McIntyre, our little battleship of a right-winger, was beginning to wreak havoc against big Davie Provan and on one attack he cut across Davie just outside the box and tried a shot. The ball hit a defender and fell to me about twenty-two yards out. I cracked it with my right foot only to see it rebound off McKinnon's leg. The bounce, however, brought it back nicely on to my left foot and I struck it perfectly into the far, left-hand stanchion. Ten minutes later (and we were now giving them a torrid time) I scored again, this time following another attacker's attempt from outside the area which the Rangers goalkeeper, Bill Ritchie, could not hold. Saints leading 2–1, this was incredible. Then I hit the bar and it seemed I could do nothing wrong. But, as is so often the case at Ibrox, they produced a goal out of nowhere and the assumption was that Ralph Brand had saved the game for them. We had other ideas. With twelve minutes to go, following a mix-up in the goalmouth, the ball broke to me and I was presented with an easy winner. Towards the end, I hit the bar again. Greed was getting the better of me.

In the bath after the game one of the older players said to me, 'Do you realise, you've created history.' Having soaked up my share of glory, I dressed and slipped out through a side door for the short walk home. As I turned the corner into Broomloan Road, which leads to Govan Road, I was caught by a reporter, Joe Hamilton of the *Daily Express*. He was the only journalist to get a quote from me that day. When I arrived home I didn't know what to expect but if my father was saying nothing, my mum was not hiding her feelings.

'Well done. Well done, son. That was great.' She went on about me being mentioned on the telly and how everyone in the street was talking about me. Then she whispered and nodded towards my dad. He was, as usual, reading a book.

'Talk to him,' my mother said. So I asked the obvious.

'What did you think of the game?'

'OK,' he replied.

He was back to his best – cool you down in case you get carried away. I just smiled at Mum, who shrugged her shoulders. Once he defrosted, Dad was into delivering one of his standard reminders: 'What did I tell you about shooting, eh? If you don't shoot, you won't score.' I don't know how many times I heard him say that. I wish I could hear him now.

The next day all the press were round and I agreed to have a photo taken outside the gates at Ibrox. I was learning to drive and the photographers posed me beside my car, with its L-plates. My life changed from that day and no matter how many twists the road took, it led upwards. In trying to make full use of my big break, the immediate problem was my slowness in recognising that my priorities had to be different from those of the mates with whom I was socialising. As a manager, I have constantly stressed to young players coming to a club that however genuine friends outside the game may be, they simply do not have the same agenda as a professional sportsman. The idea that the only danger is in mixing with worthless hangers-on is nonsense. Ordinary, decent lads, if their performance at work doesn't depend on self-sacrifice and dedication to fitness, have a right to think it is part of growing up to do some carousing. But a footballer who does not distance himself from the drinking and the late hours is asking for trouble. The lads I went around with as 1964 began were great friends and still are to this day: Billy McKechnie, Dave Sanderson, John Thomson, Eddie Hill, Rab Todd, Tom Bain, Tom McLean, Jim Bryson, Willie Dalziel and many more. We had gone on holiday together and met every Saturday in the Ingram Bar in central Glasgow to argue over the day's results and much else.

I have remained particularly close with Billy McKechnie and Dave Sanderson. They are chalk and cheese. McKechnie is a likeable extrovert who takes over the conversation and the company wherever he goes. Dave is quiet and unassuming but all three of us have always hit it off and nobody could ask for more loyalty than I have had from those two men. In fact, Billy once had to pay a horrifying price for that loyalty. It was at a time in the Eighties when Aberdeen, under my management, were beating Rangers regularly and, although Billy is an avid Rangers supporter, he defended me like a brother against bitter comments in the Mermaid Bar, a tough pub in the Bridgeton area of Glasgow's east end. The characters who had been arguing with him waited outside the pub and attacked him, leaving him unconscious and with his skull fractured. He spent weeks in intensive care at the Royal Infirmary. The Glasgow hatred of bullies and liberty-takers surfaced then and some proper hard men wanted to seek out the thugs for vengeance. But Billy refused to exploit his immense popularity in Bridgeton and asked everyone to leave the matter to the police.

There will be recurring evidence in this book that loyalty is something I regard as one of the most precious human qualities. I have frequently been accused of being over-loyal to my players when their behaviour drew public condemnation. No doubt there have been occasions when that charge has been justified but the inclination to stick by friends and allies was bred into me and strengthened by my working-class upbringing in Scotland. Where I was raised, there were good and bad, weak and strong people, as there are everywhere, but there were many you could rely upon totally if you were in trouble. Desertion was not in their vocabulary. In our contemporary society, where selfishness is rampant, such values seem more worthwhile than ever.

As the carefree outings with my unattached pals continued to take their toll of sporting dedication, there appeared to be little prospect of breaking the pattern without another touch of divine intervention – and, I'm prepared to admit even thirty-five years later, divine it was. One Friday night at the Locarno dance hall in Sauchiehall Street I spied the girl I had been eyeing up with difficulty through my plaster at the Remington Rand strike meeting. Cathy Holding's attractiveness had not diminished and after a few whirls round the floor I saw her home. That led to steady dating, so steady that we are still at it, although Cathy will insist she saw a lot more of me then than she does now as my wife and the mother of our three marvellous sons. That is probably true, since in the first flush of our romance I was seeing her every night, and during the day I would find a reason to visit her for a chat in the sub-assembly section of the factory. As our relationship deepened (in my mind the fact that Cathy was Catholic was never a serious obstacle), my zest for football and its demands was thoroughly restored and I was looking forward to gaining a transfer and starting afresh at a new club.

Strangely, my last match for St Johnstone was another victory over Rangers but this time we were helped by the contented mood of opponents who had just won the treble of League, Scottish Cup and League Cup. They also suffered from the sending off of their great centre-forward, Jimmy Millar, who was one of my all-time favourites and a really first-class guy. Those facts should have adjusted the perspective of our left-back, Willie Coburn, when he assessed his own impressive display. But no, there in the *Weekly News* was a headline: 'How I mastered Wee Willie Henderson'. At that time, Henderson had no superior in the Scottish game and I chuckled quietly to myself that Mr Coburn could expect retribution. It was swift. The League Cup draw put Rangers against St Johnstone in the first match of the season and the result was 10–2, with Wee Willie making nine and scoring one.

That summer flew by as speculation about my transfer mounted. The most persistent talk was that Dunfermline, managed by Jock Stein, had tried to arrange a swap for one of their players. But suddenly Stein left Dunfermline to take over at Hibs. That was a shock. The Fifers had progressed amazingly under Jock and were more than the equal of Hibs. A week after Jock's departure I received word that his successor, Willie Cunningham, the former Northern Ireland full-back, wanted to go through with a deal. It was an exciting development because Dunfermline had become one of Scotland's foremost teams and had enjoyed a healthy European run the previous season.

As a recently qualified driver, with a new Hillman Super Minx, 397 FVD, I was preparing to drive through to Fife for the meeting with Cunningham when it dawned on me that I had no money to fill the car up with petrol. In such a predicament, there was only one saviour – Ma. When you were skint, no matter how short of cash she was, she would always delve into one of her biscuit tins and come to the rescue. Those tins were hidden away in various parts of the house. One was for the Society Man, Jimmy Gillespie, who called every Friday to collect the premiums on a life assurance policy she paid. Other tins were for the gas bill, the electricity bill and so on. When I told her why I needed money, I could have had the moon. She and Dad were thrilled and, of course, in his case it was a cue for advice about the opportunities and pitfalls up ahead. He just never gave up on his hopes for his two sons and our debt to him is huge. I don't believe anybody's personality can ever be totally attributed to genes and upbringing. Our wider experiences, and how we handle them, also do much to forge our characters. But the influence of my dad and my ma was the kind that rubbed off on Martin and me and will be a part of us forever. Dad was the driving force but my mother had a stronger and more determined streak in her.

My conversation with Willie Cunningham at East End Park was mainly about the Dunfermline wage structure, which was disappointing. The basic pay was £27, with weekly place money if we were in the top half of the League: £14 extra for being top, £12 for second, £10 for third and so on down, plus the £3 bonus for each match win. I was already earning £27-plus as a toolmaker, having completed my apprenticeship about a year earlier. Allowing for the £16 I received as a part-time player, I would be taking a big drop by going full-time. I decided to remain part-time until the pre-season training was over and review my position then. There was no reason for regrets. I was a twenty-two-year-old with a new club, and a good one at that, and I was well pleased as I made my way back to the West of Scotland.

The Glasgow Fair undoubtedly meant a lot more to people in the Sixties than it does now that so much of the city's identification with heavy industry has been eroded and there is greater choice about when summer breaks are taken. More people can afford to escape abroad these days. In my youth there were many for whom even Saltcoats, on the Ayrshire coast, was a resort too far. The Fair fortnight in July three or four decades ago came as a massive release for the inhabitants of working areas like Govan. Families who had not gone away would be happy to gather in Elder Park or Bellahouston Park, which is close to Ibrox Stadium, and roam about on the grass or feed the ducks on the pond. The quietness that descended when the clanging din of the shipyards ceased was a rest in itself. For me, there would be no rest in 1964. The holiday gave me my first taste of full-time training. It was bloody hard but I loved it. I was determined not to be shown up and led the field in all the cross-country runs, much to the annoyance of a few of the old dogs who thought I was a smart-arse trying to impress. The only person I was out to convince was myself. All that running up and down the stairways of Hampden Park paid dividends. At Queen's Park and before, I had built a stamina base that has served me well all my life. Dunfermline was my first experience of having to punish myself every day and there were mornings when I was so stiff and sore that I could hardly get out of bed. Anyone who has endured a really arduous pre-season will know what I mean. You feel your body doesn't belong to you. Yet all of this only intensified my desire to be a full-time footballer and, after talking it over with my parents and Cathy, I resolved to go for it.

There was a little-boy excitement in me when I reported to Remington Rand at the end of the Fair holiday for what I thought would be my final day. 'No, you have to work your two weeks' notice, son,' my superintendent, Jim Cameron, told me, and I felt as if I had been kicked in the stomach. I had imagined the company would be delighted to see the back of me. After all, I was the shop steward of the toolroom and Remington was so anti-union that I was half-expecting a golden handshake. At least the extra fortnight would make it easier to arrange for somebody to take over my union duties. I hoped there would be a more widespread eagerness to serve than had been shown before I was appointed.

'There is no other bastard who'll take the job,' the vice-convenor for the factory had reported after my predecessor, Callum McKay, was sacked without a shred of justification. I had been the apprentices' shop steward, and had campaigned vigorously to ensure that our lads were wholeheartedly committed to the eight-week national strike of apprentices that secured substantial wage improvements throughout the engineering industry in 1961, so everybody knew that I wouldn't turn my back on the crisis created by Callum's dismissal. I was just twenty-one at that time, newly qualified as a journeyman, and shouldn't really have been taking on such leadership responsibilities. But nobody else was stepping forward to organise the protest against what had been done to Callum, who was factory convenor for the Amalgamated Engineering Union as well as toolroom shop steward, so there was no option but for me to accept the job and get the troops out on strike. There was no trace of a knee-jerk reaction in this. McKay was a true trade unionist, a wonderfully intelligent man who had been a source of inspiration to me. He was a Communist, so our political affiliations would always be different, but we shared a belief in getting a fair deal for working people. I concede that at times I worried about the militancy of the union at Remington Rand, where the often reactionary policies of the American owners were balanced by a willingness to pay better wages than were available in similar plants elsewhere. I learned from Granny Irwin, who was the great go-between and comforter in our family, that my mother was more deeply concerned. 'She prays every night that you're not a Communist,' my granny told me. I was able to be sincerely brusque in dismissing such fears, knowing that my vehemence would be instantly conveyed to my mum. When it came to arguing the case for a strike with the rest of the toolmakers, the fact that Callum himself was not present gave a few of them the heart to oppose the motion. I may have mellowed over the years but I could never agree with anyone declining to fight against the kind of injustice done to our shop steward. Not all of the toolmakers remained resolute and our six-week strike ended without achieving the reinstatement of McKay, who went on to work in another factory and subsequently became the AEU's district convenor for Renfrewshire. But I was proud of the workers who made a stand along with me and that period of my life gives me lasting satisfaction.

A year on, as I visited every department at Remington Rand and said my farewells to friends I knew I would sorely miss, it all became quite emotional. The six years I had spent there was a big slice of my life at that stage and when I began clearing out my bench, I appreciated how it must be for tradesmen who retire after a lifetime in one workplace. Along with the tools, you are carrying away a lot of memories. Some of the laughs we had shared came to mind. One had unlikely origins in an accident with a punch-shape machine that sliced off the tip of one of my fingers. When it happened, I ran in panic to my senior tradesman, Jimmy Junor, who rushed me off to the medical room. In we burst and Jimmy shouts to the resident nurse, Annie, 'Quick, get a brandy.'

'You can't give a young lad brandy,' says Annie.

'It's not for him, it's for me.' Jimmy Junor did like a drink, and no wonder – he supported Partick Thistle, poor soul.

— 4 —
GRIEF, GOALS AND A GOOD WOMAN

MOST of the unfading memories from a football career are created by occasions when the adrenaline is surging, and I had plenty of those in my three years with Dunfermline. It was with them that I had a season in which I scored forty-five goals in fifty-one matches, in their colours that I was introduced to the unique highs of European football and in their dressing-room at Hampden Park that I vented my rage after learning, less than a hour before kick-off, that I had been dropped from the team for the Scottish Cup final. Yet nothing that happened to me at Dunfermline comes back to my mind more vividly than a morning when East End Park was serenely quiet and the only movement in the place was that of two figures jogging steadily around the perimeter of the pitch in the pale January sunshine. It was a Wednesday, which explains the tranquillity of the scene. Whereas Tuesday training sessions under our physio-trainer, Andy Stevenson, were spectacularly gruelling, on Wednesdays the players were often allowed to relax at the local swimming baths. I was one of the two missing the outing that morning in 1967 and the other was John Lunn, a young full-back who was – I can say without hesitation more than thirty years on – the most exciting prospect I have ever seen in that position. He was a lovely lad, quiet and modest, but on the field he was brimming with aggression and his pace was extraordinary. John had recently been picked to play for the Scottish League against the League of Ireland at Ibrox and on the night of the midweek match he and two of our team-mates, the brothers Tom and Willie Callaghan, had stayed at my parents' home close to the Rangers ground. Speculation was rife that Rangers were keen to sign him and after the League international the Callaghans and I ribbed him mercilessly about his impending move into the big-time. We were not surprised when he reddened with embarrassment, for it was John's total lack of vanity that made everyone at the club delighted to see him doing so well. The future looked gloriously bright for him but tragedy was waiting in ambush and, strangely, I had a role in revealing the nature of it.

On that Wednesday at East End Park, we were lonely joggers because both of us were recovering from injuries (mine a troublesome knee, his persistent soreness in his calves). As we came round behind the goal at the town end, John suddenly asked me, 'Do you think I could be anaemic?' At the best of times he had a colourless complexion, so I found myself answering, 'Well, you're pale enough. Why don't you get a blood test?' After our work on the track, we went into the physio's room for treatment. I was having heat from a short-wave machine applied to my knee, so I was sitting up on one table, facing the door. John was face down on the other table, receiving a massage from Andy Stevenson, who was a master at rubbing away aches and tensions. The door opened and in came Dr Yellowlees, the club physician.

'There he is now, John – ask him,' I suggested. Maybe it was because he was so shy that I felt the need to act for him, I don't know, but I took on his case. 'John thinks he is anaemic and his calves are really sore,' I told the doctor.

'Well, let's have a look at you, John, when you have had your treatment.' And later that morning Dr Yellowlees conducted an examination and took a blood sample.

The players' habit of having lunch at the Regal restaurant was a highlight of my time at Dunfermline and it was probably there that the seeds of my managerial career were planted. This day was typical. Long after we had finished eating, a bunch of us lingered in the upstairs room to argue over tactics and advocate our pet theories. Bertie Paton, the Callaghans, Jim McLean, Harry

Melrose, George Peebles, George Miller and Jim Herriot were all having their say and the salt and pepper holders were shifted endlessly around the table as moves and counter-moves were plotted. At about two o'clock, just as the West of Scotland crew were readying themselves for the homeward journey, a call came through from the ground asking for John Lunn.

'I think he's downstairs playing snooker,' someone said. In addition to the restaurant, the Regal complex had a cinema and a snooker hall.

'He's got to go back to the ground immediately,' was the instruction and one of the others set off to find him.

Next day the West of Scotland lads, as usual, were last into the ground. When we made our customary buoyant entrance to the changing rooms, we were met by a deathly silence.

'What's wrong?' one of us inquired.

'There's something up with John. We don't know exactly what it is.'

Instantly I thought of the events of the day before and I felt a weight of foreboding settling on me. That morning's training was a non-event. It was two days later that the manager gave us the terrible news: 'Leukaemia.' How brutal life can be. My earlier assessment of John's potential is not exaggerated by sorrow over what happened to a truly good lad but is simply recognition of an exceptionally promising full-back who, I am sure, would have gone on to represent his country and fulfil all our hopes of him. Advanced medical procedures held the illness at bay for a while and John actually returned to play for Dunfermline, which was his home-town club, for a few seasons. When word of his death in 1974 reached me in the dressing-room at Ayr United, where I was seeing out my last year as a player, it brought deep sadness, as it did to all who were fortunate enough to have touched any part of his life. The funeral in Dunfermline, on which players from all over the country converged to pay their respects, was heartbreaking. John left a wife, Kathy, and a young family and his parents, who had worshipped him, were devastated.

John Lunn, though younger than I was, had already established himself as Dunfermline's left-back when I arrived as a twenty-two-year-old in 1964 and there was sufficient quality in other positions to guarantee a good season for the team known affectionately as the Pars (the nickname is short for paralytics and recalls how useless they were early in their existence). We emerged successfully from the sectional phase of the first competition, the League Cup, but not before I had battled through another memorable skirmish with Attila the Hun, John McNamee. Since Huns is a term applied by the Celtic faithful to Rangers, or at least to their supporters, it may seem inappropriate to link it with big John, who was never likely to have any association with Ibrox, but as a threat to the well-being of anybody who came in front of him he certainly deserved comparison with Attila. By the time of that League Cup meeting, he was with Hibernian, under Jock Stein, whose first return to East End Park gave the match an extra edge. I should emphasise that although a common-sense interest in self-preservation had persuaded me to leave McNamee unchallenged in the dressing-room corridor at St Johnstone (the best of three falls with a monster was not, as I have said, a sensible option), I never ceased to give as good as I got in our confrontations on the field. It is vital to stand up to such opponents. If you don't, they trample all over you. I stood up well enough to score in a 2–0 victory over Hibs that helped us to win our section and earn a quarter-final tie against Rangers. For that game, Willie Cunningham, with more originality than logic, decreed that I should have the task of smothering the midfield menace of Jim Baxter. I was instructed that Slim Jim must not have a minute's peace. I mentioned that when last at Ibrox I was an attacker and scored a hat trick, but I was the new kid on the block and had to do as I was told. My enjoyment of the afternoon was limited to watching probably the greatest of all boxers, Sugar Ray Robinson, who was Rangers' guest, launch the proceedings with a mock kick-off. After that, it was all downhill for me. Baxter was a magician on the park, a player who, in the words of one admiring victim, could have put a size-five football in an egg cup. Putting me in my place as a defensive influence didn't take long. Within seconds of the official start I was sprinting in on Baxter with the hopeful notion of pressuring him, or maybe even the crazy idea of winning the ball. My reward was humiliation as Jim nutmegged me and left me helpless on the ground. When I rose to my feet I was staring straight into the Rangers end and it was easy to imagine what my mates were saying. It did cross my mind in that moment that toolmaking wasn't a bad job. Rangers beat us 1–0, so at least the great man did not run riot.

The 1964–65 season was developing well for me, with no shortage of goals from the inside-left position, and when I was put out of action by a medial ligament injury, my natural eagerness to come back was sharpened by Dunfermline's involvement in the Fairs Cup (now the UEFA Cup). I had recovered by the date of the first leg of our tie with Orgryte of Gothenburg but the manager decided I was short of match fitness, so my introduction to European football was delayed until we travelled to Sweden. It was not an experience I had much opportunity to savour. Armed with a 4–2 lead from the first leg, Willie Cunningham had me playing up front on my own, with orders to harass their centre-backs for an hour and a half. If I thought he was cruel to ask me to subdue Baxter, that assignment on a quagmire of a pitch at the Ullevi Stadium came close to sadism. By the end I was functioning from memory. Afterwards, while the others celebrated the goalless draw in our dressing-room, I just wanted to sleep.

Subsequently our progress in the competition was satisfactory. We came through a little war with Stuttgart, winning 1–0 at home and drawing 0–0 in Germany. Our third round opponents were Athletic Bilbao and it was in the away leg that I first encountered, as much through smell as any of the other senses, the atmosphere that I have ever since identified with the biggest nights of continental football. There is a distinctive flavour in the air at Spanish matches, a mixture of cigar and cigarette smoke and perhaps a hint of the perfume of well-dressed women, and I have never competed in one of their major stadiums, as a player or a manager, without feeling involved in something exciting and glamorous. That romantic impression must have been strong to withstand the treatment I received from the defender Bilbao set against me, a villainous character called José Maria Echevarria. If Echevarria had applied for a torturer's job with the Inquisition, he would have been rejected as too vicious. We lost the match 1–0 and I knew we would have a grim struggle at home, especially as their goalkeeper was the outstanding José Angel Iribar, who was in Spain's national team. But a cold night and a frosty pitch helped us in Dunfermline and our inside-right, Alex Smith, managed to put the ball past Iribar to leave the sides level on aggregate. In those days that meant a third game, with the toss of a coin deciding the venue. Most of us were undismayed when we lost the toss, since we relished the atmosphere in the Bilbao stadium. The same could not be said of the result: a 2–1 defeat. Our Euro dream was over.

In the League, our form was excellent and we were in a three-horse race for the title with Kilmarnock and Hearts. It is hard to exaggerate just how unusual it was for Rangers and Celtic to find themselves labouring in the pursuing pack. In the fourteen seasons after 1965, the Scottish championship was won eleven times by Celtic (thanks mainly to Jock Stein's astonishing sequence of nine in a row) and three times by Rangers. I had a hand in ending that period of monopoly, for it was Aberdeen under my management that broke the pattern in 1980, but I am afraid I made a significant contribution to Dunfermline's failure to win the title in 1965. The prize should have been at our mercy when we found ourselves with home advantage in all of our last four fixtures. In two of them we beat Rangers 3–1 and Celtic 5–1 (thus completing home-and-away doubles over both members of the Old Firm) but we lost 1–0 to Dundee United and drew 1–1 with St Johnstone. It was the series of chances I missed in that draw with my former club in the second-last game of our league season that was reckoned to have denied us the championship, which was won by Kilmarnock, who finished a point ahead of us and beat Hearts on goal average (we had better goal figures than either of them). Those misses were untypical of the way I played against St Johnstone after leaving Muirton Park. My goalscoring record against them was remarkable. It included two or three hat tricks and in a four-year period I hit their net something like twenty-seven times, but on the occasion when I most needed to punish them I wasted a couple of clear openings and, although I did score our only goal, the accusation that I had cost Dunfermline the title was unavoidable. So was the suspicion that my performance might weigh heavily with Willie Cunningham when he came to choose the team to face Celtic in the Scottish Cup final a week later.

The excitement of our run in the knockout competition had, inevitably, intensified as each round was negotiated and our supporters were still harbouring the dream of the League and Cup double when we met Hibernian in a semi-final at Tynecastle Park. For me, the semi brought another renewal of hostilities with John McNamee. I played well on the day, making the first goal for Harry Melrose and giving big John a hard time – so much so that Attila lost his temper and was booked for a wild swing at me late in a tousy match that finished 2–0 in our favour. Willie Cunningham was due a lot of credit for the result. The manager had elected to use one of our defenders, Jim Thomson, as a man-marker on Hibernian's star player, Willie Hamilton, and Hamilton was almost invisible. Thomson was a phlegmatic individual, never up nor down, and he played that way, never losing his cool, keeping his discipline and concentration to great effect. When we faced a team with a fast, talented attacker like Hamilton, out came Thomson for the nullifying job. The scale of his achievement at Tynecastle that afternoon was underlined for me years later when I was Jock Stein's assistant with Scotland and heard him raving about Willie Hamilton. Jock regarded Willie as the most talented player he ever managed but despaired of his lifestyle. Willie never applied the brake to his self-destructiveness and he died at a relatively young age.

From outside the Dunfermline camp, it may have seemed that my form in the semi-final and my ranking as the club's top goalscorer made me a certain starter in the final. But there were other considerations that caused me to worry. I had been left out of the team when we beat Rangers 3–1 in the League and brought back for the next match against Dundee United, which we lost, and then there was my bout of poor finishing against St Johnstone. Willie Cunningham had to decide between sticking with the team that took us over the last hurdle before Hampden or bringing back our regular centre-forward, John McLaughlin, who had missed the semi-final because of injury. The natural choice would be to go for my partnership with McLaughlin, which had operated effectively for most of the season. But little Harry Melrose, who had been a faithful servant to the Pars, had scored in the semi-final and was knocking on the door. The build-up to the big game was given added intensity by the appointment of Jock Stein as Celtic manager. Optimism was running high among the players at Parkhead as they sought to win their first trophy in eight years. Dunfermline were the better team but superior ability is rarely enough in itself to beat one of the Old Firm in a final. Their history can be like an extra player to them and to overcome that inherited morale you need self-belief and a willingness to fight every inch of the way. There was a great deal of emotional pride in my desperation to play in the final but I also felt I had the right attributes for the test we would be facing. I was the top scorer and I yielded to nobody as a competitor. Forget the chances I missed a week ago. This was a different day and I was ready for it. Harry Melrose and John McLaughlin had experience but, without being unfair to them, it had to be said that they were not a partnership and in a battle they were not at their best.

On the Saturday of the match, rather crazily, the West of Scotland players had to travel forty-five miles east to meet up with the rest of the team and then return to Glasgow in the coach. Modern footballers will find it unbelievable that, after eating lunch, we simply filed on to the bus and headed for Hampden, with no mention of a team-talk. We arrived at the old ground at 1.45 p.m. and still not a word had been said about the line-up for the day. The manager was obviously shirking the responsibility of telling the unlucky player personally that he was out. As we gathered in the dressing-room at 2.10 p.m. to hear his selection at last, the tension was tearing at my insides. Standing beside Willie Cunningham as he made the announcement were the club chairman, David Thomson, and the secretary, Jimmy McConville. Moral support? I had to think so. I had never previously seen those men with the manager in the dressing-room. The first part of the team was entirely predictable: Herriot, Willie Callaghan, Lunn, Thomson, McLean, Tom Callaghan. Now the forward line and the pain in my chest deepened as each name was read out: Edwards, Smith, McLaughlin and then the hammer blow. . . Melrose. As Jacky Sinclair's name was announced as the outside-left and last player, I exploded. 'You bastard,' I shouted at Cunningham. David Thomson intervened and ordered me to behave myself. I was in no mood to quieten down and continued to berate the manager. He knew the truth about how he had treated me and never said a word.

Looking back, I make no apology for the way I reacted. My view is that when the manager is not prepared to give a dropped player his place by telling him the bad news in advance, then there can be no complaint if, when the axe falls without warning fifty minutes before kick-off, there is an emotional response. This was a Cup final, every player's dream. It is now basic to my philosophy of management to deal personally with players who might have expected to be picked for a game but are not. I let them know the position before I announce the team in front of the squad. I try to explain why I am going for a certain line-up and stress that the choice is no indictment of an individual. To be honest, I don't think the men who are dropped ever take in much of what you are saying. Reasons are of no use to them. The bottom line is that they are out and, in the depths of their disappointment, it is hard to reach them. But at least you have helped them to keep their dignity and their pride, which is more than I was left with at Hampden in 1965.

My dad and Cathy were startled when I appeared outside in my street clothes. I really felt for Dad. I knew what a let-down it was for him to discover that I wasn't playing but, putting my feelings first, he masked it well and told me not to worry and to keep my cool. A bit late for that advice, I thought. That Cup final was the last to be played without substitutes, which is why I had to suffer in the stands as Dunfermline lost 3–2. Although McLaughlin and Melrose might be seen to have justified their selection by scoring our goals, I felt we were handicapped by the absence of the determination I could have brought to the game and I think a few of the other players shared that view. No blame could be attached to the men chosen. They did their best. I simply believed that I could have added something to their game.

On the Wednesday after the Cup final, I was recalled to the team and scored in a 5–1 thrashing of Celtic but the result was academic. Kilmarnock had the championship and Celtic had the Cup and our season was over. I immediately asked for a transfer but when the request was refused I did not sulk. Instead I resolved to make the 1965–66 season the best of my career so far. It was to prove the best of my career, period. With forty-five goals from fifty-one matches in all competitions, it was never going to be easy to surpass. The determination I carried into that campaign fed on the sense of injustice left by omission from the Cup final. There was a coolness between the manager and me but there was no question of letting him down. It was always my nature to try my best. All the elements of my football life seemed to be coming together. I had one year as a full-timer behind me and had been strengthened by another rigorous pre-season preparation. My habit of practising in the gymnasium under the stands was noticeably improving my game, particularly my finishing. God only knows how many times I hit shots at targets in there. I contrived all kinds of service for myself – volleying the ball as it came off corners of the wall or rebounded from the roof, receiving it on my chest or abdomen to wheel and score, relentlessly striving to better my technique as a finisher. If ever there was proof that it is not playing games of football that makes you a player that was it. Practice makes the player. The game is the proof that you are a player. Suddenly teams were starting to plan against me and in many cases they would adopt man-marking, but that only reinforced my confidence and my ambition. I was now thinking in terms of playing at a higher level.

As that second season with Dunfermline progressed, my form

was sustained, even through the preparations that Cathy and I were making to be married on 12 March 1966. Central to those preparations was the buying of a house and after the usual frustrations of the search we made an offer for a semi-detached in Simshill, on the southern side of Glasgow, about a mile and a half from Hampden Park. The offer was £3,005, bolstered by the sale of my car, and once it was accepted we put in regular shifts of decorating and had the house in spanking shape by the date of the wedding. We were married on a Saturday morning at Martha Street Registry Office in Glasgow. A church ceremony was out because neither of us wanted to change religion, but we both felt strongly that having been brought up in different faiths would not prejudice our future. We were keen to have a wedding with the minimum of fuss. Cathy's mother, as a devout Catholic, was uncomfortable about the registry office but she did not let her disappointment disrupt her daughter's day and indeed helped enormously to make sure it was a happy occasion. My brother Martin was best man and Cathy's bridesmaid was a friend, Agnes Wishart. On hand, too, were my mates McKechnie, Todd and Sanderson; a former workmate, Bob Falconer, and his wife Alice; Clare Park, the canteen lady who had looked after me so well when I was at Remington Rand; and, of course, our parents. It went smoothly and after the ceremony Cathy and I went off with Martin and Agnes to a studio in Buchanan Street to have the photographs taken. As we were parking Martin's car, a cheeky driver tried to steal our parking place and I lost my rag and started shouting. Martin attempted to calm me down but I was off and running and couldn't be quietened until I had made my point. Cathy was not too pleased with me. Good start, Alex.

After the photographs, I went straight off to play against Hamilton on a lovely afternoon at East End Park. The game was thoroughly forgettable, although we won 1–0 with an Alex Smith goal. I played poorly and was just glad to get the match out of the way. In the dressing-room afterwards there was a sinister atmosphere and a few whispered conversations strengthened my suspicion that the other players were planning a ball-blackening.

This was the well-known ritual of stripping the victim and smearing his vital organs with boot polish and dubbin, with a bit of vaseline added just to make the results really interesting. I took my time changing out of my strip, loitering to let the rest file through to the communal bath, followed by the physio with an ill-concealed tin of polish in his hand. At that moment, wearing nothing but my jockstrap, I grabbed my clothes and sprinted along the corridor to the referee's room. The ref on the day was a friend of mine (yes, that is possible). Willie Syme's parents had at one time lived above my family in Govan Road and, although he was initially astonished by my sudden arrival in his quarters, he was soon a willing accomplice in organising my escape. Outside Martin was sitting in his car, revved up and ready to go. It's wonderful having the support of your nearest and dearest on important days of your life. I wasn't in the car two minutes before Martin announced, 'You were hopeless today.' Thanks, brother.

The wedding reception in the evening was purely for the two families and when it was over Cathy and I went to spend our first night in our new home in Simshill. There was no honeymoon, not even a short break, as the next day I had to report at Dunblane Hydro to prepare for the Fairs Cup quarter-final tie against Zaragoza. This was a new approach by Willie Cunningham and his professional outlook was appreciated by the players. Cathy was less enthusiastic but she did not complain. Throughout my married life I have marvelled at the sacrifices she has made in the interests of my football career. I shall never forget the two legs of a marvellous contest with Zaragoza, or the shock and pain of a bereavement that came between them. The first game, at East End Park, reflected the benefits of the preparation at Dunblane, where we had the chance to analyse the many strengths of our opponents and to move towards the levels of concentration and tactical discipline needed to cope with them. On the night, Bertie Paton scored to give us a one-goal victory but we realised the second leg would be an ordeal.

On the Sunday prior to the match in Spain, Cathy and I were awoken very early in the morning by knocking on our front door.

It was Martin, along with my Aunt Chrissie's husband, John Copeland. Cathy went down to let them in and I stood at the top of the stairs transfixed, bracing myself for bad news. 'Granny's dead.' I took it badly. Granny Irwin had been ill with heart problems, and had been taken into Mearnskirk Hospital, but I didn't expect to lose her so suddenly. She was a star and we idolised each other. An entire book wouldn't accommodate the love and gratitude I feel when I think of her. The outpouring of warmth and loyalty that came from all branches of her family in mourning her was a reminder of something she said frequently to Martin and me about the Catholic faith: 'It's a hard religion to live with but a lovely religion to die with.' The funeral was to take place at St Saviour's Church on the following Wednesday and, since that was the day of our return match with Zaragoza in Spain, I wouldn't be able to attend. That's not an accurate way of putting it – of course I could and should have been there. But everybody in the family insisted that Granny would not have wanted me to miss the game. When it was played, I scored twice but we lost a thriller 4–2 in extra time and it was scant consolation that Zaragoza went on to defeat Barcelona in the final that year.

At the end of the 1965–66 season I refused to re-sign, and so did Alex Smith. Both of us were determined to advance our careers. I let Dunfermline know I would not be dissuaded from leaving unless they gave me a considerable pay rise and, after an early discussion with the manager, it was clear there was no prospect of that. So it was stalemate. They had my registration and thereby held all the aces. Footballers had been rescued from the worst excesses of the retain-and-transfer system in 1961 by the landmark civil lawsuit in which George Eastham – shrewdly advised by the Manchester solicitor George Davis and supported by the English players' union, brilliantly led by Jimmy Hill as chairman and Cliff Lloyd as secretary – successfully challenged Newcastle United and the game's governing bodies in England. But years later someone like myself, in deadlock with a club, could still feel that the dice were loaded against him. Young men breaking into football now will never appreciate how privileged they are to have the freedom of movement granted by the Bosman ruling. In fact, the pendulum has now swung too far in favour of the players and unless there is agreement on a rational compromise the sensible operation of big clubs may soon become an impossibility.

As I waited, with a mixture of defiance and anxiety, for positive developments on my transfer request, I did not waste time trying to gauge the seriousness of reports that Newcastle and Rangers were interested in me. Instead, I went about furthering my plans for staying in the game as a coach or manager. I had earned my preliminary badge as a coach the previous year and now headed for the SFA coaching headquarters at Inverclyde, near Largs in Ayrshire, to gain my full badge. I found the course inspiring and considered myself fortunate to be in a group taken by Bobby Seith, who had played for Burnley and Dundee, was by then coach at Hearts and was later to have the same role at Ibrox while I was a player with Rangers. My room-mate at Inverclyde was Jim McLean, who would subsequently manage Dundee United with such conspicuous success, and we struck up a friendship that has survived to this day. Survival is the best you can hope for in a friendship with wee Jim, who makes cussedness an art form. We have had arguments over the years but the bond is still there. In that two-week period I realised what a fertile mind he had in relation to football and I never tired of the debates that stretched into the small hours.

Late in that summer of 1966 I was a qualified coach but a player threatened with unemployment. Then, in the week preceding the start of the new season, the secretary of the players' union in Scotland, Johnny Hughes, began to encourage me to re-sign for Dunfermline on the basis of verbal assurances he had received from Willie Cunningham. The essence of the new offer was that my wages would be upped from £28 to £40 a week (though the increase would not be recorded in the contract) and I had the manager's word that I would be allowed to move to another club the following season. After discussing my choices with Cathy, I signed on the Friday afternoon. The next morning my fellow renegade, Alex Smith, joined Rangers. No wonder Dunfermline were desperate for my signature. Ah well, another lesson learned.

My third season with the Pars started miserably. I couldn't score a goal to save my life. Anybody in football will tell you that strikers – more than any other players, with the possible exception of goalkeepers – live on confidence. When they are scoring, they don't think they are ever going to miss, and when they are not they wonder where the next goal is coming from. Including a carry-over from the previous season, I went fourteen games without scoring and my team-mates were probably right to suggest that I was trying too hard. Dad had a simple theory in such situations: 'If you get an opportunity near goal, blast the ball. The last thing you want to do is side-foot it and give the goalkeeper an easy job. Make him work; if he saves a hard shot, then the crowd will applaud and some of the pressure will be off you.' For front-men whose spirits are being lowered by the fans' hostility, it's not bad counsel.

As a manager, I am inclined to take suffering strikers out of the heat for a spell, hoping they will come back refreshed. Just such a rest was arranged for me by a Norwegian centre-half who did enough damage to my knee to leave me on the sidelines for five or six weeks. My return was dramatic. It was in a Fairs Cup tie against one of the outstanding continental teams of that era, Dinamo Zagreb, who were naturally red-hot favourites. The first leg was at East End Park and there was doubt, not least in my own mind, about whether I had recovered sufficiently to play. Willie Cunningham took a chance and we were both glad he did. I played exceptionally well, scoring two goals, making another and being brought down for a penalty. We won 4–2 and were justifiably optimistic about the return leg, although it was a concern that the rule giving away goals double value in the event of a draw had just been introduced. The belief that we could protect our lead owed much to the solidity of a defence organised around the indestructible Roy Barry, who had been brought in at centre-half to replace our old stalwart Jim McLean.

The second leg was a disaster for us and I take no pride in my part in it. I let my mates down on the night. The bad omens had begun to gather the previous evening when some daft pranks among the players in the team hotel ended with me crashing through a glass door with a bucket of water in my hands. Dr Yellowlees had to patch up a gash behind my ear. The wound hurt less than the deserved lambasting I received from the manager. The game itself brought no comfort. I was hounded by a man-marker who kicked, punched and nipped me all night until eventually I took the bait. With ten minutes to go, the score was 0–0 and success seemed assured. Then calamity. Europe can do that to you in away matches. Just when everything is hunky-dory and the crowd is dead, the roof falls in. Their first goal took a wicked deflection off one of our defenders and squeezed past the dive of our goalkeeper, Eric Martin. They were instantly galvanised but even so they required disgraceful assistance from the Hungarian referee two minutes later when they scored the second, decisive goal. In our admittedly biased view, it was blatantly offside. The official seemed well aware of the dodginess of his decision. He went for the centre circle like an Olympic sprinter and the chasing posse knew their complaints were pointless. I spent the last eight minutes exacting revenge on my marker. It was a stupid response and did nothing to save the game. At the end we surrounded the referee but he made off to the end opposite the tunnel. There was construction work going on at the stadium, obliging us to change in Portakabins, and as we picked our way under the scaffolding Roy Barry hid behind a concrete pillar to wait for the referee. Fortunately, one of the other players saw him and managed to drag him away to the changing room.

As we slumped in that makeshift dressing-room, Willie Cunningham was understandably furious and he rounded on me. I retaliated and argued angrily with him. I knew I was wrong. Frustration over playing badly and losing the game was no excuse and that night I went to the manager's room and apologised for my behaviour. Not for the first time, I was grateful that one of his most admirable characteristics was the refusal to bear a grudge. Dinamo Zagreb ultimately beat Leeds United 2–0 in the final of the Fairs Cup, meaning that in successive seasons we had lost narrowly to the winners of the tournament.

Disappointment in Europe was tempered by my improving form and the goals were flowing freely. We managed a good run in the Scottish Cup, reaching the quarter-finals before losing 1–0 to Dundee United. But it was an historic piece of action in the first round of that competition, an upset that had nothing to do with me or Dunfermline, which set in motion the events that would enable me to realise my dream of going to Rangers. I was in the bath at Rugby Park, after a fiercely contested 2–2 draw with Kilmarnock, when the word came through: Berwick Rangers 1, Glasgow Rangers 0. Nobody could believe it. Surely it must be a hoax, I thought, these things don't happen to the Gers. But it was true and it made news for months. The repercussions at Ibrox were severe. George McLean and Jim Forrest were put on the transfer list and quickly sold, McLean to Dundee and Forrest to Preston North End. Amid the rampant speculation about the likely replacements, I was touted as the principal target. The remainder of the season seemed to be filled with endless talk about my transfer to Ibrox.

However, there were important matters requiring attention at Dunfermline, like winning a few games of football. Willie Cunningham had increased the incentives for success by adding a bonus of £1 per goal so long as we won the match. It was uncanny how often we lost out by giving high-scoring performances that ended in defeat or a draw. The most amazing of these experiences, and probably the most amazing game I was ever involved in, was against Hibs at East End Park. After an hour we were down 4–0. That score was created by a combination of excellent play by them and prodigious blunders by us. It became 4–2, then 5–2. Then we produced the kind of fight-back that shouldn't occur outside a Hollywood sports movie: 5–3, 5–4, and it was bedlam in the stadium as Hibs hung on desperately. With ten minutes left, we equalised and our supporters went mad. We pummelled Hibs and in the eighty-ninth minute we were refused a perfectly sound goal (photographs proved next day that the ball had been two feet over the line). While we were arguing with the referee, their stylish right-winger, Jim Scott, broke clear to go one on one with our reserve goalkeeper, David Anderton. David did well to save the shot but the ball rebounded off Jim's knee and rolled into the empty goal. It was a travesty, and another bonus was down the drain, but who cared? Like everybody else on the park, I felt privileged to have been part of a drama that can still quicken my pulse at a distance of three decades. That match took you through the whole gamut of football emotions, and left you exhausted and exhilarated at the same time.

My achievements had been noted by the Scotland manager, none other than my old boss at St Johnstone, Bobby Brown, and it was a thrill to learn that I had been chosen to play for the Scottish League against the English League at Hampden, only three weeks before the full international at Wembley. A good showing would mean consideration for the big game. I thought I played respectably, and was unlucky to have a good goal chalked off in the first half, but there wasn't much chance to shine, as we were soundly beaten 3–0 by a strong English side. By the time the Wembley selection was made, two Celtic players who were on the bench at Hampden, Bobby Lennox and Willie Wallace, were picked to play alongside Denis Law. I was included in the Scotland pool, as standby in case Denis failed to recover from a knee injury that was bothering him. The remote possibility of running out at Wembley encouraged me to book flights for Dad, Martin and my mate Billy McKechnie to go to London. It was Dad's first England–Scotland match and he loved it. I didn't make the team but we were there to celebrate a famous victory: 3–2, with a performance from Baxter that could have been set to music.

Further good news came my way when I was selected to go on a world tour with Scotland in the summer of 1967. And before any wiseacre observes that Rangers, Celtic and Leeds United withdrew their players, reducing the travelling party to the status of a B squad, let me point out that I was chosen in the original pool. Israel, Hong Kong, Australia, New Zealand and Canada were all on the itinerary. I had never been further than Spain, but the Govan boy was ready for the faraway places with strange-sounding names.

Govan was a vibrant shipbuilding community when I was growing up, and our house (ringed) was close enough to the river for us to qualify as real Clydesiders.

Mum and Dad, Martin (*left*) and me – a mixed marriage and a loving family.

Above: Echoes of Govan: Queensland Star, a ship my dad helped to build, provided the name of my first racehorse.

Left: The shift is over at Fairfield's, the shipyard where Dad and Martin worked. The name lives on in surburban Cheshire.

Below: Glasgow tenement roots: a rear view of Neptune Street in 1945, when I was still a toddler.

I met my 'mate' Willie Bennett again in Peterhead prison when I conducted a quiz for the prisoners during my time as Aberdeen manager.

Four generations of my father's family (clockwise): Dad, Great Grandad Beaton, the future manager of Manchester United and Granny Miller.

Football made me a minor hero at Govan High (I'm on the far right of the middle row), but at the expense of my studies.

The urchins in sleeveless jerseys are myself and Martin at the 1953 wedding of our inspirational teacher Elizabeth Thomson.

Hectic days: I was playing for Drumchapel Amateurs (*second left, front row*) as well as for my school and the boys' club.

With my pals Ian Kirk and Dunky Petersen, braced for action in Bellahouston Park, Glasgow.

My apprenticeship as a toolmaker continued by day at Remington Rand while I learned the striker's trade by night with Queen's Park.

THE QUEEN'S PARK FOOTBALL CLUB, LTD.

1ST TEAM—SEASON 1958-59

T. & R. ANNAN & SONS   GLASGOW

Seated (Left to Right)—J. GILROY; W. OMAND; I. G. HARNETT (*Captain*); T. KERR CAMPBELL (*President*); D. H. McLEAN; I. CLARK; A. C. FERGUSON.

Middle Row—F. LYON (*Assistant Trainer*); K. G. McALPINE; R. L. CROMAR; G. FALCONER; R. McKINVEN; W. J. PINKERTON; R. K. JOHNSTONE; P. KANE; C. CHURCH; W. GIBSON (*Trainer*); A. TURPIE; W. McBRIDE; W. BELL; W. WILLIAMSON (*Coach*).

Back Row—I. K. DRAINER; M. DARROCH; R. M. WOOD; J. McQUEEN.

Joining the famous amateurs furthered my football education, and better still, our home ground was the great Scottish shrine, Hampden Park.

Football was not so much a programme, more a way of life for this raw No. 8. A week after my eventful debut for Queen's Park at Stranraer, I managed to score a header against Alloa.

With the Scotland youth team who played England, including a certain T. Venables, at Newcastle. I'm third left on the back row.

On a St Johnstone club 'break' at Blackpool in 1961; (*left to right*) Bobby Gilfillan, Doug Newlands, Ron McKinven and me.

Part-time Saint: by the early 1960s I was combining toolmaking and union activity with a different kind of striking for St Johnstone (*front row, far right*).

Friday-night fever: the Locarno dance hall in Sauchiehall Street, where I first met Cathy (*inset*).

Spiegler, who was later to play for West Ham, and his team-mates devoted the rest of the game to pursuit of revenge. It made for a lively introduction to the Holy Land.

Jerusalem was, of course, fascinating and as we interrupted our guided tour on the Wednesday to have lunch I was looking forward to the afternoon programme. We were scarcely seated at the table when we heard what sounded like the firing of rockets in the distance (swishing noises followed by heavy explosions) and before long the guide was running up to our manager, Bobby Brown, to tell him that an Arab–Israeli war was under way. As we headed back to Tel Aviv by bus, a constant stream of jets roared overhead in the direction of Jordan and we could see the smoke rising from missile impacts in the surrounding hills. Any thought of a second match was obviously history and, after hurriedly grabbing our luggage at the Arcadia Hotel in Tel Aviv, we were rushed to the airport, only to be told that the fighting made flying too dangerous and we must go back to the hotel. For Willie Callaghan and me, the immediate effect of the delayed departure was a night at the mercy of a swarm of mosquitoes that had invaded our room but it was hardly the time to complain about that scale of discomfort. Next day we flew out without further incident and it was amusing to see how certain players who had been noticeably nervous a few hours earlier had more swagger than John Wayne once the plane had been in the air for an hour.

My excitement at landing in the Far East was tinged with bewilderment when I found Hong Kong airport patrolled by large numbers of heavily armed soldiers. When Bobby Brown assembled the party at our hotel, the Happy Valley, we knew it wasn't for a team-talk. Maoist students were aggressively active in the city and we were warned that nobody was to leave the hotel without permission or without arranging proper security. Once again, the manager told us, we would be playing only one match instead of the two that had been scheduled. Next day one of the strangest occurrences I have ever witnessed took place during our training session. As the trainer, Walter McCrae, was conducting the warm-up, there was a sudden rumble of sound and a horde of students exploded into view on the rim of the hills overlooking the stadium. They were chanting and waving Mao Tse-tung leaflets. Apparently the message was that the ambassadors of capitalism should get on their bikes. Anybody who remembers the film 'Zulu' will be able to imagine the scene. At first we thought it was funny, and we were having a good laugh as we jogged round. But the noise intensified as the demonstrators got serious and we soon fell quiet. It was no surprise when, before our game against a Hong Kong Select on 25 May, high-ranking spokesmen from the army and the civil authorities lectured us on the need for good behaviour and absolute discipline. There was to be nothing that might provide the students with the slightest hint of provocation. We listened in total silence and there was no doubt that everybody got the message. The game itself was a test of endurance in a temperature of ninety-five degrees, with humidity at ninety per cent. We won 4–1 and I was pleased that I played well and scored twice.

Still suffering in the heat back at the hotel, some of us sought to break the monotony with a card school, but the real focus of our attention was 7,000 miles and several time zones away in Lisbon, where Celtic were meeting Inter Milan in the European Cup final. We were all rooting for Celtic, with the noisy exception of one Anglo-Scot, Harry Thomson of Burnley, who delighted in sneering at Scottish football. The longer the tour went on the more unpopular he became, so it was no shock that almost all of the other players took up his challenge to bet on the final. Deep down, I didn't think Celtic could win. They had already done Scotland proud but I feared that Lisbon was a step too far. This was the cosmopolitan Inter of Helenio Herrera against eleven lads drawn from around Glasgow. Could even the Messianic powers of Jock Stein overcome the odds? Maybe I wouldn't have bet on it if I hadn't been so fed up with this Harry Thomson. I piled into the wagering with all the determination that was my hallmark as a player, gladly accepting the draw in my favour. Now the card school was incidental as we strained our ears for an update from each half-hourly news broadcast on the radio. We tensed when the half-time score was due. It was a sickener: Inter 1, Celtic 0. Thomson was crowing. Goodbye to that tour fee, I conceded silently. There was no way Celtic could come back, not against the Italians. Inter would shut up shop and kill the game, exploiting their cynical mastery of negative tactics. Ah well, at least Jock had reached the final.

'I'll give 5–1 against Celtic,' boomed our bookmaker. There were no takers. We were still reeling from the half-time score. 'OK, I'll be generous,' said happy Harry. 'Forget the goal Inter have scored – straight bet on the second half.' That was too much to decline. Several of us plunged in. It wasn't defiance now. This was a good bet at 5–1. The cards carried on but all thoughts were on another continent. At last there was another bulletin, and out came the magical words: 'Glasgow Celtic have become the first British team to win the European Cup.' The rest of the news was drowned in a storm of jubilation. The cards were being tossed all over the place, mainly into Harry Thomson's face. Was he sick? He had to go to Willie Allan, the secretary of the SFA, for a loan to pay off his debts. As we collected our winnings, we knew that the significance of this victory in the wider world of football was incalculable. Eleven Scots, all born within thirty miles of Celtic Park, eight produced by the club itself, and a manager with values forged at the coalfaces of Lanarkshire, had triumphed against the might of Italy. Sport cannot get more romantic than that.

Restrictions were eased during the latter part of our stay in Hong Kong, giving us a chance to appreciate the beauties of Shekell Bay and Repulse Bay and to spend some of Harry Thomson's money on shopping trips. I bought a pair of gold cufflinks of Chinese design for my dad. After his death, they passed back to me and I wear them on big occasions.

Now we were heading for Australia and the stage of our journey that was certain to mean most to me. We were playing first in Sydney where I would be able to meet up with my great-uncle, Alex Chapman, the man I had been named after. Uncle Alex and his new wife Jean were waiting to meet me at the airport and the fact that he had negotiated himself on to the runway was a surprise only if you didn't know him. He was, to say the least, unusual. When his first wife, my Aunt Annie, who was my granny's sister on my dad's side, died in her sixties he decided to emigrate to Australia aged sixty-nine to be with his daughter, Isobel. Having met Jean at a British Legion dance, he remarried. He was now seventy-one and looked fifty-one. I adored him and was enthralled when he used his gifts as a story-teller to fill in the background of the many and varied members of our family. He nearly burst with pleasure when I scored to give Scotland a 1–0 victory over Australia before a full house at the Sydney Cricket Ground, and I was proud to have made him proud.

On the night of our win at the SCG, Rangers played Bayern Munich in the final of the European Cup Winners' Cup in Nuremberg but Harry Thomson had retired from bookmaking and there were no bets. There was, however, passionate rooting for a unique Scottish double. Sadly, Rangers lost 1–0 after extra time. In the aftermath, much of the talk was about the unlikely pair of strikers they fielded, Roger Hynd and Alex Smith. Such a choice did not discourage suggestions that I was on my way to Ibrox.

My form was pleasing as we continued the Australian tour by winning 2–1 in Adelaide and 2–0 in Melbourne. I played my best game so far in Melbourne, scoring both goals. But the memories of that night are no sharper than the less pleasant recollection of a conversation I had, before the match in Adelaide, with someone I had known in Govan. John Holmes was older than me but my friendship with his brother David made me glad to see him when he turned up with another Scot. The chat came round to the possibility of a move to Rangers and, with the second man quizzing me, I was saying I knew nothing. Then suddenly, speaking as if I wasn't there, Holmes told his friend, 'He can't sign for Rangers – his mother's a Catholic.' I was shocked that such an assumption should have survived intact on the other side of the world. Rather than enter into an argument, I just walked away.

I think everybody in our party enjoyed Australia and, in fact, I felt I could quite easily live there. My dear old Uncle Alex was at Sydney airport when we flew out for what was to be pretty much a fleeting visit to New Zealand. We barely had time to win a couple of matches comfortably, and experience the hot springs outside Auckland, before we were on the fourteen-hour flight to Los Angeles. Our onward journey to Vancouver by way of San Francisco and Seattle was delayed for ten hours because LA airport was in chaos. The reason was the massive movement of troops to Vietnam. Watching all those lads, most of them years younger than we were, being shipped out to uncertainty and danger was unbearably sad and brought a great hush over our group.

Even the beautiful city of Vancouver, and the gorgeous weather we found there, could not counter the weariness that was settling on us now. By its sixth week, the tour was wearing us down and we couldn't wait to get home. Our game in Vancouver was won comfortably and I scored again but I took a bad kick in the kidney area that caused me pain for a couple of weeks afterwards. Before we boarded a plane for Glasgow, I received a stunning piece of news. Willie Cunningham had quit the manager's job at Dunfermline. In disbelief, I put in a transatlantic call to his home. He was quite chirpy and told me not to worry, that Dunfermline would let me go. That made the long flight a lot more bearable.

On my arrival back in Glasgow, the throng of reporters swamping me with questions about Rangers was almost unnerving until I noticed, off to the side with Cathy and Martin, the reassuring figure of Jim Rodger. Jim, who died recently, was a legendary sports journalist and an invaluable friend to me. Once I knew he was on the case I was sure that, from my point of view, he would have everything under control. Cathy confirmed as much as we escaped in Martin's car. As was usual with Jim, there was to be more than a hint of the MI5s about our dealings, with him contacting me by making calls under a false name to a neighbour's house in Simshill. There was still no development by the time I had to report for training at East End Park but I had the Rodger guarantee that Rangers were negotiating and I had no qualms about resisting the efforts of Dunfermline's new manager, George Farm, to persuade me to drop my transfer request. When genuine progress came it was in a way that showed Jim was not the only one with a taste for secrecy. I was at home watching athletics on television on a Saturday afternoon when a car rolled up outside and a young, good-looking man emerged and started up the steps leading to the front of the house. As I went down the path to meet him, he motioned me towards the car and said, 'My dad would like to speak to you.' His father was Scot Symon, the Rangers manager.

'I think it's better I don't hang around in case anyone sees us,' he said, after handing me his address and asking me to go to his house that night.

I was high with excitement as I travelled to the Symon home in the evening. I had supported Rangers all my life, was born within a mile of the stadium, and here I was going to the manager's house to talk terms. When his wife had made me welcome and left us to chat, he told me the two clubs were close to a deal and then spelt out his offer to me: £60 a week and £80 in the playing season (double what I was getting with the Pars) and he was willing to give me a £4,000 signing fee. We shook hands on that package but I did say before leaving him that I was going to ask Dunfermline for a percentage of the fee.

'Good luck,' he said with a smile.

What George Farm said after I had raised the issue with him as we prepared to complete the transfer at Ibrox on the following Monday morning was rather less bland. The former Blackpool and Scotland goalkeeper could swear in technicolour. But he knew I was adamant and relented to ensure that the deal went through. I admired his parting words to me: 'Please do your best for that man. He is a real gentleman.' George Farm was, of course, referring to Scot Symon, who was under pressure from the Rangers board and the media.

'Don't worry about that,' I said.

— 6 —
SHATTERED
DREAMS

THE boots I carried under my arm when I stepped through the front door of Ibrox for the first time as a Rangers player were dumped in the rubbish bin within minutes. How could I know then that there were certain people inside the great club who would make it their business to do the same with the dreams I had cherished since playing street football as a boy a few blocks away? No other experience in nearly forty years as a professional player and manager has created a scar comparable with that left by the treatment I received at Ibrox. My form in the two and a half years I spent there was by no means all I would have wished it to be – I had good games, decent games and bad games – but the humiliations eventually heaped on me could never be justified on the basis of my playing performances. I finished my first season as the club's leading scorer, with twenty-three goals, but already I felt a powerful current of rejection from Davie White, who had taken over as manager by that time. What I sensed coming from Willie Allison, the former journalist who was in charge of Rangers' public relations and who had an alarming influence on the thinking of the club's elderly chairman, John Lawrence, was something different. It was nothing less than poisonous hostility. Allison was a religious bigot of the deepest dye. I had a thoroughly Protestant upbringing but, of course, Cathy is Catholic and so were my mother's family. Such facts were sure to count for much in the twisted mind of Allison and, as an intriguer behind the scenes at Ibrox, he was as dangerous as he was despicable.

Perhaps I should have foreseen trouble when, on the day I signed for the club, one of the directors, Ian McLaren, asked me about Cathy's religion. When I confirmed that she was Catholic, McLaren, who had been a famous rugby player and had a big building business in Glasgow, wanted to know where we had been married. After I told him it was in the registry office, he said, 'Well that's all right then.' I don't know where my tongue was. How could I, who consider myself a strong character, have refrained from delivering a furious blast in response to such offensive questions? But that's what happens when you desire something as badly as I wanted to join Rangers. You are willing to dilute your personality to make the dream come true. Anybody who suggests that I had become paranoid towards the end of my time at Ibrox should try explaining the circumstances that prevailed immediately before I left the club I grew up idolising and for which I never took the field without giving every ounce I had. In my final months there in the autumn of 1969, I was reduced to turning out for the Rangers third team on Saturday mornings against opponents like Glasgow Transport, Glasgow University and Queen's Park's Hampden XI, for whom I had played when I was sixteen. To add a further slight, I was obliged to report in the afternoon for the reserves, with no prospect of playing. My hopes and ambitions were being buried alive. Yet other clubs were keen to buy me. Paranoia? I don't think so. I had a right to suspect that somebody up there didn't like me.

In spite of everything that was to happen subsequently, my first arrival for work at Ibrox, on a Tuesday morning in the late summer of 1967, remains one of the brightest memories of my life. As I was warmly welcomed by the members of the first-team squad, and allotted peg 27 in the dressing-room, I felt there was nowhere else in the world I would rather be. Even something as trivial as being issued with new boots added to my excitement.

'How can you score goals with these things?' Davie Kinnear, the trainer/physiotherapist, had asked with a grimace after looking at my old pair. The replacements were nowhere near as stylish or expensive as the footwear you would find most public-parks players wearing nowadays. They were J.S. Symon boots, endorsed by my manager and made by the Co-operative Society. I couldn't possibly foresee that they would far outlast J.S. Symon's reign at Ibrox or that the unfair dismissal of that conscientious and dignified man would lead to terminal trouble for me. Symon's critics on the Rangers board and in the media were feeding on the unprecedented success brought to Celtic by Jock Stein, who had just led our ultimate rivals to a first British triumph in the European Cup. The pressure on the manager naturally increased when the draw for the first competition of the season, the League Cup, put us in a tough section with Celtic, Aberdeen and Dundee United.

I had already tasted action in two contrasting pre-season friendly matches with Arsenal and Eintracht Frankfurt. Our trip to London was pleasant (we were given £20 a day spending money, compared with the £3 that was standard on continental trips with Dunfermline and on that global trek with Scotland); at least it was pleasant until we took the field at Highbury. There our form was miserable and we lost 3–0. My introduction to the fans at our own stadium was a different story. We beat Eintracht 6–3 and, with my family and friends present in force, I scored a hat trick.

On the opening day of the season we ground out a 1–1 draw at Pittodrie against a strong Aberdeen team predictably well organised by their manager, Eddie Turnbull, and on the following Wednesday, in the League Cup, I faced my first Old Firm game. Rangers had a right to go out with optimism on that warm, sunny evening, having spent big in the summer to strengthen the team. Apart from me, they had brought in the skilful Swedish outside-left Orjan Persson from Dundee United; another forward, Andy Penman, from Dundee; and the goalkeeper Eric Sorensen from Morton. The build-up had more electricity than the National Grid, with the gates closed at 6.30 p.m. and 98,000 crammed into Ibrox. There are people who insist that other great rivalries in football can generate as much intensity as the collisions of Rangers and Celtic. Well, I have been in San Siro for the Milan derby, in Barcelona for the visit of Real Madrid, I have seen Benfica–Porto and all the big derby games in England and have been involved with Manchester United against City, Liverpool and Leeds and, believe me, there is nothing, just nothing, to compare with the atmosphere of Rangers–Celtic. Since sectarianism is at the centre of that blood feud, it is not something on which Scots can congratulate themselves. The consequences are sometimes frightening and disgusting, but there is no denying the unique sense of drama. A sense of proportion is less noticeable. Often in the past it would have made sense to leave the ball in the dressing-room for the first half-hour of these matches, since players used about that much time to warm up by booting one another. During one Old Firm game I remember from my second season with Rangers, there were nine bookings in the first half and the senior police officer on duty at the match came into the dressing-rooms at the interval with both club chairmen and warned the players that if we didn't calm down we would be inviting a riot. My introduction to the conflict in that League Cup match of 1967 wasn't quite as hair-raising but it did have its moments. In the frenetic opening exchanges, wee Jimmy Johnstone had a kick at me off the ball, accompanying the blow with a tirade identifying me as a 'big blue-nosed bastard'. It was pretty much the initiation I had expected. Play continued to be hectic until a goal by Celtic settled us down and we began to dominate. But we couldn't gain full reward for our supremacy. We equalised through an Andy Penman free kick but a missed penalty by the same player cost us a valuable victory. However, we went on to beat Dundee United and Aberdeen and, with Celtic falling a point behind us by losing to Aberdeen, our return fixture at Parkhead was going to decide qualification from our League Cup section.

In that match I contributed to the first-half attack in which Willie Henderson put us ahead, and our lead was still intact with twelve minutes to go. Then came as weird a conclusion to a game as I have known. Everything was normal enough as Kai Johansen, our right-back, hit a long high ball up the inside-right channel and I rose for it with Billy McNeill at my back. Big Billy was the best header of a ball I ever played against and you had no chance of beating him in the air unless you timed your jump perfectly. On this occasion, I got it right and headed the ball on for Willie Henderson to scamper clear, with John Clark in pursuit. Well inside the box, Clark brought Henderson down. What a chance we had: 1–0 up with twelve minutes left and now a penalty to seal the win. After Andy Penman's miss at Ibrox, it was Kai Johansen's job to take the kick. At penalties, I always made a point of pacing the same number of steps back from the edge of the box as the kicker did from the ball, so that I could synchronise my strides with his and be first into the area if there was a rebound. Kai's shot hit the underside of the bar and as I followed up to head the rebound into the net he jumped in front of me and headed it in himself, thereby giving away a free kick. Could you believe it? He didn't know the laws of football. It wasn't long before he knew the cost of his ignorance. I am sure Celtic's equaliser should have been disallowed because of Bobby Murdoch's charge on Eric Sorensen but the referee let it stand and suddenly we collapsed under pressure and finished 3–1 losers.

That defeat meant elimination from the League Cup and I am sure it put the mark of doom on Scot Symon's managership, and was therefore a turning point in my own fortunes with the club. Losing out to Celtic yet again had given Symon's enemies the ammunition they needed to complete the destruction of his credibility, although the process would stretch over a number of weeks. As an intensely private man, who was never adroit with the press, he was ill-equipped to counter the criticisms levelled at his methods. Much of the fault-finding was unfair. For instance, I thought it was wrong to condemn him for not being a tracksuit manager who worked with his players on the training ground as Stein did. Symon had brought in Bobby Seith as club coach, and my old mentor from the SFA school at Inverclyde was doing a good job, sensibly ignoring Rangers' silly prejudice against afternoon training by taking individuals like myself for special sessions. With Seith so active, and another hands-on influence provided by Davie White, the reserve team coach and assistant manager, was it necessary for Symon to be the third man in a tracksuit? Given that he was in his office every day by 8 a.m. and did not leave until well into the evening, and that he had only his secretary, Isobel, to help him run the club, I have nothing but admiration for the job he did on behalf of Rangers.

Any reasonable outsider might have thought the league form that had carried us to the top of the table by September would have offset any damage done to the manager's position by our removal from the League Cup. But the deadly ingredient was that we had been killed off in the cup competition by Celtic and when a league meeting with Stein's prodigies loomed there was obviously more than points at stake. We reckoned it was a good time to take on Celtic, as they had just lost their World Club Championship match in Buenos Aires after dismissals reduced them to eight men in a pitched battle with Racing Club. That First Division encounter at Ibrox was shaped by a sad and ugly moment midway through the first half when Davie Provan, our big and likeable left-back, went for a ball with Bertie Auld. Davie was favourite to win it but, as he swung his left foot to make a clearance, Auld, in keeping with his reputation, went in a fraction late over the ball and there was the loud crack of a leg breaking. My dad, who had gone to the game with Davie's wife, Lillian, instantly recognised the seriousness of the injury and took her down to the dressing-room. The incident fired us up and, having switched John Greig to left-back and moved Dave Smith from midfield to play in central defence alongside Ronnie McKinnon (Smith performed so well there that he carved out a new career for himself as a defender), we had a clear edge. Every time Auld went near the ball there was a blue jersey after him, but he was crafty and kept quiet for the rest of the ninety minutes. Early in the second half a brilliant individual goal from Orjan Persson gave us the lead and we put Celtic on the rack. I had to admire the ferocity of the Celtic players' efforts to stave off defeat. Under Stein, these men had convinced themselves that losing to Rangers, or anybody else, was unacceptable and their spirit was impressive. On this day, however, it was thwarted.

In our dressing-room afterwards it was not hard to tell that we were celebrating our first Old Firm victory for quite a while. Two of the directors danced fully dressed under the showers. I didn't begrudge them their happiness but my main satisfaction was that we had won for Scot Symon. Once the emotion had subsided, our immediate thoughts were for big Davie Provan. His injury was no less terrible than we had feared. The leg fracture was to end his career at the top level. He battled back but was never the same and eventually left Rangers for a spell at Crystal Palace and then Plymouth Argyle. Davie deserved better. He was a true Ranger, one of the most popular players, and one of the most underrated, in the history of the club.

I had now come through three Old Firm matches and, although as a supporter since boyhood I had always understood the significance of these meetings, nothing had prepared me for the pressures experienced by the players. I felt I was carrying a burden of a kind never before piled on my shoulders. Immediately before we went on to the park, the tension in the dressing-room produced a deafening silence, as each man readied himself mentally for what was ahead. Out of the demands of facing Celtic came an intensity of concentration and a unity of purpose that were often missing in other games, where the substantial talent of the players might be let down by inadequate team spirit. Nevertheless, we were stringing together good results in the League and Scot Symon was definitely being given more support on the field than was forthcoming from the boardroom. That much was emphasised when a Saturday home match with Dunfermline found us struggling and the manager decided in the second half to put on a substitute for the popular Alex Willoughby. The angry reaction of the fans was worsened when Alex chose to run straight up the tunnel but Dad told me later that far more questionable behaviour had come from the Rangers vice-chairman, Matt Taylor. As supporters in the stand hurled abuse at the directors' box, Taylor had turned round to them and pointed down at the dug-out as if to say, 'It's nothing to do with us.' What a disgraceful thing to do to Scot Symon, who had served Rangers magnificently for thirteen years. I think when directors are being appointed they should be interviewed to gauge their character and the dignity they can bring to a club. Directors are entitled to make decisions about whether they support or don't support their manager but their views should be conveyed in the privacy of the boardroom. What Taylor did was an invitation to a public hanging.

The days that followed brought further discredit to Rangers and made me sick at the treatment inflicted on the manager. Around midday on the Tuesday, as we returned from training at the former Albion dog track across the road from the stadium, there were TV vans drawn up in front of Ibrox and a curious crowd had gathered. Scot Symon had been sacked. I was shocked, disillusioned and in a way frightened. How could Rangers Football Club do this, with the team undefeated in the League and sitting on top of the table? The day could only get worse. We were told that after we had changed we should wait in the dressing-room to be informed of developments. About an hour later, Davie White and Davie Kinnear came in to complete silence. White told us that he was in charge for the time being and, to be fair, he looked a bit perplexed. In that gathering, I was alarmed at the lack of concern over what had been done. Next morning's papers revealed just how badly Scot Symon had been treated. Rangers had sent an accountant to deliver the *coup de grâce*. How could a club of great tradition be capable of such horrible behaviour? On the following day I went to see Bobby Seith to tell him that I wanted away. I just couldn't stomach what had gone on. Bobby went berserk and pulled me into the quiet of the gymnasium, where he gave me such a telling-off that it stunned me. I had always considered him a sedate man.

'You are only starting a career – do you want to throw it all down the drain?' he shouted at me. 'Do you think Scot Symon would want you to behave like that? The best thing you can do for him is to play well.'

I went away chastised and confused but the proof that Bobby's advice had registered with me was seen that evening when I delivered one of my best performances for Rangers in the first leg

of a Fairs Cup tie against Cologne at Ibrox. I scored twice and
had another goal disallowed for some unknown reason (all right,
that complaint may have a familiar ring). My second goal was
the most incredible header I ever struck. As our left-back, Billy
Mathieson, shaped to cross from near the by-line, I launched a
run from about thirty yards out and met the ball on the edge of
the penalty area. It was a classic example of what timing can do
for you and the header flew like a shell into the top corner of the
net from all of eighteen yards. We won the match 3–0 and suddenly we were a great team again. Davie White did not have any
real impact on that game but, as so frequently happens, a change
at the top had evoked a positive response from the team. I was
enjoying the European adventure, having scored with a right-foot
volley to give us a vital 1–1 draw in Dresden in the previous
round. But I knew that Cologne, with World Cup players of
the calibre of Overath, Weber and Lohr, would be dangerous in
Germany. What I didn't know was that White would take a leaf
out of Willie Cunningham's book and give me a marking job, this
time on Wolfgang Weber. I thought I handled a difficult task fairly
well and when I was pulled off after Lohr hit a late equaliser for
Cologne there were encouraging words from White. Fortunately,
Willie Henderson scored in extra time to send us through to the
quarter-finals.

As we maintained our unbeaten run and retained leadership of
the League, it was impossible to discern any change the new
manager had made in the way we were playing; nor had he done
anything to improve the training format, which was an archaic
mixture of track work and uninspired physical exercises. Perhaps
the afternoon sessions with individuals that Seith and White had
organised were considered so revolutionary that any further mod-
ernising would have been too much of a shock to the ancient
system. It was utterly absurd that a club as big as Rangers should
have remained mired in such outdated methods while there was
so much evidence of progress elsewhere, not least on the other
side of Glasgow.

When the different approaches of Rangers and Celtic were again pitted against each other in the Old Firm's New Year fixture, I was in the stands because of a suspension that was the punishment for being sent off in a match with Hibs. I watched as Celtic's seemingly unassailable 2–0 lead was wiped out by remarkable mistakes by their goalkeeper, John Fallon. We didn't squander the fruits of that lucky draw and as Easter approached we were still undefeated and increasingly optimistic about the championship. Confidence was, however, severely jolted by losing a Scottish Cup quarter-final to Hearts after a replay that was, without question, my poorest game in the blue jersey. Our Fairs Cup quarter-final with Leeds United was another downer. After a goalless first leg at Ibrox, we lost 2–0 at Elland Road, where I gave away the first goal by blocking a header from Billy Bremner with my hand to present Leeds with a penalty that John Giles stroked into the net. A cloud of disappointment settled over us and, to my mind, Davie White was wilting under the pressure as the media began to doubt our capacity to last in the League. Then, just as we were shaking off the effects of the Leeds defeat, Jock Stein gave an interview to the daily papers in which he surrendered the championship to Rangers. 'It is Rangers' title now, unless they throw it away' was the gist of his statement, and somehow the onus he put on us proved unnerving and we went into free fall. Stein had employed his cunning and experience against the youthful uncertainty of Davie White, whose previous managerial experience was a year with Clyde. It was no contest. I shall never forget those headlines Jock instigated. The trick was instantly lodged in my memory.

The struggle for the title was still undecided when Celtic and Rangers each had two matches to play. In the second-last games, we took our unbeaten record and a one-point lead in the League to Rugby Park for a dangerous meeting with Kilmarnock, and Celtic were at home to Morton. We scored a late winner against Killie and, when supporters came on the pitch to tell us Celtic had drawn 0–0, we danced in celebration. Then in the dressing-room we were shattered to learn that Stein's men had scored in injury time. 'Lucky bastards' was the nicest comment we could muster, but we were still sure we could clinch the championship when we met Aberdeen at Ibrox in our final match.

I'll forget my own name before that decisive Saturday fades from my memory. The Rangers legions, expecting a coronation, packed the stadium to overflowing and it seemed that our day would be perfect when Dave Smith strode forward and hit one of his specials into the corner of the net to send us deservedly in front. We were at full surge and a second goal for us appeared imminent until our goalkeeper, Eric Sorensen, went for a harmless high ball and, with nobody near him, managed to fumble it into an equaliser. Ibrox was stunned. All through matches players make mistakes and recover but when a goalkeeper blunders there is rarely a reprieve, and you had to feel for Sorensen as he sat in the dressing-room at half-time with his head down. He never did regain his composure during the rest of the afternoon. But it looked as if we could live with his problem as we pummelled Aberdeen after the interval. Nine minutes into the second half, I scored with a header and once again the title was in our grasp. Soon after, I was pulled down so crudely by their centre-half, Tom McMillan, that the shirt was nearly ripped off my back but no penalty was given. If that was peculiar, what happened next was crazy. From an Aberdeen attack down their right flank, a cross was directed to their centre-forward, Davie Johnston, who rammed a shot through Sorensen's hands. In the last minute, there was the same move along the right and across came the ball to Ian Taylor – 3–2. The game, the championship and our proud undefeated record were all gone.

Predictably, there was an angry response from the Rangers support. Dressing-room windows were broken and a protesting crowd milled around the main door of the stadium for hours, forcing the players to wait inside until the trouble died down. A former team-mate from my St Johnstone days, John Bell, had come home from Australia and we had planned to go out that night. Our arrangement to meet at the front entrance now seemed impossible. I risked sticking my head out to look for him. He was there and I asked him to bring his car to the door in ten minutes so that I could make a dash to join him. The clock was striking seven when I made my escape and just as I was climbing into John's car a supporter ran up and kicked me hard on the calf. I couldn't really blame him. I felt as sick as he did.

The final chapter of that season was completed four days later when Celtic beat Dunfermline 2–1 at East End Park in a match that was postponed because the Pars had been busy winning the Scottish Cup on the Saturday of our débâcle against Aberdeen. Rangers' failure led to a feeding frenzy in the media and quite a few of the critics sank their teeth into me. But much more serious than that was the evilly intentioned gossip about Cathy's religion that was swirling around Ibrox and the other gathering places of the supporters. I knew that the principal muck-spreader was Willie Allison, the bigoted public relations officer, who clearly felt that anybody married to a Catholic was not a fit and proper person to play for Rangers. Later, after our first son was born, Allison peddled the tale that Mark was christened in the Catholic church. To most normal people, where a child was baptised – in Mark's case it happened to be the Church of Scotland parish church in Croftfoot – would have no relevance to the father's membership of a football team but a diseased zealot like Allison was prepared to tell lies about the matter. Because of his appearance (florid complexion, glasses and standard uniform of pinstriped suit and bowler hat) and his tendency to bluster, I had taken to calling him Colonel Blimp but he was much more sinister than the nickname suggests. The malevolent rumours were already circulating while Cathy was pregnant with Mark and, naturally, I did my best to keep that nonsense away from her.

It was a trying time for me and worse was to come in Denmark on the club's summer tour. Without warning, on a day when we were in Copenhagen, the Scottish papers carried a story that tore the heart out of me. 'Ferguson finished at Ibrox' was the consensus of the headlines. I went straight to White and, caught off guard, he admitted that this effort to undermine me bore the mark of Allison's hand. Still in a rage, I went to meet the journalist Ken Gallacher at a bar in the Tivoli Gardens to discuss what, if anything, I should say in response to the vilification. Although I was not a drinker, I was in a mood to make an exception that afternoon. John Greig and Alex Smith were also in the company and we sat in the bar for hours, more than long enough for me to be well gone. When we returned to the King Frederick Hotel I sought out Allison. He was in the dining-room and as I started to let him know what I thought of him the players grabbed me and hustled me off to my room. Allison showed up at my door as the lads were opening it and I gave him another blast. Once in the room, Greigy undressed me, got me into my pyjamas and shoved me into bed. But when John and the others had left, the irrational urge to have my say drove me out of bed and I went storming back downstairs in my pyjamas to resume the verbal attack on Allison. So my team-mates had to do another removal job and this time they succeeded in getting me off to sleep. About four hours later, I was awakened by John, Orjan Persson and another team-mate, Dave Smith. They had brought me steak and chips and a glass of milk. I demolished that lot in no time and when I had finished John asked how I was feeling. As soon as I indicated that I was all right, he said, 'Right, get dressed. We are going out.' We spent the whole night clubbing in Copenhagen. Next day I trained from memory, and a pretty fuzzy memory it was. Whatever the manager thought of my behaviour, he must have realised that boozy indiscipline was totally out of character for me and that the aberration was triggered by the evil doings of Willie Allison.

On the summer tour I had been used just once, as a substitute, so I had a close-season fraught with anxiety, lightened only by the exciting prospect of starting a family. As I tried to make sense of the decline in my fortunes, I kept coming back to Allison. After all, I had finished the season as top scorer and in amassing those twenty-three goals I had played some good games, and always I had worked my tripes out for the team. When I analysed why we had lost the League, the explanation was simple: our squad did not have the collective character of Celtic. Yes, there were excellent individuals in Johansen, Henderson, Penman, Dave Smith and Persson, but when the chips were down they did not have the grit and team spirit that

Jock Stein had instilled in his men. Petty jealousies were rife at Ibrox. A glaring example was the running feud between Willie Henderson and Ronnie McKinnon. They were continually bitching about which of them was earning more and each was scathingly insulting about the other's wife. Wee Willie was also a key participant in card schools that frequently cost players extravagant sums of money. He would set a trend by betting £20 blind in a game of three-card brag and it was not unusual for somebody to win £2,000–£3,000 in one session. Davie White socialised with some of the players and seemed unable to bring strong discipline to the club. Firm control might have worked wonders with the rich talent at the manager's disposal. I longed to see the good players around me fulfil their potential. I had built strong friendships in the dressing-room and I loved playing for Rangers. Just going into the stadium every day gave me a thrill. I was convinced that with better team spirit and organisation we could accomplish much. Above all, we needed more of the determination embodied by John Greig. He was, beyond any doubt, the most influential player at Rangers then. He drove them on and at times he went close to achieving the impossibility of being a one-man team.

My summer misgivings were more than justified. To call the 1968–69 season an unmitigated disaster for me would be to let it off lightly. I knew that the club chairman, John Lawrence, with Allison at his ear, had no enthusiasm for employing me and it was soon obvious that the ineffective Davie White would comply with their wishes to see me on my way. At the end of our pre-season preparation, he called me into his office and informed me that I had been offered as part of a deal to secure the Hibs centre-forward, Colin Stein. White's confident manner indicated that he had expected meek acceptance but instead he was told I had no intention of leaving. His response was to confine me to training with the reserves for several weeks. Then, plainly under pressure to get Stein, the manager suddenly became quite friendly for a day or two and I guessed he was up to something. So it was no surprise when he called me in again and, with a more humble demeanour, suggested that it would do no harm to go through to

Edinburgh and talk to the Hibs manager, Bob Shankly, brother of Liverpool's immortal Bill. I was still determined that I wouldn't sign for Hibs but agreed to meet Bob Shankly, if only as a courtesy to a fine gentleman. Bob and his wife made me very welcome at their home on the outskirts of Edinburgh and he and I were in the middle of a pleasant (if, to my mind, rather meaningless) chat when the phone rang. Bob picked up the receiver, listened for a couple of minutes without speaking, then put it down on the table and carried on talking to me. But I couldn't concentrate on what he was saying because I could hear a voice coming in a steady flow from the phone. Eventually I had to say to Bob that the caller was still on the line.

'Oh that's my brother Bill,' he said. 'He rings me every Sunday and I can't get a word in edgeways, so I just lift the phone now and again and say "Aye".' I suppose Bill would be quite satisfied with the odd monosyllable, so long as it endorsed his eulogies of Liverpool. Was there ever another football family like the Shankly clan?

The Fergusons had good reason to think they were pretty special themselves on 18 September 1968, when Cathy gave birth to a healthy son. She went into labour a month ahead of schedule and I was down at Largs on the Ayrshire coast, where Rangers were preparing for a Fairs Cup tie with Vojvodina of Yugoslavia, when an urgent phone call from Bridget, Cathy's sister, sent me rushing by taxi to the Queen Mother's Hospital in the Yorkhill district of Glasgow. My idea of rushing and that of the taxi driver were, I must admit, rather different. We were in constant danger of being passed by lawnmowers. Soon after entering the hospital, I saw a doctor coming towards me with a huge grin on his face. His appearance, bald with glasses, meant nothing to me but he greeted me warmly.

'Hello, Alex. Cathy is all right. We have her settled in bed and there is no problem. How's your mother?'

That really baffled me and I was floundering until he offered his name. Frank Sharpe had lived two tenement closes from me in the Govan Road and we grew up together. Not recognising him was embarrassing but I am sure he understood. He had lost his hair and acquired glasses since I had last seen him. Frank was the head gynaecologist at the hospital and he organised the Govan version of VIP treatment – a trolley from the canteen bearing eggs, chips, beans, sausage, tattie scones, bacon, bread and butter and a pot of tea. The modern trend for husbands to be present at the birth was not in evidence then and, in fact, I began to feel about as useful as a trapdoor in a rowing boat. At around 2 a.m. I was advised to go home (I discovered later that an outbreak of infection had caused the staff to quarantine the wards) and at 5.30 the phone went to tell me that our first child, a boy, had weighed in at 6lbs 8oz.

After Cathy came out of hospital with our son, we discussed names and I insisted the choice must be Alex.

'None of this Wee Alex and Big Alex – not on your life,' Cathy declared.

'Look,' I said, 'the firstborn in the Ferguson family is called Alex.' My wife was taken aback by that pronouncement and when my parents came to see their grandson she tackled Dad.

'Mr Ferguson, what was your father's name?'

'John,' Dad replied. So we called the boy Mark. It's not hard to see who's the boss in our house.

In spite of my refusal to be a pawn in their manoeuvres, Rangers signed Colin Stein for £100,000 and that pushed me down the pecking order. But, with the season at a critical stage and the team not playing particularly well, I regained my place and began playing really well into the bargain. Yet, after scoring our opening goal and generally having an important impact in a Fairs Cup quarter-final against Bilbao, I had to make way in the second half for Orjan Persson. The crowd let the manager know what they thought of that substitution and I had every reason to be disappointed. It was, however, a far bigger blow to be left out of our Scottish Cup semi-final with Aberdeen on the following Saturday. I felt my form merited selection and my misery was compounded when Aberdeen's feeble opposition made that semi-final a canter. Rangers won 6–1 to qualify for a meeting with Celtic in the final.

Injury ruled Colin Stein out of the final and throughout the preceding week I was left to stew in doubt about whether I would be handed the No. 9 jersey. It was not until the Friday morning that I was told I was playing but the uplifting effect of being chosen was somewhat dampened by the incredible team-talk White held on the afternoon of the same day.

'I can't believe this,' I said to myself as he outlined his plan. He had decided that our full-backs should man-mark Celtic's wide attackers, Auld and the young George Connelly, who were not natural wingers in the mould of their regular pair, Jimmy Johnstone and John Hughes, who were both suspended. The consequence was that our two centre-backs, Greig and McKinnon, would play against the two Celtic fliers, Chalmers and Lennox, and that was a recipe for disaster. Lennox and Chalmers would thrive on the space they were to be granted. At the end of the team-talk, McKinnon raised the subject of Billy McNeill's threat in the air at corner kicks. Ronnie was not confident he could cope with McNeill and suggested I should man-mark Billy in these situations. I wasn't happy, pointing out that Ronnie was two or three inches taller than I was, but I accepted the responsibility on the understanding that Ronnie would attack the ball. On the more serious problem of the overall tactics, some of the players pressed John Greig, as captain, to talk White out of his wilder notions.

'You've got to speak to him or we'll get slaughtered,' I told John.

But Greigy was uncomfortable about interceding, perhaps because voicing apprehensive thoughts was contrary to his nature. Nothing was done to correct the manager's folly and the slaughter duly materialised. I freely confess that I was culpable when McNeill headed the first goal in that 4–0 calamity. I lost big Billy at a corner after only a couple of minutes had gone but McKinnon's failure to attack the ball was equally conspicuous. The other three goals exposed the comical ineptitude of our tactics as Lennox and Chalmers strung out Greig and McKinnon. Auld repeatedly took our right-back, Johansen, for a walk, which allowed Tommy Gemmell to attack at will along Celtic's left flank. You could have driven a fleet of buses through the gaps in our defence. Davie

White's naïve theories had been savaged by the master, Jock Stein. Our shame was complete when fighting broke out among the spectators at the Rangers end and the match had to be stopped for about five minutes. My personal torture continued into the evening. That final on Saturday, 26 April coincided with the marriage of Cathy's sister, Bridget, to John Robertson and most of the men attending the reception in the Grosvenor Hotel in Glasgow, including the groom and his best man, had been at the game. What should have been an enjoyable occasion became an ordeal of embarrassment.

There had to be a scapegoat at Ibrox in those days and I was aware that I fitted the role. On the Monday morning, White summoned me to his office and demanded to know if I had been criticising him in the press. I answered truthfully that I had spoken to one reporter long before, at the start of the season, when efforts were being made to offload me to Hibs. That was his opening and he told me that I would not be involved in our semi-final of the Fairs Cup against Newcastle (Rangers lost 2–0 on aggregate). It was going to be another bleak summer but I took comfort from the knowledge that I was a stronger man than Davie White. My analysis of him was that, while not a bad man, he was essentially weak. Strangely enough, I had some sympathy with him but I became unforgiving when I considered his lack of appreciation of my efforts. The players knew how much pride I took in wearing the jersey and how hard I worked for the team, and so, quite definitely, did the fans. (On the night of the kick on the calf, every player was a villain.) During my time at Ibrox the supporters were great to me and at the beginning of the 1969–70 season the general buzz among them was, 'What is going on?'

The answer, as it turned out, was a great deal. Glasgow was electrified by the news that Jim Baxter, one of the greatest footballers Scotland has ever produced, was returning to Rangers on a free transfer from Nottingham Forest. Opinions about what that would mean for the club were mixed. Slim Jim's dazzling talent had been eroding for several seasons but he was so gifted and such a talisman for Rangers that nobody could dismiss the possibility that he would help to bring back glory to Ibrox. The main doubt we all harboured concerned Davie White's ability to handle such a notoriously undisciplined genius. There are countless stories about Jim's capacity for drink and I am glad to say I had only one experience of him in action with the booze. After an away match, our players ended up in John Greig's room and most of us were having a beer or two when the bold Baxter entered with a bottle of Bacardi, a few Coca-Colas and a large ornamental glass of the type that was often on display in hotel lobbies back in the late Sixties. In little over an hour, Jim had drunk the full bottle of Bacardi and, according to some of the lads, he had a night out afterwards. In fairness, no one could have worked harder than he did in the pre-season of 1969 and I must say I found him to be a really good team-mate, with a generous heart and a shrewd knowledge of the game.

With the season under way, it was immediately clear that my days as a Rangers player were effectively over. I was separated from the first-team squad and for a time I trained with the apprentices. One of the assistant trainers, Joe Craven, a wonderfully pleasant and funny veteran, showed the substance of his character by refusing to treat me as a leper and instead giving me consistent encouragement, even deputing me to organise a session with the apprentices. I devoted the whole morning to possession of the ball, which by then was central to my vision of the game. It was hardly surprising that I had a good response from the lads, given that the group included such future notables as Kenny Burns and Alfie Conn. White's reaction, after coming upon the scene, was to insist that I train entirely on my own. If that was meant to dishearten me, it didn't. Each day I worked like a beast on the track and then went into the tunnel to practise playing the ball against the wall, which had ringed numbers as targets. On one of those mornings, as I was wearing out the wall, I was approached by Colonel Blimp. I suspected he was checking to see if I had broken down. In fact, Willie Allison had stopped to tell me he had cancer. I know it is a terrible thing to say, but I did not have a crumb of pity for him.

In the midst of my final phase with Rangers, that humiliating period when I was condemned to third-team football against the likes of Glasgow Transport and Glasgow University, somebody less depressed than I was might have recognised the signs that Davie White's regime was far from secure. As they say in Scotland, his jacket was on a shoogly peg. Men within the Ibrox organisation who carried far more respect than White or Allison, particularly two who had been outstanding Rangers players in their day, Bob McPhail and Willie Thornton, were giving me generous moral support. But I did not read enough into their advice that I should keep my head down and soldier on. For obvious reasons, they were never explicit about the weakening of the manager's hold on his job and I was so sick at being denied a decent standard of football that oblique hints were lost on me. Towards the end of November 1969, I was at a low ebb when Jim Baxter told me he had been talking to the Nottingham Forest manager, Matt Gillies, and that Gillies had asked why I wasn't playing. I think Jim must have put in a good word on my behalf because a few days later White called me upstairs to talk about a Forest bid for me. I knew I had to accept the move but I laid down a final challenge to Davie White by telling him I wasn't going unless I received ten per cent of the fee from Rangers, which meant £2,000. White exploded but, after the intervention of the club's vice-chairman, Matt Taylor, it was agreed I would get the percentage. Cathy was reluctant to leave Scotland but she realised what I had been through and, as always, her support was rock-solid.

When I went to see White next day to learn details about reporting to Forest, the light outside his office showed he was engaged and while I was waiting Willie Thornton came out and there was another of those puzzling conversations. He kept asking me if I was sure I wanted to leave but my mind was in a whirl over the move to England. Then the manager's light turned green and I entered his room to be met with a bombshell. Willie Cunningham, my old boss at Dunfermline and now in charge of Falkirk, had been on the phone wanting to buy me. I had made up my mind that I was heading for the Midlands. Falkirk were in the Scottish Second Division and I wasn't interested in dropping a grade. But I had a lot of time for Willie Cunningham, so the least I could do was take a call from him.

'Look, Alex, I'll give you anything you want,' Willie said. 'Just don't move and I'll drive through now.' About an hour later he arrived to confront me with an offer that was quite incredible. In a real quandary, I contacted Cathy for her opinion.

'Does that mean we don't have to leave Scotland?' It was a question that amounted to a vote. I phoned Matt Gillies to apologise profusely for changing my mind, and I was on my way to Brockville.

After picking up my boots and saying my goodbyes to Joe Craven and the physio, Laurie Smith, who were two splendid men, and Davie Kinnear, I walked to the front door for the last time as a Rangers player. The door was manned, and I mean manned, by a real character called Bobby Moffat, whose parting line was, 'So you've escaped, have you?' There were some wonderful people on the staff at Ibrox, stalwarts like Bob Dinnie, Lizzie Love and Derek Manly in the ticket office, and I found it difficult to walk out of the place. I hung about talking to Jock Shaw, the former captain, who was another terrific person, and, of course, old Bob McPhail. To be honest, I was scared to go outside because I knew that when I did it was over – forever. Eventually it was getting dark and I was worried that Cathy would be fretting, so I forced myself out into the November night.

On the following Wednesday night, Rangers lost a Cup Winners' Cup match to Gornik Zabrze at Ibrox and the great Polish forward Lubanski tore them apart. I was at the game and everything Willie Thornton had been trying to say to me became clear. Writing in the *Daily Express* next morning, Willie Waddell summed White up perfectly under the headline: 'The Boy David'. Before the day was out, White had been sacked. You're an idiot, I kept telling myself. Idiot, idiot, idiot! A week later, when Waddell had been installed as manager, I dropped in for my £2,000 cheque and all was revealed about his disappointment over my departure. Who knows what would have happened if I had stayed? Waddell had always championed me as a player. He was my kind of man: strong, single-minded and one who would brook no interference from doddering old chairmen. Luckily, he would yet have a major influence on my football life.

— 7 —
A FINISHER FINISHING

EVEN when there is mutual respect and liking, the relationship between a manager and a player can be complex. Success for the team is their shared objective but there is an obvious difference in the pressures and anxieties they experience and that difference contains the seeds of conflict. The manager must think collectively, sometimes being hard on the feelings of individuals in the interests of fielding an effective unit, and he has to live with the frustrating knowledge that ultimately his reputation is at the mercy of the talent and the will-to-win of other men. A player, however honest his commitment to the team ethic, is bound to have a narrower view. Every game he plays is a statement about himself and any outside threat to his own perception of his worth, especially if it comes from his manager, naturally stirs resentment. Some of the best alliances between players and managers have been volatile and that was certainly true of my association with Willie Cunningham. We were good for each other but we did not always get along cosily. The inclination to have rows that had been conspicuous at Dunfermline was never likely to fade away after I rejoined him at Falkirk (in fact one of our quarrels at Brockville would have degenerated into a fight had the club physio not intervened) but none of those angry exchanges ever lowered my opinion of Willie as a man or a boss. I admired his toughness and his willingness to say forthrightly what was on his mind, although occasionally I thought his stubbornness was destructive. When he was confident he was a good manager, with sound tactical knowledge, but he suffered strange bouts of insecurity, and his innate suspicion of people he didn't know well could be a problem. He cared about his job and deserved greater loyalty than was shown to him by the players who I thought contributed to his sacking at Dunfermline, or the Falkirk directors who were to drive him out of Brockville. I had a warm regard for Willie back then and still do now and it was a pleasure to meet up with him again when he and Mrs Cunningham came down from their home in Dunfermline for a weekend in Manchester late in 1998, bringing their son and his wife, their daughter and her husband, and three grandchildren. I arranged the hotel for them and got them tickets for our match with Wimbledon at Old Trafford. My players arranged the right result, too: a 5–0 win.

When I reported to Falkirk in November 1969, Willie Cunningham's was just one of several familiar faces that greeted me. George Miller had been a valued team-mate at Dunfermline; Andy Roxburgh, who was later to manage Scotland, had been a Queen's Park Youth Team player in my last year at the famous amateur club; and my connection with Craig Watson went even further back, to the days when we both played for Govan High School. These reunions were pleasant but the acquaintance I was most determined to renew was with First Division football. Soon after my arrival the manager asked me how I came to be so fit in spite of seven months out of the Rangers first team. The answer was that I had resolved to prove to myself and everybody at Ibrox that I was still a player of substance. Helping Falkirk towards promotion from the Second Division was the immediate priority. Not surprisingly, the standard of the team was inferior to that I had known at Rangers and Dunfermline but I was pleased to see that my presence in the dressing-room lifted the confidence level and we brought a consistency to our performances that carried us all the way to the championship. I became leading scorer and rediscovered all my old joy in playing. It turned out to be a wonderful season for us, as we also reached the quarter-finals of the Scottish Cup, where we were unlucky to lose 1–0 to Aberdeen, who went on to beat Celtic 3–1 in the final. All the players took immense satisfaction in providing the faithful supporters of the club with such cause for celebration. There was no shortage of passion among the hard-core fans and none expressed it more vociferously than Ruby Connell, a formidable lady from the nearby village of Bonnybridge. Ruby's comments evoked dread in many a referee at Brockville and I am told her capacity for terrifying officials did not desert her when, in later years, she became manager of Bonnybridge Juniors. Yet, far from being a virago, she is a diamond of a woman. Cathy and I became quite friendly with her whole family. Ruby and I still write to one another regularly and her letters are amazing. They are small works of literature, six to eight pages crammed with sparkling accounts of all the latest happenings in her busy life, and they make me feel totally inadequate when I have to reply. Having a talent like that isn't fair on the rest of us.

The Falkirk directors were so delighted to gain promotion that they set up an excellent bonus system for the 1970–71 season. It not only rewarded us healthily for wins and draws but gave us an extra £40 for every week we were in the top ten of the First Division. With the squad strengthened by some good signings, notably Alex Scott, the former Rangers, Everton and Scotland winger, we never fell below the required level, so it was a prosperous as well as a happy dressing-room. Alex had lost a yard or two of pace but he was still a magnificent crosser of the ball and his service helped me to be top scorer for the second year in a row. He used to tell me that whenever he got to the by-line I should be ready to receive the ball just inside the penalty spot, and he never let me down. We struck up a good friendship, probably because I like people who keep their promises. Falkirk at that time, under Willie Palmer, a chairman with genuine concern for his club and his players, had the pleasant and positive atmosphere of an organisation moving in the right direction.

To be truthful, however, when I think back to that football season all other memories tend to be swamped by the emotions of a single day: 2 January 1971. On that date, sixty-six people died in a crowd disaster at the traditional New Year Old Firm match at Ibrox Stadium. I was a spectator at the game along with two of my Falkirk team-mates, Andy Roxburgh and Tom Young, but we left just before the final whistle without an inkling that anything untoward was happening. When I had dropped Andy and Tom off at their homes and was driving back to my parents' house in Govan Road, taking a slightly complicated route to avoid the match traffic, I passed the Southern General Hospital and saw ambulances queueing at the entrance to the emergency department. Even then the worst thought that crossed my mind was that there had been some violence among the rival supporters. It wasn't until I saw my father's face when he opened the door to me that I realised something truly awful had happened. My mother and Cathy were also in the house and our horror at the news coming from the television – the death toll had already risen to forty – was deepened by personal dread because my brother Martin had been on the terracing at the Rangers end, where the fatal crush occurred, and nothing had been heard from him.

After trying to reassure my parents by telling them that Martin had probably left the ground early and gone for a drink, I suggested that it made sense to go and look for him. So Dad and I went off with a friend, George Glover, to search the pubs in the Govan Cross area and I shall never forget the growing anxiety on my father's features as we hurried from bar to bar without success. He was strong but he could not hide the depth of his fears.

'I think we'll have to go to Orkney Street,' he said at last. That meant the police station and the thought of what we might learn there was frightening. I felt a terrible helplessness as we joined the throng of people inquiring about family and friends. We lived almost opposite the station, so the desk sergeant knew us and dealt with our worries sympathetically, but the best advice he could give was that we should check at Ibrox, where the bodies were being kept. If there was no sign of Martin there, the next step would be to contact the hospital but it had to be Ibrox first.

We were making our way round to the house to get my car when George Glover suddenly screamed out Martin's name. As Dad and I spun round, George was off and running down the

Govan Road, pursuing a Skoda that we recognised as Martin's car. I had often cursed the unreliability of that Skoda but I was grateful for it now as the engine spluttered and gave George the chance to reach out and hammer on the boot. Martin stopped and got out, puzzled by the assault on his car, just as Dad and I arrived on the scene. With a mixture of relief and anger that was natural in the circumstances, Dad hit out at Martin.

'Where have you been?' he demanded. On other occasions I would have enjoyed Dad having a whack at my younger brother but this time my only reaction was pleasure at seeing him. My mother, of course, was ecstatic.

Amazingly, Martin was totally unaware of the disaster. He had left the ground about two minutes from the end of the match, when Jimmy Johnstone scored the goal that appeared to have won it for Celtic, and gone to the Rolls-Royce Social Club in Paisley Road. I had waited long enough to see Colin Stein equalise a minute later but had known nothing of the consequences. Rangers fans who had been streaming disconsolately towards the exits were so excited by the eruption of celebration behind them that they tried to rush back up the stairways to the top of the terracing. They met the others who were still pouring down and produced a murderous jam of humanity.

Willie Waddell was rightly praised for the sensitivity with which he, as Rangers manager, responded to the most harrowing episode in the club's history. I received a call from his assistant, Willie Thornton, to join other former players in attending funerals. It was the least we could do and as I went to those burials (one of the victims was someone who had been at school with me) I reflected on how strange my involvement with that tragic weekend had been. Falkirk had played Rangers at Brockville on the day before the disaster. On the eve of that game, Hogmanay and my birthday, I had discovered in conversation with one of my former team-mates from Ibrox that Rangers were resting a handful of players against us so that they could be strong to face Celtic, who would be fresh as a result of being spared a 1 January fixture. My inside information about the weakening of the opposition stirred my old ally George Miller, a Lanarkshire man whose love of his native Larkhall was equalled only by his passion for punting, and the outcome was a bet organised on behalf of our team by one of the directors. The odds were 3–1 and so was the score in our favour. That defeat of Rangers meant we turned up in good spirits for our away match with Airdrie on 2 January but a waterlogged pitch forced a postponement, sending Roxburgh, Young and myself on the short journey to Glasgow to watch the Old Firm game. It was a roundabout way to find ourselves present at a calamity.

There is no doubt that the greatest source of happiness for Cathy and me in 1972 was the arrival of our twin sons, Jason and Darren, on 9 February. It was a difficult birth but Cathy coped bravely, which is more than could be said for her man. Before she went into theatre, frequent contractions were causing her severe pain and I held her hand to comfort her. Then her face turned purple and that was too much for me. I fainted. The first voice I heard as I came round was the Sister's: 'Get him out of here.' Trotting off meekly, I called back to Cathy, 'You'll be all right.'

'Yes,' she said. 'But will you?'

When the boys were born, Jason was fine but Darren, who was much smaller and had a touch of jaundice, had to be put into an incubator for a while. As for the fainting father, he had to go off and play a Scottish Cup replay against Rangers. Obviously I had been given my quota of joy for the day at the hospital, for Rangers beat us 2–0.

Earlier in the season we had reached the semi-final of the League Cup, removing Aberdeen and Hibernian along the way. In the first leg of our quarter-final, Hibs opted to man-mark me with a promising young player, John Blackley, and John still insists that I did more than anyone else in football to educate him. Funnily enough, Martin Buchan, who was with Aberdeen at that time, says exactly the same. Are these compliments double-edged? I must sit the two of them down one day and get them to explain themselves. I scored in our 2-1 win in that first leg and the second meeting was a battle as we hung on to progress 2-1 on aggregate. Bertie Auld was in midfield for Hibs by then and he was up to all his tricks but I had warned my team-mates to be wary of Bertie's methods, always ensuring they showed their studs and avoided going in first. I didn't want any repeat of what had befallen Davie Provan.

The prospect of a Hampden semi-final with Partick Thistle electrified the population of Falkirk, proving how much potential the town and its surrounding district had for supporting a major football club. The Thistle, one of my native city's great institutions, would be interesting opponents. They had a popularity that did not rely on achievement. For decades they had been a favourite target of every comedian working the Glasgow theatres, but their loyal fans regarded them with loving indulgence, gladly tolerating rapid fluctuations of form that took them from the scintillating to the abysmal. Ideally, the club should have had joint chairmen – Dr Jekyll and Mr Hyde. They had earned any number of nicknames, some straightforward, others mockingly fanciful: the Jags, the Harry Wraggs, the Maryhill Magyars, the Partick Hungarians. At their best, they might have given Puskas and his 1950s Hungarians a fright, but at their worst a team picked from drunks leaving the pub at closing time might have beaten them. To support them or play for them was to be on an emotional rollercoaster, as I was able to confirm when Martin wore their colours in the early Sixties. I was confident Falkirk could handle the Thistle, especially as I had been able over the years to score plenty of goals against them. So much for assumptions. At Hampden on the big night, Thistle were in their Magyar mood and their two wingers, Lawrie and McQuade, tore us to ribbons. Our only consolation was that they did the same to Celtic in the League Cup final, beating Jock Stein's men 4-1.

In March of 1972, Hibs were eager to sign me and I was ready to go to Easter Road, convinced that at thirty I should take the opportunity to move to a big club that was again flexing its muscles under a new manager, Dave Ewing, the former Manchester City centre-half. Willie Cunningham opposed the idea with sullen determination. I was equally unyielding and our confrontations became so heated that, in a Brockville toilet long after one Saturday match was over, we were at the point of fisticuffs when the physio came between us. Willie broke the deadlock by drawing up an improved contract and promising me assistance with my plans to stay in the game after my playing career was finished. Unfortunately, the 1972–73 season brought troubles for both of us. Another nasty knee injury was a specific problem for me and the manager was burdened with the more general worry of a series of bad results for Falkirk.

During my weeks on the injured list, Willie took to sending me to study future opponents and it was on a night when I watched Hibs play Aberdeen in Edinburgh that my own team suffered a humiliation in Perth that was to have controversial repercussions. Nobody could blame Willie for being enraged by the 6–0 loss to St Johnstone but his reaction went too far. There would, he ordered, be morning, afternoon and evening training sessions and expense allowances for travel and lunches would be cancelled. The night training was a bit much and so was the withdrawal of payment for the appreciable amount of travelling some of us had to do. When the first morning of the new regime subjected the players to such intense work on the running track that they were exhausted at the end of it, there was good reason to believe that a three-sessions-a-day schedule would drain away the energy they needed to start winning matches. As players' representative at the club and a member of the national committee of the SPFA, I conveyed the complaints to the manager but he refused to soften his attitude to men he branded 'non-triers'. The response from our side was a decision to go on strike. I wasn't entirely happy with the action. It was hasty. My knowledge of Willie Cunningham told me that he would eventually calm down and that life would get back to normal. The question was when.

The dispute turned messy over the next couple of days as two directors, Alex Hardie and Jim Manson, took a hand and held meetings with some of the players. At one of these, Hardie suggested to me that I should pick the team for the Saturday but I knocked that notion on the head immediately. After all, we were on strike and there was nothing wrong with the manager other than that he had lost his temper. The stand-off persisted until lunchtime on Saturday, when Willie Cunningham climbed down. I felt for our manager. He plainly believed he had been let down by the players but his own stubbornness had pushed him towards the crisis. From where I am now, I can well understand his behaviour. A manager has a hard job and when you have bad results you can feel isolated, betrayed and helpless and sometimes you create demons in your mind. For my part, perhaps I should have been stronger in arguing against the strike but I would not ever have wanted to be known as a boss's man. To someone with my upbringing, that would have been a heinous crime.

Although I had been the spokesman for his mutinous crew, Willie Cunningham showed that he did not see me as an enemy by appointing me the first-team coach. With Falkirk at the foot of the table, and the threat of relegation biting deep into confidence, the job might have struck many as more of a headache than an opportunity. But, having been granted responsibility for every aspect of match-preparation except picking the team (and even that Willie had promised to discuss with me), I relished the chance to prove that my coaching badge wasn't an empty qualification. I reorganised the training so that it included work in the afternoons, particularly for the younger players in the squad, and I took charge of the part-timers on Tuesday and Thursday evenings. My changes appeared to have an impact and, as March approached, we were off the bottom of the First Division and had reached the third round of the Scottish Cup. To go forward in the competition, we had to beat Aberdeen at Pittodrie and we went there full of confidence for the Wednesday night game.

We began well enough and were causing them all sorts of bother until one moment of indecision permitted their centre-forward, the former Rangers man Jim Forrest, to put us behind. As we fought to recover, the match became increasingly physical but with a notoriously strict referee, John Gordon of Newport, it was no time to turn reckless. Yet I did. After a bout of sustained pressure on Aberdeen's goal, I challenged their main central defender, big Willie Young, for a corner and the two of us ended in a heap on the ground. Willie had a kick at me as we landed and I kicked back. John Gordon saw my swing and promptly sent me off. It wasn't my first taste of returning alone to the dressing-room but the miserable longing to have the ground open up and swallow me was stronger than ever before. Having worked tirelessly with the team on the training ground to bring about a revival of our form, I had undone all our efforts with an act of gross irresponsibility. Would my coaching career be derailed before it was properly under way? At half-time there was a hush among the players and the manager gave me one of the special looks that often served him better than speech. I could not bear to watch the second half but the noises above me said more than I wanted to know about how we were doing. After a 3–1 defeat, the atmosphere in our hotel was icy. Being dumped out of the Cup was a serious blow for a club struggling in the League. Willie Cunningham did not say a word to me until around midnight. Then he summoned me over to a corner of the lounge, where he was having a drink with an old mate of his, and the firm words he spoke could not have been more appropriate. He acknowledged that my conduct had left a cloud over my position with the club but made it clear that it was up to me to demonstrate from the next day that I was made of the right stuff. 'I can handle it, but can you?' was the kernel of what he said to me.

The following morning I apologised to the players and set about making sure we would not let the setback interfere with the vital business of protecting our First Division status. Playing solidly in the ensuing league matches, we edged to safety and I honestly felt that, with the exception of my costly stupidity against Aberdeen in the Cup, I had done a good job since becoming first-team coach. There had been a marked improvement in the team and I had taken enormous satisfaction from working with the young players. Outstanding among them was a full-back who had been developing as a part-timer and was now nearing the end of his apprenticeship and clearly ready to step up to full-time football. Stuart Kennedy first impressed me with his resolution and the application with which he answered every demand made of him. He thrived on challenge and nobody could beat him at anything in training. It is a joy to come across such raw talent and help to shape it into the finished article. During the latter part of the season I kept pestering Willie Cunningham to play Stuart but the manager was reluctant to risk overtaxing him. However, with our survival in the First Division assured, young Kennedy was drafted in for a late league game against Aberdeen. It was fitting that he should have his debut at Pittodrie, where he would subsequently have a truly wonderful career in the Aberdeen shirt and render monumental service to me during my years as manager there.

After the nightmare of my previous visit, that match at Pittodrie might have been an ordeal for me but Willie Young set a sensible tone at the start.

'I'm sorry about the last time, Alex, so let's have a quiet game for a change,' said the big man and I was delighted to agree.

Yet my earlier sins did come back to haunt me when Jimmy Bonthrone, the Aberdeen manager, mentioned that he had considered offering me a job as his assistant but that my sending-off had not gone down well in the corridors of Pittodrie. That was bad news but not nearly as bad as the abrupt announcement a few days later that Falkirk had sacked Willie Cunningham. I knew he had been having arguments with Jim Manson and Alex Hardie, who were by then the controlling influences in the boardroom, and that on at least one occasion they had tried to interfere with team selection. The manager gave them the brusque rebuff they deserved but there was little he could do to counter their long-term campaign to undermine him. The club had suffered a grievous loss when Willie Palmer ceased to be chairman. He was a man who could be trusted, which is something I never felt able to say about his successor, Alex Hardie. While I was commiserating with Willie Cunningham, he found time to show an interest in my position at Falkirk, telling me that I was highly regarded by the directors and should apply for the vacant post. I was rather nervous about that idea. At thirty-one, I was intending to remain a player for a few more seasons. There seemed to be backing for Willie's assessment of how the board viewed me when Alex Hardie asked me to take charge of the players until a manager was appointed and then advised me to apply for the job. But I had sufficient scepticism about Hardie to wonder, 'Is he at it?' I didn't have to wait long for an answer.

When the Scottish season was over for the players, there was still plenty to occupy managers, scouts and coaches. Tournaments in schools football and in the 'juvenile' grade, which caters for amateurs young and old, came to a climax at that time of year, with finals being staged all over the country. One juvenile final played at Brockville in 1973 drew the attention of senior clubs because three particularly promising lads were in action. I had learned that it paid to have my card marked by the older scouts, who had usually made it their business to know which players were already out of reach. The word was that David Narey had signed for Dundee United and Davie Cooper was joining Clyde-bank but a little slip of a lad who had seriously impressed me, chasing and harrying all night, was apparently still considering offers from Dundee United and Hamilton Accies. His name was Andy Gray. Exploiting the privileges of the Falkirk coach, I was able to linger around the corridors until Andy came out of the dressing-room and then usher him and his young girlfriend of the time into the manager's office. There I made a strong pitch on behalf of Falkirk and, having convinced the boy that he should listen to further argument, I was excited as I went to beckon Alex Hardie out of the boardroom to enlist him as the final persuader. I was stunned when Hardie rounded on me.

'You've no right to talk to players about joining Falkirk Football Club. That's the manager's job and until we appoint one there will be no signings.' I was flabbergasted and had to go into the secretary's office to gather myself before returning sheepishly to Andy to explain that we were interested but had to wait for the new manager to arrive. That appealed to Gray so much that he went out and signed for Dundee United that night. Alex Hardie had done his best to harden my opinion that Falkirk had fallen into the hands of the wrong directors.

What the fans thought of the board was unmistakable after John Prentice was named as the successor to Willie Cunningham. Prentice had already been in charge at Brockville but had walked out to take over at Dundee. The supporters saw that as a treasonable offence and the directors who brought him back were damned for compounding the treachery. I have never known more bitterness about the appointment of a manager. Such public feeling does not always have a sound basis but it must be said that Prentice's second term did nothing but damage. His return sent a good little football club into chronic decline. I sensed early that I wouldn't have much enthusiasm for working with him and I was doubly glad that I had enrolled on a summer course for managers and coaches at Lilleshall in England. There was much to be learned on that course and the star of the show for me was Jimmy Sirrell, the Scot then managing Notts County. It was instantly obvious that he commanded the respect of everybody at Lilleshall and I decided that I wouldn't neglect any opportunity to listen to him. He did not disappoint me. The principles of management he laid down with such emphasis were often simple but their importance was so undeniable that I have always tried to adhere to them. 'Don't have the contracts all running out at the same time' was one of his tenets. 'Watch the ages of your team' was another. It was a reminder that common sense, when there is enough of it, amounts to wisdom. Another demonstration of Jimmy's substance came when he was asked to take a coaching session based on methods he applied with his successful Notts County team. At first he was finding great difficulty communicating with the men at his disposal, so he stopped the play and gathered all the players and other coaches and managers together and explained his problem. He told us that he would use a Notts County player's name for each of those involved in the exercise, suggesting that familiarity would lead to smoothness of execution. It did. Here was an utterly genuine person, one honest enough to admit his difficulty and deal with it. Over the years I have come to know this fanatic of a football man quite well and, like everybody else who ever met him, I have been infected by his passion.

Having had no word from John Prentice by the start of preseason training, I knew everything about my future as first-team coach at Falkirk. I didn't have one. But I insisted that he tell me the facts face to face and the meeting was more uncomfortable for him than for me. He found it hard to look me in the eye. What he told me ultimately was that he wanted to bring in his own man. That was fair enough. In his place, I might have done the same. It was agreed that Falkirk would release me from my contractual obligations to let me negotiate my own terms with another club. But Prentice soured the parting by trying to deny me my last payment of the signing-on fee associated with my contract. I was not about to tolerate that, and a phone call to the ex-chairman, Willie Palmer, confirmed that I would receive my due. There is an interesting division of opinion when the worth of John Prentice's contribution to Scottish football is discussed. If you listen to his admirers, such as Jim McLean, he was a marvel, but in my short spell with him I found him to be lazy and uninspiring. I was not at all surprised when Falkirk were relegated that season, having failed to win a game until New Year's day. When they came calling on my next employers, Ayr United, I scored the winning goal against Prentice's team. One good turn deserves another.

I realised that my playing career must be nearing its end but if I had been looking for a gentle transition to retirement I would have stayed well away from Somerset Park, Ayr, where the manager was that irrepressible enthusiast Ally MacLeod. A handful of years later Ally's extreme optimism would run into the buffers when the Scotland team he said could win the World Cup were embarrassed in Argentina. Even in the humble context of Ayr United, whose players were part-timers, he was already proclaiming extravagant ambitions when he offered me a two-year contract in 1973. As soon as our business was completed, he produced a fixture list and began reeling off the successes that would take

Ayr to the League championship: 'First game, Dumbarton at Bog-head, no problem. They are just promoted and they don't have enough experience – two points. Clyde at Somerset. We always win our first home game, and anyway that big Willie McVeigh is useless. You're bound to score against him – two points.' Having swept us through the first six matches without a hitch, collecting the maximum twelve points, he was ready for the crunch games. Rangers: 'Well,' said Ally, 'they won't enjoy coming to Somerset with us top of the League – two points.' Celtic at Celtic Park: 'We are due a result there – two points.' He drew energy from such fantasies and his capacity for producing them was boundless, as he proved again with a tale that never failed to enthrall the group of promising young players he had gathered round him at United. It was a story from his playing days as a lanky left-winger for Blackburn Rovers in the Fifties and concerned a confrontation with Newcastle United's Jimmy Scoular, who was rated by many as the hardest man of his era in English football.

'Yes,' Ally would say, 'it was an FA Cup tie and there were sixty thousand in St James' Park when Scoular and I went for a fifty-fifty ball and I sorted him right out and he never came near me the rest of the game.' According to what I have heard from reliable witnesses, if Scoular had been waiting at the OK Corral, Wyatt Earp wouldn't have turned up, so the only reasonable response to Ally's account of their collision was a quiet chuckle.

Some might have been put off by the dream factory Ally carried in his head but I was stimulated by his bubbling enthusiasm. He had the same effect on many others and the team he built at Ayr United showed that he had an eye for character as well as ability. I enjoyed my time with him and had reason to be grateful that he had rescued me from the feeling of neglect which was closing in after I left Falkirk as a free agent. There was no danger in that pre-Ayr United period of my door being battered down by managers clamouring for my signature and I was glad I had added another string to my bow by learning about the licensed trade over a year and a half as a part-time helper in a friend's pub and restaurant. Rather than risk idleness, I considered several tenancies offered by Drybrough, the Edinburgh brewery firm, and decided on one in Kinning Park, which is just along the road from Govan. The pub was in a dockland area where, it was said, the lamp-posts were taken in at night. But I wasn't looking for a place that was genteel, just one that was busy. Of course, I still regarded myself as a footballer rather than a publican but a conversation with my old pal Jim McLean made me wonder. Jim had become manager at Dundee United and I welcomed a call from him until he started talking about having me along to Tannadice for a trial. For Christ's sake, I thought, a trial! I had been a professional with St Johnstone, Dunfermline, Rangers and Falkirk and had been top scorer at every one of those clubs. It wasn't the CV of a triallist.

Fortunately, if wee Jim had doubts about my usefulness, Ally MacLeod did not and I like to think I repaid his confidence. Although it was a strain to divide my efforts between part-time football and running the pub, I finished the season with fourteen goals, which put me second in Ayr's scoring table behind the one and only George 'Dandy' McLean. Anything ever said about the outrageousness of Dandy's character could be multiplied by ten without getting near the truth. He had been on his travels since being unloaded by Rangers in the aftermath of the Scottish Cup disaster against Berwick Rangers and wherever he went managers struggled to cope with his dual identity as a talented player and a world champion playboy. Yet Ally MacLeod, typically, insisted that he had Dandy under control. It was a claim that was put to the test on a day when Ayr's Glasgow players were told to rendez-vous with the team bus in Hope Street to make the journey to Edinburgh for a Cup quarter-final with Hearts. 'Where's Dandy?' was the question as the rest of us settled on the coach. At first nobody was too perturbed but the calm did not last. 'I'll fine him' was Ally's initial reaction, delivered with cool firmness. Then he became increasingly feverish as he moved among the players and directors, ranting about Dandy in terms that suggested the electric chair would be lenient punishment. Just as the coach was prepar-ing to leave, an open-topped sports car zoomed right in front of it. The driver was a gorgeous blonde and in the passenger seat, unshaven and tieless but looking perfectly happy with the world, was Dandy. As he stepped on to the bus, it seemed that every one of us already there had stopped breathing.

'Morning lads,' he said brightly.

'Where have you been?' Ally shouted, and then answered his own question. 'Don't dare lie to me. You've been out all night. Look at the sight of you.' Dandy's response was immediate.

'Well, Boss, I can't lie. I was out. I went into the Muscular Arms [a fashionable Glasgow pub at that time] for a quiet drink last night and this young girl came up to me and said, "Dandy, I want you to sleep with me." So, Boss, what could I say?' Ally couldn't think of anything to say. The Dandy-controller was dumbstruck. When the bus pulled away, big George turned to the other players and winked. He was some man, lovable and impossible. As a team-mate, I found him great to have around. As a manager, I would have had to forego the charm of his company.

My year had been interesting and I had done quite well but towards the end of the season I was having trouble with a groin injury. Maintaining fitness as a part-timer was difficult and my thoughts were turning to management. That process was accelerated when I had to take one of the rigorous medical examinations the insurance companies demand for anybody working in the pub trade. The tests were conducted by a Dr McIntyre, who happened to be an ardent Rangers supporter, and he alarmed me with the revelation that my arteries were enlarged. He added that, unless I was desperately in need of the wages, he did not think I should be punishing myself at my age for the £60 a week Ayr were paying me. I was only thirty-two but the doctor's opinion convinced me that I should retire immediately. Not until some time afterwards did he admit that his advice had been influenced by the protective feeling that it was demeaning for somebody who had been with Rangers to be playing out the last phase of his career with Ayr United. Apparently, the condition of my arteries was quite common among sportsmen in their thirties and certainly it has created no problems for me since then. I wasn't too pleased when

I thought back on the panic the doctor's rather unscientific approach had caused me but, considering how my life in management has gone, he obviously did me no great harm. Ally MacLeod's reasonableness did me a great deal of good. The manager had given me a £6,000 signing-on fee and I was concerned about still having a year left on my contract. But Ally insisted that what I had done in one year more than justified the fee. He also turned up at the pub in Kinning Park to hand over ten weeks' wages that I had not expected to be paid. In addition to all that, he actively encouraged my plans to become a manager, channelling inquiries that had been made about me by Queen's Park and East Stirlingshire and urging me to go for interviews with both.

First, however, I was due to play my last official game as a pro and it was at Somerset Park on the final day of the season against East Fife reserves. All players remember their last one and mine, quite appropriately, was brightened by a scoring header. East Fife that day had a young centre-half by the name of Colin Methven, who later moved to England and had a decent career in the lower divisions. I particularly recall him because he seemed to be afflicted with temporary blindness. He kept running through me to get to the ball. I had to smile as I looked at the enthusiasm of a young lad who reminded me of many of my own attitudes when I was starting out. There was never a chance that I would become embroiled with him, as I was too busy reliving my sixteen years as a senior player in the space of ninety minutes. It is interesting to think of just how many professional footballers have experienced the private emotions of that hour and a half at the finish. You wonder where the years have gone as you reflect on the great moments, the goals, the regrets, some of the characters you played with and against, and it is not easy to come to terms with a permanent parting from it all. However, in my case, it was not really an ending but a beginning.

The day after I shed my striker's L-plates with a hat trick for St Johnstone at Rangers of all places, and I'm starting to believe in miracles.

Brothers-in-arms: Martin and I have always remained close.

Willie Cunningham (*left*), who signed me for Dunfermline, talks tactics. I'm fifth from the left among the players.

Early days at Dunfermline and the goals are flowing for me.

After a lean spell and an injury layoff, I had a good time in the October 1966 Fairs Cup home tie against Dinamo Zagreb – played well and scored two goals.

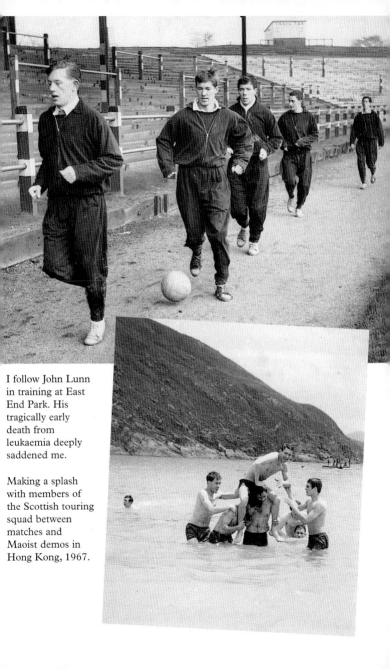

I follow John Lunn in training at East End Park. His tragically early death from leukaemia deeply saddened me.

Making a splash with members of the Scottish touring squad between matches and Maoist demos in Hong Kong, 1967.

Above: Scot Symon (*right*) was the manager who brought me 'home' to Ibrox, but within months he was disgracefully sacked.

Right: Deceptively close to the ineffective Davie White in this Ibrox squad shot. John Greig, a great Ranger, is on his other side.

Below right: My shot is blocked on the Airdrie line soon after I joined Rangers in 1967, which somehow typified my time at Ibrox.

Below: Back to Govan: I have just signed for my childhood heroes, Rangers, a few blocks from where I played street football as a boy.

Rangers' manager Davie White (*right*) has just told me he wants to offload me to Hibs in part-exchange for Colin Stein, but I'm having none of it.

Willie Johnston and I celebrate a goal for Rangers at Hearts.

Playing for Falkirk in 1971, against Rangers appropriately enough.

Our first son, Mark, is born a month ahead of schedule in 1968.

The day I got steaming at Falkirk – in the sauna with my team-mates, I hasten to add.

Willie Cunningham, now my manager at Falkirk, waits to have a polite word as I take the walk of shame after being sent off in 1972.

— 8 —
LIFE AT FERGIE'S

I HAVE had a few original ideas in my time but running a pub would not qualify as one of them. Among past generations of prominent footballers, when careers began to run down it was almost a reflex to take over licensed premises. With the money successful players earn nowadays, they would probably turn up their noses at anything less glamorous than Planet Hollywood. You were not likely to find Sylvester Stallone, Bruce Willis or Arnold Schwarzenegger in my place, though you might have encountered the odd customer who, single-handed, could have put the three of them to flight. In an earlier period of its existence the pub had been called 'Burns Cottage' but, since it was located at the junction of Govan Road and Paisley Road West and drew much of its clientele from a dockland area, whatever charms it now had were not rustic. It had once been a thriving establishment, with a reputation for launching musicians and entertainers towards success, but by the time it came under my control its biggest celebrities were the members of the darts team.

As with everything else I turn my hand to, I worked extremely hard to get the business up and running and that meant a lot of late nights and little time at home. I had taken pains to learn the ropes of the licensed trade and I knew it was one in which there is no substitute for putting in the hours and paying attention to detail. There are many stories of poor publicans and rich bar managers, so another imperative was the recruitment of someone I could trust as my charge-hand. On the advice of a friend who was an experienced publican, I hired George Hope. George had a desperately bad stutter but there was no reason why that should be a significant problem. Renamed Fergie's, the pub began to pick up encouragingly. We had two darts teams and a dominoes team and I found that cribbage was a great attraction for the many sailors and dockers who came in. Nobody who knows me will be surprised to learn that I made it my aim to be able to hold my own at all these games and would have backed myself against any of the crib players. Entertainment of a more stylish kind was provided in the downstairs lounge, which had been refurbished with a loan from the brewery company, who were very helpful. I christened the lounge 'Elbow Room', a popular choice given my awkward way of running as a player. Some marvellous bands and solo performers played there before a pretty exacting audience.

Just when I had come to appreciate fully the value of George Hope, I was rather dramatically deprived of his services. He disappeared from my life because of a chain of events which was a reminder that having a pub in the Kinning Park/Govan district of Glasgow was no occupation for anybody who cherished tranquillity. Stealing is inseparable from the docks but the episode that led to George's departure had nothing to do with petty theft. There had been a whisky heist and a cargo valued at about £40,000 had been stolen and then re-stolen from the original thieves. The result was a gang war which involved my pub. One of my regular customers was a massive man with a face that had seen any number of confrontations, both in the boxing ring and in the street. Somehow the grapevine became alive with the word that the big man was involved in the heist and its aftermath. After training one night at Ayr United, where my playing career was drawing to a close, I was told by the manager, Ally MacLeod, that George Hope had been seeking me on the phone. Since my home in East Kilbride was only half an hour away, I decided to wait and contact George from there. When I did, his stutter was worse than ever but soon enough the message came through – there was someone in the bar with a shotgun.

'You'll need to come down,' George pleaded.

'What can I do against someone with a shotgun?' I asked rather lamely.

I managed to calm him down and told him that someone from the local CID would be there shortly. A phone call to Govan police station did send the CID to the scene. When they arrived the gunman had gone but George was able to give them a detailed description of the man. Early next morning, I received a call from a Detective Inspector to let me know me that the information from my barman seemed to identify a particularly notorious character from the east end of Glasgow. The news chilled me to the bone and that old line about your whole life passing in front of you was never truer. Later that day, I told George about the CID's strong suspicions, and the implications of being their one solid witness apparently sank in. Quite simply, that's the last time I ever saw him. I believe he went to Wales. Had I been in his shoes, it might have been Tristan da Cunha.

The vendettas he left behind persisted for quite a while. The big man who was my customer survived an attempt to run his car off the Kingston Bridge and then his lorry business was burned to the ground, with all his trucks destroyed. It was serious stuff. Every time the door of the pub swung inwards people immediately scanned the new arrival and things became a bit paranoid for a time. Then, at lunchtime one Friday, we were paid a visit by a contingent from Customs and Excise. It was always a hectic hour for us and I was busy working away when a well-dressed gentleman stepped forward to announce who he was and show me his warrant card.

'You will have to close your doors and no one will be allowed to leave,' he said. Two policemen stood firmly at the entrance to the pub as a painstaking search was conducted. It was all done with courtesy, and much apologising. The search was, of course, part of the pursuit of the whisky taken in the heist. All the pubs in the dock area had come under scrutiny and, with a customer who was tied into the surrounding violence, mine was obviously high on the list. Everybody in the pub appeared to enjoy the excitement of it all but I was glad when my involuntary brush with the underworld was over.

Life at Fergie's was never dull. How could it be with so many of those wonderful dockers on hand? They represented every character you are liable to come across in a city full of special people. There were historians, poets, psychiatrists, bums, would-be millionaires, fighters, lovers, fantasists, all with a shared gift for entertaining their listeners. To enhance business in an area where there is a pub every fifty yards, I decided in my wisdom to have a tick book, that is to operate a system that allowed customers to borrow money during the week and repay on a Friday. It is common practice in pubs but the snag is that after a while you don't know if the money passing to and fro is yours or theirs. On Fridays I felt like a millionaire as all the repayments rolled in, but by Saturday evening most of the cash had gone back out again. Saturday mornings were hilarious. That was when the dockers would bring their wives in for a weekly treat and the patter was terrific. But as the morning gave way to early afternoon secret distress signals would be communicated to me. A roll of the eyes, a nod of the head or a number of fingers held up, all in a way that ensured the gestures would not be detected by the wives, conveyed the scale and urgency of the financial help required. The confidentiality of the tick book was sacrosanct but the women weren't fooled.

'If I thought my man's name was in that book, I'd cut the balls off you, Alex,' Ann Armour once said to me.

'Would I let you down like that, Ann?' I replied, laughing off the possibility. They knew what was going on but they also knew I wouldn't take liberties with them by allowing their men to get into a mess and so they played along with the pretence. Those guys were the salt of the earth and they would warn me about some dockers who made a habit of moving from pub to pub, leaving debt in the tick books.

Once enmeshed with life in dockland, you became used to the bartering system and there were days when my pub was like a market as goods that had made an unofficial exit from the docks were sold off. I must confess that I fell prey to many of the wheeler-dealers and Cathy used to go off her head when I brought home clothes, binoculars, lengths of silk, china, cutlery and all sorts. On one occasion, as we were preparing to go out for the evening, I was preening myself before a mirror in a smart suede jacket I had just acquired. With a last little touch of vanity, I gave the cuffs a tug to bring everything into line and the sleeves came away in my hands. Cathy was in hysterics as I stood there, sleeveless and dumbstruck. Maybe I should have stuck to the pub-market's specialist service, which was providing wedding presents. All you had to do was put in an order for cutlery or china or crystal and the next week, without fail, there it was all gift-wrapped and ready to be conveyed to the happy couple.

At first glance Jimmy Campbell, who had been recommended as a replacement for George Hope, looked like an unlikely collaborator for the docker-entrepreneurs. He turned up for his first morning at work wearing a bow tie. 'A bow tie in a pub in dockland,' I said to myself incredulously. A few of the wags were having a field day but Jimmy kept the place immaculately clean and everything seemed to be fine and dandy until one Friday night I arrived to sort out wages and expenses. The place was absolutely heaving and the two part-time barmen were working their tails off. But the bold Jimmy was splendidly aloof from all the sweaty activity, standing at the end of the bar in his suit and bow tie. As I went towards him, I noticed that he was filling paper bags with something he was taking from a large sack under the counter.

'What the bloody hell is this?' I said, pointing at the sack.

'Bird seed,' he answered nonchalantly, as if nothing could be more normal than selling the stuff over my bar.

'This is a bloody pub, not an aviary,' I told him, adding a few comments that are better left unrecorded. Needless to say, that was Jimmy's last night, but he wasn't a bad lad. He had merely succumbed to the charms of one of the dockers who had brought in a consignment of seed and enlisted his help with the merchandising operation. I can laugh at that bit of madness now, but on the night I was not amused.

Some would say I was asking for a comeuppance when I had

the rather corny notion that I could edge Fergie's up-market by ordering a huge delivery of cocktail glasses. After the first Saturday night of their use, eighty per cent of them were gone. One Saturday night a few weeks later, as we were seeing the last customers out, one of my waitresses stopped a girl from leaving the lounge on the grounds that she had been seen filling her bag with glasses. When asked to surrender the booty, the girl refused to do so and within seconds her husband and friends had started one hell of a fight. There were bodies everywhere as my staff and a number of helpful customers struggled to force the troublemakers up the stairs and out into the street. One big fellow was in his element and sorted out more than a few of the rowdies. Once we got them into the street we bolted the doors and made our way back to the public bar to congregate with some of my friends, the customers who had helped and members of the staff. Cathy was also there and for a few minutes peace reigned. Then suddenly the door was burst open and a barrage of bottles came crashing into the room, somehow missing everyone but smashing into the bar. Immediately the big fellow snatched one of the dockers' hooks that were often left behind the counter and headed towards the besiegers. I phoned the police and made my way out on to the pavement and what I saw appalled me. One of the group who had attacked the pub was prone on the ground with blood gushing out of his face and neck; his wife was bending over him, screaming wildly. At first I thought he was dead and it was a tremendous relief to discover that he was not. He was, however, in a serious condition and was taken to the Southern General Hospital. When the police arrived on the scene there was complete bedlam and it was intensified rather than diminished by the efforts of everybody to calm everybody else down. The upshot was that I had to go to Govan police station and lay charges against one of the crowd who had stormed the bar. The next day someone from the station warned me that if the man who had grabbed the hook was ever seen in my pub again I would lose my licence. The point was taken.

One of my happier memories as a landlord concerns the sub-scription club I ran for regulars with the object of having an annual outing. Customers who wanted to participate would chip in a little money each week, I would match every sum contributed and we would use the total kitty for a trip to a hotel in Darvel, Ayrshire. It was always a wonderful day out. After an early lunch, the women would all go to Ayr for the afternoon while the men stayed in the hotel to participate in a series of competitions I had organised: dominoes, cribbage, pool and darts. In the evening the prizes would be given out and we would have a party with a sing-song. This event became a highlight of my time at Fergie's and quite a few of the locals in Darvel looked forward to our arrival. One in particular, George Young, the postie, took part in our competitions. He was quite a character and kept in touch with me regularly until he died just recently. The star entertainers at our evening get-together were invariably a couple who were regulars in Fergie's. They were forever arguing and then having loving reconciliations and that pattern was certainly not interrupted by the outing. Both were magnificent singers, with voices so remarkable that their solos and duets commanded respectful attention even when their audience had left sobriety far behind. Unfortunately, during one of the Darvel expeditions their inevitable argument reached an unusually violent pitch and the wife hit the husband with a beer glass and cut him badly enough to necessitate rapid transportation to the nearest hospital. Yet a few hours later there they were, hand in hand, singing love songs to one another, completely unabashed by the massive bandage encircling the husband's head. Even by Govan standards, they had a strange way of being romantic.

With Fergie's in good shape, I agreed to go into partnership with a friend, Sam Falconer, in a pub called Shaws in the Bridgeton area. It cost us £22,000 but we put up only £2,000 each, with a loan from Drybrough providing the other £18,000. The idea was that Sam would be in charge but I would call in regularly in the hope that my presence would give the place a lift. Partnerships are difficult and this one turned out in time to be a nightmare. But I did enjoy meeting the customers in the Bridgeton pub, who were completely different as a group from those I had in Govan. In a city like Glasgow, districts have their own distinctive pride and tribalism. For instance, the Gorbals was traditionally an Irish and Jewish community with a predominance of Irish Catholics. Bridgeton was the bedrock of militant Protestantism in Glasgow. Although many other areas had mainly Protestant populations, Bridgeton saw itself as being in the vanguard of Orange fervour. That identity was very marked in the Bridgeton Cross area, where Shaws was located, and there was never any doubt that our premises would have to make special arrangements for the twelfth of July, the anniversary of the Battle of the Boyne. 'What time are we opening on the twelfth?' was a loaded question when put to you by a regular. 'We usually open at seven thirty,' was the answer supplied by another customer. This was the accepted procedure and I was not about to question it. When the doors were opened at half-past seven in the morning, those who would be marching later in the day filed in with almost regimental precision and, having folded their Lodge colours and sashes neatly and placed them in a corner, immediately began drinking in earnest. On these occasions in Bridgeton, the local constabulary were expert at turning a blind eye. As the morning wore on and the tempo quickened, I was urged to take part in the singing of an Orange song. It was no time to offer my thoughts on the selection of music. Joining in was not a matter of choice but of common sense. In fact, the early morning revellers were as good as gold and, before departing for their parade, they all thanked me for the food we had laid on for them.

In early 1978, I decided that managing St Mirren, being involved in the running of two pubs and attempting to be some sort of reasonable father amounted to an impossible combination of responsibilities. Fergie's had to go. The enjoyment I had once derived from it had been replaced by an almost permanent headache. Maintenance problems were never-ending and a prolonged period of bad stock returns severely reduced my profit margin. On top of those worries, I was sick of having to come home at weekends with a cut head or swollen jaw from trying to keep the peace in the pub. Mayhem didn't erupt every week but from time to time a fight would break out and my efforts to quell the disturbance would put me in the middle of it. One night, after a skirmish with a bunch of brothers that featured flying glass and left another bad gash on my head, I returned home to tell Cathy, 'That's it. I'm definitely getting out.' She was relieved.

That summer, when I took over the managership of Aberdeen, I also agreed to sell my half-share in Shaws bar to Sam Falconer, but some months later I still hadn't been paid. That was just the first chapter of a long and miserable story. The essence of it was that Sam had plunged the business into considerable debt and, although he was eventually obliged to sever his connections with the pub, my endeavours to resurrect it as a going concern were unavailing and it went into liquidation. In spite of the financial loss I suffered, I was relieved that this outcome at least meant I was rid of a gnawing distraction 140 miles away from Aberdeen and could concentrate on my real job. Overall, my experiences of the pub trade were a mixture of fun and pain, a bit like that worthy singing with the bandage on his head.

— 9 —

MANAGING TO MOVE UPWARDS

EVERY one of the twenty-five years I have spent as a club manager has been a learning experience but some of the principles I brought to the job as a raw, thirty-two-year-old recruit are as important to me now as they were on my first day in charge of East Stirlingshire in July 1974. Prominent in that category is the certainty that good coaching relies on repetition. Forget all the nonsense about altering training programmes to keep players happy. The argument that they must be stimulated by constant variety may come across as progressive and enlightened but it is a dangerous evasion of priorities. In any physical activity, effective practice requires repeated execution of the skill involved. Why do you think the greatest golfers who ever lived have devoted endless hours to striking the same shots over and over again? Yes, I know golf, where the ball always sits still to be struck, is so different from football that technical comparisons are foolish. But the link is the need to concentrate on refining technique to the point where difficult skills become a matter of habit. When footballers complain about the dullness of repetitive passing exercises it is usually not monotony they resent but hard work. David Beckham is Britain's finest striker of a football not because of God-given talent but because he practises with a relentless application that the vast majority of less gifted players wouldn't contemplate. Practice may not make you perfect but it will definitely make you better and any player working with me on the training ground will hear me preach the virtues of repetition – repeatedly.

I battered a few eardrums with the message at East Stirlingshire and it had its effect, although there was no Beckham available to me there. In fact, when I arrived the club did not have enough players of any kind to field a team. We had a total of eight on the books and they did not include a goalkeeper. When I looked at the list, and reminded myself that East Stirlingshire had finished bottom of the Scottish Second Division in the previous season, which made them the worst senior team in the country, I had to wonder why I had chosen to launch my management career at Firs Park. One simple reason was that my interview with Queen's Park had been a disaster. Ally MacLeod had given me a glowing recommendation. But everybody on the board at Hampden had played with me and in front of the interviewing committee I surrendered to nerves and failed to offer a shred of justification for employing me.

It was mainly a desire to be courteous that made me accept East Stirlingshire's invitation to talk to them but when I met their chairman, Willie Muirhead, the honesty in his face and the ease I felt in his company persuaded me to take a chance. Once he revealed the poverty of the playing resources, the decision began to look suicidal. When Willie was obliged to own up to an awkward truth, his smoking action accelerated dramatically and he was puffing at a hectic rate as he delivered the facts of life at Firs Park.

'Do you know you need eleven players to start a game, plus two subs?' I asked him. He tried to console me with word of a board meeting that had been arranged to see if some money could be allocated for strengthening the squad, at least to the level of a quorum. That meeting came immediately after my first training session – where the players, whatever their limitations, encouraged me by being receptive and enthusiastic – and when summoned I fought my way through the billowing cigarette smoke to await the good news. Willie showed all his admirable forthrightness.

'Two thousand pounds, Mr Ferguson. I know it's not a lot but it is all we can afford.'

With that budget, the only place to start was among the men who had been granted free transfers. My phone was almost too hot to touch as I went wheeling and dealing through the bargain basement. My first essential was a goalkeeper. As I mentioned to the board, it always helps if you start a match with a goalie. The strongest candidate was still contracted to Partick Thistle but was in the reserve team. Tom Gourlay was useful, had good presence and was utterly fearless. He was also a minimum of two stones overweight. The Thistle manager, Bertie Auld, waived the right to a fee, I was able to agree a £750 signing-on payment with Gourlay and we had the luxury of a man between the posts. Tom, I was confident, would improve his condition sufficiently to do a job for us. Other handy acquisitions from Partick were Jimmy Mullen, a clever little centre-forward, and George Adams, a tall midfielder who had looked set for an outstanding career with Aberdeen until a succession of knee injuries blighted his progress. Both had been freed and a total of £300 in signing-on fees secured them. I had slightly less than £1,000 left to spend and my target was a centre-forward Clyde were willing to release. His name was Billy Hulston and whenever I had seen him play he had done well. My first offer to him was £300. His initial demand was £1,500. We met halfway, at £900, and with the addition of a couple of provisional signings I had a squad of fifteen. It was enough to send a man power-crazy.

In pre-season training, I started every session with 'the boxes', a routine in which perhaps five or six players are deployed in a group surrounding two other men. The players on the outside play the ball to each other while trying to defy the efforts of the pair in the middle to intercept it. I still use the exercise at Old Trafford but there it is done as a bit of fun to help with motivation. At East Stirlingshire, where the technical standard was light years behind that at Manchester United, its purpose was more basic. I used it to improve touch and to develop the movement that gives the man on the ball an angle to make a pass. At first the quality of passing and movement was depressingly poor but within a few weeks it had risen noticeably, thanks to the healthy influence of that old ally repetition. A pre-season game against a young Celtic team produced a 3–3 draw and, more importantly, proof of a gathering confidence among my players. They all wanted the ball and they were ready to express themselves. In another friendly match, Tranmere Rovers, managed by the former Liverpool centre-half Ron Yeats, beat us 2–0 with the help of a goal from an energetic striker by the name of Steve Coppell. I was pleased with the way we had passed the ball during much of the game but stressed to the players that we had lacked penetration. You can have all the possession in the world but if you end up going nowhere and don't finish with a positive attack in the last third of the field, what is the good of it?

Applying another of my early principles that has remained close to my heart, I sought to create a youth policy at East Stirlingshire by inviting local young players to Firs Park for coaching. To further the scheme, I paid the travel costs of bringing Glasgow United, a well-known boys' club team from my home city, through to Falkirk to test our crop of hopefuls. Some time afterwards, when that boys' game was the last thing on my mind, I was called before the board to find Willie Muirhead pouring out the smoke signals that meant he was preparing for a momentous declaration. Then he announced that I had committed a serious breach of club policy by authorising the £40 payment to a Glasgow bus company. I was flabbergasted and, once the truth had sunk in, I lost my temper.

'I did that to try and improve this club, but if that's the way you want it then stick the club up your arse.' Throwing £40 on the table, I stormed out. It was necessary to cross the pitch to leave the ground and, as I was marching over the turf in the dark, Willie came chasing after me.

'Alex, please, listen to me,' he said. 'I was forced by Jim Hastings to bring it up. You have to understand – he's an old man.'

Jimmy Hastings was, indeed, one of the oldest directors in the history of East Stirlingshire and, if my outburst destroyed his daft complaint about the bus money, I didn't fare as well on the occasion when I collided with him over the issue of the team's strip. They wore a replica of Queen's Park's narrow black-and-white hoops and I couldn't wait to tell the board that there should be a change to white shirts, black pants and red socks. The suggestion was greeted with silence, then a few coughs from Willie Muirhead before old Jimmy addressed me.

'Look, sonny, that strip was here when my father was a young man and it will be here long after you've gone.' That was the end of the debate. I don't think Jimmy was too fond of me after that. One day I stopped to offer him a lift about three miles from the ground.

'No thanks,' he barked, and strode on.

Beginning the season with the League Cup, we won three and drew one of our first five matches, but in the other we could not cope with the speed of Albion Rovers' centre-forward, Peter Dickson, and took a pasting. When we met Rovers again, it was to decide the winners of our section and a lucrative tie against Rangers in the next round was the prize. In the first half, our players did not heed my instructions to sit off Dickson and allow him to receive the ball, and instead left space behind them and became easy prey to his pace. We were down 2–0 at the interval and, as we pounded away at them to no avail in the second half, my annoyance was not lessened by the sudden appearance of my wonderful chairman in the dug-out.

'What are you going to do?' Willie asked.

'I'm going to throw you out of this fucking dug-out if you don't move NOW,' I said.

He made himself scarce and no East Stirlingshire director ever again interfered with the playing side of my work. Perhaps I should say that none ever interfered directly. One of them, Bob Shaw, was a background figure in a serious test of my authority that came from our centre-forward, Jim Meekin. Players are always trying to take liberties, checking how far they can go before you come down on them. If somebody who fancies taking up management asks me about discipline, I have a simple piece of advice: 'Don't seek confrontation. It will come to you anyway.' Martin Buchan asked such a question soon after taking over at Burnley and I made my point about confrontation.

'Too late,' said Martin. 'I hung one on my centre-half an hour ago.'

My problem with Jim Meekin arose when he informed me he would be missing Monday training because he was going to Blackpool for the weekend with Bob Shaw, who was his father-in-law.

'I don't care if you are going with the Queen,' I told him. 'You are training on Monday. End of story.'

I got on well with Shaw but when he phoned me on Meekin's behalf I wouldn't listen to the director's pleas. At about four o'clock on the Monday afternoon there was a call from Meekin to say his car had broken down on the way home and he wouldn't make training. I asked him to give me his number, so that I could ring him back. After a prolonged silence, he meekly admitted that he was still in Blackpool.

'Don't come back,' I said. 'You're finished.' I meant it. I was not willing to be messed about by any player and this was as good a time as any to prove it. On the journey back from a game weeks later, and with Meekin still suspended, I was alone in a restaurant lavatory when the chairman arrived amid a cloud of smoke to stand in the next stall. He asked me solemnly if I would do him the favour of permitting Meekin to return 'to get this man Shaw off my back'. Being in a mischievous mood, I said, 'Oh, I don't know about that.' At which point Willie comes away with one of his classics: 'I am asking you as a decent, God-fearing man.' I had no answer to that, so I nodded and said, 'OK.' And he kissed me, the silly old bugger. He must have been getting some grief from Bob Shaw.

Our form in the League was good and by the end of September we had climbed to third place in the Second Division and East Stirlingshire (known to their supporters as The Shire) were preparing for the biggest game they had faced in years. My old club, Falkirk, under John Prentice, had been relegated in the 1973–74 season and now the town rivals were in direct opposition. For obvious reasons, this was a match I was particularly keen to win and I had spent weeks building my players up for it.

'There is not one thing I don't know about this mob,' I assured them. 'I can tell you which side of the bed they lie in.' I did a detailed analysis of Falkirk's weaknesses and worked on the elements of our game that could hurt them. Above all, I took pains to rid our lads of the feeling that Falkirk were the town's big team.

'I know them and they are useless,' I said. The board gave me permission to have the players in for training on the Saturday morning and to take them for lunch. Long before nutritionists came on the scene, I had strong views on eating before games. 'What the hell is this?' was a common reaction to the grilled fish, toast and honey that were served up, but they accepted that I knew what I was doing.

As it happened, I was rather nervous. But I reminded myself of how well we were playing and of the good level of skill ensured by players like George Adams, Ian Browning, Jim Mullen and Bobby McCurdie. All they required was direction and somebody to say 'well done' from time to time. Those are the best two words in football. There is no need to elaborate. 'Well done' says it all. On the day, everything we planned became reality and the 2–0 scoreline did not reflect our superiority. We gave Falkirk a drubbing.

I was learning something new about management every day and, although I was making mistakes, I was not repeating them. In the main, I was acting on instinct but I discovered that when I reached decisions quickly I was drawing a positive response, especially from players. I tested myself all the time. When a player was talking to me, I was making rapid analyses and assessments in my head so that I could give quick, clear answers. If I was unsure, I would encourage more dialogue until I worked out a sound reply. As a player, I was never happy when a manager responded with vagueness or groping indecision. There is nothing wrong with requiring time to consider a question or an argument and you can gain it without appearing to be a dithering idiot. I might say, 'I've never considered that angle – can I give it some thought?' By praising the other person's ability to make me think, I increased his willingness to wait for an answer.

Just when everything was going along fine at Firs Park, I received a call in October 1974 from my former boss, Willie

Cunningham, who was then managing St Mirren. He suggested that I should call on him at Love Street and I drove the few miles from my Glasgow pub to Paisley, expecting nothing more than a nostalgic chat. But I soon realised the big man had more serious business to discuss. He told me he was quitting St Mirren in a few days and had recommended me for the job. Was I interested? Willie said he was leaving because he had had enough of football but painted an attractive picture of St Mirren as a club ready to be revived by someone with ambition and drive. Although flattered, I was not convinced. I was enjoying the challenge at East Stirlingshire and felt strong loyalty to a great bunch of players who were giving me their all. Even when Willie's departure became official and I was invited to meet the St Mirren chairman, Harold Currie, at his Glasgow office, I went to the meeting intent on declining the offer of the job. I understood the arguments about the club's potential – Paisley is the largest town in Scotland – but I had noticed that the most recent attendance at Love Street was 1,200. Living in the shadow of Glasgow guaranteed that, every match day, bus after bus would leave Paisley Cross carrying fans to watch Rangers and Celtic. Yet Harold Currie made a point that gave me pause: 'Can East Stirlingshire become a big club? If not, why do you want to stay if you are ambitious?' As I pondered, I had a brainwave, or so I thought. I phoned Jock Stein at Celtic Park.

'Mr Stein, I wonder if you could give me a bit of advice?' I said.

'If I can,' he replied and let me explain my difficulty. His advice was succinct.

'Go and sit in the stand at Love Street and look around, then do the same at Firs Park and you will get your answer. All the best.' And he put the phone down.

Willie Muirhead was typically marvellous when I told him I was moving on after just three and a half successful months with his club. In their last match for me, the players produced their best performance since my arrival, a 4–0 thrashing of Alloa, which made delivering my subsequent announcement all the tougher. Mute shock was the general reaction until our wing-half Tom

Donnelly said: 'You bastard!' Tom was a good lad and showed his disappointment as honestly as he lived his life. I shook hands with all the players and made my way to the boardroom, where I thanked the directors for the opportunity and support they had given me. As I left East Stirlingshire for St Mirren, there was no trace of exhilaration but rather a dull sense of failure, of a task unfinished. I had no right to assume that the players awaiting me at Love Street would serve me as well as the diamonds I was leaving behind at The Shire.

Sometimes I feel that I have known nearly as many scouts as Baden-Powell. If the kind familiar to me were seen escorting a frail old lady across a busy street, it might be because she had a grandson who was scoring a barrowload of goals for the local boys' club. Good scouts in football are masters at gaining the trust of the families of promising players. That is only one of a wide range of qualities a man must possess if he is to be successful in searching through schoolboy teams, the amateur, youth and junior ranks and every other lower grade of the game to find talents he can recommend to the professional club employing him. Obviously he should be able to judge a player but when the quarry has been identified the scout must ward off the other pursuers, and that calls for resourcefulness, perseverance and often a little low cunning. All of those attributes, and a few more, were conspicuous in Archie 'Baldy' Lindsay, who did wonders for me at St Mirren and was perhaps the most remarkable of the countless scouts I have used during my career in management. Baldy was a taxi driver from the Kinning Park district of Glasgow and he had made a name for himself as manager of a well-known juvenile team called Avon Villa. My relationship with him was nothing short of tempestuous, frequently punctuated by the weeks of estrangement which followed one of his storming exits ('You know damn-all about football'). But he was a vital ally once I decided that most of the thirty-five players I inherited at Love Street would have to go and that fresh young blood was the only hope of raising standards to an acceptable level.

Baldy's commitment to lads he had spotted was total and even when I put him on the track of somebody drawn to my attention in other ways he refused to be denied. An example occurred when a boys' club final was played at the St Mirren ground and an outside-left named John McDonald scored seven goals in a sensational performance for Leeds United BC. I furnished Baldy with details of McDonald's school in the Knightswood area of Glasgow, his father's Christian name and a couple of further facts but could not give him a home address. Baldy's solution was to go to the Knightswood police station and tell the desk sergeant there had been a death in the family and he needed to contact his nephew. Out came the voters' roll and a process of elimination produced the required street and number. Another prospect, Phil McAveety, a centre-half who was captain of Scotland Schoolboys and played for Celtic Boys' Club, was wooed to St Mirren after Baldy used his cab to ferry the lad to and from school and persuaded me to buy his family a turkey for Christmas. Probably the greatest Lindsay triumph was the remorseless pestering he applied to me on behalf of a beanpole of a midfield player called Billy Stark. I took a while to share Baldy's enthusiasm and when Stark signed provisional forms for Rangers I was again blasted as an ignoramus. Then, in the summer of 1975, Rangers let young Billy go and, having had another look at him in action, I put him on our books to begin a senior career in which he matured into a player of exceptional grace and skill.

After a particularly ferocious barney over something or other, I lost contact with Baldy altogether for some years and I was manager at Aberdeen the next time I heard the familiar voice on the phone.

'Hello, Boss, how are you?' he inquired, as if we had been speaking the day before.

'Fine, Baldy, how are you?' He admitted that he had 'not been keeping too good' and I could tell that was an understatement of his health problems. But the real subject of his call was his nephew, a genuine one, who was playing with St Mary's Boys' Club in Bridgeton, Glasgow. The nephew was Joe Miller, who went on to play for Aberdeen, Celtic and Scotland. A few weeks after the phone conversation, I signed Joe, and Baldy died less than a week later. I was proud that when he did his last scouting mission, he chose to do it for me.

My use of Baldy at St Mirren, and of all the other willing and knowledgeable men I engaged to scour the playing fields at weekends, was part of my wholehearted commitment to youth development at the club. Fortunately, though most of the players I found when I arrived at Love Street were in my eyes inadequate, there was at least one jewel among them. Tony Fitzpatrick was not immediately available to me because he had been laid low by pneumonia, but as soon as he was healthy I drafted him into a specially arranged reserve fixture on the same day as the first team were confronting my previous club, East Stirlingshire, in the opening round of the Scottish Cup. Davie Provan, my former team-mate at Rangers and as conscientious and trustworthy a man as you could ever have at your side, had joined me as assistant manager and I asked him to study Fitzpatrick's contribution carefully. The assessment could not have been simpler.

'Brilliant,' said Davie. 'He is the best player we have at the club.'

Having watched East Stirlingshire dismiss us contemptuously from the Cup, with a 2–0 scoreline that might have been tripled, I wasn't going to hesitate about giving Fitzpatrick a first-team place for our next league match. He was outstanding in that game, driving himself over every blade of grass and showing wonderful care in his passing. I was so impressed that I instantly made him captain for our visit to Dumfries to face a strong Queen of the South team that included a newly signed centre-forward, Peter Dickson, whose deeds for Albion Rovers had brought me pain in my few months with East Stirlingshire.

When I took over at St Mirren in the 1974–75 season, my overriding concern was to ensure that they finished in the top six in the Scottish Second Division. In 1975–76 the League was to be restructured, changing from First and Second Divisions each containing eighteen clubs to three twelve-club divisions. The

Premier Division would be formed by the top twelve finishers in the old First Division in 1974–75, and the new First Division would be drawn from the bottom six in the old one and the top six in the Second Division. We were determined to claim one of those half-dozen places but it did not look like a good bet as we headed into that away match with Queen of the South, who were sitting pretty at the top of the table with Hamilton Accies. If we were to avoid dropping into the lowest of the new divisions, that game at Palmerston had to be a turning point. It was. Our 1–0 victory led to a run of eight wins in a row that secured the coveted top-six finish.

Equally important was the way Tony Fitzpatrick's enthusiasm spread through the club, reinforcing my resolve to bank on young players. An increasing supply of worthwhile talent was emerging from our vigorous youth policy. Intensified scouting was paying dividends and splendid work was being done by the St Mirren Boys' Club, which was run by good and responsible people and was starting to attract the best boys in the Paisley area. An expanding network of contacts also helped and the goodwill of established figures in the game was a welcome bonus. One day early in 1975, Willie Thornton, who had been so supportive throughout my troubles at Rangers, surprised me with a phone call.

'There's a young lad playing for Kilsyth Rangers who is well worth signing,' he told me, and added, 'He's no use to us but he is a very good player.'

When Willie said the boy was no good to Rangers, I knew he must be a Catholic. I dispatched one of our scouts, Maxie Gray, to see a young Frank McGarvey excel, and within a week Frank had been added to the corps of highly promising footballers we were now assembling. Considering that McGarvey would ultimately win seven Scotland caps, Willie Thornton's tip was a valuable one. While passing it on, he revealed that Willie Waddell, the Rangers manager, had recommended me for the St Mirren job and intended to smooth my progress whenever he could. I remembered how grateful he had been when, on my departure from Ibrox, I assured him that I would not be tempted by newspaper offers to pay me handsomely for throwing mud at Rangers. 'I'll not forget this, Alex,' he said then. Willie Waddell was a man of his word.

Consolidation rather than success was the theme of our 1975–76 season in the First Division. We were challenging for leadership for a while but had to settle for fifth position in the end. What mattered more was that we were rousing the population of Paisley from years of apathy towards football. Those were long and demanding days for me, as I fitted the running of the pub business into whatever gaps my football responsibilities allowed and at the same time tried to give Cathy such assistance as I could with the raising of our young family in East Kilbride. But my energy was constantly recharged by the entire community's response to the happenings at Love Street. In our eagerness to spread the message, we started our own newspaper and then an electrician at the ground, Freddie Douglas, had the idea that he and I should go round the town in his van and address potential supporters through a loudspeaker. I was gaining a reputation for innovative management but to me it was simply a case of being willing to try anything that might make the club more successful. At least, as canvassers, we were better received than election candidates. I have to confess that Freddie did most of the hailing, but I was good at waving.

My strong rapport with the fans brought a practical benefit almost as soon as we were into the 1976–77 season. I had begun to realise that to make St Mirren capable of winning the First Division title and earning promotion, I had to introduce more experience to the team. That reasoning focused my attention on Jackie Copland of Dundee United, who had achieved the far from impossible feat of falling out with United's manager, Jim McLean. Jackie was a seasoned centre-half with the necessary toughness and he had the extra advantage of being a Paisley lad. The obstacle to my plan was that the club coffers were virtually empty and the transfer fee was £17,000. So I put my case to the Supporters' Association and they generously provided a loan of £14,000. The club raked together the additional £3,000 and the deal was sealed.

By January, we were at the top of the Division and playing some excellent football, with attendances showing a tenfold increase on the 1,000 or so that had been commonplace before my arrival. There were 19,000 at Love Street when we gained a superb 4–1 victory in the Scottish Cup over Dundee United, who were edging towards a position of strength in the Premier Division. The possibilities of the team were further indicated by the selection of four players – Fitzpatrick, Stark, McGarvey and Robert Reid – for a Scotland Under-21 XI. We and the 15,000 fans who travelled with us to Fir Park for the next round of the Cup deserved better than the refereeing that I felt left us at the mercy of a harshly aggressive Motherwell team. When we had collected our wounded, having lost 2–1, I had a go at Willie McLean, the Motherwell manager, and conveyed my disgust so forcefully to the referee, Ian Foote, that I was reported to the SFA. Losing is never palatable to me but I am ready with sincere congratulations when beaten fairly and squarely. Fir Park was the scene of a sporting atrocity.

If my mood was foul on the way home, it was worse later when I received a phone call from one of my best friends, John Donachie. John had been with me at Harmony Row Boys' Club in Govan and had been vice-chairman during my chairmanship of the Scottish PFA between 1969 and 1974 (his own pro career took him to East Stirlingshire and Queen of the South). When he told me that he had seen Frank McGarvey the worse for wear in the Waterloo Bar in the centre of Glasgow on the evening before the Motherwell game, it was the same as having witnessed the scene myself. McGarvey, when challenged, promptly confessed and I told him that he would be withdrawn from the Scotland Under-21 game, that he was finished with football and I never wanted to see him again. For an entire week, team-mate after team-mate pleaded for leniency and on the Saturday night, at a supporters' dance to which Cathy and I were invited along with all the players except Frank, he jumped out from behind a pillar in Paisley Town Hall and showered me with declarations of contrition and repentance. Cathy sympathised and I relented.

The point had been made – and there was still a championship to be sewn up. Our closest challengers, Clydebank, were due at Love Street the following week. Reconciliation with a chastened McGarvey was something I could bear.

St Mirren delivered some stunning performances on the road to the title and I found it no hardship that three of the most devastating were against Dundee, who were managed by Davie White, whose regime had turned joy to misery for me at Rangers. The aggregate score in those three matches was 11–1 and the last of them, a 4–0 win at Dens Park, clinched the championship. It was an unforgettable season for St Mirren, with our young team suffering just two defeats in thirty-nine games. Their achievement was a source of cheer for a town increasingly hurt by rising unemployment. My own satisfaction was doubled by the evidence that the flow of youthful talent towards the club was swelling. Davie Provan and I were conducting coaching sessions for lads from far and wide and additional scouts like Billy Duncanson, Harry McIntosh and the legendary Sam Beck were reaping a rich harvest. One of my many extra duties was ferrying three young players from East Kilbride every week and there is a member of that group who, whenever we meet these days, berates me for not signing him. At that time he was a midfield player with nice skill but he was small and I was unconvinced that he would grow sufficiently to make the grade. His name was Alistair McCoist. Ally never tires of telling me that I am the worst manager he ever encountered.

In fact, that was a period when my development as a manager was accelerating. Sheer hard work was a huge factor in bringing success but I am sure that sticking to my beliefs was equally important. I believed strongly that being able to pass the ball well was crucial and I don't think there was a training session that did not incorporate passing. But I was also trying to add imagination to my coaching, emphasising the need for players to have a picture in their minds, to visualise how they could have a creative impact on the shifting pattern of a game. Of course, my drive to extract the best from myself and those around me didn't always show in sweetly acceptable ways. The quickness of my temper and depth of my anger often worried me. On one occasion, prior to a match with Partick Thistle at Love Street, my brother Martin phoned with word that some of my players had been frequenting that pub again, the dreaded Waterloo. As if that wasn't bad enough, they had been mouthing off about the amounts they were being paid in bonuses. I was furious and after the match, which we won 1–0, I told the culprits to sit on one side of the dressing-room so that I could let rip at them. My anger intensified with each decibel until I lost control, lifted a bottle of Coca-Cola and smashed it against the wall above their heads. Not one of them moved as the Coke ran down the wall and the glass dropped on to their strips. I told them that the whole team would be staying at Love Street all night, training, unless they signed an agreement never to enter the Waterloo pub again. I then made my way to my office, leaving behind the sheet of paper with the guarantee typed on it. Half an hour later Jackie Copland, the captain, came to the office and asked what it was all about.

'Were you not listening?' I asked.

'Yes,' he said, 'but you were in such a temper that nobody was taking it in. I think they are all shitting themselves down there.'

I explained exactly what the problem was and reiterated my demand – that sheet had to be signed or they would be training every Saturday night. Ten minutes later, big Jackie came back with the form duly signed. I was determined to fight the drinking culture that has always been a curse in British football. It can take a damaging hold at any club, as my initial experiences at Old Trafford were to confirm, and any manager who turns a blind eye shouldn't be in the job. Far from being a teetotal zealot, I love to see people enjoying themselves by having a pleasant drink, and if there is good red wine available I won't be slow to hold out my glass. But boozing should have no place in the lifestyle of a professional sportsman. Any footballer who thinks otherwise won't last long with me.

After my first two and a half years at Love Street, much had changed, on and off the field. When I went there, St Mirren operated like a strange little social club and, but for my aggressive interventions, would have continued to do so. There was such wholesale avoidance of responsibility that the non-playing side of the club was run by the groundsman and his family. Jimmy Ritchie was a good man but he became a victim of the ridiculous latitude and power given to him by default. He was left to order all the cleaning materials from half a dozen different companies, he was in control of catering, of programme sales and of supplies for the pitch. Visiting the ground on Sunday morning, as a break from the pub, was an eye-opener. Hanging out to dry was a full set of strips, the property of the local police team. Jimmy's brother, Willie, was busy servicing cars under the main stand and his sister was upstairs in the kitchen, making lunch for her family and the police. Those arrangements came to an end that day. I ordered Jimmy to return all unsold programmes along with the money raised by the sales and for the first time there was actually a profit from programmes.

A separate concern was my knowledge that substantial numbers of fans were entering at matches by jumping over the turnstiles, with the connivance of some gatemen, who were doing friends a favour or possibly pocketing tips. Since establishing proof of that scam was difficult, I brought in joiners to lower the roof in the turnstile booths, so that jumping over was impossible.

You could say that I was a hands-on boss. Somebody had to be. Most of the directors were visible only on match days and at least one of them, John Corson, did not seem to absorb much while he was there. 'Alex, which one is Tony Fitzpatrick?' he once asked me, two years after I had installed Tony as captain of the team.

There were two factions on the board, always at loggerheads, and Corson had allied himself with Willie Todd, who succeeded Harold Currie as chairman. To be fair to Todd, he was seen at Love Street far more than any other director and not just because his business supplied the painters to do all the work around the place. He was a genuine fan. But from the moment of my arrival, when he was all over me, I suspected that his ego might easily run wild. If there was a hint of glory, nobody could beat him at basking. Todd was constantly bombarding me with tales of how resolutely he was supporting me against the rival boardroom faction, Yule Craig and Fraser Mackintosh. I was consequently wary of Craig and Mackintosh until, in 1976, Yule was the only director who accompanied the team on a three-week Caribbean tour that was apparently made possible by Harold Currie's contacts in the whisky export trade. The tour, which involved one game in Barbados, two in Trinidad, another in Guyana and the last one in Surinam, had several useful effects. It did a lot to strengthen the camaraderie of our squad and gave them the feeling that they were worthy of the big-time treatment. Our travels – and especially the final five days we spent relaxing in Barbados after a 4–0 slaughter of Surinam, whose media had astonishingly dismissed us as cannon fodder – also left me with an opinion of Yule Craig that was vastly different from Todd's characterisation.

Not everything about the tour was positive. In Guyana I had an experience that illustrated the frustrations which can beset a manager who has recently stopped playing for a living. During games, Davie Provan and I would strip as subs and we had some fun in Barbados and Trinidad. That wasn't quite the case in Guyana, where the national team were managed by a likeable Scot, John McSeveney, who had them wound up for a forthcoming World Cup qualifying match. From the start of our game with them, I was complaining to the referee about the cruelty their big centre-half was inflicting on our young centre-forward, Robert Torrance. Half-time came and went without any sign of improved protection and as young Torrance was hacked down yet again, I said to Davie Provan, 'That's it. I'm going on. That big bastard is taking liberties.' Davie tried to dissuade me but I was fired up. In the first contest for a cross, I exacted a bit of revenge on the centre-half, whose squeals caused the referee to point at me ominously. The confrontation became fierce until I nailed Torrance's abuser perfectly. As he rolled about like a dying man, the referee sent me off. At the end of the match, I delivered a warning to my players, pointing to a different individual as each word came out: 'Don't ever let anyone know about this sending-off. Do you understand?' They never did tell the tale.

I was dismissed six times in my sixteen years as a senior player. Obviously I don't accept that the sentence was always justified and I can say with my hand on my heart that, until the Guyana incident, I never took the field with the intention of damaging an opponent. During my playing career my offences were invariably reactions, perhaps overreactions, to violence administered to me. When opposing players were fair, I responded in kind. Disciplinary records often relate to temperament or cunning more than morality. There are players who can be philosophical in the face of abuse, others who instinctively hit back. Some of the assassins in the game are so subtle that their list of convictions is surprisingly short. As a manager, I have always put my faith in skill, never in rough or dirty tactics. I have also preached the value of self-control, which is not only more creditable than the alternative but infinitely more profitable in practical terms. I have to admit, however, that as someone who contrived to be sent off as a manager, I cannot quote my own example as ideal.

I have no doubt that the Caribbean tour in the summer of 1976 brought our players together and matured them to an extent that helped us to win the First Division championship in the following season. In turn, the winning of the title created an immediate opportunity of advancement for me. Ally MacLeod was by then the Aberdeen manager but he was about to take over Scotland in preparation for the 1978 World Cup and he phoned to ask if I fancied being his successor at Pittodrie. Like an idiot, I replied that I wanted to build St Mirren into an Aberdeen and therefore must turn down the offer with sincere thanks. Later I would understand that there are fundamental distinctions of scale that apply to football clubs. Just as East Stirlingshire cannot be a St Mirren, so St Mirren cannot be an Aberdeen and Aberdeen cannot be a Manchester United. Had I recognised that when Ally spoke to me, I would have saved myself a great deal of heartache, much of it associated with Willie Todd and his growing hunger for power.

It had long been my aim to bring St Mirren into full-time football and we took an important step along the way when a scheme was devised to permit players to have jobs in the mornings and train in the afternoons. But that progress was meagre compared with the leap Todd had planned for himself. Arriving one morning for his daily visit, he announced that he had terrific news and, just as I was imagining an injection of cash for transfers, the chairman unloaded the glad tidings: 'I'm going full-time.' Just how unterrific that news was became apparent after a really exciting 3–3 draw with Rangers at Love Street. The match was marred by the misbehaviour of a section of the Rangers support and some of the fans, mainly young lads, spilled on to the pitch and forced a stoppage. I ducked the press's attempts to embroil me in follow-up stories but our full-time chairman plunged arrogantly into the fray. He was quoted as saying Rangers supporters would be banned from Love Street and offering to 'sit down and talk with Willie Waddell about Rangers' problems'. Naturally, when the famous Waddell blast came, I was in the firing line. 'You bloody big-timers,' was the opening line of a justified tirade from a man who had been extremely generous to me and to St Mirren (once handing back Rangers' half-share of the gate money from a friendly between the clubs that drew 9,000 spectators). I am sure my relationship with Willie Todd was permanently soured when I expressed my disapproval of his presumptuousness. At his request, I arranged for him to meet Waddell at Ibrox and was horrified to discover that Todd had forgotten all about the meeting. I shudder to think of how he was received when he eventually turned up.

Inconsistent results, and a tendency to squander leads, made the 1977–78 season a struggle to escape relegation. With three or four games to play, and our position in the Premier Division still in doubt, we were able to field our strongest team for the first time in weeks against Ayr United at Somerset Park. Ayr were also candidates for demotion, so our 1–0 win lifted us towards safety.

Willie Todd and I were no longer talking to each other and when Aberdeen made another approach to me there could be only one reaction. They had a vacancy because Billy McNeill, having taken Aberdeen to within a whisker of the League and Cup double, had been recruited by Celtic, who had dismissed the great Jock Stein and then guaranteed his departure by shabbily offering him a position in their commercial department. My position was complicated by the fear that St Mirren might have enough of a contractual hold on me to encourage them to sue. So I foolishly delayed announcing my decision to leave and thus gave Todd a chance to implement his plans to get rid of me. Perhaps I should have recognised omens in a slanging match I had with John Corson at a board meeting but, in truth, nothing could have prepared me for what unfolded when I was called into the boardroom one weekday morning. Todd had a sheet of paper bearing a long typewritten list of numbered items. Its significance emerged when he told me I had broken my contract and proceeded to read out fifteen instances. One of the more serious accusations was that I had sworn at a female secretary. What happened was that she took Todd's side against me in an argument we were having and on the next day I told her: 'Don't you bloody do that again to me.' Another item on the list referred to a £25 expenses payment I collected every week. This had been negotiated as part of my salary and a back-letter from the club, confirming it, had been put into the contract. There was never any doubt that the arrangement was maintained with the club's knowledge and permission. A third offence mentioned on the list was that I had advised a bookmaker friend that we would beat Ayr United. Now anybody with any sense will realise that a football manager's opinion that his team will win is not exactly pure gold to a betting man. A manager giving an assurance that his team will lose is another matter. I had been friendly with the bookmaker in question, Davie McAllister, for many years. We socialised quite a bit and regularly exchanged views about what we thought were the good bets on the coupon. I always fancied St Mirren, so my comment about the Ayr match was hardly precious inside information, and to define it as a breach of contract was, I thought, absolutely ludicrous.

The other twelve reasons for the sacking struck me as farcical. They included allowing the groundsman to drive my car and attending the Liverpool–Bruges European Cup final of 1978 at Wembley without permission (at my own expense, by the way). By the time the whole list was read out, I couldn't hold in my laughter. Willie Todd was thoroughly annoyed and asked me to stop laughing.

'I can't help it,' I said. 'I thought you needed only one reason to sack anybody – that he's not good enough at his job.' I went through to my office, cleared my desk and went home to see Cathy. When my thoughts had settled I was really angry but I had learned the lesson that my attitude to management could make me excessively vulnerable. Even if you hate your chairman, you have to find a way of getting on with it. My single-mindedness meant I was always ready to argue my corner with Todd and in the power struggle I had no chance. The weird exercise in the St Mirren boardroom had opened the way for my move to Aberdeen and for that I was grateful.

Ten minutes in the Aberdeen office of Dick Donald, the club's redoubtable chairman, produced agreement on my contract. Then there was lunch with Dick and his vice-chairman, Chris Anderson, and later my appointment was announced to the press. Within a couple of days I was off to the United States to join up with Chris for a three-week trip on which we studied the commercial initiatives associated with the North American Soccer League, which was at its most vigorous around 1978. The time spent in the States gave me a chance to get to know the vice-chairman and to gather valuable information about my new club. I set out for a family holiday in Malta with the feeling that I had prepared myself for what lay ahead. My sunbathing was interrupted by sessions in front of the television, watching the World Cup in Argentina, and on the phone to Scotland to take soundings before appointing an assistant manager. Davie Provan had impressive credentials but I was worried about possible resentment of our shared Rangers connection, something that had been discernible at Love Street, from the boardroom to the terraces. Telling Davie

I wasn't taking him with me was difficult but we have remained the firmest of friends. My first choice as right-hand man was Walter Smith, who was doing splendid work under Jim McLean at Dundee United, but efforts to negotiate with Jim met a brick wall. So I went for Pat Stanton, who had just ended his playing career. Pat did not have the coaching experience but he had everything else and it was a major extra asset that he had been such an exceptional player for Hibernian. Though Cathy was very apprehensive about moving to Aberdeen, as ever her support for me was unwavering. The boys looked upon the move as a big adventure. So did I.

10

LIGHTING UP THE NORTH

ONLY fifteen times this century has the Scottish League championship been won by a club other than Rangers or Celtic. That statistic alone should explain the priority I saw as crucial to success at Aberdeen. There was simply no hope of making my team major contenders for honours unless we could beat the Old Firm on a regular basis. It was a straightforward ambition but I knew I would have to develop the players' minds to the point where they shared my belief that it was possible. The dominance established by the Glasgow giants virtually since the beginning of professional football in Scotland infects the mentality of other clubs with resignation, an acceptance that it is their destiny to be the supporting cast. Passivity of that kind is alien to me. I had no intention of letting Aberdeen settle for isolated moments at centre-stage. I wanted sustained achievement. I wanted trophies. As far as Rangers and Celtic were concerned, I meant to be the man from the Monopolies Commission, putting a stop to their comfortable sharing of the spoils. Much of that would happen in my eight years at Pittodrie, and no matter how well things go at Old Trafford it will be difficult to surpass the satisfaction of turning a provincial club, for a few seasons at least, into the benchmark of quality in the Scottish game. But, although I had reason to be grateful for the sound foundations left to me by Billy McNeill, whose regime had taken Aberdeen within touching distance of notable successes, the early phase of my management in the North East was a troubled time. On the personal front, I took an emotional battering. Some of the pain I brought upon myself by taking St Mirren to an industrial tribunal over that bizarre catalogue of charges Willie Todd, the chairman, used to dismiss me. My determination to clear my name created additional pressure in a period when I was already under stress because of my father's rapidly deteriorating health. With the squad, too, I made my life more trying than it need have been. I had not yet fully absorbed the lesson that it is usually unnecessary to seek direct confrontation and I was often too impetuous in my attempts to instil discipline. It was definitely a time when I needed all the staunch support that has always come from my family and friends and when I was particularly appreciative of the calibre of men I had backing me at Aberdeen.

Before Pat Stanton arrived as my assistant manager, none of the backroom staff was more important than the amazing Teddy Scott, who was the reserve team coach, kit man and general oiler of the wheels at Pittodrie. Teddy has now served Aberdeen for forty years as a player and coach with a level of dedication that I deeply admire. He is a country loon from Ellon, about twenty miles from the city, and in the days before he had a car he frequently worked so late at the ground that he missed the last bus home and had to sleep on the club snooker table. In January of 1999 it gave me immense pleasure to take Manchester United up to play in a sell-out testimonial for Teddy.

As for Pat Stanton, I could not have asked for a better lieutenant. It was invaluable to be able to bounce ideas off him as we discussed the merits of the players on our staff and the structure and playing style I planned to introduce to the team. My main initial concern was that Aberdeen were inclined to defend too deep. The tendency was understandable, given the attributes of the key players in defence. Our two centre-backs, Willie Garner and Willie Miller, had formed a solid partnership and their tactic of defending in their penalty box was logical, since neither was particularly quick and it was essential that they should avoid giving attackers space behind them. But Willie Miller was underestimating himself at that stage, as his subsequent development would prove. In any case, the excessively deep defending was incompatible with my basic commitment to positive play. I wanted the team to declare themselves through creative aggression.

After a couple of months we hit something of a bad patch and I ran into criticism. One complaint in the dressing-room was that I kept comparing my former players at St Mirren with the men at Aberdeen. That was ill-judged on my part, since the footballers at Pittodrie were far more seasoned and successful than the young lads I had at Love Street, and I resolved to be more careful about how I talked to the players.

The only individual who seemed to present a long-term problem was the little front-man, Joe Harper. Joe was a hero with the fans but for me, whether he was on his own two legs or on four wheels, he was a worry. I had misgivings about him as early as pre-season training, when I found myself lapping him during an endurance run (three and a half years after I had stopped playing seriously), and the suspicion that he was an artful dodger was strengthened one day when he stopped me outside the back door of the dressing-rooms to tell me how much the players were enjoying my coaching.

'We never got any coaching when Big Billy was here,' he informed me.

I have no time for such nonsense and Harper's motives for peddling it were exposed the following week when he came to me with a request for a testimonial. I marked him down as somebody to watch. Apparently the local constabulary did the same. Not long after taking over, my phone rang in the small hours and the police told me they were holding Joe on a drunk-driving charge and asked if I would accept his call. He wasn't exactly incoherent but his plea was close to madness: 'Will you please contact the Chief Constable, Alex Morrison, and see if they will drop this charge? I've had only three pints.' I took the liberty of waking Chris Anderson and the vice-chairman, predictably, rejected Harper's crazy idea about appealing to the Chief Constable.

'Don't even think about it,' Chris said. 'We have had these problems with Joe in the past and for him to try and use you in this way tells you everything about him. Go back to sleep.' Soon afterwards, having received another call from the police station telling me Joe was two and a half times over the limit, I did.

December of 1978 is etched with particular clarity in my memory. Our League Cup semi-final against Hibs at Dens Park, Dundee, was the last match ever attended by my dad and I can still see him waving back to me from the directors' box, wearing the Crombie coat I had given him and with a smile on his face. He was so proud of our 1–0 victory. Two weeks later the verdict of the industrial tribunal was delivered, and it was a hammer blow. My lawyer, Malcolm McIvor, made sure I was sitting down before telling me the tribunal had found against me. I couldn't take it in. 'How could they?' He said they had decided that the acceptance of the expenses constituted a breach of contract and that finding, together with the swearing incident involving the secretary, amounted to grounds for dismissal. It was Malcolm's opinion that we would win hands-down if we went to a court of law but I was too worried about my dad to consider that. My thoughts were already on the shattering effect the tribunal's decision would have on him. Cathy and my mother would be hit hard by it but they had the strength to cope. My father was desperately ill. He faded badly after hearing the news and two months later he died, at the age of sixty-six, on the very day we were playing St Mirren at Love Street. I had travelled down to see him on the Friday and was shocked at how much he had deteriorated in the previous two weeks. As I sat with him, all I could do was hold his hand and look into his eyes. They had gone a very pale blue, which was actually quite beautiful.

'It's just one of those things, Alex,' he said to me as I left.

In that match with St Mirren on the Saturday afternoon, we were 2–0 ahead and coasting until a series of unlikely events transformed it between 4.20 and 4.25. The referee sent off Willie Miller and Ian Scanlon and awarded St Mirren enough peculiar decisions to let them salvage a 2–2 draw. At time-up I went wild at the referee, who announced that he was reporting me to the SFA. Minutes later my old friend Fred Douglas, the Love Street electrician, was shepherding me into a small room to tell me of my father's death. I was completely broken up. Fred, the Aberdeen chairman Dick Donald, and Chris Anderson all did their best to console me but, like most of us at such times, I was beyond consoling. When I reached the Southern General Hospital and asked Martin when Dad had died, he said: '4.23.' It was strange that Dad had slipped away just when all that mayhem was breaking out at Love Street. At the funeral on the following Wednesday, Martin and I welcomed all sections of the Govan community. Father's workmates from the Fairfield shipyard turned up and so did my friends from schooldays, Duncan Petersen, Tommy Hendry and Jim McMillan, which was especially pleasing to me. Their respect for Dad went back a long way. Later on the Wednesday, I drove to Aberdeen (we had a game with Partick Thistle that night) and I stopped in a country lay-by to have a good greet.

My first major final as a manager came on 31 March 1979, the climax of our run in the League Cup. We were facing Rangers but, as someone who had been a player at Ibrox, I was in no danger of being in awe of them. I took the squad down to Largs for preparation and it was at our Ayrshire base on the eve of the match that I learned that Ian Scanlon, our talented but emotional left-winger, had decided he would not play. He wanted to leave the club, saying he had stopped enjoying his football. It was a nice time to reveal his feelings (they turned out to be temporary) but I was never one to show distress at the loss of any player and I set about rearranging my team plans and tactics. I had just completed my first transfer deal on behalf of Aberdeen, the £70,000 purchase of Mark McGhee from Newcastle United, but Pat Stanton and I reckoned that he was too short of match sharpness to be risked in the final. The team we sent out at Hampden performed well, with Steve Archibald providing unmistakable evidence that he was about to become a top-class front player. We went into the lead through a goal by Duncan Davidson, who was playing wide on the left in place of Scanlon, and refused to be demoralised by the highly controversial sending-off of our left-back, Doug Rougvie, in the second half. Then, with twelve minutes remaining, Bobby Clark in our goal received an elbow injury and was signalling frantically for the game to be halted so that he could have treatment from the Aberdeen physio, Brian Scott. Brian was standing by a goalpost, waiting to come on, but play was not stopped until Alex McDonald, Rangers' dynamic midfield player, struck a shot from twenty yards that was deflected beyond the struggling Clark. We still seemed assured of a replay but, with seven minutes of injury time played, Colin Jackson scored the winner for Rangers. That final gave John Greig his first trophy as a manager and he was to collect the Scottish Cup later in the season. Our own interest in the latter tournament ended when we lost a semi-final 2–1 to Hibs before a meagre crowd of 9,900 on a wet Wednesday at Hampden. Bobby Clark was unfit for that game and the inexperience of his stand-in, John Gardiner, was a handicap. The natural successor to Clark was waiting in the wings. Jim Leighton had already made his debut in the first team against Hearts on a sodden pitch at Tynecastle. In conditions that were dreadful for goalkeepers, with the ball flying off the greasy surface, he had served notice of his exceptional talent.

As my first season with Aberdeen drew to a close, my main worries about the team concerned the need to achieve a better balance of talents in midfield. We had gifted lads in Gordon Strachan, Dominic Sullivan, John McMaster and Drew Jarvie, but they did not produce the right blend. Pat Stanton endorsed my diagnosis and his assessment was underpinned by the fact that he had been a top player in that area of the field. But we agreed that there was promise. When I arrived at Pittodrie it was widely accepted that Strachan had not lived up to expectations. The chairman went as far as asking me if I would 'like to sell little Gordon'. 'Let's see how he does in training,' was my answer, and after a few weeks I was satisfied that he had ample ability and was well worth developing. His endurance work in the pre-season programme was good, his application to anything I demanded of him in training was above reproach and he had excellent ball control, with a marvellous first touch. As the season progressed, he had become a regular in the team, but there were parts of his game that required improvement, especially his passing. Essentially, he was a player who loaned the ball to a team-mate for a few seconds and took it back. So in essence, although he was bringing great enthusiasm to his play, he was not demonstrating the range and penetration that the best midfield players have. That would come through coaching him on longer and more effective passing. I was confident that Gordon would meet our needs on the right side of midfield but centre-midfield was a problem we had to address. We had no one who found it natural to go and win the ball and also defend. In John McMaster we had one of the finest passers I ever had at my disposal but his inability to get to opponents quickly enough when they had the ball was one of the main reasons why Miller and his co-defenders were always in our penalty box. We simply didn't defend early enough. Young Andy Watson was impressive in the reserves but Teddy Scott felt he required time to build up his confidence.

I was keen to put the emphasis on youth, and vigorous scouting in my first season had enabled me to sign up a promising collection of schoolboys. Neil Simpson had already been signed the week I arrived and was now a first-year apprentice. My boy recruits included the midfielders Ian Angus and Neale Cooper, the forwards Ian Porteous and Eric Black and the goalkeeper Bryan Gunn, and I brought the schoolboy centre-forward Steve Cowan and the teenaged midfielder Doug Bell in from St Mirren on free transfers. All of those lads were to have successful careers with Aberdeen and other clubs and five of them would be involved when we won the European Cup Winners' Cup in Gothenburg in 1983. Another youngster who was to contribute memorably to that wonderful night in Sweden was John Hewitt and the securing of his signature, in the face of opposition from any number of other clubs, was one of many triumphs for the charm of our chief scout, Bobby Calder, a genial gentleman whose immaculate dress was invariably topped off with a pork-pie hat. 'Let me get to the mother and we'll be all right,' was his slogan and the approach paid off yet again with the Hewitt family.

Entering the 1979–80 season, my insistence that we defend the ball early meant increased demands on the front players, who had to do their share of harrying. I knew that, in the long term, the unathletic Joe Harper would not fit into this system and my reasons for signing Mark McGhee would become obvious. My decision to draft in our up-and-coming centre-half Alex McLeish had immediate impact. Alex thought like a defender, he could tackle and he was a really enthusiastic young lad. His presence improved the balance of the team, as did the deployment of Gordon Strachan wide on the right. Gordon hated being called a winger, so I spared him the use of the term, but at the time that is exactly what he was. There was plenty of development still to come from him. Sadly, it must be said that misfortune for Joe Harper brought a breakthrough for the team. Nobody likes to see a player suffer injury but when Joe was unfit I was able to press ahead with my intended striking partnership of Archibald and McGhee. They played a vital part in turning my second season at Aberdeen into a highly successful one. But there were disappointments along the way, none more hurtful than losing a second successive League Cup final, this time to Dundee United after a replay. In the first game at Hampden we absolutely hammered them but it finished goalless. Our miseries in the replay on a Wednesday night at a rain-drenched Dens Park were not eased by the fact that I was confined to the directors' box because of an SFA ban and was unable to communicate instructions to Pat in the dug-out. United won easily by 3–0 and, with my respect for Jim McLean's shrewdness and hard work, I had no hesitation in offering the sincerest congratulations on his triumph.

That night I did not sleep well, which is unusual for me. Whatever the pressures of management, I am normally able to drift off as soon as my head hits the pillow. But on this occasion I had a hundred and one ideas going through my mind. By early morning I was up with a renewed vigour, ready to attack the day, and when the players reported for training I was waiting to shake each of them by the hand. We then had a brief meeting in which I told them they would not lose another final. I meant it. On the next Saturday, in a game against St Mirren, I made a declaration of my commitment to young players by giving sixteen-year-old John Hewitt his debut. He did extremely well. I was more than pleased with the progress he was making under the guidance of Teddy and Pat. The same was true of the other boys of similar age and they were filling me with that priceless positive feeling that had been engendered by the youth policy at Love Street. There is nothing more uplifting for a manager than the emergence of young players of talent. With their innocence and energy, they bring back to you the freshness and excitement of your own early days in the game.

By the beginning of 1980 our league form had gathered momentum but the postponement of some games complicated our position in the table. We were ten points adrift of Celtic, with three matches in hand, when we had to face a tricky fixture against our bogey team, Morton, at Cappielow. Any game away from home is difficult but travelling to face Morton was a small nightmare. Our record against them was appalling. I tried every ploy imaginable in an effort to overcome them but time and again that big overweight genius Andy Ritchie would score a brilliant goal to do us down. This match was no exception, although in this instance Morton were helped by a serious mistake from our left-back, Doug Considine. Whereas I had found on my arrival at Aberdeen that the right-back position was ideally filled by Stuart Kennedy, who had made such a profound impression on me when he was an apprentice at Falkirk, left-back was a persistent worry and a succession of players were tried there. But Doug Rougvie soon regained the position and, after losing to Kilmarnock on 23 February, we remained unbeaten for the rest of the season. That run of fifteen games without defeat carried us to the League championship and, if our most significant victims were our closest rivals, Celtic, a win at last over the bogey boys from Greenock was a tremendous boost. It was not so much our 1–0 victory as our refusal to allow severe winter weather to prevent the scheduled playing of the match that reflected our determination to let nothing stand in the way of our march on the title. A motley army of shovellers and sweepers, with even old Dick Donald pitching in, worked from seven o'clock on the Saturday morning to clear six inches of snow off Pittodrie and the reward was a dogged performance from the team, crowned by a goal from Drew Jarvie. Celtic's match had been frozen off, the gap was narrowed, and now there was a real challenge on for the championship.

Twice on the run-in a testing away match against Kilmarnock was swiftly followed by a visit to Celtic Park and the feat of collecting maximum points from those four fixtures did much to win us the title. We bounced into the last of those four games off a 3–1 win at Rugby Park, while Celtic came to it licking their wounds after being savaged 5–1 by Dundee, but on a warm night in Glasgow we were not surprised to find the Celtic supporters at their most defiant and vociferous. The ground was packed and the atmosphere was electric. Far from being intimidated, our players raised themselves for a wonderfully positive performance and the 3–1 scoreline did not flatter them in the least. I had said that the only way to succeed in Scottish football was to beat the Old Firm. We had beaten them. Who could stop us now? Nobody was the short answer. We confirmed ourselves as champions at Easter Road with a 5–0 demoliton of Hibs (who were already relegated) on a day when Celtic were held to a goalless draw at Love Street. One of our goals was scored by Andy Watson, who was vindicating Teddy Scott's faith and patience as the final piece of the jigsaw in that particular team. Andy's willingness, determination and tackling ability made him a good foil for the other midfield players: Strachan, McMaster, Jarvie and Scanlon. Big Doug Rougvie was established at left-back, with Alex McLeish replacing Willie Garner in central defence and forming a partnership with Willie Miller which was to be the bedrock of Aberdeen's success for years.

After the game at Easter Road, as Martin and I embraced, we did not mention Dad but we felt he was with us. He just had to be. He deserved it. Martin travelled back to Aberdeen on the team bus, leaving his car with Gordon Strachan, who was staying down in Edinburgh with his parents. I didn't envy Gordon the job of phoning Martin's wife, Sandra, to tell her that her husband was heading north. We two brothers sat up until dawn, celebrating and reminiscing, interrupted only by a couple of supporters who somehow arrived at my house to join us. I had no idea who they were. Given the delirious goings-on in Aberdeen that night, it's not a certainty that *they* knew who they were.

Winning the League inevitably publicised the talents of the players, notably Steve Archibald. He had decided months before that he wanted to leave and, with freedom of contract due to be introduced the following year, a concrete offer of £750,000 for him from Tottenham Hotspur was impossible to refuse. Our relationship was often one of conflict but I truly admired Steve. He was single-minded, stubborn, awkward, determined – he reminded me of someone! And what a player he was! Of the strikers I have worked with, he undoubtedly belongs in the top echelon. He rated high on the defiance chart, too. Once, after scoring a hat trick against Celtic in a 3–2 victory at Pittodrie, he took the match ball home with him. That was not a common practice then and next morning in my office I reprimanded him while he sat in what had become known as the 'Archibald Chair', because he was in it so frequently. Twenty-four hours later, as Pat, Teddy and I were enjoying a quiet cup of tea, the office door burst open and Steve booted the ball into the room, sending it ricocheting off the walls so violently that it smashed the fluorescent light. 'There's your fucking ball,' he said and marched off. Yes, those were interesting days with Steve.

The other great loss that summer was the departure of Pat Stanton, who decided he wanted to move back to Edinburgh. I believe that Margaret, his wife, was missing her home town and her family. It was a terrible disappointment to me. I loved Pat. He was a truly honest and trustworthy lieutenant. Even now, when I think of him, it is always with immense fondness. In contrast with the Stantons, my family were settling happily in Aberdeen. My work was going well, illustrating one of the fundamental truths of football management: the only possibility of controlling a football team is by winning. Cathy and I were becoming friendly with some lovely people and these friendships have lasted and strengthened over the years. The boys were growing up and they, too, gathered friends who are still special to them today. You cannot put a price on the kind of warmth we encountered in that marvellous city. The people who offered it to us – and there are too many to name here – know how much regard and affection we have for them.

Aberdeen began the 1980–81 season as we had finished its predecessor, going fifteen games before losing. There was the promise of another championship. It was, however, the club's first tilt at the European Cup that had my concentration, particularly after we knocked out Austria Vienna 1–0 on aggregate and were drawn next against the team of teams in England then and for some time to come: Liverpool. Bob Paisley was the all-conquering manager, of course, but Bill Shankly was still around and when Archie Knox, who had succeeded Pat Stanton as my assistant, joined me on a trip to watch Liverpool play Middlesbrough at Anfield we were thrilled to meet the great Ayrshireman.

'Hello, Alex, good to see you – you are doing a terrific job up there,' was Bill's greeting and I was still stuttering my thanks when he went on, 'So you're down to have a look at our great team?' Archie and I, behaving like a pair of groupies, could only mumble an affirmative. 'Aye, they all try that,' said Bill.

What we tried on the field certainly did not work. We lost the first leg 1–0 at Pittodrie and the 4–0 beating we suffered in the second was far too emphatic to allow us to plead mitigating circumstances on the basis of the players missing because of injury. All we could do was try to ensure that we learned from painful exposure to proven masters of the techniques and discipline required in European competitions. Above all, our players had to appreciate that there is no forgiveness in such games for teams who surrender possession cheaply.

If injuries did not explain the scoreline on Merseyside, they had a lot to do with our failure to sustain our form in the League. Just a few matches into the campaign, a bad back had incapacitated Bobby Clark, McMaster was removed for the rest of the season by knee damage suffered against Liverpool and Strachan was unavailable to us after 30 December because of hernia problems. At times we were without half the players who had won the championship and, as the five-point lead we held at the turn of the year evaporated, we had to settle for second place behind Celtic. But there was comfort in the valuable experience being gained by young hopefuls like Leighton, Cooper, Angus, Bell, Simpson, Cowan and Hewitt. Having completed three seasons with Aberdeen, I was sure I was making progress, even if there was only one Premier Division title to show for it. What pleased me most was that when we went head-to-head with the Old Firm we were making a habit of coming out on top. In that period there was, without question, a relocation of power in Scottish football. Aberdeen and our fierce rivals on the east coast, Dundee United, had cut confidently into the dominance of Rangers and Celtic. We now relished any meeting with them, as we showed against Rangers in the Scottish Cup final of 1982. The first half was quite even but we overran them in the second half and it was only the squandering of excellent chances that kept the match tied at 1–1 and took us into extra time. In the additional thirty minutes we translated our superiority into goals and crushed Rangers 4–1. Since we had killed off Celtic in the fourth round, nobody could question our right to the trophy.

We began our UEFA Cup challenge that season of 1981–82 by defeating the holders, Bobby Robson's Ipswich, comfortably over two legs. But when people remember our run in that competition it is because of something which happened in the second round, a dressing-room incident that has been embellished over the years until it resembles the Mad Hatter's Tea-Party, Govan-style. It happened when we went to Romania with a 3–0 lead to play the second leg of our tie with Arges Pitesti. My tactics for capitalising on that advantage required Gordon Strachan and Peter Weir, a brilliantly penetrative left-winger we had signed from St Mirren in the summer, to play out on the touchlines, with Mark McGhee operating as a lone striker. But little Strachan had ideas of his own and in the first half he played anywhere but wide right. We were in such disarray that I was glad to go in at the interval only 2–0 down. In the dressing-room I set about Gordon in a manner that could fairly be described as blunt, demanding that he concentrate on giving us width to our game. The wee man was, however, in one of his nippy sweetie moods, full of caustic comments. What he regarded as smart ripostes struck me as senseless meanderings and as I intensified my onslaught I swung a hand in anger at a huge tea urn that was nearby. It was made of pewter or iron and striking it nearly broke my hand. The pain caused me to flip my lid and I hurled a tray of cups filled with tea towards Strachan, hitting the wall above him. The other players and Archie Knox were also sitting on that side of the room and a fair amount of the tea dripped down the wall on to Archie, who sat motionless. Strachan obeyed instructions in the second half and we scored twice to coast through to the next round, with an aggregate score of 5–2.

In the next round we faced Hamburg, who had the great Beckenbauer playing sweeper at the time. They were a powerful team, and were to be losing finalists in the UEFA Cup that year, and yet we should have left them for dead at Pittodrie. We were up 2–1 when Strachan missed a penalty but Hewitt made it 3–1 with nine minutes left. Insane self-destructiveness yielded a last-gasp goal to Hamburg and the complexion of the tie was changed entirely. On a cold night in Germany we were well beaten 3–1, and that was that.

Another disappointing two-leg defeat came in the semi-final of the League Cup. We beat Dundee United 1–0 at Tannadice but were stuffed 3–0 at home. It was annoying that Dundee United so often held the upper hand in Cup games, since our form was much superior in the League, where we had been known to slaughter them 5–0 and 5–1. The matches involved a great deal of tactical sparring between Jim McLean and me, with each of us reacting to a setback by trying to outsmart the opposition next time. Our collisions were enthralling and demonstrated quite clearly that we were the New Firm.

It was the perfect prelude to my most exciting season at Aberdeen when I attended the World Cup finals for the first time. In

Ayr's veteran centre-forward is poised to pounce but Davie McCulloch (white shirt, *left*) heads home against Stranraer, while Dandy McLean looks on.

My first manager's job, at humble East Stirlingshire in 1974. When I arrived we had a £2,000 transfer kitty and no goalie.

Dividing my time between managing a football club and managing a pub proved to be a challenge. We had some terrific times at Fergie's but, in the end, I had to sell it.

I take over at St Mirren, flanked by
Willie Todd (*left*) and John Corson,
the directors behind what proved a
beneficial dismissal for me in 1978.

Billy Stark: Rangers' loss was our
gain as he blossomed at St Mirren.

Davie Provan, a former colleague at
Rangers, became my trusted
assistant manager at St Mirren.

I was delighted to join Aberdeen and never had anything but marvellous support from worldly-wise chairman Dick Donald (*centre*) and vice-chairman Chris Anderson.

Bobby Calder: Aberdeen scout.

Archie Knox: my assistant at Aberdeen and Manchester United.

Watched from the stands by my dad, for the last time as it transpired, I urge the Aberdeen players to greater efforts before extra time against Hibs in 1978. There is able support from Pat Stanton.

Aberdeen began 1980–81 as holders of the Drybrough Cup, as well as champions, after winning the pre-season tournament.

Calmness itself – on the outside at least – as Aberdeen gain the first of two crucial wins at Celtic during April 1980 *en route* to the title.

Gordon Strachan, pictured against Rangers in the 1978 Scottish Cup final, oozed ability but it needed to be properly channelled.

My old Ibrox colleague John Greig and I lead out Rangers and Aberdeen before our 4–1 victory in the 1982 Scottish Cup final.

Neale Cooper in control against Rangers as we take the Scottish Cup in 1982, having already knocked out the other half of the Old Firm.

Doug Rougvie was an Aberdeen cult hero and fancied himself as a TT racer until I threatened to get rid of him unless he got rid of the bike.

I brief Aberdeen sub John Hewitt before extra time against Real Madrid, scarcely imagining he would clinch the Cup Winners' Cup for us.

Cathy, Mark, Darren and Jason settled well in Aberdeen – and so did I. Winning trophies with them was special.

that summer of 1982, I combined watching Scotland's matches with a family holiday in Malaga and, although Cathy had her complaints about the intrusions of 'that stupid game', the boys were as thrilled as I was, especially by the opportunity to see Jock Stein's team in action against Brazil. There was a carnival atmosphere among the mingling supporters of the two countries at the stadium in Seville and national colours were freely exchanged. But our Darren defiantly refused to swap his Scotland shirt for a Brazilian one. Sean Connery was in our party at the game and ten years later he reminded me with amusement of Darren's boyish patriotism.

I had a special allegiance in Seville to two of my own players who were on the field. Although I was equally proud of Strachan and Miller, Willie's achievement in establishing himself in central defence for his country gave me particular pleasure. He had been obliged to overcome considerable scepticism, none of which I shared. The man was one truly exceptional player, so much so that when I was asked recently to select a dream team of Scottish greats from the post-war era, I included him alongside more glittering talents like Law, Dalglish, Mackay, Souness and Baxter. His timing of tackles was superb and so were his powers of anticipation and concentration but what set him apart was the strength of his will as a competitor. Among all the footballers I have managed, Willie and Bryan Robson stood out as men for whom winning was almost as important as breathing. After Scotland yet again narrowly failed to survive the first round of the World Cup – drawing 2–2 with Russia when a win was imperative – I looked up my old sparring partner Steve Archibald at his hotel, which was next door to our holiday apartments. I found him near the pool, ordering a hamburger and a bottle of Dom Perignon. He deserved to be back in the 'Archibald Chair' for mixing those two.

Nobody who has the slightest interest in football will have to be told that Aberdeen's 1982–83 season was dominated by our exploits in the European Cup Winners' Cup. We went close to winning another League title and did win the Scottish Cup for the second year in a row but it was the continental adventure that stirred us, our city and eventually the entire nation. We were disappointed that we had to play a preliminary round against Sion of Switzerland but scores of 7–0 at home and 4–1 away made it a formality. The second stage was much more nervy and we were glad to squeeze through by the only goal scored in our tie with Dinamo Tirana of Albania. Lech Poznan of Poland were seen off 3–0 over the two legs and when the draw for the quarter-finals paired us with Bayern Munich, the first signs of the coming frenzy began to appear in Aberdeen. The music-hall jokes that tease Aberdonians for being mean could not be further from reality but when it came to our meeting with the Germans at Pittodrie in March of 1983, anybody who had a ticket guarded it like a miser. That match was the second leg of the quarter-final and, having given a remarkably disciplined performance to draw 0–0 in Munich, we entered it under a crushing weight of expectation.

Archie Knox and I had taken turns travelling to Germany on scouting trips long before a ball was kicked in the tie and we knew how dangerous Bayern could be on our ground. In the first game, we had coped well with Paul Breitner's ability to control the tempo of their play and the threat posed by Karl-Heinz Rummenigge, who was adept at dropping deep and then arriving late in attacking positions. But at Pittodrie they sprang a surprise by playing their tall left-back, Pflugler, at outside-left. His height advantage severely troubled our right-back, Kennedy, particularly when every Bayern defender, including the goalkeeper, made a point of targeting Pflugler with high balls. Our problems became a crisis after only ten minutes when Breitner tapped a free kick to Augenthaler and the big centre-half blasted a tremendous shot into our net from twenty yards. Now we were suffering for our failure to score in Munich. A draw would put Bayern through.

Just before the interval we took a first step towards recovery when Neil Simpson's thunderous challenge on a hesitant German defender forced the ball over the line for an equaliser, but we were again in agony early in the second half as Pflugler volleyed Bayern back into the lead. Our hopes were draining away. Kennedy was still struggling and over on the other side of the field Del'Haye, a small and skilful winger, was torturing Doug Rougvie. Something drastic had to be done. It was time to gamble and I did so with a vengeance. I took off Kennedy and switched Rougvie to right-back to deal with Pflugler's aerial menace.

Neale Cooper was moved to left-back in the hope that he would make a better job of handling Del'Haye and John McMaster was sent on to restore some composure to midfield. All that gave us an improved response to the Bayern tactics and we attacked more convincingly, only to be thwarted by good goalkeeping from Muller, and by his crossbar when he was beaten by an Eric Black header. I made a last throw of the dice thirteen minutes from the end, replacing our excellent midfield battler, Neil Simpson, with an additional attacker, John Hewitt. Almost as soon as Hewitt was on the field we gained a free kick on the right-hand side of the opposition's penalty box and Strachan and McMaster launched into a well-rehearsed routine. Having both shaped to take the kick, they pretended to get in each other's way and began arguing. Then suddenly Strachan whipped the ball into the six-yard box and, with the Germans foxed into casualness by the phoney row, McLeish was allowed to score with a header – 2–2. Pittodrie went mad. Exactly thirty seconds later the place threatened to explode. A throw-in on the halfway line was directed to McMaster, who used his refined left foot to flight the ball deep into Bayern's box for Black to rise and deliver a header that Muller could only parry towards the feet of Hewitt, who scored. The two substitutions had worked out pretty well but I wasn't likely to start congratulating myself too soon, since my gamble had left me without a recognised tackler in midfield and that made the remaining thirteen minutes nerve-racking in the extreme. However, the wave of sound coming from our ecstatic supporters was just about enough in itself to hold our opponents at bay and soon the roars of encouragement had become a din of celebration.

After the exhausting dramas of the contest with Bayern Munich, it was a pleasant relief to have a one-sided semi-final against Waterschei of Belgium. A 5–1 victory in Aberdeen meant that a 1–0 defeat in the second leg was irrelevant. But the occasion was far from painless, for it brought to an end the magnificent career of Stuart Kennedy, who suffered a dreadful injury when his studs caught on wooden boarding attached to the boundary wall beyond the edge of the pitch. Stuart was a first-class player and a man you could trust implicitly. He had real pride and belief in himself and was quite simply one of the strongest and finest characters I have come across in football. I think I made one of my best-ever decisions in management by listing him among our official substitutes for the final against Real Madrid. Naming somebody who couldn't play was a risk, but Stuart deserved no less.

I felt it was essential to bring some light relief to the build-up to the final in Gothenburg and decided to wind up the players' wives about their travel arrangements. The girls were sent an itinerary that told them they were lodged in chalets. It gave them a chalet number and listed items they must bring with them: two mugs, knife and fork, sleeping bags and other basic camping equipment. Apparently the joke worked better than I could have hoped. There were phone calls between wives complaining about the stinginess of the club. As the players began to be given severe earache, they transmitted it to me, so I suggested that the wives should come into Pittodrie for a meeting. When the families, children included, gathered in the players' lounge one afternoon, I ordered the men out but I was well aware they were eavesdropping at the door. What they heard amazed them. Their women-folk, who had seen through the mickey-taking itinerary by then, were all sweet reasonableness as I explained how important their support was for men preparing for the most important match of their lives. I expected Claire Miller or perhaps Brenda Rougvie to say something but no, not a questioning word came from any of them. 'If you have a problem, come to me,' I said, and they just sat and nodded agreement. If that wasn't a triumph, what is?

Even Cathy, who is not interested in football, was touched by the fever of excitement that spread through Aberdeen. Maintaining our sons' concentration on their schoolwork was her biggest problem. Every conceivable mode of transport was called upon to convey 14,000 of our fans across the North Sea and their presence was naturally a precious boost to the team, who had settled two days ahead of the game at a pleasant hotel in a hamlet outside Gothenburg. A valued friend of mine in Sweden, Nestor Lauren, had everything flawlessly organised for us in advance. I invited Jock Stein, the Scotland manager, as our guest and my opinion of the big man rose even higher on that trip. He gave me plenty of good advice without ever trying to push himself forward. It was Jock's way to be there for you if you needed him. One interesting suggestion he made was that I should buy the Real Madrid manager, the great Alfredo Di Stefano, a gift of good whisky. 'Let him feel important,' said Jock, 'as if you are thrilled just to be in the final and only there to make up the numbers.' Di Stefano was certainly taken aback when I presented him with the whisky on the eve of the match. By that time, picking my team was straightforward. With Stuart Kennedy and Doug Bell injured, I had only John Hewitt to disappoint.

A night of incessant rain created a heavy pitch for the final but that did not stop us from outplaying our opponents. The first goal was from another of our rehearsed set-pieces. Gordon Strachan hoisted a corner out to the edge of the Real penalty box and Alex McLeish arrived really late to head the ball. I think it was probably going in anyway but it struck one of their defenders and fell nicely for Eric Black to score. Later in the first half, big Alex made a different kind of contribution when he was short with a pass back to Jim Leighton which allowed Santillana a chance. Leighton brought down Santillana and the penalty was efficiently converted. I was worried about how the mistake would prey on McLeish's mind but I should never have doubted such a strong character. He was determined to compensate for the blunder and hardly put a foot wrong afterwards. I had seen Alex grow up in football, admiring his hard work and eagerness to learn from coaching, and it was a joy to see him fulfil his potential in such a setting. The fact that the game went into extra time was a tribute to the resilience of their defence, in which Stielike, who was a pillar of the German national team, gave a performance that was astounding for a man who had been out of action for seven weeks. An injury to Black near the end of the regular ninety minutes had obliged me to replace him with John Hewitt and John proceeded to have such a nightmare that I was considering a substitute for the substitute in the second half of extra time. It was then that Hewitt chose to write himself into the history books. Peter Weir, who had been giving Real Madrid's right-back a roasting for most of the night, set off on a run from close to our box. He beat a couple of opponents and played a lovely ball up the line for Mark McGhee to take in his stride. Mark had such strength and stamina that challengers were by that stage simply unable to stay with him as another lung-bursting effort carried him to a good position near the by-line. Meanwhile, I was watching Hewitt, who was making his way into their box in a straight line, with no thought of bending his run as he had constantly been told he should. As McGhee crossed, I was muttering all sorts of abuse of Hewitt. So, of course, the ball landed on his head and he won the Cup for us.

The reception when we returned to Aberdeen after the 2–1 victory was unforgettable. All the schools in the North East had declared a day's holiday and it was estimated that half-a-million people were on the streets of the city to welcome its heroes. The emotional current passing through those crowds and linking them with the players reminded me of a remark Di Stefano made after the game. It was not just a football team Real Madrid had met, he said, but an unstoppable spirit. At the club, that spirit was nourished by many stalwarts who were never on the field. The players are the most important people in any football set-up but at Aberdeen they received heroic support from those working selflessly behind the scenes, from our worldly-wise and drily humorous old chairman, Dick Donald, to the pensioners who cleaned the ground after matches and came to be regarded as members of the staff. I would need more than one alternative team-sheet to include all the non-playing stars who helped to make my years at Pittodrie so memorable. Perhaps the most amazing figure was Barbara Cook. She and Brenda Gosling were assistants to Ian Taggart, the secretary, and all three did terrific work, but Barbara more than anybody ran the club. On the football side, there was the indispensability of Teddy Scott, and I was lucky, too, in having a physio as good as Roland Arnott. Archie Knox was, of course, closest to me in day-to-day operations. We had our disagreements but in the main we got on well together and my respect for him was huge. It was said that we were too alike but that was nonsense. We had practically nothing in common other than a burning desire to succeed and the energy to work whatever hours our jobs demanded. We drove everywhere and anywhere to watch games and, when Aberdeen became the first club in Scotland to start coaching clinics outside its own area, we travelled to Glasgow once a week to tutor promising youngsters at Helenvale, an all-weather pitch that happened to be next door to Celtic Park. Maybe that was something else that Archie and I shared – cheek.

After Gothenburg, there was still a faint mathematical possibility of winning the championship. If Dundee United drew with Dundee on the last day of the league programme, and we beat Hibs 7–0, we would have the title. Lifting themselves unbelievably just three days on from the European Cup Winners' Cup final, our team had a good crack at that outrageous target, finishing with a 5–0 victory over Hibs. But a late winner for Dundee United at Dens Park kept them a point in front of us and, in fact, goal difference put us a fraction behind Celtic. It was frustrating to reflect that, but for the missing of crucial penalties during the season, we would have been in first place instead of third.

One week later we met Rangers in the Scottish Cup final and, having beaten Celtic in the semi-final, I expected a massacre. But, of course, it was foolish to underestimate the delayed backlash from events in Sweden. The final was an awful game that laboured into extra time before we broke the deadlock with an Eric Black goal. In spite of all my cajoling and bullying, the team stayed absolutely flat. At the final whistle, while they were being presented with the trophy, I castigated their performance on TV and said that Leighton, McLeish and Miller had won the Cup; the rest hadn't turned up. That was grossly unfair and next morning, as the celebrations were about to begin back in Aberdeen, I apologised unreservedly.

The following week I was lying in bed on a Saturday morning, reading the paper, when my phone went. The caller was a Rangers director, Jack Gillespie, and he offered me the manager's job at Ibrox. I was flattered but declined with thanks. John Greig, the Rangers manager, was a good friend of mine and I had no intention of being involved in ousting him. His task had never been easy. He took over from Jock Wallace after Wallace had won the treble during his last season in charge. Greig's own outstanding record as a player for the club increased the pressures on him and these had been worsened by the emergence of Aberdeen. I had nothing but admiration for John as a person and for the manner in which he carried out his duties at Ibrox. He was one of the greats of Scottish football and will always remain so in my eyes.

— 11 —
JOCK STEIN – LEARNING FROM A MASTER

FOR any young manager seeking to further his education in football, Jock Stein was a one-man university. After my successes with Aberdeen in the League, Scottish Cup and the European Cup Winners' Cup, I suppose I had to be considered a graduate student but I had no doubt there was still a great deal I needed to learn. I realised, too, that if I searched the whole world I would not find a better source of instruction than the big man from Lanarkshire. So after Jim McLean resigned from the position of assistant to Jock with the Scotland team, I was silently praying that the job would be offered to me. I had heard all the negatives about being dangerously distracted from my duties as manager of Aberdeen but I was so keen to work with Jock that I was shoving all other thoughts to the back of my mind, and within a few days I was given the thrilling news that he wanted me at his side. Before accepting, I had only two questions to ask him. Can I be responsible for the training preparation, and can I be involved in picking the team? Jock had no problem with my first request but there was a significant pause before he responded to the second.

'What do you mean about picking the team?' he said at last.

'I mean, can I have some dialogue or input with you?'

'Well, I know you wouldn't let Archie Knox or Willie Garner pick your team,' said Jock, 'but I'm sure you have always given them their place as your club assistants and have listened to them with respect. That's how I would want it – I'll pick the team but I'm happy to listen to you.' Deal done!

Everybody in the game knows that Jock Stein's record as Celtic manager was as triumphant as any ever achieved in the history of club football. The best tribute to his genius is not the winning of nine successive league championships, the countless other trophies he collected or even the historic breakthrough that made Celtic the first British club to lift the European Cup. What sets him apart more than anything else is the fact that the team who devastated Inter Milan in Lisbon on a magical evening in 1967 consisted of ten players born within a dozen miles of Celtic Park and one outsider, Bobby Lennox, who came from thirty miles away in Ayrshire. Jock won the European Cup with a Glasgow and District Select. At no other time, before or since, has one of the greatest competitions of world football been blitzed by such a concentration of locally produced talent. It was as close to a miracle as management can go. So who could blame me for being excited by the prospect of working with the man who created it?

Stein had just about every attribute required of a great manager but none of his talents was more significant than his judgement of players, not only as performers but as people. Whether a man was playing for him or against him, Jock specialised in probing assessments of strengths and weaknesses. He had worked underground in the pits until he was twenty-seven and he had a wider, richer experience of human nature than is readily available to somebody confined since schooldays to the enclosed, insulated world of professional football. I am sure I have been helped by the fact that I served a full apprenticeship as a toolmaker, that in my formative years I was exposed to the values of a workplace other than the training ground and the football field. His talent for dealing with all kinds of men probably counted as much as his technical knowledge and his advanced ideas on the game in enabling him to establish himself quickly as a manager. He matured to greatness very rapidly.

Big Jock never took his coaching badge but I can understand that. He was an established manager when the enthusiasm for coaching first took hold in Scotland. The earliest coaching school I can remember was around 1962–3. Coaching only really gained momentum in Scotland when the likes of Eddie Turnbull and Willie Ormonde and Jimmy Bonthrone became the teachers around 1967 and '68. That was when people were asking why Jock Stein didn't have his full badge. Willie Waddell, the great right-winger who became manager of Rangers, was the same. It was a generational thing. The minute I became a full-time player I made up my mind I was going to be a manager and by then such a decision made it natural for me to go to all the coaching schools. I started taking down notes about training programmes and so on. I was twenty-two in 1964 when I went full-time with Dunfermline and the next summer I went to my first coaching school. The following year I took my full badge as a coach. That also happened to be the year I got married, 1966. I used to go back to Largs every summer for a refresher course. I'd have a fortnight's holiday with Cathy and then two weeks at Largs. In that way, I tried to give myself at least some trace of preparation for management. Jock, having shown himself to be a manager of the highest calibre, had nothing to prove. If they asked me to go to a coaching school now I would find it difficult because you are exposed to the criticisms of people who couldn't live with you when it comes to preparing teams to play at the highest level. Jock didn't need a badge. His credentials were there for all to see in what was happening to Celtic Football Club. I was prepared to go to Largs and get my full badge because I felt at the time that it was going to be important. Word was that it would become an official requirement. Jock emerged in a different era, so I don't think there is any substance in efforts to criticise him for not going to Largs. I can well understand why he didn't go.

Stein was the big man in every sense. When he came into a room he dominated it. You always knew when Jock was present. He seemed to know everybody's first name and that's a wonderful asset. Matt Busby had it. When Jock left Dunfermline to manage Hibs he had a wee share in a bookie's in Dunfermline and I remember going into the betting shop one day when he was there. He said: 'Hello Alex, are you enjoying playing at Dunfermline?' It made me feel really important. When people treat you that way you are instantly in favour of them. I had never spoken to Jock in my life, but he knew me. Of course, he was a familiar figure to me but I wouldn't go and say, 'Hello Jock, how're you doing?' I was only a young man at the time. He was an established person. It's about respect. Coming up the stairs at Old Trafford recently, a young player, one of the sixteen-year-olds, called me Alex. I said, 'Were you at school with me?' He said, 'No.' I said, 'Well call me Mr Ferguson or Boss.' Some of the senior players were drawing desperate faces. They were thinking, 'He'll kill 'im.' 'Hi, Alex.' Sixteen years of age! Brilliant. With Jock, it was almost a case of 'I wouldnae hear a bad word about Jock Stein – he said hello to me.'

I think he used his power to make him better at his job. His network of informants enabled him to know just about everything that was going on in Scottish football. I find I don't have the time to do that. At Aberdeen I tried to know everything that was going on. I had a good network there. At United it seems to run away from you at times. The scale of the operation makes it impossible to keep in touch with every detail and nuance of what is going on around you. Jock would phone you up on a Saturday night and you felt duty-bound to tell him everything about your business as a club manager because you suspected he probably knew anyway. He would say, 'You're not in for such and such a player, are you?' You would think, 'How the hell does he know that?' I'd finish up telling him everything, how much we'd offered and all the details. The journalists in his network thought he was doing them favours, and he was, but they were doing more for him. His system of dealing with the Celtic board, of putting rhetorical questions, using terms that left the others with hardly any choice but endorsing his suggestions, was classic Stein. I do that myself. I think your personality has got to force things because sometimes you cannot wait for decisions. I don't generally ask for anything at a board meeting. Maybe I go to the chairman. For instance, anything for the youth programme usually gets passed without fuss because they know how much it means to me and they have seen the benefits. They obviously think, 'If we don't give him this he will just keep on about it until he gets it.' Originally, in Jock's early days as Celtic manager, old Bob Kelly, the chairman, would try to pick the team, which was accepted practice at a lot of clubs. I'm sure Jock soon sorted that scene out.

There is no doubt that by the time he was in charge of Scotland the vigour that had been so overpowering at his peak as a club manager had been severely reduced by health problems. The serious angina attack he had suffered and the car crash that almost killed him in 1975 inevitably took a lot out of him. I noticed when I was his assistant with Scotland that his voice had become much softer. When he was younger, I had only one period of competing against him. It was while I was manager of St Mirren and at that time there was a hard edge, real authority in his voice. Of course, he never lost the ability to make what he said produce an impact, whether he was expressing anger or dispensing grandfatherly wisdom, and there was never a greater exponent of the quiet put-down. He could embarrass people into behaving and performing well. With Scotland, his mind was as sharp and fertile as ever and he compensated for loss of energy by being a wonderful observer. But, yes, he had mellowed.

People say I'm mellowing and it's true you do change over the years. You are less inclined to lose your temper as you become older. When I was younger, a bad pass during a game could get me ripping into people. The cup-throwing stories are exaggerated but they are not entirely fictitious. In my younger days, particularly at Aberdeen and in the early phase at Manchester United, I still had that burning desire to change the world. You are driven. People like Stein and Shankly were driven. Fear of failure is part of it, but the drive comes above all from the positive determination to be outstandingly successful, to be good at what you are doing. I'd come in at half-time sometimes and I'd say, 'What about that pass you gave there. I am fed up telling you not to give straight passes. Pass the ball to help your man make progress or do damage, not to put him in trouble or stop him dead.' And we'd be winning 3–0. When you are older you become a little more tolerant of mistakes, you become more understanding because it's the end product, the overall effect, that you are looking for then. You do mellow a bit. You can diminish players by emphasising mistakes too much. With those who fancy themselves you might dwell on the shortcomings but with others you offer encouragement. For instance, with John Hewitt at Aberdeen, I knew that if I looked at John during a team-talk he would fold up. I never involved him in a team-talk because I knew it could destroy him. He was really scared of me. So I would only say to John when they were going out, 'Now you go and enjoy it – you are doing great.' That's all I would need to say to him.

I think Jock liked me. Some of the players used to say that. Our shared West of Scotland working-class background made us comfortable together and he liked my energy. It brought back his early years, that drive, and as a result it was a good partnership. It goes without saying that Jock's knowledge of the game was tremendous and everything he did tactically was attuned to the capacities of his players, which he understood better than they did themselves. Through everything Stein did with football teams he wanted to be positive. That applies to me, too. Go and win the game, that's my philosophy. With the best of his Celtic teams, Jock achieved an almost perfect balance of skills. They had a marvellous variety of ways to hurt the opposition and they played at pace. They had a controlled and sustained tempo that suited them and disrupted opponents. I noticed that nearly all the players Jock brought in at Celtic had decent pace about them. He knew what Celtic were good at and the message to his team was, if they are going to beat us they will have to run. I have urged the same attitude on my team many times. Opponents come to Old Trafford expecting an onslaught. 'Why disappoint them?' I say to my players.

My first assignment as Jock's assistant with Scotland was a friendly match against Yugoslavia in September 1984, and I feel the preparation was good. Well, it couldn't have been too bad – we won 6–1, with Kenny Dalglish and Graeme Souness both at their majestic best. I revelled in the opportunity to operate from an assistant's position, blissfully free of all the extra responsibilities

that crowded in on me as a club manager. I did not have to handle
the press, deal with directors or cope with the countless obligations
that go with being in overall charge of a group of players. Big
Jock was a master in all those departments, so I was able to
concentrate on working with some great footballers in training
and studying how they applied themselves. In the main they co-
operated very well and gave me no problems whatsoever. Graeme
Souness was the most interesting one for me. Having 'Champagne
Charlie' as his nickname didn't encourage the suspicion that he
was a lifelong member of the Temperance Society, so to see the
discipline of this man's preparation for a game was a real pleasure.
I soon realised that many of the prevalent perceptions of Souness
seriously underrated the man. I was impressed and I could understand why Jock had great faith and trust in him. Only fools could
have underestimated Souness's talent on the field. He was by any
standards a great midfield player, brilliantly effective both as a
winner and a user of the ball. The quality of his play invariably
helped those around him to raise their levels of performance
and that is one of the hallmarks of a truly exceptional footballer.
What prevented many people from wholeheartedly applauding
Graeme's skills was, of course, the ruthless streak that made him
such an intimidating opponent in physical confrontations. I was
embroiled in my share of rough stuff as a player but I must confess
that the sight of Souness in his assassin's mode could send a
shudder through me. He could be cruel. But he is a more complex
man than his critics imagine and, like Jock Stein, I warmed to
him.

At that time Scotland had a good squad of players, good enough
to nourish hopes of reaching the 1986 World Cup finals in
Mexico. Although it would not be easy to negotiate a qualifying
group that pitted us against Spain, Wales and Iceland, we felt we
had a right to be optimistic. But I could see how difficult picking
the team was going to be. For instance, the balance of the midfield
was difficult, given our abundance of creative types like Gordon
Strachan, Paul McStay and Graeme. In the match against Yugoslavia, Gordon and Paul did very well but tended to try to play

in the same area. I knew from my experience with Gordon at Aberdeen that he wanted to be involved all the time. Another of my Aberdeen men, Jim Bett, was someone who looked capable of bringing variety to our midfield. There were many facets to his game. His acceleration and ability to run consistently from box to box was a major strength I felt we could utilise. He could also sit in front of the defenders, as Souness could, and give you good balance and the capacity to keep possession and be patient. Bett was a player I honestly believe should have been absolutely top drawer. However, like Paul McStay, he was a very shy and quiet individual and among men like Souness, Dalglish, Alan Hansen, Willie Miller and Richard Gough, all strong personalities, he was always in danger of underselling his abilities. It was reassuring to have him available and the same could be said emphatically of the rich skills and wonderful left foot of Davie Cooper. He could give us some natural width on the left-hand side.

After some chats with Jock it was clear to me he was an admirer of Alex McLeish and Willie Miller as a partnership. As I said to him some time before they were regulars, it was a partnership made in heaven and although neither was blessed with pace they were, unquestionably in my mind, the best twosome in Britain; Jock was coming round to that way of thinking. There was, however, the major complication of Alan Hansen's powerful claims to be one of the centre-backs. We both admired his talent and Jock at the time was doing his best to keep him in the right frame of mind and perhaps privately he was preparing to give him a regular run. Alan and Willie had played together before, but in a vital match against the USSR at the World Cup finals in Spain in 1982, a moment of desperate confusion between them had led to a goal that was instrumental in preventing Scotland from progressing beyond the first stage of the competition (a humble distinction that still eludes the Scots). There were doubts in my mind about whether Hansen and Miller were basically compatible as defenders but Jock was prepared to have another go with the partnership. Most countries would have been happy to have three centre-backs as good as Hansen, McLeish and Miller but with

Scotland Richard Gough was also in the frame. Gough was a man with many assets: determination, pace, mobility, single-mindedness and good leadership qualities. He was a winner.

All in all I was more than pleased about the squad in general, and the challenge of identifying the strongest formation merely made my involvement more exciting. The hottest debate of all revolved around a fundamental question: who the hell was going to partner King Kenny? There were plenty of candidates: Maurice 'Mo' Johnston, Charlie Nicholas, Frank McAvennie, Steve Archibald, Mark McGhee, Graeme Sharp, Paul Sturrock, David Speedie – even Andy Gray was showing a resurgence in form, having moved to Everton and overcome some long-term knee problems. They were all going to get a chance, but the World Cup finals in Mexico were two years away and plenty of obstacles lay in our path. Given the aptitude for self-destruction tradition-ally associated with Scottish footballers, some of the biggest diffi-culties were likely to be created by our own troops. The away games ahead of us didn't pose a problem in terms of player discipline, since it is usually easier to maintain control of a close-knit group in a foreign country. At home it was a different, more worrying story. We always stayed at the McDonald Hotel at Eastwood on the road out of Glasgow towards Ayrshire. The hotel was run by a very capable manager, John McGuinness. Jock got on well with McGuinness and if the players were getting up to mischief a report would go straight back to the Big Man. It never ceased to amaze me how widespread Jock's intelligence network was.

The Scotland get-togethers were an absolute revelation for me, priceless access to the mind and personality of Jock Stein. I am sure there were times when he got fed up with my incessant barrage of questions. I was so determined to find out as much as I could about one of the greatest managers of all time that I used every moment to draw enlightenment from him. On general football matters he was always forthcoming and educational but the brick wall went up if there was a hint of a negative about Celtic. I felt – and it wasn't exactly an isolated opinion – that Celtic had treated him disgracefully in failing to reward the years of inspired management that brought the club the greatest run of success in its history. So I could not resist asking him how he felt about the insult of being offered a job supervising the Celtic development pool, which amounted to reducing a supreme football man to a fund-raiser. His reaction was astonishingly low-key and devoid of bitterness. He said: 'When you are successful it is fine for a time and then they maybe think you are too successful and that the success wasn't really due to you at all.' End of story. In all my experience of him, I never once heard Jock criticise Celtic. It made me realise how much he loved that club and I found a deep sadness in the contrast between his devotion and the treatment he received. They say something similar happened to Bill Shankly and Don Revie and there have even been mutterings about Manchester United's appreciation of Sir Matt Busby being a lot less than it should have been. I think if I were as badly used as Jock was at the end by Celtic, I would find it hard to be as philosophical or as generous as he was.

Another subject that Jock consistently refused to expand upon was how he went about making Celtic the first British club to win the European Cup. Everybody knows that his contribution – in finding and developing the players and then supplying them with tactics brilliantly devised to suit their strengths – was utterly crucial, but he shrugged off any attempt to give him a substantial share of the glory. His modesty was extraordinary, and it was sincere. When the European Cup was mentioned, he would eulogise the players who won it and launch into some of the marvellous human stories surrounding that great team. We would be sitting in the reception lobby of the hotel at 2 a.m. with one hilarious tale following another. Many involved wee Jimmy Johnstone. According to Jock, when his phone rang at home late on a Friday night a picture of Jimmy would leap instantly into his mind and his first thought would be: 'Which police station this time?'

These were golden times for me, sitting to all hours in the morning, arguing, debating, enjoying the story-telling, with the talk frequently punctuated by the teetotal Stein's urgent command: 'Steely, get another pot of tea.' Jimmy Steel, one of the world's great human beings, was the life and soul of Scotland's get-togethers. He was officially masseur to the party, as he was at Celtic, but he spent much of his time leaving the players helpless with his renderings of the dressing-room fury of a Czechoslovakian team manager he had once observed, of a tout at the Epsom Derby ('No, I'm not Prince Monolulu, I'm Tam the Tipster') or of the boxing commentator at Madison Square Garden. At the Garden, his listing of the film stars and other celebrities at ringside would invariably include a few unlikely interlopers from our own ranks: 'Yes, they're all here tonight and would you believe who's down there in the front row, no less. It's Jock Stein and Alex Ferguson. Must be complimentaries.' Although he is not at his sprightliest, Jimmy still raises himself whenever I phone him at his Larkhall home. Jock once said of him that he had never committed a sin in his life and I would agree with that – a truly great man. So, apart from being the best masseur in the business, the entertainments officer and general confidant to everyone, on these nights Steely's most important job was getting that tea!

We usually assembled on Saturday nights, which meant players would arrive at different times, depending on where they had been playing. But in the main they would be in the hotel around 9.30 p.m. After checking in, some of them would go for a beer and be back by midnight. That was the arrangement and the players were pretty good but we had one or two energetic young men like Charlie Nicholas and Mo Johnston and, well, they were different. When they were room-mates, Nicholas and Johnston sometimes took the view that their quarters were inadequately furnished if they did not have a little female company. After their antics had got out of hand on one occasion, obliging Jock to soothe and placate a girl whose late-night visit had ended in tears, it was plain that the disciplinary boot would have to be swung. In such circumstances the principles of justice were rarely applied without a heavy taint of pragmatism. Jock felt, as I did, that although Charlie was a smashing lad, intelligent and definitely not a bad sort, he was too big an influence on Mo. Since Jock had

Mo very much in his plans – whereas Charlie was seen as sufficiently similar to Kenny to make playing them together difficult – it was Nicholas who had to go, temporarily as it turned out.

Our first World Cup qualifying match was against Iceland and it was a good performance, featuring two goals from Paul McStay that made him the talking point of the 3–0 victory. Paul was highly talented, with a good range of passing, but would his introvert nature prevent him from fulfilling his potential? Could he take the big step forward and join Strachan and Souness? Those thoughts were troubling me, but he was young and I had to be hopeful.

The next game was against Spain and we secured an important 3–1 win with a vintage Dalglish performance. There have been many great British players who, because of the standard of the national team they played in, have been denied an appearance on the World Cup stage. So trying to assess footballers as world-class can be a confusing and sometimes pointless exercise. But if the term means anything, there are some men from the weaker football nations who clearly qualify for its use. George Best, who never played in the World Cup finals, is undeniably one and I am convinced that Denis Law and Kenny Dalglish are two Scots who deserve the description. It can be argued that Kenny played in three World Cups – 1974, 1978 and 1982 – and did not set the heather on fire in any of them. But I believe he became a truly world-class player in the later years of his playing career and that he was in his prime at the time of the qualifying campaign for Mexico. Looking at Dalglish in training and in the games, there was one quality that struck me even more forcefully than his technical excellence. It was his enthusiasm. He just loved playing and in many ways was like a little boy with his toys when he was out there with the ball and the other players. He was, in my opinion, the best bum player in the game. If he got that broad backside into opponents in or around the penalty box they were dead. One certainty was that no defender would frighten him. Because he was so skilful, Dalglish's courage was seldom stressed, but he had the heart of a lion. I must say he and the rest of the squad brought a good attitude to their work with me. Naturally, every one of them had enormous respect for Jock.

After we had won our first two qualifying games in the build-up to Mexico, the commercial wagon started to roll and one promotional idea created an embarrassing scene at our headquarters in the Turnberry Hotel on the Ayrshire coast. Big Jock had been approached by one of the famous tea companies about allowing members of their organisation to have a photograph taken with the team. For this the team would receive £5,000 and a further £5,000 if they reached the finals in Mexico. Jock phoned Graeme Souness, who put it to the committee the players had formed to deal with such proposals. Apparently the committee, which I think included Willie Miller, Richard Gough and Roy Aitken, agreed the terms and so when the tea company men turned up for their photo they were shown into a lounge where their cameras were set up while we were finishing our lunch. Everything seemed to be fine until Graeme approached Jock to inform him that Kenny would have nothing to do with it and wanted a deal for himself. Jock was not a happy man and immediately called a meeting in the kit room. I attended the meeting but kept in the background, as Jock was pretty angry and made it clear to Kenny he thought £5,000 just for a photo was a reasonable deal. I couldn't make my mind up whether Kenny's concern was strictly financial or whether he was annoyed about not being fully consulted in advance. Anyway, the debate went on for nearly an hour, with all the experienced players having their say. At one point Mo Johnston, who idolised Kenny, made a comment but the brusqueness of Jock's reaction discouraged Mo from further displays of his debating technique. Thankfully, the matter was settled when Kenny relented and the photo was belatedly taken. The incident made it clear to me that Kenny's admirable resolution on the field was more than matched by his stubbornness off it, particularly when it came to arguing his corner, about money or anything else.

The more time I spent with Jock Stein, the greater my affection for him became, and I found it increasingly easy to understand why he had been so immensely successful. I loved being in his company, savouring the extent to which his beliefs and ideals and humour corresponded with my own. Politically, we were soulmates. The vehemence of Jock's loyalty to his roots in the Lanarkshire coalfield was demonstrated by something that happened at the height of the miners' strike of 1984–85. As the Scotland team were driving to a game, some of the lorries used by scab operators to bring in coal from Belgium and other countries drew close to our bus. Jock told our driver to pump his horn to draw the lorry drivers' attention, at which point Big Jock engaged in what Glaswegians call 'giving them pelters', shaking his fists at the strikebreakers and letting them know exactly what he thought of them. On another occasion when we arranged to meet at Tynecastle Park, I got there ahead of Jock and was walking in front of him. I passed some miners who were campaigning for strike funds with their cans and buckets and, to be honest, I didn't have any idea they were there until I heard Big Jock's voice.

'Alex,' he called and as I turned round he beckoned me back to where the miners stood. 'Have you got a fiver?'

'Yes,' I said.

'Then give it to me.' He took out a tenner from his own pocket and dispatched the £15 into the can. 'I'm surprised at you of all people forgetting these lads.' I offered no apology or excuse. It was an important message he was giving me and I have never forgotten it. In fact, I go out my way if I ever see anyone in that position or selling the *Big Issue*.

Our next game in the qualifying series brought the kind of experience I never thought I would have while involved with Scotland. It made Jock and me deeply angry. The game was against Wales at Hampden and, inevitably, Ian Rush and Mark Hughes were much on our minds. So when it came to the tactics talk, we got round to discussing the best way to handle the pair of them. I asked Kenny for an expert insight into Rush's talents, his strengths and weaknesses, but all I got was the bland acknowledgement that yes, he was a good player. Alan Hansen was equally unforthcoming and likewise Steve Nicol. The room was absolutely dead and the silence was broken by Jock asking Arthur Albiston (as a Manchester United team-mate) about Hughes. Arthur gave a detailed appraisal of Mark, which took a lot of strain out of the meeting. After the team-talk, Graeme, Jock and I had a chat and Graeme suggested we had encountered the Liverpool version of *omerta* – say nothing about anything. Graeme said he didn't want to say a lot at the time as he preferred to wait and not disrupt the harmony. It was important to keep Kenny happy.

Graeme gave us his own opinions of Ian Rush but we were still disappointed in the general Liverpool response. The game itself hardly made us feel better. Rush and Hughes battered us in the first half and Wales deservedly went in front. In the second half we brought on Hansen as a third centre-back in order to contain them and try to edge our way back but we never looked like winning or even squaring the game. The match ended on a sour note when for the final ten minutes Souness and Peter Nicholas, Wales's terrier in midfield, intensified a feud which seemed to have been simmering throughout the game. I have to say all the same that Nicholas's choice of enemy was a brave one.

I can well understand the frustrations of a national team manager at times like this when players disperse into the night and he is left to his own thoughts. For Jock it must have been a long night and, knowing him, I'm sure it would have been sleepless. He was never a good sleeper. It wasn't so bad for me as I had the company of McLeish, Miller and Leighton on our way back to Aberdeen and I could release some of my frustration and anger on them.

World Cup qualification was plainly our overriding priority but when the inauguration of the short-lived Rous Cup thrust us against England at Hampden in May 1985, it was more than a sideshow. Facing the English always quickens Scottish blood but when Gough headed the only goal of the match I managed to contain my pleasure. I was only doing my third somersault when England centred the ball. Oh, you beauty! So I fulfilled a dream in a way, being involved in beating England. In the dressing-room after the game the atmosphere was electric and Big Jock was elated.

Immediately after the game we headed for the airport to fly to Iceland for the return of the World Cup match and it was a happy flight. The unfading memory for me is of us sitting in the rooftop restaurant in the Hotel Saga at three o'clock in the morning in broad daylight, sipping a glass of wine, congratulating ourselves on a wonderful day and thinking that this certainly was a great life. I still think the football man's lot is a wonderful one but while you are enjoying the highs you had better be ready for the lows. We had only three days to wait for one of those. Iceland absolutely pulverised us but we stole a result with a Jim Bett goal four minutes from the end. That was a nice twist as Jim used to play there and his wife is Icelandic. Jim Leighton saved a penalty and there was an ugly incident in the first minute of the match when Graeme Souness made a thudding tackle on the blue-eyed boy of our opponents, Siggi Jonsson. Had the foul come later, there might have been a red card flourished instead of a yellow. Soon after Souness's moment of mayhem, out of the corner of my eye I caught sight of an Icelander apparently intent on indirect retribution. It was the president of Akranes Football Club, whom I knew from meetings between his club and Aberdeen in European competition, and he was moving aggressively towards Jock. He was, however, immediately accosted by Steely, who was seventy-two and giving away perhaps thirty years to his opponent but was nevertheless all for the fisticuffs. Steely's fighting blood was cooled by a typical Stein rebuke: 'Sit down you silly old bugger!' Steely complied reluctantly, muttering: 'Well, nae wonder.' Yes, it was all rather different from the euphoria of Hampden a few days before. Incidentally, when everything had calmed down there was an analytical discussion of Steely's boxing technique. Was it that peek-a-boo style perfected by Floyd Patterson or was he just hiding behind his hands? What a lot of people don't know is that Jimmy Steel had a long connection with boxing through the army, and I believe he acted as a second for the great Freddie Mills.

Having lost the second of our World Cup matches with Spain by 1–0 in Seville three months earlier, we now found that qualification for Mexico would hinge on our final group fixture against Wales at Ninian Park on 10 September 1985. We needed at least a draw to earn a play-off with the winner of the Oceanic Group, Australia. Cardiff was sure to be a hostile place and we would be handicapped by the absence of Souness, whose booking in Iceland had given him a suspension. But that and every other football consideration would become utterly trivial before Tuesday, 10 September was over. Having an exceptional memory has greatly enriched my enjoyment of life. I have always had excellent recall of places, incidents, detail. But when I think of Cardiff I always want to forget it. I have never watched the video of the game and don't intend to, and it has been painful to regurgitate in my mind what happened that night. The actual day of the game I remember clearly, the game itself is something of a blur and other parts I can't put in place. It is a strange mixture of the vivid and the vague.

We had decided to stay in Bristol and prepare at the Rovers training ground. Bobby Gould was their manager and he came to watch the training. On the Monday, Jock had asked me to take some of the squad and do whatever I wanted with them. He needed to talk to the defenders about his plans to play McLeish, Hansen and Miller as a three at the back with Gough and Nicol as wing-backs. About ten minutes after we had broken off our warm-up and split into the two groups, Jock shouted me over.

'You'll not believe this,' he said. 'Hansen says he is injured and wants to go back to Liverpool for treatment!'

I looked and Hansen was walking away. Jock was right. I couldn't believe it. This was the day before the game. Christ, why hadn't he said anything before now? Neither of us was pleased but if there is one strength I've always had it is not showing panicky anxiety if a player is injured and on this occasion, to be honest, my feelings were mixed. Since the previous game with Wales, I wasn't sure how to talk to Hansen about Rush.

The practical effect of the departure was that Jock switched Nicol to right wing-back, with Maurice Malpas as his counterpart on the left. We used Gough against Rush, McLeish on Hughes and Miller as the free player at the back. Souness's suspension meant he would be watching the match from the stands, so we had Gordon Strachan and Jim Bett in the middle of the park. All that was straightforward enough but the repercussions of how Hansen had left us were bound to be more complex. Jock had always had reservations about the attitude of Liverpool and their players to Scotland's needs and about the number of times Hansen in particular had withdrawn. That night, when the two of us went to see Bristol Rovers play, Jock did say that if we succeeded in qualifying Hansen would not be going to Mexico. I said nothing but I remembered his words.

There were several things that had upset Jock on the day of the match but they were minor problems. One or two in the media were having a pop and, although he did not complain, he did mention the fact. He also made reference to some interview in which the Wales team manager, Mike England, had been quite critical of Scotland. After lunch the Big Man was in good form as we played pool against John McDonald from Inverness, who was one of Jock's closest friends and allies at the SFA. McDonald's partner against Jock and myself was an old friend of mine, Willie Purdie, and there was something like £20 a side at stake. The little wager put Jock in his element. McDonald was badgered mercilessly by the Big Man. His whole repertoire of gamesmanship was on show: shakes of the head, tut-tutting over McDonald's choice of shot just as he was about to play were all part of the kidology and it paid off, as we collected the money. We went to our rooms for a rest and I was just settling into a nice little sleep when there was a knock on my door. It was Jock. 'I was just thinking . . .' and in he came in his boxer shorts for a chat about the game and I could sense that, although he was extremely positive, there was a trace of tension. After a while I suggested we have a nap and freshen ourselves up and he agreed and off he went. Seconds later, back he came.

'I've locked myself out.'

It took a phone call to the porter to get us into his room. At that point, sleep was completely off my mind and I joined him in his room. He had the symptoms of a heavy cold and I noticed that on his dressing-table he had a medicine bottle and two small bottles of tablets. Jock had laid out all his clothes for the game and on his bed lay a pair of Bukta shorts with a broad green panel, and I thought to myself that he must carry them for luck because they were out of fashion at the time. Later he took some medicine and a tablet from one of the bottles and we had another run-through on the game. When eventually I went off to get ready for the journey into Cardiff, I kept thinking of those Bukta shorts. Even great men have their little superstitions.

The trip to Ninian Park was quite normal. Tapes were played on the bus and Jock went through his usual ritual of complaining about the choice of music. 'What kind of music is that?' he was asking in that dismissive tone that was a speciality of his. Then he would get Steely to give us a few of his routines. The atmosphere was good.

The damage Rush and Hughes had inflicted on us at Hampden ensured that they would dominate my team-talk for this decisive match. But after the refusal of our Liverpool players to talk about their team-mate before that game, I wasn't interested in asking them for any help this time around. I made it my aim to avoid letting the players become apprehensive about what Rush and Hughes might do to us in Cardiff. I said, 'Get right into this Rush. He's a coward.' Now I don't believe that for a minute but I was determined not to let our lads build those two up in their minds. I said of Hughes, 'He can't run, get in front of him.' I underplayed Wales's most dangerous men to boost the morale of our own players. It's true that Mark comes to the ball all the time; running beyond an opponent isn't his strong suit. But I was exaggerating negatives about both of them because there was no doubt that they were the key to our chances of coping with Wales. They were the Welsh team. There were other decent players in their side, like Peter Nicholas and Kevin Ratcliffe, but if we did not allow Rush and Hughes to dominate we would be in good shape.

There were, naturally, signs of nerves at the start of the game. I don't care what anybody says, when the crowd in Cardiff start singing that Welsh national anthem it creates some atmosphere. It's such a magnificent anthem that you can hardly stop yourself from singing along. There were 35,000 in the ground that night and when they gave voice it was bound to stir their players. That was real motivation. The Welsh team were revved up and in the first half they gave us a hard time.

In a playing sense, the drama of the match all centred around Jim Leighton and the fact that he lost one of his contact lenses in the first half. To say I found that dramatic is an understatement, considering that Leighton had been playing under me for seven years and I never had the faintest inkling that he used contact lenses. To my dying day I shall be haunted by the worry that Jock left us believing that I had let him down, that I knew about the lenses and hadn't told him. It still strikes me as incredible that Jim kept it a secret for so long. I knew there was something wrong with him in the first half. I couldn't believe how much trouble he was in. Balls were bouncing off him, he was miskicking, he was all over the place. Wales went ahead when the ball was driven in from the left-hand side and Sparky Hughes took the goal brilliantly. So at half-time we were 1–0 down and in the dressing-room Jock got stuck into wee Gordon Strachan. Gordon had not played well, had not expressed himself as effectively in the game as you would expect from a player of his quality, and Jock had a real go at him. He was going to take Strachan off and bring Davie Cooper on at that point. Gordon was upset but there was nothing new in that.

Then all of a sudden Jock left the main part of the dressing-room. Hugh Allan, the physiotherapist, had called him into the bathroom area. I went across and sat down with Gordon.

'What Jock is saying is for the sake of the team. You're not playing as well as you should.'

'I can't believe he is saying that to me,' Gordon responded.

'Look,' I said, 'he's right. Just settle down. You're not coming off. He'll give you ten minutes. Get your game together.' Then big Jock called.

'Alex, come here.'

I walked into the bathroom area and I'll never forget the scene that greeted me. There was a kind of wooden plinth and Jim was half-sitting on it with an expression that told me straightaway there was a serious problem. He has a face that can assume a real hangdog look and the one he had then was a classic.

'He's lost his contact lens.'

Jock said it in a way that suggested he was assuming I had known about the lenses and hadn't told him. I swear I had absolutely no idea that Jim used them. I was so dumbfounded and there was such a swirl of anger and embarrassment going through me that at first I didn't say a word. I remember giving Jim a look that was like a string of curses. When I did speak it was to ask him if it would be better to take the second lens out and play without any. He admitted that having one made his vision hopelessly distorted but added that without lenses he simply could not function as a goalkeeper. 'I wouldn't be able to see the ball,' he told us. That meant we had to put Alan Rough in goal for the second half and, as it happened, the change turned out to be a good one for us. Rough's temperament proved to be a godsend in the difficult circumstances we were facing. But at the time what happened with Leighton was a horror story. Jock gave me one of those long hard looks that amounted to saying: 'You're going to have lot of explaining to do.' There I was, Leighton's club manager, somebody with a reputation for maintaining strict control over my players and for making it my business to know everything worth knowing about them. Jock was entitled to suspect that I had been holding back about the lenses. In fact, nobody at Aberdeen knew about them. When I got back up north, I checked with our physiotherapist and he was as stunned as I had been. When I had a showdown with Leighton in my office, I annihilated him. Obviously, had I known, we would at least have carried a spare pair as a precaution, which is what we did with Aberdeen afterwards. I think the secrecy represented terrible selfishness on Leighton's part. For seven years he had kept me and his team-mates and everybody else at the club in ignorance. Whether he did it because of worries about a threat to his career (which his longevity in the game has shown to be groundless) or for reasons of vanity I don't know. But in football, where it should be all for one and one for all, that kind of behaviour is out of order.

The drama of the lost lens definitely sent a wave of panic through our dressing-room. We were a goal behind, with just forty-five minutes in which to earn the draw we needed to qualify for the World Cup finals. Big Jock was desperate to get there, obviously, and during that interval we knew we were up against it. We had the Strachan issue to sort out and when the Leighton problem hit us it meant there was no possibility of having the composed team-talk we needed. Even with all the experience Jock and I had, bringing calm to those players was never going to be easy. We were soon grateful for the help that came from Rough. I was never a great fan of his goalkeeping but he is a very likeable person and his laid-back attitude was perfect for the predicament we were in. In the midst of all that tension, he managed to laugh and joke while he was saving balls and those qualities were invaluable for us.

The strains of that second half were extreme. Cathy was watching the game on television and she told me afterwards that when the cameras were turned on the Scotland bench I looked awful, as if *I* was liable to have a heart attack. Part of the trouble was that I was already worrying about Jock. He had begun to sweat and his face was grey. He was sitting with Hugh Allan on one side of him and me on the other. Steely was next along from me and beyond him was Stuart Hillis, our doctor. I was sufficiently concerned to indicate quietly to Stuart that he should check on Jock. The doctor looked along the bench and said yes, he would keep an eye on him. When Jock decided to make a substitution about a quarter of an hour into the second half, initially I misunderstood what he had in mind. Looking back on it now, I think the confusion probably had something to do with the fact that he was already unwell at that point and therefore wasn't as clear and authoritative as he would have been normally. I was well aware that, in advance of the game, he had been favouring the option of replacing Strachan with Cooper in the later stages. He had said to Davie Cooper, 'I think you will be better coming on as a sub in this match because by the second-half Joey Jones will be struggling.' Jones had just been brought back into the Welsh side at right-back and it was a reasonable assumption that he wouldn't stay the course. That was how it worked out. Cooper did really well along the left wing for us and gave Jones a nightmare in the last half-hour. But at first when a change was mentioned I thought Jock wanted to take Steve Nicol off and I got the wrong board out.

'No, keep Nicol on,' Jock said. 'Take Strachan off and put Cooper on.'

We were by then the better team but it was no certainty that we would get the equaliser we needed and with about twenty minutes to go Jock started stressing to me that we must keep our dignity if we lost. I shall never forget how much importance he attached to that, how he made the point to me several times.

'Look, Alex,' he said. 'If we get beat here, I want you to take the team to the centre circle and acknowledge the fans. And we must not lose our dignity.' He kept saying that. 'Ignore everything else. Just don't let us lose our dignity.'

As everybody knows, we didn't lose the match. With ten minutes left, David Speedie was going through on a ball when it bounced up and hit David Phillips on the arm and we were given a penalty. It was a break for us because, although we were clearly superior by that time and largely controlling the play, it was a fairly soft penalty. The contact was accidental but it was a blatant hand-ball and the Dutch referee, Mr Keizer, did not hesitate over the decision. Davie Cooper stayed cool and directed the ball low away to Neville Southall's left into the corner of the net and we were on our way to the next summer's World Cup finals in Mexico.

When that equaliser went in, Jock didn't say a word. Shortly afterwards the referee blew for a free kick but Jock thought it was the full-time whistle. There were actually a couple of minutes to go but the Big Man rose to move towards Mike England, the Wales manager. Jock was annoyed about a lot of the stuff England had been quoted as saying about the Scotland team and I am sure the idea was to go across and say, 'Hard luck, son.' It would have been a touch of the old sharp-edged commiserations, doing things right but letting Mike know he didn't fancy somebody running off at the mouth. Jock had no masters when it came to remaining polite while having a dig. But as he rose from the bench he stumbled. I had been keeping an eye on him throughout the second half and when he began to fall I grabbed for him and shouted to Hughie Allan to do the same. The doctor joined us and the medics came out of the tunnel immediately. Hughie and I held him up until the others took over and helped him inside. I went back to the bench and at the end of the game I told the players to stay on the pitch. We didn't know whether Jock was in the dressing-room or what was happening. We were given the signal that it was all right to go in and when we asked how he was the first impression we received was that he was recovering. There were no real celebrations in the dressing-room but I felt reassured enough to start saying 'well done' to the players and telling them that the Boss had suffered a heart attack but was going to be all right. Everything appeared to be OK and when I was told I would have to deal with the press, I was starting to warm to that job. Some of the reporters had been a bit critical of Jock and I was relishing addressing a few words to them. But when I came out I saw Graeme Souness at the door of the medical room and he was crying.

'I think he's gone,' Graeme said. I couldn't believe it.

'Where is he?' I asked and when Graeme said Jock was in the medical room I made to open the door and go in. At that moment Ernie Walker, the secretary of the Scottish Football Association, stepped out and told me I couldn't go in there. It seemed that Ernie was more or less dismissing me but I could understand it. He was under huge pressure, trying to compose himself to deal with all the things that had to be done in the immediate aftermath of Jock's death.

'Look,' I said, 'somebody will have to phone Jean.'

'God, of course,' Ernie said, 'we've got to do that right now. Could you go and do that, Alex?'

I got on the phone and there was no answer. So I rang Jack Flynn, knowing he and his wife Lela were neighbours of the

Steins and very friendly with them. Jack told me Jean and Lela had gone to the bingo and said he would drive to the hall and get to them before Jean heard the news by any other means. As he was on his way there, however, they were coming back and he missed them. Meantime, Ray, Jock's daughter, had learned from television that her father had been taken seriously ill and had headed for her mother's house. She was waiting there when Jean arrived back with Lela. They all went into the house and it was Ray who answered the phone when I eventually got through. Ray said to me, 'Alex, don't tell me, please, please don't tell me.' But I had to tell her that her father was dead. Then David Will, who was the president of the SFA, took the phone from me. No doubt as president it was his place to do that but I knew the family really well and, although nobody could do anything about the depth of grief they were suffering, it might have been better if they'd had a familiar voice on the end of the line.

Soon we had to go through and tell the players and the other members of the backroom staff. Old Steely was in a dreadful state. He had been very close to Jock and he was inconsolable. I managed to hold my feelings in check. I didn't shed a tear until I had flown from Cardiff to Glasgow the following day and set out on the drive up to Aberdeen, where we had a game against Partick Thistle that night. On the way up, I pulled into a lay-by and I just broke down. Then, when I reached home much later and Cathy asked me about Jock's death, I really collapsed. The full weight of what had happened came down on me and I just gave way to my emotions. At Ninian Park I had been determined to keep control. I had absorbed what Jock said about maintaining dignity and I was making sure the players were all right. When we filed on to the bus there were thousands standing outside the ground and the quiet sadness of the atmosphere was unforgettable. There were one or two shouts of 'God bless you, Jock' and 'Well done lads, he would be proud of you'. But the abiding memory is of a solemn silence. It was as if the king had died. In football terms, the king *had* died.

— 12 —
MEXICO 1986

JOCK STEIN's death shook the whole of Scotland and, for the football community especially, recovering from it was a slow process. Everybody accepted that the first obligation to Jock's memory was to complete the national team's qualification for the World Cup finals in Mexico in 1986. I was delighted and honoured when the Scottish Football Association decided that I should take over as manager on a part-time basis, with an agreement that both sides would review the position after the finals.

Before we could be sure of competing in Mexico, we had to survive a play-off with the winners of the Oceanic Group, Australia, but a fairly comfortable 2–0 victory in the first leg at Hampden on 20 November 1985 left us confident that we could tidy up the loose ends in Melbourne a fortnight later. Loose cannons turned out to be more of a problem. Our preparations for that last qualifying match were irritatingly disrupted by some typically irresponsible shenanigans from those specialists in boozy bad behaviour, Maurice Johnston and Frank McAvennie. With the game scheduled for Wednesday, 4 December I implemented medical advice about acclimatisation by arranging to fly the main party to Australia on the previous Thursday, training the players on the Friday and giving them a day off on the Saturday. I knew the hazards of granting such freedom but it is unrealistic to expect young lads to cope with being confined in their rooms day after day. We had to guard against the danger that the undisciplined minority would go on the rampage and we seemed to have found an acceptable compromise when an old friend of mine, Hugh Murney, who had a pub in Melbourne, offered to provide private facilities for the squad. Hugh, who had played with St Mirren and Morton, came from a tough, down-to-earth family and would never let me down in circumstances like that. He gave them a room to themselves, hired a wee band and put a man on the door to vet everybody coming in. It was an ideal set-up.

I felt reasonably relaxed as I headed down to Sydney for the day to see my Great-uncle Alex. He was ninety and I assumed this visit to Australia would be my last meeting with him. (It was, although he lived to be ninety-seven.) After a marvellous day with Uncle Alex I went back to Sydney Airport, only to discover that my flight had been cancelled and I would have to spend the night in a hotel before flying back to Melbourne next morning. Settled in a lovely big room, watching the television, I made a call to my assistant, Walter Smith, to make sure that everything at the camp was all right. It was a huge relief to hear reassuring words from Wattie and I went back to the telly. Half an hour later, the phone rang and this time Wattie's voice was not at all reassuring. Usually his tone was deadpan but now it was tortured.

'You'll not believe this,' he said. 'Those clowns Johnston and McAvennie have brought three birds into the bar, they're buying everybody drink. They're going off their heads.'

'Stupid bastards – I'll kill them when I get back.' Verbally I did. I got right in about them. 'You're on your last warning, the two of you,' I said. 'Once more and you're out.'

The game was no triumph for us but the 0–0 result was perfectly satisfactory. We were a bit disappointing in the first half, then improved after the interval, but the truth is that Jim Leighton ensured our passage to the finals with four outstanding saves. My Uncle Alex had taken the train up from Sydney to see the game – fourteen hours at ninety years of age – and after it was over we gave him a lift back to the station on our bus. Ernie Walker, the chief executive of the SFA, was sitting in his usual seat at the front but Uncle Alex said, 'Come on, young man, move along.' Ernie was terrific.

'I don't want to argue with *you*, auld yin,' he answered and transferred to another seat.

After we had dropped Uncle Alex at the station and seen him on his train for Sydney, it was time for everybody to have a night out. The players did not have a game on the Saturday, and surely the wild men had gathered sense, for this trip at least. Some chance. Next morning Ernie was sitting on his own at breakfast and I went across to thank him for being so pleasant to my uncle. The moment I approached, Ernie said, 'I warned you about that shit, Johnston.' He told me that halfway through the night there was a tremendous battering on his door and a burst of expletives from the other side of it. When he went to the door and looked through the peephole he saw Mo Johnston, starkers, with a girl. I think she, too, was naked. Ernie asked me if I had heard the racket but I had not.

'Alex,' he said, 'I'm giving you a bit of advice. He's bad news.'

'Well, I know that,' I said, 'but he can play, and that's the problem. But I'm not standing for that behaviour.'

I was already thinking of my list of players for Mexico and Mo had more or less put a line through his name. He had ability. He had good movement and an excellent goalscoring record but his conduct off the field made him a liability. If you are taking players away for four or five weeks to Mexico, it's not the same as just travelling up the road. You can't say, well, get on the bus and go home. There was also the growing inclination in my mind to bring Charlie Nicholas back into the fold because World Cups demand players with brilliance and Charlie had his share of that. Although Johnston had a notable talent for scoring goals, he did not have the all-round talent of Nicholas and I thought that a World Cup platform would bring out the best in Charlie. Whereas Mo was a silly boy, Charlie was bright and intelligent and he had an engaging personality that enlivened everyone around him.

Having strong personalities among my back-up staff was also important to me. I wanted Walter as my assistant and I chose Craig Brown and Archie Knox as coaches because I knew them and was certain they would be able to work well with everybody else in the group. Considering the importance of our challenge in Mexico and the amount of money generated by it, there was no point in going out there without sufficient people to cover all the essential requirements. Ernie, characteristically, was totally supportive of my refusal to skimp. His attitude was that anything I felt I needed, I should have. He believed there should be a place for Andy Roxburgh, who was the SFA's director of coaching and, after listening to his case, I agreed. On the medical side, we could not have been better served than we were by Dr Stuart Hillis, whose contribution was always first class. I decided that our veteran masseur, Jimmy Steel, should have the help of Teddy Scott, a stalwart on my Aberdeen staff, because Jimmy was in his seventies and there was the obvious possibility that the heat and other unfamiliar conditions in Mexico might take their toll. I also enlisted an extra physio, Eric Ferguson from Dundee. From what I knew of past World Cups, particularly the Scotland party Ally MacLeod led to Argentina, Scotland had suffered from undermanning but there was to be no chance of that in 1986. Even when we learned that we had been drawn in the toughest imaginable group – bloody Denmark, West Germany and Uruguay – I was determined to meet the challenge of the World Cup positively and enjoy every minute of it.

I travelled down to Ipswich to talk to Sir Alf Ramsey at his home. His response was tremendous and he could not have been more helpful. He pointed out the difficulties that could arise with unfamiliar food in Mexico and, on his advice, we arranged to take considerable supplies with us. Other valuable hints he passed on were concerned with altitude training and the general handling of players during a World Cup in a foreign country. When I told him that we were going to Santa Fe, New Mexico, for ten days and then down to Los Angeles for some hard work on fitness levels before returning to altitude in Mexico, he was pleased and impressed. I was glad and grateful to hear him say that we deserved to do well because we clearly cared about how we were approaching the job and had tried to cover everything.

When it was time to address the most vital issue of all, the composition of my squad, I recognised immediately that no decision would be more controversial than the one I had to take about Alan Hansen. Nobody with any sense could ever doubt his quality as a central defender but his tendency to pull out of Scotland matches had raised a question in my mind about his reliability and perhaps his attitude. His deserved reputation as a marvellous player was based on his achievements with Liverpool. I have to say that, to me, he was never as remarkable with Scotland, but I was certainly in no hurry to turn my back on him. We faced two testing pre-World Cup matches, against England at Wembley and Holland in Eindhoven, within a week in late April of 1986 and he was called up for those. While we were training at Luton Town's ground for the England game, however, Alan walked up to Walter Smith and said, 'I can feel my knee – I'll need to go back.' Then, without any real discussion, he left for Liverpool and I felt instantly that it was all too much of a re-run of the episode in Cardiff, when his late withdrawal from the crucial qualifying match with Wales so annoyed Jock Stein. What happened there had such an effect on Jock that I am fairly sure, had he lived and remained in charge, Hansen would not have been on the plane for Mexico. My own thoughts were rapidly hardening against taking him. But I admit I was concerned about how Kenny Dalglish would react to the omission of Hansen. Kenny was by then the Liverpool player-manager but the bond between them was even stronger than that implies, because they were close personal friends. In the interests of the Scotland team, I was anxious to respect Kenny's position. He had just gained his hundredth cap for the country and I believed that in this late phase of his career the combination of his rich skills and unrivalled experience was capable of making him more important to us than ever before.

Nevertheless, Hansen's withdrawal from the England game, and the manner of it, encouraged me to think about alternatives in central defence and in that context I had a chat with David Narey of Dundee United. Narey had opted out of Scottish squads but his club form was impressive. He was extremely quick, a good tackler and a good reader of the game and he had the precious additional advantage of versatility. He had played centre-midfield as an anchorman and had served as a right-back for Scotland in the past. In my view, a man with his talent should not be missing out on the World Cup finals, provided he had the urge and the will to be involved. When I met him I told him I wanted him to be with us and, while I could not promise him a place, I would guarantee him absolutely fair consideration. He satisfied me that his enthusiasm was rekindled, so I fielded him in our second preparatory match against Holland and he was brilliant. The Dutch put out a strong team against us and we did well in the scoreless draw. It was a good performance.

During the trip to Holland, another player who had been out of the reckoning for some time thrust himself on my attention. Steve Archibald, who had been missing from football for six or seven months and had been seeking to speed his rehabilitation by having sessions with a celebrated Dutch physiotherapist, sought a meeting with me. The physio accompanied Steve and said he would vouch one hundred per cent for his fitness. It was a difficult call but I was swayed by my high opinion of Archibald as a striker. Steve had a bit of everything. He was two-footed, had great balance, he was good in the air, he was quick, he was a good finisher, he was brave. Even with the doubt about his condition, all those assets would keep him at least on the fringe of consideration. It was comforting to have him there if any of the strikers I had now decided to take to the finals could not go. Paul Sturrock had qualified as one of those front players because he was the best available to me when it came to moving defenders and I included Graeme Sharp as someone who could make a telling difference in the air. Charlie Nicholas was given a place because he had exceptional skills and the capacity to be inspired. The earlier worry that he might be too similar to Dalglish faded before the thought of what both could do in the World Cup. None of our other strikers could run through the middle with the penetrative effect of McAvennie, so he was in, in spite of the worries about his discipline. I had given up on Mo Johnston. Although Nicholas and McAvennie could be jack-the-lads, they weren't stupid. I wasn't sure that could always be said of Mo. I knew I could control Frank and Charlie but Mo's record condemned him. David Speedie struck me as a serious moaner and I suspected that if he wasn't playing he would give me problems, so he was left out. Davie Cooper, who was to die so young and so tragically, had done much to seal our indispensable victory over Wales the year before but the case for selecting him had a much broader basis. There had been a trend with Scotland to favour all-round players – midfielders who could play out wide if required – at the expense of real wingers. Davie Cooper represented a justification for bucking that trend. He was a beautifully balanced outside-left. He had a superb left foot, was a tremendous striker of the ball who could deliver splendid crosses. There was no certainty that he would be a constant element of the team but I thought he could play a valuable part. I was convinced I had to bring him in.

Among the defenders, too, one of my choices, Arthur Albiston, owed his inclusion to the fact that he was naturally left-footed. There was an inevitable preponderance of right-footed players, including two who regularly operated at left-back, Stevie Nicol and Maurice Malpas, and I was anxious to have the option of balancing that, which Arthur gave me. McLeish, Miller, Narey and Richard Gough had persuaded me they were the men to cover the centre-back positions and I was also going for Roy Aitken because his unbelievable enthusiasm and energy made him an uplifting influence around the squad. He wasn't the most brilliant player but he could always give something to the cause and he was a good foil for others. Graeme Souness, Gordon Strachan, Paul McStay and Jim Bett would be the core of the midfield and, of course, Jim Leighton picked himself as the number one goalkeeper.

So, having weighed and sifted all the evidence to the point where my squad was virtually complete, I came back to the thorny question of Alan Hansen. In fact, it had ceased to be a question. I was leaving him out. I had not looked for a reason to do so. I had never fallen out with him and had no axe to grind. He was always quite receptive to me. There was no personal animosity tainting the decision. My criteria were strictly those of a football manager and there is no contradiction in adding that the memory of how Alan dropped out of the Cardiff game and then the England game loomed large in my thinking. I simply felt that he did not deserve to go to Mexico. But I realised that Kenny Dalglish would take a different view and made sure Kenny was the first player I contacted on the day before the squad was announced. I had sat down in my house in Aberdeen to spend the afternoon making a long series of calls. After telling Kenny how pleased I was that he would be with us, I gave him the news that I would not be taking Alan Hansen. Kenny made the expected response.

'He's a great player, Alan. You can't leave him out.'

'Well, look, let me think about it,' I said. That was essentially a matter of showing respect for what Kenny was saying but, after phoning a number of other players to let them know about their selection or exclusion, I went back on to him.

'No, I can't change my mind about Alan,' I told him. 'It's silly to go back on your own feelings. It's sad but that's the way it is.'

Kenny's reaction was muted. 'Well, OK. It's your decision.'

When I gave the bad news to Alan Hansen himself, he handled it well.

'Fine,' he said. 'I understand it's difficult. You can't take everybody.'

Shortly before we were due to fly out, Kenny called off. We were informed that he was going in for an operation on his knee. In his autobiography, Kenny wrote: 'People claimed I was snubbing Fergie out of spite over Alan. That was not true. Those who said I pulled out because Alan Hansen wasn't picked were not only libelling me but impugning the integrity of the surgeon who told me not to go. I was hardly going to be able to play in a World Cup finals with the ligament detached from my knee.' Dalglish was a massive loss to us. He blossomed magnificently in his early thirties and was fit company for the very best players in the world. His extraordinary talent was matched by unbreakable courage, an attribute the importance of which is often overlooked when great players are dazzling us with their skills. Kenny was physically and mentally tough and he had an aura around him that would have been priceless in the Scotland camp. He would have given all the others a lift just by being there. I know Graeme Souness missed him in Mexico. But Souness is one of those shrug-of-the-shoulders types. 'Ach, well, if he's not here, he's not here. Let's get on with it.' He has the kind of nature made to handle setbacks. So he was quite pragmatic about Kenny's absence but he was definitely disappointed. Once the World Cup finals were under way, Souness had his own problems.

After we were thoroughly unfortunate to lose our first match against Denmark by 1–0, having played well and had a perfectly legitimate goal by Aitken disallowed, we went one goal ahead against West Germany in our second game. Then they equalised and, immediately after the interval, Rudi Völler shot them into the lead and left us with an uphill struggle as we chased the game in the second half, to no avail. They won 2–1. That was when I realised how badly Graeme was tiring in matches. He was losing so much weight during games, up to twelve pounds in ninety minutes, and his stamina was visibly draining away in the later stages. He had suffered an injury with Sampdoria that had kept him out of action and away from training for a while and the reduction of his fitness was telling on him in Mexico.

Scotland's hopes of progressing beyond the initial round of the World Cup finals for the first time were still alive as we entered our third match, against Uruguay. We had to win, whereas a draw would put our opponents through, and I knew the limitless cynicism of the Uruguayans would make our confrontation with them a bitter and exhausting war of attrition. I had to worry about Souness's ability to last through it. But this was a player of the highest calibre and not somebody any manager would drop without regret. Walter Smith, who was assistant to Graeme at Rangers, where he had taken over as player-manager the previous April, urged me to play him against Uruguay but the probable character of the match argued against that option.

'The way I see it, there is going to be a lot of grim toil,' I told

Walter. 'They're going to defend for their lives; they're going to kick us; they're going to destroy the game. If we need him in the last part of the hour and a half, he may not be there. I'd rather have him as a sub.' It was Walter's opinion that being a substitute would be seen by Souness as an unbearable insult and when I mentioned the idea to Graeme he confirmed that he felt that way.

'It's hard enough being left out but being a sub would kill me,' he said and I had to respect the feelings of a truly great footballer.

I think I can claim that my management over Scotland's first two matches in Mexico was good but I am less than happy with my memories of how I handled that decisive third game with Uruguay. My team selection could have been better, although it is true that I was handicapped by the physical difficulties being experienced by Souness and an injury sustained by Charlie Nicholas. Against Denmark and West Germany we had performed pretty well and our lack of luck showed not only in the run of the ball and the results but the ugly foul that curtailed the severe trouble Nicholas had been creating for the Danes. Combining well with Sturrock, Charlie was dropping into the hole behind his team-mate and the opposition didn't know what to do with him. When we had to take him off with about half an hour to go, it was a blow to our prospects in that and succeeding matches. I brought him on late against Uruguay as a last throw of the dice but would probably have made far more use of him if he had been fully fit.

There were, however, other weaknesses in the selection, some of which could be traced to a foolish sense of guilt I had begun to develop about having so many players in the squad who were associated with my reign at Aberdeen. I should have played Archibald, for a start. Stevie, who was brought in after Kenny Dalglish withdrew, had done really well against West Germany but fears that his recent seven-month absence from action might cause a dip in his form if he were asked to face Uruguay five days later counted against him, and so, perhaps, did the nagging embarrassment about the Aberdeen connection. That factor certainly prevented me from implementing my gut inclination to play Jim

Bett in midfield. Instead I opted for Paul McStay and, for all his wonderful talent, his contribution was disappointing. To say that of Graeme Sharp would be an understatement. I had thought of him as an aggressive attacker of the ball but he was surprisingly soft in that game. Uruguay had José Batista ordered off after only forty seconds for a desperate foul on Gordon Strachan and subsequently their packing of their penalty box was screaming out for our forwards to go and attack headers. I was expecting Sharp to lead the charge but he succumbed to the practised bullying of the South Americans.

Maybe our players would have coped more effectively with the frustrating skulduggery of the Uruguayans if my team-talk had been more inspired. I confess that it was, by the standards I expect of myself, distinctly poor. On my way in to deliver it, I had a blazing row with Archibald, who did not take kindly to being told that he was on the sidelines. I was not astonished by Stevie's attitude. He is not a selfish person but he is single-minded and not likely to remain quiet if he disagrees with you. After our argument I should have given myself a break to regather my thoughts and look at my notes again before joining the team but instead I launched straight into the talk. The result was that I failed to emphasise the important points. I ended up offering nothing more relevant to the players than some words to the effect that if they played to their form they could beat anybody in the competition. It was all a bit emptily Churchillian. A team-talk should always contain a healthy dose of realism, should encourage your men to recognise their strengths and work to exploit them. We had good players and I should have been giving them mature advice about patience, maintaining possession, how to initiate counter-attacks and to avoid being provoked and led into unproductive activity by the cunning of the opposition. It was no time for the kind of rhetoric that is meant to convince moderate players they can transcend their limitations. That was all right when I was manager of St Mirren but was out of place with Scotland.

Having admitted all that, I must say that the players could not be proud of how they performed. They did not come anywhere near their true standards. As soon as the Uruguayans were down to ten men, we became nervous and revealed that old Scottish inability to produce the killer thrust. Enzo Francescoli was magnificent for them, playing up front on his own with endless resourcefulness and composure. He stood out in a team notable mainly for their malice and the shamelessness of their tactics. The French referee, Joel Quiniou, had started off like a hero with that first-minute expulsion but later on he was blatantly intimidated by the Uruguayans' unadulterated mischief. They were ready to descend to any level of connivance and deceit to gain the draw they required and the referee fell victim to their methods. They made unorthodox use of the little cone-shaped bags of drinking water that had been supplied to us to help combat dehydration. As the referee and linesmen came in at half-time, the Uruguayan subs were hitting them with those bags of water. At the end of ninety minutes, most of their team were hounding Quiniou to blow for time-up – pushing and shoving at him, pulling his jersey, pointing to the clock – and ultimately he succumbed to the pressure and blew the whistle when there must have been at least five minutes of stoppage time to be played. At the post-match press conference their coach, Omar Borras, made a statement of historic hypocrisy.

'I don't know what all the fuss is about,' he said. 'We played a fair game.'

I lost my temper and refused to shake hands with him. FIFA showed what they thought of Borras's protestations when they fined Uruguay 25,000 Swiss francs and threatened to eject them from the tournament if they did not improve their behaviour. Football was done a favour when they were knocked out in the next round by Argentina. But none of that helped us. Yet again Scotland's participation in a World Cup had been brief and far from glorious. It pained me deeply that I had been unable to improve upon a depressingly familiar script.

— 13 —
MORE SILVER FOR THE SILVER CITY

THE success that at first fosters a powerful spirit of comradeship in football teams may ultimately splinter them apart. As the honours accumulate, individual ambitions grow and nobody can blame players for seeking opportunities to earn more from their talents elsewhere. Accusations of disloyalty are hard to sustain against the reality that the most compassionate clubs will jettison anybody who has ceased to serve their needs. When managers and players who have achieved much together find their paths diverging, the most either side can expect is that the parting will be conducted with mutual respect and transparent fairness. I found little evidence that those were Gordon Strachan's priorites once he had made up his mind to quit Aberdeen. His intentions were conveyed to me in the 1983–84 season by a statement I considered ridiculous. 'I'm bored – I want to leave,' he said. My advice was uncomplicated: 'Go and get yourself unbored.' But there was no escaping the evidence that his heart was not in what he was doing and several times I thought of dropping him.

Since he had made it clear he was in his last season with Aberdeen, it was imperative that I try to sell him to an English club. If he went abroad, the so-called 'multiplier system' in force at the time would restrict our fee. For a player moving outside Britain, the maximum that could be charged was a sum produced by multiplying his annual wage by a figure governed by the man's age at the time of the transfer. Thus it was ten times salary for somebody of twenty-one or under and then on a sliding scale which, if I remember correctly, would have entitled us to ask for seven times Gordon's wages. That would have been less than a quarter of the £800,000 valuation I had placed on Strachan, who was twenty-six. I was therefore keen to develop the interest shown by Arsenal and Manchester United. My price seemed to discourage United but Arsenal gave the impression they were poised to make a deal until, having checked his medical records, they informed me they were withdrawing because they were unhappy with reports about his pelvic area. Lazio made vague inquiries and Cologne came forward with an offer we could not take seriously; by the end of the season we were surprised and worried by the lack of interest in Gordon from England. There was a real danger that we would be short-changed by a transfer to the Continent. We had heard so many rumours that I had to ask him outright if he had signed any agreement with a foreign club. He strongly denied that he had, so I felt free to encourage potential buyers in the south. After all, the little man had been a brilliant player for Aberdeen and it wasn't as if we were trying to sell somebody a pup. I phoned Ron Atkinson at Manchester United, pointed out that it would suit both of us to do business before a foreign club intervened, and said that in the circumstances we were ready to lower our asking price to £500,000. Later that day Ron agreed to the fee and I gave him phone numbers for Strachan and for his accountant, Alan Gordon, in Edinburgh. Next day Alan Gordon called to tell me there was a problem.

'What is it, Alan?' The pause was long.

'He has signed a pre-contract with Cologne.'

You get used to surprises in football but this was a belter. I was so stunned I couldn't even lose my temper. Though I always felt there was a cunning streak in Strachan, I had never imagined that he could pull such a stroke on me, not after everything I had done for him, particularly in my early days at Aberdeen when he was in the reserve team and most people at Pittodrie had given up on him. The revelation of his dealings with Cologne necessitated lengthy consultations between Aberdeen, Manchester United and the SFA and it was decided that the move to Old Trafford should go ahead on the assumption (which proved sound) that the Germans wouldn't regard it as worthwhile to make trouble. In the week he joined United, Gordon apologised to me for his behaviour and I accepted. I rationalised it as an indication of inexperience and possibly insecurity but still felt he should have trusted me as he knew I was striving to convince all and sundry about his worth to any team in England. I accompanied him to Old Trafford to complete the formalities and watching him sign made me proud of him and also a bit proud of myself for contributing substantially to his development into an established international player. Yes, we had had our disagreements but that was all in the past. 'I don't think he would ever let me down again,' I told myself. I was always an optimist.

While the Strachan saga was unfolding, we had progressed into the semi-finals of the Scottish Cup and European Cup Winners' Cup and were clear at the top of the League. The Scottish Cup assignment pitched Archie Knox and me, formerly such staunch allies, into direct opposition. He had resigned as my assistant at Pittodrie in December 1983 to become manager of Dundee, who had abruptly sacked Donald Mackay. Archie's departure was something I expected as I had sensed a restlessness in him and knew he was drawn by the challenge of revitalising the proud traditions of the Tayside club. If anybody could do so, it was most definitely the Knox man. But we put his aspirations on hold, beating Dundee comfortably by 2–0 to qualify for a third successive appearance in the Cup final.

Our quiet conviction that we could retain the European Cup Winners' Cup was shaken when we played disappointingly in the first leg of our semi-final with Porto in Portugal. There was a conspicuously lacklustre performance from Strachan and we were fortunate to lose by a single goal. We went down by the same margin in the second leg on a night of almost eerie anti-climax in Aberdeen. The fog that descended on Pittodrie seemed to dampen our support and neither they nor the team could raise themselves. It was one of only two losses suffered at home in European competition during my tenure at Aberdeen.

We settled the league race at Tynecastle with a goal by Stewart McKimmie, a quick and aggressive left-back I had signed from Hearts before Christmas, and that set us up nicely for a Cup final with Celtic. Our challenge was eventful even before we reached Hampden. Three days prior to the game, Jim Leighton was cutting his grass with an electric mower and when he stopped to clean the blades his daughter pressed the starter button and almost took his fingers off. There was also a road accident that was to affect Doug Rougvie's form but he kept it to himself until after the Cup had been won. Leighton's hand needed quite a number of stitches, and a special strapping fitted by our physio on the Saturday morning obviously did not prevent Jim from suffering severe discomfort. His sterling display epitomised the grit and courage that were never in question with Jim Leighton. The match itself was marred by the controversial ordering-off of Celtic's Roy Aitken after he brought down Mark McGhee when he was clean through. We were leading 1–0 from an Eric Black goal but, as often happens, the ten men rallied defiantly and gave us a terrible fright. The end of the ninety minutes could not come soon enough for me, but Paul McStay equalised for Celtic with four minutes remaining. The introduction of Doug Bell in extra time swung the game our way. At last we produced something like our genuine form and the winning goal came when Bell had a fine run and a shot which hit the inside of a post. The rebound was picked up by Strachan, who crossed for McGhee to score the winner and his last goal for Aberdeen.

That season was historic – it was the first time a club outside the Old Firm had completed the League and Cup double in Scotland. It also signalled the fragmenting of an excellent football team whose players had grown up together and were almost like a family. Gordon Strachan's move to Manchester United was followed by the transfer of Mark McGhee to Hamburg for £300,000. Both were influential players but I feared the loss of McGhee more, simply because Strachan's preoccupation with leaving had made him a ghost of his true self for most of the season. In contrast, although McGhee knew he was going, he had continued to work ardently for the team and had been a huge asset through to the last minute of his service. A totally honest player with splendid balance, strength and running power, Mark was not a natural finisher and yet managed to score over a hundred goals for us. He would leave a massive hole.

The third player on the way out, Doug Rougvie, who had been bought by Chelsea, would also be missed by us. But perhaps not as much as he would miss Aberdeen. In my opinion there are some players who are tailor-made for certain clubs and who are diminished by going anywhere else. Tommy Gemmell was a giant for Jock Stein's Celtic but looked ordinary at Nottingham Forest. I suspected that Rougvie would struggle at Chelsea. Undoubtedly Aberdeen would have been wise to accede to the requests for more money presented by Rougvie and McGhee but the Gothenburg success and its consequences had not fully registered with the club. We were, in a way, ill-prepared for the sudden elevation and the way the rising profile of the players had altered their earning capacity. Nevertheless, it was silly of Rougvie to leave. He was a cult hero with the fans and could have ended up with a great testimonial. I appreciated the valuable service he had given me, although it is hard to exaggerate how infuriating he could be. Once I returned home from holiday to find the *Aberdeen Evening Express* carrying a front-page photograph of Rougvie on a motorbike under the headline: 'Doug signs up for the T.T. races'. I was flabbergasted to learn that he fancied himself as a daredevil. A quote in the final paragraph of the story summed up his naivety: 'I don't know what the manager will think but I am looking forward to seeing him tomorrow.' Really? There was much hilarity among his team-mates next morning when he turned up in full leathers and helmet. But he discovered how unamused I was when I summoned him to my office and told him: 'I'm putting you on the transfer list until you get rid of that bike.' Can you believe that he actually looked startled and asked why I objected to the machine?

'Why?' I shouted. 'Why? If you think I'm going to sit in my house worrying about you speeding through Aberdeen on a motorbike you have another think coming. Incidentally, do you have insurance for that contraption?' It turned out he had a cover note and my warnings about the likely cost of insurance had a sobering effect. Within a week he had replaced the motorbike with a bicycle but that brought its own disaster. On the Thursday before that 1984 Scottish Cup final with Celtic he was knocked off his bicycle by a lorry and had to be taken to hospital. Typically, he told neither me nor our physio about the accident. No wonder he had a nightmare of a game and had to be substituted.

Collecting trophies is marvellous but I always feel a special tingle when there is a chance to make a little bit of history. Aberdeen had another opportunity to do that in the 1984–85 season. No club, not even Rangers or Celtic, had ever won the Scottish Cup four years in a row but in the spring of 1985 we should have had the record at our mercy when we qualified for a semi-final tie with Dundee United. Again, however, we showed the familiar tendency to stumble when opposing United in a knock-out competition, losing 2–1 after a replay. It was not simple disappointment that made our dressing-room resemble a morgue afterwards. Our players knew they should have won. I am sure the result would have been different if one of the main elements in the reconstruction of the team, Frank McDougall, had not been denied to us in the semi-final because of injury.

Frank was the latest proof of how much Aberdeen had benefited from my awareness of the bargains that were available at the club I had formerly managed, St Mirren. In the previous season I had paid £70,000 to bring Billy Stark (Baldy Lindsay's favourite discovery) from Love Street as long-term insurance against the impending departure of Gordon Strachan, and Billy was more than justifying my confidence in him. My other acquisitions from St Mirren – Peter Weir, Doug Bell and Steve Cowan – had been successful, so when I required a goalscoring centre-forward it was natural that I should return to the seam that had yielded so much. In the gossip of the game, McDougall had been branded an unreliable character and many suggested I was buying nothing but trouble in paying £100,000 for him. But my brother Martin, who was assistant to the St Mirren manager, Alex Miller, provided reassurance. Martin offered glowing praise of Frank's abilities and added that his behaviour was not a serious problem. All he needed was firm handling. I thought I could guarantee that small item, so I went ahead with a deal I came to regard as one of the best pieces of business I ever did. From the moment of his arrival until his career was prematurely ended by a spinal injury, shortly before I left Aberdeen, Frank was a magnificent asset to me. His glorious consistency as a finisher was crucial to the winning of our third championship. In two runs of victories we had, one of eight matches and the other of seven, he scored in every game. Of course, he had to be watched off the field. I found that basically he was too obliging to fairweather friends and from time to time I had to bring him to book. 'I'll show this bastard,' was his usual response, and the more he showed me the better I liked it. These days he lives in Clitheroe, near Manchester, and we often have a laugh about our skirmishes.

With the McDougall fee and the £70,000 paid to Clyde for their left-back, Tommy McQueen, a stylish footballer with a nice left foot and excellent stamina, we had an outlay of £170,000 to set against more than £1 million received for Strachan, McGhee and Rougvie. Old Dick Donald was ecstatic. I was less so after an abortive attempt to make an impact on the European Cup. The first-round dismissal (by Dynamo Berlin in a penalty shoot-out) was bad enough but when we were done in at the same stage of the League Cup by Airdrie, managed by my old boss, Ally MacLeod, embarrassment was severe. Then there was that sickening loss to Dundee United in the Scottish Cup semi-final. It was a relief when our young players reversed this trend in sudden-death tournaments by taking the inaugural Scottish Youth Cup with a thrilling comeback against Celtic. As the lads arrived in the dressing-room after their 5–3 win, every first-team player was there to congratulate them. It was a moving reminder of the family feeling at the club. When those first-team men had a success it was an outstanding one. They captured the championship with a massive total of 59 points from a possible 72, winning twenty-seven matches and losing only four during the league campaign.

The death of Jock Stein in September 1985 overshadowed everything else that was happening in Scottish football that year. Jock was a true working-class hero and the whole country was in mourning. My association with Jock is described elsewhere. Had I devoted a whole book to it, I would not have overstated its importance to me. On the following Saturday, Aberdeen played a league match at Celtic Park, where Stein had made himself a football immortal. I don't know whether that emotional week was having a cumulative effect on me but I felt a real heaviness in my chest on the Saturday and had to get the Celtic doctor to examine me. Dr Fitzsimmons passed me fit, advising me to ease up for a little while. The game was easily forgotten, apart from the heartfelt solemnity of the minute's silence.

For Aberdeen, it was time to call a halt to our repeated failures in the League Cup. It had been irritating to find that trophy so elusive and when we laid hands on it in the 1985–86 season it was satisfying to do so with the unprecedented feat of going through every round without losing a goal. My appetite for history-making persuaded me to plan specifically for a clean sheet against Hibs in the final by playing three central defenders. Hibs' main threat came from Gordon Durie and our old warrior, Steve Cowan, who had been transferred to Easter Road, and they were thoroughly contained by McLeish and Neale Cooper. With Miller tidying up the loose ends and springing many of our attacking thrusts, we had no trouble in winning 3–0. Willie, by then, was the outstanding player in Scotland, with a presence matching that of the great captains of the recent past, McNeill of Celtic and Greig of Rangers. Like them, he had developed the ability to dominate not only the game but the referee. The only criticism outsiders levelled at Willie was that he introduced the principle of the fourth official long before governing bodies ever thought of it.

After we had the League Cup in the cabinet, our spirits were high. We were sitting second in the League, were once again drawing a bead on the Scottish Cup and could look forward to a

European Cup quarter-final. You might say it was business as usual at Pittodrie. What made the circumstances unusual for me was that, after Jock Stein's death, I had agreed to take on the management of the Scotland team through to the World Cup finals (another episode covered elsewhere) and combining the two jobs proved more difficult than I had anticipated. Completing qualification for the Mexico finals involved going out to Melbourne and securing a result against Australia and that kind of absence on international duty deepened my doubts about my choice of Willie Garner to succeed Archie Knox as my assistant at the club. Willie, who had been Aberdeen's centre-half, was a lovely lad and possessed good qualities, particularly his knowledge of the game. But he was young and was, at that stage, far too easy-going to suit my ideas about management. I like the hungry ones who are always on the go. In the eyes of the older players, Willie was still one of them and he found it hard to command the necessary respect. If I had acted sooner to replace him with a more authoritative assistant, my international commitments would have done less to undermine Aberdeen's bid for a treble of championships.

Our cause wasn't helped by the rumours circulating about the probable defection of Eric Black, whose contract was due to expire at the end of the season. He had become evasive and secretive but as early as January I had reliable information suggesting that he was making clandestine trips to the Continent to talk to other clubs. I was inclined to accept that he would be leaving and, apart from trying to generate interest in England to combat the penalties of the multiplier system, I focused my mind on more positive issues, like the European Cup. With the attacking quality of gifted footballers like Stark, McMaster, Weir and Jim Bett to complement the defensive solidity built around Miller and McLeish, I was confident we could do well in the tournament that season. Bett's introspective personality was a handicap but he was a major talent. Blessed with a wonderful awareness of space, whether passing into it or running off the ball, he rarely cost the team possession. As for Weir, I always believed that when he was on

song Aberdeen were a great side. His powerful, penetrative running along the left had flourished in the company of Strachan and
now that little Gordon was gone I was looking for maturity from
Peter, waiting for him to assume an influence befitting his abilities.
But there seemed to be self-doubt lurking in him and when expectations were highest he would go into his shell. I hoped the European stage would stir him, as it had done in the Cup Winners'
Cup final of 1983 in Gothenburg.

As it happened our opponents in the European Cup quarter-
final of 1986 were the team carrying the pride of that Swedish
city and my first disappointment with the occasion was the meagre
attendance of 17,000 at Pittodrie on that March evening. It
crossed my mind that perhaps the Aberdeen supporters were
spoiled and took success for granted, and the suspicion planted
seeds of restlessness in me. The game was tremendously exciting.
Instead of being ahead by the hatful of goals our chances justified,
we were leading 2–1 with a minute to go when, uncharacteristi-
cally, Willie Miller made a charge upfield and was dispossessed
far out of position. The ball was immediately dispatched through
the middle for Gothenburg's flying machine, Johnny Ekstrom, to
equalise with the last kick of the match. Gothenburg cannily
ensured that the return leg was a non-event, achieving the 0–0
draw that exploited the away-goals rule and dumped us out of
the Cup. That result did nothing to lessen the discontent that
had begun to take root when I surveyed the crowd of 17,000 at
our own ground a fortnight before.

Back in 1984 I had resisted a second approach from Rangers.
It was made by John Paton, a director who subsequently became
chairman, and when I sought the advice of my former mentor,
Scot Symon, he said he would be uneasy about any overtures that
did not directly involve Willie Waddell. The truth is that I was
already reluctant to entertain exposing my family to the risk of a
recurrence of the bigotry I had encountered at Ibrox in my playing
days. Even without Scot Symon's words of caution, Cathy's
religion would probably have been enough in itself to convince
me that returning to Rangers was not a good idea. In addition to

the approaches from Ibrox, during my time at Aberdeen I had turned down serious offers of the manager's job at Arsenal, Tottenham Hotspur and Wolverhampton Wanderers. Now, however, my thoughts were dwelling increasingly on a change of some kind. I was finding that the afternoons at Pittodrie were becoming a bit of a drag. The club was so well run that the challenge for me had diminished and I can honestly say that I was feeling the need for the painful stimulation of again having to build a successful team. A smooth 3–0 victory over Hibs in a Scottish Cup semi-final, which took Aberdeen into their fourth final in five years, was small comfort and at one of my daily meetings with Dick Donald I told him I was thinking of moving on at the end of the season. He shook me slightly when he said categorically that there was only one job I should consider preferable to the one I held at Aberdeen. Asked to name the club, he said, 'Manchester United. If you really want a challenge, that is the biggest in football.' It was a remarkable declaration to hear at that stage of my life and somehow it gave me a lift.

That was not at all the effect of a meeting I had in my office with Eric Black a fortnight before we were scheduled to face Hearts in the Scottish Cup final. He had come to tell me he had signed for Metz in France. My reaction was naturally one of anger. I had looked after him since he was thirteen years of age. Yet rather than show trust by talking to me, he had plotted in secret to quit Aberdeen. I didn't think I or the club deserved such treatment. But the cloak-and-dagger behaviour had extended even to the fellow players who knew him best. If Eric imagined that by telling me two weeks before the Cup final he was setting up a grand exit, he had a rude awakening. After training that day, I called him in to tell him there was no need for him to come back. So his career with us came to a sad end but the manner of the parting could not detract from the value of the service he gave to Aberdeen. It was remarkable. He scored important goals in all the four finals he played for us, including the night of nights in Gothenburg. In addition to good pace and control, he profited from an extraordinary ability to hang in the air, as if levitating, before striking deadly headers. But for an unfortunate back problem, he would have gone on to play a lot of games for his country.

Our task in the Scottish Cup final was made easier by the morale-sapping blow inflicted on our opponents when they were undeservedly deprived of the championship by losing 2–0 to Dundee on the last day of the league season. That result allowed Celtic to swoop on the title and I felt sincere sympathy for the Hearts manager, Alex McDonald, and his assistant, Sandy Jardine. Their team's chances of shaking off the gloom in the final were wrecked when they started brightly and hit the bar, only to find John Hewitt putting us ahead from the immediate counter-attack. By the end of the game, Hearts were disheartened and ragged and could have lost by a wider margin than the 3–0 scoreline.

On the Monday, Cathy and I went to visit Chris Anderson, Aberdeen's deputy chairman, who was dying of motor neurone disease. We took the trophy to his home and Chris became really emotional. It was heartbreaking to see how he had been ravaged by that dreadful wasting disease. I never saw Chris alive again after that visit. He died while I was with the Scotland team in Santa Fe, New Mexico, preparing for the 1986 World Cup. He was a gentleman and his unfailingly progressive thinking brought huge benefits to the club. His modern attitudes balanced perfectly the more traditional approach of Dick Donald and I realised how lucky I had been to serve under two such splendid men.

On my return from the World Cup finals in Mexico, I decided that I could not continue with Willie Garner as my assistant. He was too young for the responsibility attached to the job. I am glad that Willie has not harboured any grudge towards me over the action I had to take. Archie Knox was keen to come back and that was, of course, the ideal solution for me. Since Archie had recently been in the manager's chair at Dundee, it was worth taking care about the classification of his position at Pittodrie. I advised that we call him joint manager and that was agreed.

If I had remembered the story of Guy Fawkes, I might have known that the fifth of November was not a good day for keeping secrets. It was on that date in 1986 that I tried to protect the privacy of my meeting with the chairman and three directors of Manchester United by taking them to the home of Cathy's sister in Bishopbriggs, on the outskirts of Glasgow. But going unnoticed is not easy if you are in the company of one of the most famous figures in sport. A neighbour recognised Bobby Charlton the moment he arrived in Bridget's driveway. Fortunately, however, we did escape the attention of the media and the most momentous discussions of my career remained confidential.

There have been so many fanciful versions of when and how Manchester United first approached me that it is probably time I put the record straight. If I avoided specifics in the past it was out of consideration for the feelings of other people, not least Dick Donald. Ron Atkinson, my predecessor at Old Trafford, insists in his autobiography that it was Bobby Charlton who offered me the job during the 1986 World Cup. That is not true. Although Bobby did speak to me at the side of the pitch before Scotland's fiasco of a game with Uruguay, the furthest he went was to ask that if ever I decided to move to England I should let him know. I don't think that can be considered an offer and it did not send any signals to me that I was bound for United. Apart from that brief contact with Bobby, there was nothing but rumour to link me with Old Trafford before 5 November.

In the phone calls he made to me almost weekly, Gordon Strachan kept telling me the word in Manchester was that I would be the next manager. There was not the merest hint of an official approach to support these stories and I was left musing on some of Gordon's comments on how the great club was being run. He cited all sorts of problems with the team, particularly the drinking that was going on among the players and the alleged indifference of Big Ron to its damaging effects. The training, Gordon suggested, was a shambles, with nothing done until Ron had a session on his sunbed as a preliminary to joining in a small-sided practice game.

When the approach did come it was a surprise. Admittedly, I realised that Ron would be under pressure when I read on teletext on the night of 4 November that Southampton had beaten Manchester United 4–1 at the Dell. United were lying second-bottom of the English First Division and that thrashing would emphasise how far they had sunk. But I was hardly likely to have those events in my mind when I was buzzed in my office about two o'clock the following day and asked if I would take a call from Alan Gordon, Gordon Strachan's accountant. I had always got on well with Alan and lifted the receiver immediately with the kind of greeting he would expect: 'How are you doing, you ugly bugger?' It wasn't Alan's voice that came back from the other end of the line but an exaggerated impersonation of a Scottish accent. I discovered later that the speaker was Mike Edelson, the United director. He asked me to hold on, and when somebody else spoke it was Martin Edwards. He gave me his number, so that I could ring him back and thus be assured of the authenticity of the call. I could scarcely contain myself as I dialled the Manchester number. Would I be interested in the job at Manchester United? Yes, I told him without hesitation. Could we meet that night in Scotland, at a place safe from prying eyes? I said I would ring him back in an hour.

My next move was to inform Archie Knox of developments. We had an agreement that if I joined a club in England he would come as my assistant. Then it was home to do the hard part – tell Cathy. She was devastated, completely against the idea of leaving Aberdeen, a city she had grown to love. Our boys had grown up there and their lifestyle was as close to perfect as they could ever hope to find. But Cathy knew what the Manchester United offer meant to me and could guess the outcome of the meeting I now arranged with Martin Edwards's party for 7 p.m. at the motorway service station at Hamilton in Lanarkshire. My other call at that juncture was to Jim Rodger, my old journalist ally, to check whether there was any speculation in England and to seek advice on how I should handle the media if I took the job.

Bang on time at 7 p.m., Martin Edwards arrived in the services car park and got into my car while his companions, Bobby Charlton, Mike Edelson and Maurice Watkins, the United director who is also the club's legal adviser, used Martin's to follow us to Cathy's sister's house in Bishopbriggs. Our meeting there covered the main subjects of concern: players, staff, the money available for transfers, which – surprisingly enough – was nil, although Martin did say he could raise some if I was desperate. The salary was disappointing. I had earned more that year at Aberdeen, where I had a healthy bonus arrangement. I mentioned the difficulties involved in organising a quick sale of my house and asked Manchester United to buy it from me but that proposal met with a blank. There was the other problem of a £40,000 loan I had been given by Aberdeen, and which I thought United might undertake to clear, but again there was a refusal and I was told I should talk to Aberdeen about it. From all of this it will be seen that financial inducements had nothing to do with my enthusiasm for going to Old Trafford. To a great extent I was a captive candidate, and happy to be so. The Manchester United job was a dream opportunity to fulfil the grand ambitions I had nursed since entering management and I eagerly accepted the terms presented to me. Formalities were concluded the next day when Martin Edwards and Maurice Watkins flew to Aberdeen to meet Dick Donald and his son Ian, who had become a key member of the Pittodrie board after the death of Chris Anderson, and a compensation figure was agreed.

In a last attempt to keep me, Dick said, 'You can have the club if you want it.' We both knew he was dealing in gesture rather than reality but a pretty wonderful gesture it was, and entirely typical of a priceless man. As a chairman, he was a colossus and nobody had to tell me that I had little chance of ever working for his like again. Dick's support for me when my father died is something I will always cherish. Professionally, too, he was a bulwark when things were not going well for me in my early period at the club. The quality of men Aberdeen had drawn together as directors was remarkable and there was never a hint of unrest from the boardroom. Dick Donald set the supportive example. After a defeat, when the press were milling around the foyer, waiting for hints of disarray, out would come Dick and he would start dancing in front of them. 'Good day, gentlemen,' he would say. 'What a great game.' He had been an outstanding performer on the ballroom floor in his youth, when a dance hall was the foundation of the business interests that extended into cinemas, bingo halls and property and made his family rich, and he was liable to waltz without warning into a display of fancy footwork. Sometimes he would make a twinkle-toed entrance to the dressing-room as the players prepared themselves for the game.

'Good-day, Mr Ferguson. How are you today?'

'Fine, Mr Chairman. How are you?'

'Fine, fine, and what's your team today?' As I recited the names, I would come to someone Dick didn't fancy and he would stop me. It was a ritual.

'You're not picking him, are you?'

'Yes I am, Mr Chairman.'

'Ah well, it's your team.' And off he would waltz out of the dressing-room, with hardly a pause.

Dick's wealth was usually well hidden behind his frugality. One day I happened to look down at his shoes and noticed that he had a black lace that was joined to a brown one and then back to a black lace again. When Cathy and I first moved to Aberdeen and were looking for carpets for our house, Dick volunteered his help.

'Come up to my warehouse,' he said expansively. 'I've got heaps of the stuff.'

Cathy did not like the idea of having her choice narrowed but she had no inkling of just how narrow it would be. All the carpets Dick showed us had a large letter C emblazoned on them. They had been made for his theatre, the Capitol. Cathy and I were glad to escape from the warehouse. Dick's mood could be accurately read from the positioning of his brown trilby hat. If in a contented frame of mind, he would place it jauntily on the side of his head. If something was bothering him, the hat was planted firmly on the back of his skull. On return journeys from Hampden, where we won all four Scottish Cup finals we contested in my time with the club, there was never much doubt about the angle. But even in his happiest mood his shrewdness (no man I ever met had more of it) did not desert him and he took mischievous pleasure in letting you know that he missed nothing. There was invariably a bit of nonsense about how much champagne we would take on the team bus to the Cup final. I would order six cases, but as we prepared to leave for Glasgow on the day before the final, the chairman would tell Ian Taggart, the club secretary, to put five cases in store and load only one on to the coach. As soon as Dick went off to change for the trip, I would reverse the ratio, hiding five cases away on the bus and putting one in store. On the way north after beating Celtic in the Cup final of 1984, the players and their wives were making good use of the generous supply of bubbly but trying to be secretive as they passed bottles around freely. Cathy and I were sitting at the front with Dick and his wife, Betty. As the celebrations quietly gathered momentum behind us, Dick leaned over to me.

'Mr Ferguson,' he said.

'Yes, Mr Chairman?'

'How many cups were we playing for today?'

— 14 —
DRINKING TO FAILURE

I WAS nervous and I had drink on my mind but it wasn't because I was entertaining any crazy idea of bracing myself with something out of a bottle. As I travelled towards my first working day at Manchester United, my thoughts on alcohol were all about the damage it could do. Gordon Strachan's accounts of excessive drinking by some United players had been confirmed by the chairman, Martin Edwards, and I realised the problem was so serious that it had to be confronted without delay. The prospect of starting off with a showdown hardly eased the edginess I was feeling. On my first day at St Mirren and at Aberdeen, there had been no misgivings, only an eagerness to get started and show what I could do. My belief in my abilities had not diminished but this time there was an anxiety about how I would be received. I had never managed in England and now here I was taking charge of the biggest club to be found there, or anywhere else. There was no guarantee that I would be given the most positive welcome by all the established international players who were waiting for me, especially as several of them were about to be clearly informed that I didn't think much of bending the elbow as a form of exercise.

For longer than anybody cares to remember, boozing has been a blight on the discipline of British footballers. Maybe in earlier generations the drinking culture carried over from the working-class origins of the players. Most of them came from families where many of the men took the view that if they put in a hard shift in a factory or a coalmine they were entitled to relax with a few pints. Some footballers seem determined to cling to that shift-worker's mentality, even to the extent of persuading themselves it is all right to go straight from the training ground to a bar. Also prevalent is the notion that Saturday night is the end of the working week and therefore a good time to get wrecked. The obvious truth that a professional athlete has no right to take liberties with his physical condition at any time is not always readily accepted within the game in this country. British players who have gone to continental clubs have often been jolted by the discovery that their socialising ways are frowned upon not only by the management but by their team-mates, who resent having to rely on somebody whose performance might be impaired as a result of escapades in the small hours. Our clubs and their managers have frequently shown a weak-kneed reluctance to deal with the menace of boozing. When I arrived at United, I was astonished to find that there was a club rule forbidding players to drink alcohol 'less than two days before a game'. I replaced that feeble prohibition instantly with a rule that made it an offence for any player to drink while he was in training. Of course, I knew there was no hope that the ban would be observed but at least the new wording was a declaration of my attitude, whereas the previous version almost suggested that there were times when it was permissible to go on the tiles. Yet even the latitude granted by that old rule wasn't sufficient for some of the players I inherited.

My appointment was formalised on a Thursday in Aberdeen, and in Manchester that very night, on the eve of my first meeting with them and less than forty-eight hours before they were due to play an away match at Oxford, certain members of the squad were doing some serious drinking. Apparently Ron Atkinson, as outgoing manager, had thrown a farewell party. I gather that Big Ron did not invite all the players but a few of those who were excluded seem to have had no difficulty in generating a celebratory spirit among themselves. I don't think Ron's timing was very good, considering that there was a game to be played on the Saturday. He knew that the group of footballers who worked under him contained a number who were unlikely to limit themselves to a couple of toasts. When I heard about these activities (and there is always someone ready to pass on information to the manager of Manchester United) I could hardly bear to contemplate the implication that the players involved did not care a monkey's about the fact that I was arriving as their boss next morning.

Unaware of the insult on that Friday of my first meeting with them, I contented myself with the briefest of introductory speeches. There was no trumpeting of my ambitions. The main point I made once they were assembled in the gym at the Cliff training ground was that I hoped they regretted the departure of Ron Atkinson, since that would show they had a proper commitment to the man who was managing them. If they did, we would have a chance. They must have thought I had very little to say for myself and if they suspected that it was all a bit nerve-racking for me they were right. They encountered a different Ferguson when they were summoned to the gym again at the beginning of the following week, after I had sat through a 2–0 defeat at Oxford and had learned about the boozing on the previous Thursday. I made it plain that I meant to put an end to Manchester United's reputation of being almost as much of a social club as a football club. I told them that they would have to change their ways because I certainly wasn't going to change mine. The confrontational approach raised a few eyebrows but that didn't bother me. To hell with soft-shoeing around such a major issue. I had been depressed by the poor standard of fitness United revealed at Oxford and, while I accepted that the introduction of a far tougher regime of endurance training would have to be gradual, I was in no mood to be similarly patient about the destructive drinking habits. Of course, tackling the problem was one thing, eradicating it was quite another. That would take time, as would attending to all the other areas of concern I had identified within two or three weeks of moving in at United.

In addition to a lack of fitness, our squad suffered from having too many players who were physical lightweights, who simply did not have the bodily strength to compete forcefully throughout the long battle for a League title. Too many of those who might have been strong presences on the park were forever on the treatment table. We could hardly have had more casualties if the opposition had been firing guns at us. Another alarming weakness was the way the playing staff had been allowed to age without sufficient care being taken to ensure that younger replacements of the right quality were ready to stake claims for regular places in the first team. That worry was compounded by the glaring inadequacies of the scouting system and the absence of a comprehensive and carefully structured youth policy. My aim in management has always been to lay foundations that will make a club successful for years, or even decades. Flash-in-the-pan achievements, such as some good runs in cup competitions, with perhaps the odd winning appearance in a final, could never satisfy me. They are exciting and can do wonders for morale but the true indication of worth is to be in contention for the championship season after season. When I joined United on 6 November 1986, they had gone nineteen years without a title and nobody had to tell me that if I did not end that drought I would be a failure. Putting them in a position to challenge consistently would, I knew, be a long haul. I would have to build from the bottom up, rectifying the flaws I had recognised and spreading my influence and self-belief through every layer of the organisation. I wanted to form a personal link with everybody around the place – not just the players, the coaches and the backroom staff but the office workers, the cooks and servers in the canteen and the laundry ladies. All had to believe that they were part of the club and that a resurgence was coming. But unless the rebuilding was accompanied by a measure of success, there was bound to be doubt about whether I would be given enough time to fulfil my plans.

Looking back, most outsiders would say that my survival came down to a photo-finish, that if we had not beaten Nottingham Forest 1–0 at the City Ground in the third round of the FA Cup in January of 1990, I would have been doomed. Such assumptions are understandable (our league form in that season was often abysmal) but they are contradicted by what happened on the Friday prior to that Sunday Cup-tie, when Martin Edwards invited me into his office for a talk. In the days before the club grew into the corporate monster it is now, such chats with the chairman were an enjoyable feature of my routine but that one had more significance than most. 'Even if you lose, it won't cost you your job,' Martin Edwards told me. His words were comforting but only a fool would deny that, without the series of events triggered by that victory at Forest, the pressure to sack me might eventually have become irresistible. Going on to win the Cup, and then beating Barcelona in the European Cup Winners' Cup final in the following season, gave me security and provided a platform from which I could launch United towards an increasingly successful future. So it is natural for me to see the period between my appointment and that European triumph in Rotterdam as the first phase of my management at Old Trafford. Those four and a half years brought me far more lows than highs as I struggled to cope with the forbidding list of problems I mentioned earlier. A glance at where we finished in the league table in my first five seasons will show why I sometimes felt that I was taking one step forwards and two backwards. Reaching eleventh place in 1987 was tolerable, since we had been second from bottom when I took over. Being runners-up to Liverpool in 1988 represented a highly encouraging improvement, even if the nine points separating us testified to a gulf in class. But finishing eleventh in 1989 and thirteenth in 1990 was miserable and having to settle for sixth in 1991 did not reflect the standard that had given us glory on the Continent that season. Yet, as must be obvious, these bare statistics do not begin to tell the story of the tide of change that swirled through the club in those years, or of the strengthening process that would become evident when we went within a hair's breadth of the title in 1992. Much of the change was painful, never more so than when famous players had to be jettisoned or promising youngsters had their dreams shattered by injury. But before I had time to be concerned with any of that, I was experiencing the deepest possible pain of my own.

Just over a fortnight after I became manager of United, I made my daily phone call to my mother in Glasgow and got no reply. Earlier in the year she had been diagnosed as having lung cancer, so when further calls went unanswered there was cause to be worried. Soon I was being told by Sandra, my brother Martin's wife, that Mother had been taken into the Southern General Hospital. I immediately booked a flight to Glasgow and communicated the bad news to Cathy, who was staying in Aberdeen until Darren and Jason completed their schooling the following summer. Flying north, I recalled a conversation I had with Ma after first hearing from Martin that she had cancer. 'Oh, by the way,' she had said casually, 'I've stopped smoking.' Well done, Ma, I said to myself, you're just fifty years too late. My mother had smoked since she was fourteen and had now paid the price. At the hospital, my feeling of helplessness deepened when the specialist treating her told me she was not expected to live more than four or five days. Mother, I found, was a strange mixture of perkiness and resignation. It was a paralysing thought that the woman who had brought Martin and me into the world, who had been our rock throughout our lives, was preparing to leave us. If she was ready for it, we were not. I decided to stay up in Glasgow, at my brother's house, so that I could make regular visits to the hospital. My mind was filled with wistful reflections about where Ma's life had gone. She had worked nearly all her days and had devoted herself to my dad, Martin and me. People who know our family often make the mistake of seeing me as purely a mirror of my father. It is true that he passed on many attributes to me. There is no doubt I have his temper and his stubbornness and I hope I have inherited some of his intelligence. But my mother had incredible courage and determination and if those qualities have helped me to succeed, I am sure I have her to thank.

On one of my visits to the Southern General, a woman who was a close friend of my mother's asked to have time alone with her and, as I stood around out in the corridor, I became aware of just how disastrously a once-great hospital had deteriorated. It was appalling. The images of decay and neglect have remained with me and I have never ceased to curse the Tory government for vandalising the National Health Service. Margaret Thatcher's aggressive efforts to privatise health care in this country were a betrayal of a service that has been one of the proudest achievements of our society. Facilities were run down and doctors and nurses were taken for granted. In that corridor at the Southern General, I was ashamed to have my mother living out her last days in such surroundings. She deserved better and I felt for her and for the medical staff, who were absolutely wonderful.

On the Friday, three days after she had entered the hospital, Martin and I were shocked to see how far she had sunk. Her little body had shrunk to a terrible frailty and only her spirit and her faith were still strong. On Dad's death, she had returned to the Catholic religion with great commitment, first having asked my permission to do so.

'Ma, for goodness sake, you don't have to ask me that,' I told her.

'Well, I don't want to embarrass you in any way,' she said.

'Ma, that's the last thing you could ever do. I want you to go back to church. It will make you happy.' As we sat at her bedside, she told us that she was looking forward to dying so that she could rejoin our dad. She had a simple last request: 'Just have a wee greet and think of me.'

Proof that her faculties were intact came when she urged Martin and me to go on home and get a night's sleep so that we could cope with our responsibilities at games the next day. During the night the phone went in Martin's bedroom and we knew instantly what that meant. I just lay there and thought about my mother until dawn. There were no tears. There would be plenty of time for that. I just wanted to savour her in my thoughts.

Plunging back into the world of football was not easy but it had to be done. I returned to a fixture that was sure to lay bare the physical inadequacies of the 1986 Manchester United. The Wimbledon of that era, with their emphasis on aerial bombardment and the undisguised delight they took in intimidating opponents, had no trouble persuading me that trying to win a championship with my lightweight crew would be like going to war with a pop gun. It was hardly a comfort to reflect that three of our players who were equipped to compete in the toughest company were injured so often that it was a luxury to have all of them fit at the same time, and not a rarity to have none of them available. Bracketing Bryan Robson, Paul McGrath and Norman Whiteside together would be foolish. They were very different footballers and very different characters, but they did share a tendency to spend a lot of time in the physio's room. Something else they had in common, it must be said, was that none of them could ever have been mistaken for a teetotaller. There were, however, clear distinctions in the drinking department, too.

Robson's professionalism and his fierce dedication to turning in match-winning performances kept him well short of the extremes to which the other two's binges could take them. It would have been impossible for any manager to avoid thinking of Robbo as a hero. He was a miracle of commitment, a human marvel who could push himself beyond every imaginable limit on the field. Of all the players I have worked with during forty years in the game, he ranks among the three or four who impressed me most. Technically, it was the range of his skills, rather than the capacity of any one of them to take your breath away, that made him so special. He had good control, was a decisive tackler, passed the ball well and had a remarkable engine. The combination of his stamina and perceptive reading of movement enabled him, in his prime, to make sudden and deadly infiltrations from midfield into the opposition's box and score vital goals. Above all, as a competitor he had no superior. At Old Trafford he carried an aura about him and it was understandable that, when I arrived, there was a feeling around the club that winning or losing largely depended on whether or not he was playing. The notion of a one-man team has always been repellent to me. It is a nonsense that can lead only to grief. But there is no denying that on the park Robson had far more impact than any one player, however outstanding, could normally be expected to have. He was just as much Captain Marvel for us as he had been so frequently for England. Sometimes I worried that his determination to fill the role could make him too rash in his challenges for the ball. There were times when a little more weighing of the odds might have saved him from injury, but it was fruitless to try to temper the courage that was basic to the man and his game. I did not hold back when it came to demanding restraint with his drinking. Sharp words were delivered on the subject. In particular, I stressed how harmful boozing was in the period of recovery after injury. When he was fit, the masochistic zeal of his training helped to sweat the alcohol out of his system more effectively than was ever possible for the less vigorous McGrath and Whiteside. Drinking is unacceptable at any time but in spells of enforced idleness it is even more of a menace and certain to slow the process of rehabilitation. Bryan's unwillingness to give up booze altogether caused our relationship to be fraught now and again. But the occasional anxiety was a small price to pay for the magnificent service he gave me.

It was, of course, with my two wayward Irishmen that alcohol would eventually become an unmanageable problem for me. Although Norman Whiteside's drinking never struck me as being as serious as Paul McGrath's, he was a worthy companion for the big defender when it came to carousing. I was saddened as well as infuriated by the way they abused themselves, since both had the sort of talent given to only a tiny élite of footballers. When I first saw Norman on the training ground at the Cliff, I felt the excitement that is stirred by watching a player of the highest class. I knew about him as the prodigy who had been introduced to the Northern Ireland team at the age of seventeen, and had seen him play at the World Cup finals in Mexico, but I would never have appreciated how good he was without the advantage of studying him at close quarters. He had a self-assurance that was extraordinary in a twenty-one-year-old. The excellence of his technique gave him easy mastery of the ball and he had the gift of making time for himself that is the stamp of quality. No matter how fast the game was or how much pressure was on him, he was an island of composure, looking up and unhurriedly making his decisions. He very rarely surrendered possession and he measured the angle and the weight of his passes so well that the receiver never had to fight the ball. His eyes were as cold as steel and he had a temperament to match. There was no hint of viciousness in him off the field but when he was out there he could be hard enough to make you shudder. Having seen how much Whiteside had to offer, I set out to discover why he had so many injuries. As a player, he was close to the genius category and if there was anything more we could do to get him on the field regularly, I wanted it done. According to Norman, his tale of woe began when, around the age of fifteen, a physiotherapist gave him treatment that went horribly wrong and left him with permanent trouble in his hips and other joints. Later he was to have a dozen operations, and the most serious were probably on his knees, but he blames that course of manipulation for the lack of pace in adulthood that was his one noticeable deficiency. When I heard that he had been a sprint champion at school, I began to picture the player that real quickness would have made him. There was no difficulty about doing so, no need for silly guessing games, because the addition of pace would have meant that Norman had absolutely everything. I honestly believe he would have been world-class, one of the finest players we have seen. It was natural to wonder if the pain of thinking about what might have been had something to do with the contempt for his career that was implied by his consumption of booze. He was intelligent and would hold his hand up when called to account over his drinking. My rebukes did little good but at least in our talks I felt I was communicating with Norman.

That was never true with Paul McGrath. I found him unreachable. Time and again I would have him in my office, attempting to bring home to him the damage that alcohol was doing to his life. He would sit there and just nod in agreement, then walk out of the door and carry on as before, seemingly indifferent to the threat his behaviour posed to a career already jeopardised by chronic knee problems. The methods that had served me so well over the years in dealing with the serious personal difficulties of players achieved nothing with him. But I went on trying, for my sake as well as his. I knew that a fit McGrath who had his

head straight would be a huge asset to Manchester United. He
was an exceptionally skilful and stylish defender, with marvellous
innate athleticism, a man whose abilities stood comparison with
those of any central defender in the game. But his dishevelled
lifestyle had taken its toll. In the match that was my first as United
manager, that 2–0 defeat at Oxford, I had been advised to play
him in midfield but he did not have the stamina for the job. He
was so knackered that I had to take him off. Centre-half was the
right position for him and, if he had given himself a chance, he
could have flourished there, especially after he was provided with
a stalwart partner when we secured Steve Bruce from Norwich
City in December 1987, for what proved to be the bargain price
of £800,000. McGrath, however, continued to give abstinence a
wide berth. Admitting that his troubles were too much for me, I
enlisted the assistance of people I thought might be more persuasive. Sir Matt Busby talked to Paul but even the warmth and
wisdom of that great man had no effect. Francis McHugh, our
club doctor, had a try and so did the parish priest, and I had
several conversations with Paul's wife. It was all wasted effort.
The big man went lurching on as if we had never spoken to him.
Maybe I should have sought professional psychiatric help for
Paul. At times I felt I could almost do with some myself as I
struggled to cope with the aftermath of the latest drinking marathon. The worst binges usually occurred when McGrath and
Whiteside took to the bars as a double-act. As swallowers, they
could have been backed at even money against W.C. Fields and
Rab C. Nesbitt. Once when McGrath hurt himself quite badly
by crashing his car into somebody's garden in Hale after a session
in the nearby Four Seasons Hotel, my concern about his injuries
was compounded by fears of what he might get up to when his
release from hospital reunited him with his amigo, Whiteside, who
was recovering from Achilles tendon damage. The less active they
were professionally, the more hectic they tended to be socially. It
was a pattern which made me suspect that we were approaching
a painful parting.

The reckoning drew nearer in January 1989 when the two

Irishmen broke all their own records for irresponsibility during the week of preparation for a third-round FA Cup-tie at Old Trafford against Queens Park Rangers. I first became aware that they were heading for an epic bender on the Tuesday afternoon, when I started receiving calls from disillusioned supporters who reported that the pair were moving from pub to pub in the Cheshire area. I was able to chart their erratic course throughout the day. At training on the Wednesday morning I read the Riot Act and fined them the maximum allowed under the ludicrous agreement with the Professional Footballers' Association that restricts a manager's powers of punishment in such cases. Considering the wages most top league players were on, the kind of offences committed by Norman and Paul warranted far more stringent deterrents. They showed how much the fines bothered them by again hitting the drink in a big way on the Wednesday evening. Next morning on the training pitch, McGrath could hardly jog properly. He was obviously the worse for wear and I had to send him off the field. It was truly shocking to realise that these men had so little respect for themselves or the club that they were ready to scorn every boundary of responsible conduct. The antics had immediate practical consequences, since my squad for the Cup-tie had already been alarmingly depleted and now my hopes of including McGrath in the team were evaporating. But I was so badly off for fit players that I had to keep him on the periphery of the squad. Then, on the Friday evening, Granada screened an interview with Paul and Norman in which both were on Planet Zigzag. It was disgusting, and I have to say that Granada were out of order in going ahead with the interview. They must have known, as their audience certainly did, that the two players were seriously affected by booze. Just when it seemed that the handicaps we were carrying into the QPR match could not get any worse, they did. At lunchtime on Saturday the group of players available to me shrank even further as one of them dropped out with flu. I was down to thirteen men and then McGrath put the final insulting touch to his disgraceful week by reporting unfit to the club physio, Jimmy McGregor. I was furious. I had sacrificed my principles by even thinking about him, let alone including him in the squad, so I suppose I asked for the kick in the teeth. But who could have foreseen that McGrath's disdain for the needs of the club would stretch to withdrawing a couple of hours before kick-off? His conscience should have made him strive to be involved. Instead, yet again, he had let me and his team-mates down. The inescapable conclusion was that neither he nor Whiteside had a future at Old Trafford.

Fittingly, McGrath's transfer to Aston Villa for £400,000 in the first week of the following August came only two days after Whiteside went to Everton for roughly twice that figure. I wished both of them well and hoped that separation and a change of environment would stimulate them to rededicate themselves to their careers. In spite of everything, I had retained a soft spot for Norman and I was delighted when his initial season with Everton brought him thirteen goals. But soon afterwards the injuries he had been battling for so long finally overwhelmed him and one of the most talented footballers I have known was forced into retirement in his mid-twenties.

Fortunately, Paul's association with Aston Villa was a longer, happier story. Graham Taylor, his new manager, deserves credit for helping McGrath to pull himself together so successfully that he shone over a number of seasons not only for Villa but for Jack Charlton's Republic of Ireland team. Apparently, Graham gave him a minder to reduce the risk of backsliding and cosseted his ravaged legs by confining his training exertions to gymnasium work. Such easing of the load would have been hard to sustain at United, where every match has the intensity of a Cup-tie and players must be rigorously trained to meet extreme physical demands. The improvement in McGrath's performance record after he went to the Midlands must, however, have had less to do with his limbs than with his head. He was reluctant to leave United and the jolt of having to move may have prompted some private owning up about the dangers of his downward spiral, and caused him to re-examine his priorities. I am convinced the changed McGrath we saw at Villa would not have materialised at

Old Trafford, where he hid in a cocoon of unreality, surrounding himself with people who encouraged him to retreat to his drinking hideaways. It was, presumably, his attachment to that make-believe world that was the main reason for his keenness to stay at United but I knew that he and we would suffer if he did. I always sensed a fragility about the man and it was easy to feel sorry for him as a victim of his own nature. I did not for a moment begrudge him the success he enjoyed after he left me. Most of the acrimony was on his side, as he demonstrated by blasting me in the *News of the World*.

I may have been at fault in tolerating his outrages as long as I did. What he accomplished at Villa never evoked the slightest regret in me about letting him go. Transferring him made sense, as did the decision to sell Gordon Strachan four months earlier, in March 1989. Strachan rediscovered excellent form at Leeds but I am sure that in his case, too, such a rejuvenation would not have occurred if he had remained with Manchester United, where he had given too many indications that his enthusiasm for our cause had dwindled irretrievably.

I had first managed Gordon in 1978 and we had been together through some glorious years with Aberdeen. He had gone to Old Trafford in 1984 and it was disappointing when I went there a couple of years later to come upon a player who bore scant resemblance to the man I remembered at Pittodrie. On the field there was little evidence of the zest and cocky assurance that characterised his play in Scotland. Verbally, he was as assertive as ever, with an acid wit that was often used in criticism of his team-mates. But in matches he appeared to be diminished by living in the shadow of the likes of Robson, Whiteside and McGrath. Aberdeen had been a terrific team, with no shortage of strong personalities, but he had always been able to stand out, certainly in the eyes of the press. He had drawn nourishment from his status and now he seemed to be suffering from being rather submerged at United. But I thought enough of his abilities to have no doubt that it was worth persevering with efforts to bring him back to his best. When the wee fellow's contract was up at the end of the 1987–88 season, we were anxious to keep him. So our chairman had a busy summer negotiating a new deal. We had started pre-season training before Martin Edwards rang me with the news that Gordon had agreed on a revised contract and was coming in the next day to sign. I was pleased, and relieved that I didn't have to go looking for a replacement. However, when Strachan did turn up next morning it was to inform me that he was heading for France to sign for Lens that day.

'Wait a minute,' I barked at him, 'you can't do that. You agreed firmly on a deal with the chairman yesterday.' His reply was dismissive.

'That's a figment of the chairman's imagination,' he said, and left immediately.

I sat quietly for a minute, absorbing the strangeness of that brief encounter, then phoned Martin Edwards to check his version of events. He could not have been more categorical.

'Gordon Strachan and I came to a definite agreement and he promised he would come in the next day to sign.'

My mind went back to the similar stroke Gordon had pulled at Aberdeen, where his cloak-and-dagger manoeuvrings committed him contractually to Cologne while I was trying to find a buyer for him in England. I forgave him then and refused to let the incident affect my judgement of him as a person, preferring to put it down to immaturity and insecurity. But he was now a seasoned pro in his thirties and if he could break his word without a qualm it was sickening. I decided that this man could not be trusted an inch. Our lives had been enmeshed for most of a decade but I knew in that moment that I wouldn't want to expose my back to him in a hurry. It looked like end of story as far as our association was concerned, but there was to be a further twist. That weekend I read a piece in one of the Sunday newspapers which stated that Lens had sacked their coach and that the man taking over did not want Strachan. It will serve him right, I said to myself, if that proves to be true. Sure enough, the same evening my phone rang and Strachan's chirpy voice said: 'Are you interested in a broken-down winger?' The new coach at Lens had declined to offer him a contract, which meant that he was still our player. With mixed feelings, I told him he should come into training and that I would speak to the chairman. Martin Edwards and I were both sick that his French arrangements had fallen through, not because we did not value him as a player but for the obvious reason that we assumed he would never have come back to us if there had been a better alternative open to him. Yet, when everything had been settled and Gordon had agreed to a new contract, my attitude towards him was not one of bitterness. I would never be able to have full trust in him again but a productive working relationship was possible if he strove wholeheartedly on the park to be the Gordon Strachan of old.

For a while in the 1988–89 season my hopes were high. I recall particularly a game at West Ham when he gave an inspired performance in a 3–1 victory, scoring a cute goal and tantalising the opposition with his ball-skills. We were labouring in the League but I believed he could help us to gain a measure of compensation in the Cup. After two replays, we survived the third-round tie against QPR that is forever linked in my memory with the drinking Olympics staged by McGrath and Whiteside. Then we beat Oxford and Bournemouth and found ourselves at home to Nottingham Forest in the quarter-finals. In my pre-match press conference, I singled out Gordon as the player who could take us to Wembley. I did that to elevate him in his own mind as the star of the team, to give him that feeling of being special which I felt had meant a lot to him at Aberdeen. To say my ploy came unstuck is a monumental understatement. United were lamentable in losing that quarter-final 1–0 and Strachan, to me, was like a triallist who had found himself completely out of his depth. He seemed to be intimidated by Stuart Pearce, the Forest left-back. That was not a treasonable offence, considering the physiques of the two players, but the real Strachan had always wanted the ball and had refused to be subdued. Subsequently, he claimed that he had become bored with life at Manchester United, that he had played for me too long. I detected an echo of sentiments he had

Substitute John Hewitt (*left*) heads Aberdeen's historic goal in Gothenburg, moments after I had cursed him and considered taking him off.

Gordon Strachan (*centre*) with Ron Atkinson (*right*) and Sir Bobby Charlton. Gordon left Aberdeen for Manchester United – but soon Big Ron moved on and I was his manager again.

Willie Miller (*foreground*) and Alex McLeish after Willie's goal for Aberdeen against Celtic in 1985 brought our third title in six seasons.

In Seville with Jock Stein before the 1985 World Cup qualifier. Working under Jock was like taking an honours degree in management.

Before they heard the news of Jock Stein's collapse, Alan Rough (*left*) is congratulated by Mo Johnston after Scotland's draw with Wales, but my face betrays my fears.

Frank McAvennie (dark blue shirt) takes on Australia in Melbourne in 1985, having first taken me on with some boozy pre-match nonsense.

Above: Alan Hansen: doubts about his durability cost him a World Cup place.

Left: Jim Bett: too quiet to get the best from his exceptional talent.

Below: Kenny Dalglish (*centre*, against Spain) matured into a truly world-class Scot like Denis Law – even his backside was skilful.

It may look as if I'm leading the pipers, but I'm actually soaking up the unique Hampden atmosphere before the 1986 Cup final.

The Scotland line-up before our World Cup opener in Mexico. Roy Aitken (*back row, far right*) had a goal disallowed as Denmark won 1–0.

Graeme Souness, seen tussling with Denmark's Soren Lerby, suffered in the heat and humidity of Mexico in 1986.

Scottish inquisition: I face the media after our opening match of Mexico '86 ends in a narrow and unlucky defeat by Denmark.

Harald Schumacher blocks from Frank McAvennie while a colleague uses Murrayfield methods on Steve Archibald in our 2–1 defeat by Germany.

Gordon Strachan is the meat in a South American sandwich as my selection mistakes and Uruguay's cynicism conspire to eliminate Scotland.

Above: To say I was disappointed by Graeme Sharp's lack of aggression in this World Cup game against Uruguay would be putting it mildly.

Left: No way, José: Uruguay's Batista (No.2) is ordered off after forty seconds but even against ten men we cannot rise above their spoiling tactics.

Below: Enzo Francescoli, a skilful exception to Uruguay's skulduggery, takes on Paul McStay as our World Cup adventure ends in frustration.

once expressed at Aberdeen. Wee Gordon could be quite boring on the subject of boredom.

Well, I wasn't bored by what I saw from Manchester United against Forest. I was angered and embarrassed. Where was the passion that was supposed to run through Alex Ferguson teams? This team had decent ability but too many of the members lacked the burning desire to be winners. The collective morale was poor. There was far too little of the mutual respect and the all-for-one-and-one-for-all spirit needed to dominate in a highly competitive league week by week. On one of my more philosophical days, I tried to define the feeling that should exist among footballers aspiring to reach the heights: 'When you can look round this dressing-room and be glad that every player you see will be out there shoulder-to-shoulder with you, then you will know you really do have a team.' In that period at Manchester United, I couldn't look round the dressing-room and say, hand on heart, that the team mirrored me in any shape or form. I was certain in my own mind that most of them lacked the resolve and endurance to challenge for a title. It was time to act. Minor tinkering would not suffice. I had to take a number of hard decisions and one of them was that it would be better for Strachan and for us if he continued his career elsewhere.

I did not have long to wait for inquiries about him. On the Monday after that depressing defeat by Forest, Ron Atkinson, now managing Sheffield Wednesday, phoned to talk about buying Strachan. It is an old trick to press a manager to do business soon after a setback, when he might be vulnerable, and I was a bit annoyed with Ron for subjecting me to it. But that wasn't a serious matter and Wednesday's interest was welcome. In a book published in 1998, Ron claimed that I accused him of tapping Gordon about going to Sheffield and added that he had given me a rocket over the phone, letting me know in no uncertain terms that I wasn't dealing with any stupid footballer. I find the idea of me staying quiet to take a roasting from Ron Atkinson totally hilarious. The truth is that I had no preference about which club Strachan joined and I definitely had no prejudice against Ron. I always got on well with him. The complication was that, months before, Howard Wilkinson had inquired about Strachan's availability. I told Howard then that Gordon was not for sale but assured him that if the position changed Leeds would be notified. When I did as promised and mentioned a fee of £300,000, which was £100,000 more than Ron had offered, Howard instantly agreed to the figure. In my opinion, I had done good business for Manchester United over a thirty-two-year-old player whose contract was due to expire at the end of the season.

When Atkinson came back to say he would match whatever Wilkinson was ready to pay, it was obvious that the choice of clubs lay with Strachan. At first Gordon had no intention of speaking to Howard. Probably he had set his mind on going to Hillsborough to rejoin his former manager. But I stressed that the courtesy of a conversation could do no harm, and once Gordon had listened to the enticing details of Wilkinson's offer he could not wait to sign. It was a coming together that neither Leeds United nor the player ever regretted.

Strachan contributed substantially to their promotion in 1990 as Second Division champions and he continued to play a key part in their surge to the First Division title in 1992, when they held off Manchester United in an agonising photo-finish. As we reeled away from that narrow failure to end a championship drought that had lasted a quarter of a century, there were many who sneered that I had helped Leeds to thwart us by providing them with such an influential player. That simplistic nonsense did not bother me. How a player performs in one environment is not necessarily how he will peform in another. Nobody knows that better than Howard Wilkinson, who would later sell me Eric Cantona. Strachan's rebirth as a footballer at Elland Road, which owed much to the exemplary care he had always taken over his diet and conditioning, was something to be celebrated by everybody in the game. Only the hopelessly mean-spirited would not be thrilled by the sight of a man fulfilling his possibilities. If Strachan inflicted some damage on us along the way, that was fair enough. It did not weaken my belief that the policies I was putting in place when

I transferred him would bring long-term dividends. Letting Leeds have a title did hurt but our aim was to take championships by the handful.

Pursuing that aim was bound to mean heavy traffic in players, inward and outward, in those early years of my management in Manchester, and severing connections is often painful in football. I could live with the occasional sourness from men who were sold. They were moving on with their careers and there was always the chance that they would improve their fortunes as McGrath and Strachan had done. I had much more emotional involvement with players whose dreams of a big future in the game were taken away from them by injury. Remi Moses was a notably sad example. He had impressed me from the moment I arrived and his competitiveness, organisational ability and good passing would have made him an important element of my rebuilding programme but for the fact that recurring ankle injuries prevented me from fielding him for more than a handful of games at a stretch. When bad knee trouble completed his nightmare, he had to retire. He was a tremendous midfield player and one I missed personally and professionally.

Other sad losses were Nicky Wood, a forward who was barely into his twenties and had shown great promise in his two appearances in the first team, when he was finished by a chronic back problem, and Tony Gill, a right-midfielder who was a shade younger. Tony had broken through and was establishing himself at the top level when his prospects were ruined by a horrible leg fracture. Billy Garton, a centre-back of talent, was only in his mid-twenties when he succumbed to the debilitating effects of myalgic encephalomyelitis, the mysterious condition known as ME. Two goalkeepers also suffered serious physical mishaps. At least Gary Bailey was a mature man with a lot of action behind him when a training accident while he was with England at the Mexico World Cup in 1986 caused difficulties that put him out of football at the end of the following season. Misfortune struck Gary Walsh soon after he had become the regular first-team goalkeeper at the age of nineteen. Short of halfway in the 1987–88 season, two severe bangs on the head hurt him so alarmingly that his mother asked me to talk him into retiring. The second occurred on a trip to Bermuda that was supposed to give the players a break from the pressures of the League but proved instead to be an unmitigated horror story. Gary was kicked on the head so violently that the Bermudian striker responsible broke his ankle in the process. The damage kept young Walsh out for the rest of the season and he took years to recover from it. After a spell on loan to Airdrie, which was meant to help him regain his touch, he returned to us with an ankle injury, and a series of abortive comebacks left the outlook gloomy. A pioneering bone-graft operation on the ankle came to the rescue but by then Peter Schmeichel was unchallengeable as our goalkeeper and Gary was transferred to Middlesbrough. From there he went to Bradford City and it gave me a thrill in May of 1999 to watch him do well for City as they were promoted to the Premiership. He has shown as much courage in overcoming adversity as he always brought to his performances for us.

Gary's experience in Bermuda was by no means the only grim episode on that trip. My involvement with another began when I was summoned to the telephone at our base in the Elbow Beach Hotel. A Scottish voice identifying itself as that of Detective Sergeant Wallace from the police station in Hamilton, the capital of Bermuda, immediately made me suspect that I was being conned, and I responded with some dire warnings for our physio, Jimmy McGregor. But soon I realised that the speaker was indeed Detective Sergeant Wallace and he had a message to freeze my blood. Clayton Blackmore had been arrested on the strength of allegations that he had committed rape. Fortunately, Maurice Watkins, who was our club solicitor and a member of the board, was in our party and so was Les Olive, a wonderful man who was secretary at United in those days. The three of us rushed to police headquarters and there we were briefed on the details of the charge and informed that, if convicted, Blackmore faced ten years in jail. When we were allowed to see Clayton, he broke down in my arms, telling us a version of the circumstances that convinced us he had been set up by the two girls whose combined evidence was the basis of the charge. We stayed with him, giving comfort, for as long as we could and when he walked away in his prison garb the dreadful implications of his plight were driven home to us.

Maurice Watkins has consistently earned my respect during my time at the club and he excelled himself in that emergency, working non-stop to secure Clayton's release. I am sure that, like me, Maurice was galvanised by absolute belief in the lad's innocence. Anything less than certainty would have put us in an impossible position where such an accusation was concerned. One of my worst tasks was phoning Clayton's wife to let her know what was going on before the press came out with the story. How do you tell a girl that a rape charge, however concocted, is hanging over her husband? Thanks to Maurice's efforts, there was quick progress in the case, and no charges were brought against Clayton. Sitting on my hotel verandah next day, looking out at the sea for the first time since landing on the island, I remembered telling Dick Donald, my chairman at Aberdeen, that I had to leave my attractive life in that northern city because I was missing the agonies of being challenged to my limits. I had not been thinking of the kind of agony I had encountered in Bermuda.

— 15 —

FEW HIGHS AND A TERRIBLE LOW

B IG miseries can make your everyday worries seem almost comforting. After Bermuda, it was a relief to be back among the less weighty dramas of the 1987–88 football season, in which we maintained the reasonable league form that would eventually leave us a distant second to Liverpool but found our best hope of silverware crushed in a controversial ending to an FA Cup fifth-round tie at Highbury. We had a chance to equalise with a last-minute penalty but, just as Brian McClair was taking the kick, Nigel Winterburn engaged in some antics to put him off. I was, however, more angry at Bobby Robson and England for arranging a friendly match in Israel three days before our big Cup engagement in London. Sod's law took a hand and Bryan Robson received a calf injury at England training which ruled him out of the game against Arsenal that just about held the key to our season. Why do international managers infuriate and alienate those of us in charge of clubs by complicating our lives with such unnecessary demands on players? I was disappointed that Bobby Robson of all people failed to be more considerate. He is a real football man and should have known better.

Brian McClair was far too intelligent to let that penalty incident be anything more than a temporary annoyance. He was my second signing for United, in July 1987, and one I had plenty of reason to celebrate for a decade afterwards. My first buy for the club was Viv Anderson, whose resolute professionalism at right-back and bubbly, contagious enthusiasm in the dressing-room were worth a lot more than the £250,000 we paid Arsenal. Viv, a man I am always happy to see, was prevented by injury from being as valuable to us as he should have been. One of McClair's many assets was that he was hardly ever injured and I never had a doubt that the £850,000 it cost to bring him from Celtic was money well spent. He was strongly built, had terrific stamina and had proved in Scotland that he was a scorer of goals. He never stopped moving on the field and he read the play so well that he constantly put himself in good positions. His qualities as a footballer were the kind that helped other players around him to thrive. Over his years at Old Trafford, I asked Brian to handle a wide variety of functions in the team. The tendency to exploit his versatility, and to pick him or leave him out on the basis of what was required on a given day, was not always fair to him but you could count on Brian to be there with one hundred per cent commitment. His contribution was sometimes undervalued by people on the sidelines but never by me, and he knew that. When major success came to Manchester United in the Nineties, nobody deserved it more than the good soldier McClair.

While I was preparing to recruit McClair, during my first close season as United manager in the summer of 1987, I told Martin Edwards that I really needed about eight new players and, to my surprise, he was taken aback. You could say I was shocked at how shocked he was. It was hardly cheering to hear the chairman say that the club did not have the resources to finance the purchases I knew were necessary. He reminded me that there was no Jack Walker around to reach into an endless store of personal wealth. That conversation might have astonished all the outsiders who, even back then, thought of United as an organisation rich enough to attack problems with a blitz of cash. Having learned otherwise, I had to forget about trying to cure all the ills I had diagnosed and decide on priorities. So I concentrated on strikers. The two I had at the time, Peter Davenport and Terry Gibson, were talented but physically they did not fit with my vision of a team that would win the League. I wanted powerful, durable performers. Securing McClair was straightforward but trying to bring about

Mark Hughes's return to Old Trafford from Barcelona (where he was patently unhappy) ran us into tax complications that ruled out a quick transfer. When I turned my attention to Peter Beardsley, who was doing great things at Newcastle United, I met with a distinctly frosty reception from their manager, Willie McFaul. He said there was no way Beardsley would be sold to us even if we offered £3 million. The next week the little forward went to Liverpool for £1.9 million. Can I be blamed for feeling bemused and disappointed?

In that eventful summer of 1987, I might have beaten Liverpool to another attacker who was to be a star with them for years ahead and I acknowledge my failure to do so as a serious mistake. Graham Taylor had recognised that he could not keep John Barnes at Watford and Graham phoned me to say I could have the exciting young winger for £900,000. I passed up the chance. Part of the explanation was an exaggerated faith in Jesper Olsen. The Dane had shown some excellent form for us and, as he returned to fitness after a long spell out with injury, his outstanding work on the training ground suggested that the best was yet to come. It proved to be false promise and before long Olsen had left us for Bordeaux. My idea of a replacement was Ralph Milne, whose name has become enshrined in the fan folklore of United as the symbol of bad buying. I don't pretend that it was the best piece of business I ever did but the fact is that Ralph was a hell of a winger in his days with Dundee United. Old Trafford was simply too much for him and he faded into the shadows. He was a likeable lad and I was sad when personal troubles hit him hard. Meanwhile, John Barnes made us pay more than once on the field for missing the chance to grab him. Without looking for excuses, I can say truthfully that, as a manager new to English football, I could have done with stronger guidance. When Barnes first became available, I had not seen him play, so Tony Collins, our chief scout, went to study him in action against Norwich. Big John scored and did well. But the opinion of the scouting department was that he was up and down, not very consistent. Then he played against us at Old Trafford and performed creditably at centre-forward. He definitely interested me but I received little encouragement to sign him. We later parted company with Tony Collins, who had many qualities but was too cautious for my liking. Les Kershaw, who took over as chief scout, and is now Director of our Academy, would throw his hat in the ring and make a judgement and that is a way of working that suits me.

John Barnes would have been a wonderful player for Manchester United. So would Paul Gascoigne but his was an entirely different case. The fact that he never wore the red shirt was his mistake, not ours. As far as I am concerned, I had a solid promise that he would sign for me and I think that his change of mind hurt both of us. I had been determined to bring Paul to United ever since he had tortured us with a devastating performance for Newcastle at St James' Park. We sent out the powerful midfield of Moses, Robson and Whiteside that day but the twenty-year-old Gascoigne outplayed them, crowning his precocious display by patting Remi Moses on the top of the head like a headmaster mildly rebuking one of his pupils. I was as angry as Remi at such patronising treatment of an experienced pro and jumped out of the dug-out, begging for the young upstart to be put firmly in his place. But nobody could get near him. What a performance, and what a player! 'I'm going to sign him,' I told my assistant, Archie Knox, on the way home.

It was when that season was over, in the summer of 1988, that I set about living up to the promise. Newcastle were no more co-operative than they had been about my approach for Beardsley but I wasn't going to let them frustrate me again, so I made direct contact with Gascoigne and his agent, Mel Stein. Paul was a player I had no intention of losing and I pursued the negotiations with him through a series of meetings, anxious to conclude an agreement before I took Cathy and the boys to Malta for a holiday the family badly needed. We had come through a worrying time when Cathy was seriously ill and in intensive care for nearly a week. For three weeks my sons and I virtually lived in the Alexandra Hospital in Cheadle, praying day by day for good news. Our prayers were answered when Cathy pulled through, and we were all looking forward to relaxing in the sun. My spirits were lifted further on the night of our departure by a phone call from Paul Gascoigne.

'Mr Ferguson, you go and enjoy your holiday,' he said. 'I am signing for Manchester United when you come back.'

'Great, son, you'll never regret this,' I told him. 'You will become one of the greatest players this club has ever had, I assure you of that.' And off I went to Malta to enjoy the hospitality of a truly marvellous set of people who have become close friends of our family. On one perfect day I was lying by the pool, dreaming of next season's line-up. 'I'll have Gascoigne and Robson and if I get Hughes we'll take a bit of beating,' I was musing to myself, when I was interrupted by a tannoy announcement that I was wanted on the phone. As I wandered into the hotel, nothing could have been further from my mind than the words I was about to hear. It was the chairman on the line: 'Gascoigne has signed for Spurs.' I was stunned and as Martin Edwards filled in the details I wasn't really absorbing what he was saying. The explanation of the late switch was said to be that Paul's feelings were swung when Tottenham bought a house for his parents. I wonder if his advisers ever consider what a boob they made, taking a lad of Paul's background and temperament to London. Maybe his self-destructive nature would have brought him trouble anywhere, but it is my belief that if he had signed for United he would not have had nearly as many problems as he had in London. I know managing him would have been no joyride but the hazards that went with the talent would never have put me off. I still don't know Paul well but at our meetings I warmed to him. There is something strangely appealing about him. Perhaps it is his vulnerability. You feel you want to be like an older brother or a father to him. You might want to shake him, or give him a cuddle, but there is certainly something infectious that gets you involved with him. To this day I regret being denied the chance to help him to make better use than he did of his prodigious abilities.

One consolation at the time was that, within a week of the Gascoigne let-down, we did succeed in bringing 'Sparky' Hughes back from Barcelona for a fee of £1.5 million. Apart from believing that Hughes would significantly strengthen the team, I saw the transfer as repaying the fantastic loyalty of our supporters by restoring one of their heroes to them. I had heard all sorts of stories about why he had been sold. The most popular was that the chairman had grabbed at the first big-money deal that was put on the table, but I must say that Martin Edwards placed no obstacles in the way of bringing Hughes back. It was a source of encouragement to me in those early years that the chairman provided good backing without ever interfering with the running of the team. There was no problem about the way we worked together but the same could not be said about his relationship with the supporters. From many of them he evoked a feeling strong enough to be called hatred. In a way, I found myself piggy-in-the-middle and soon after reaching Old Trafford I felt I had to start building a bridge between the club and our followers. Our fans had maintained United's status as the best-supported team in England, in spite of going without the League title since 1967. The links with them had to be strengthened. Martin was never going to get them on his side, no matter what he did. Their resentment of him was too deep-rooted. Perhaps it had something to do with the family connections that had brought Martin to his position and with his father's regime as chairman in the era of Sir Matt Busby. As an incomer, it was not for me to judge such matters. I did not know enough about my chairman to offer a considered opinion of him. That would come much later. It was sufficient for the moment that I was getting on well with him and enjoying our regular meetings as I continued with the task of reviving a great club. Reintroducing Hughes to the attack represented a substantial advance. Physically and technically, he was equipped to trouble any defence and he had the heart to thrust his sturdy body in where it hurt. Mark was taciturn and withdrawn in the dressing-room and, when off form, he could suffer a loss of confidence. But no opponent could ever intimidate him and he was liable to be most assertive when the stakes were highest. It was no accident that he specialised in scoring vital goals on big occasions. You just had to look at the determined set of his strong features to know you were dealing with a Welsh warrior.

There is, of course, no point in being effective at the front if you are rickety at the back and I had been working steadily to improve our defence. It is essential to have defenders who play regularly together over long periods, developing the understanding to operate as a cohesive unit under pressure. Forwards, too, need to be on the same wavelength as each other but for them a failure of communication usually means no more than the wasting of an opportunity, whereas a similar breakdown among the men protecting your own goal can cost you a match. I inherited a United defence in which, mainly because of a seemingly endless plague of injuries, there was a constant shuffling of personnel, especially in the central positions. In one emergency, I even played Bryan Robson as a centre-back and, although he was unhappy with the role, he performed magnificently. But he was required elsewhere and I knew that to produce the spine which is indispensable to a good team, I would have to find a centre-back partnership that would turn out consistently, week after week.

Steve Bruce was the first element of such an alliance. Considering that durability was one of the characteristics which made Steve a cornerstone of so much of my success at Old Trafford, it is amusing to remember that medical doubts arose before we signed him. Some discolouring was detected on the X-rays of his knees. I felt that more telling evidence was supplied by his appearance record during his time with Gillingham and Norwich City. How often a man is fit to go on the park is the best guide to his soundness. The number of games Bruce had played for Norwich City was greater than the aggregate appearances of Paul McGrath and Kevin Moran at centre-back for United. Far from being a risk, the big Geordie was a banker, one of the dourest and most dependable defenders ever to play for me. His resolution was mingled with warmth and modesty, so that he commanded respect and affection in equal measure. He led by example and fully deserved the honour of going on (after Robson bowed out) to become the most successful captain in United's history. Bringing a man of Bruce's calibre into our ranks gave me huge satisfaction. Releasing a diamond of a fellow like Kevin Moran was painful. We had sold Graeme Hogg and one of our goalkeepers, Chris Turner, to help balance the books but we did not think it would be fair to ask for a fee for somebody who had been as loyal as Kevin, one of the bravest and most admirable men I have known. I was particularly pleased that Kevin, like Arthur Albiston, a full-back who had grown up at Old Trafford and was United through and through, was awarded a testimonial as well as being able to go on with his career elsewhere.

With Moran and Hogg gone, and young Billy Garton only sporadically fit, I needed another centre-back. In October 1988, I did a deal with Luton for the transfer of the Ulsterman Mal Donaghy, a veteran with plenty left in the tank. But it was ten months later that the quality of partnership in central defence that I had sought for so long at last became possible. The signing of Gary Pallister took a long night of frequently abrasive negotiating, with Maurice Watkins helping me to cope with the aggressive tactics of the Middlesbrough chairman, Colin Henderson, and at the end of it we paid the asking price of £2.3 million, which was several hundred thousand above the ceiling we had in mind entering the talks. But anybody who thinks we didn't emerge from those exhausting exchanges as winners should take a look at how much Pallister contributed to the trophy-gathering exploits of Manchester United in the Nineties. He came to us as a twenty-four-year-old beanpole with a rich talent that was flawed at times by rawness. But his physique and his football both matured rapidly and, unusually blessed with balance and pace, he became a centre-half I wouldn't have swapped for any in the game. As a combination, he and Bruce gave us a sense of assurance and authority in defence that spread confidence through the whole team.

Behind them by that time was Jim Leighton, the goalkeeper who had achieved so much with me at Aberdeen. With injuries clouding Gary Walsh's future, I had brought Jim south in the summer of 1988. He was a gifted goalkeeper, extremely courageous and with a level of concentration that enabled him to make breathtaking saves in the middle of long spells of idleness. My only fear concerned his ability to handle crosses in the context of the English game. I would have been even happier if I could have made further defensive improvement by luring Stuart Pearce away from Nottingham Forest. But Brian Clough ensured that I was given no chance to woo his left-back, a player I had long coveted, one whose courage, confidence in his own ability and competitive temperament suggested he would be an ideal wearer of United's colours.

In fact, Cloughie showed a pronounced reluctance to have any dealings with me at all. Once when Martin Edwards and I called at the City Ground, admittedly on an impulse and without an appointment, we did not get further than the reception window. After our identities had been confirmed, there was a delay of about ten minutes and then we were informed that Brian was not available. It was not the kind of behaviour football people expect of one another but Cloughie could never be relied upon for the norms of courtesy. I had my first experience of his ways when I went with Archie Knox, who at the time was my assistant at Aberdeen, to a Forest–Celtic UEFA Cup match in Nottingham. After the game, we fell into conversation with Brian's assistant, Ronnie Fenton. I had come across Ronnie on several occasions while he was manager of Notts County and I was at St Mirren. He was friendly and, when he discovered I had not met his boss, he said, 'Come along with me and I'll find out if he can see you for a minute.' There was the feeling that we were being granted a privilege akin to an audience with the Pope. We were taken to what I assumed was Cloughie's office and must have been there for well over thirty minutes, chatting away happily, before the great one popped his head round the door.

'Alex Ferguson from Aberdeen, Brian,' said Ronnie. Cloughie responded by coming in, shaking my hand and sitting down beside me. He looked tired and I felt he needed the break from the circus outside. In addition to the gamut of emotions managers go through during big games, they have to cope with the build-up beforehand and then the post-match demands of TV, radio and the press. It is exhausting. So I was thinking sympathetic thoughts as Brian seated himself. But I did not have time to dwell on them.

'What did you think of the game then?' he asked me. Since Celtic had lost when they should have won, an honest answer was not likely to please. But I gave one anyway.

'I thought Celtic played well and that you were a bit lucky,' I said. 'But I do think it will suit you better at Celtic Park in the second leg.' Cloughie got up off his chair and made for the door.

'Ah well, I've heard enough,' he tossed back over his shoulder. Archie and I were left in fits of laughter. What Brian was trying to prove I'll never know. All he contrived to do was embarrass Ron Fenton, who could not stop apologising. Brian Clough provided ample proof that he was one of British football's greatest managers. That he was almost certainly its rudest is perhaps another distinction he is proud to claim. He is welcome to it.

The week after Martin Edwards and I were turned away at the City Ground reception window, I tried to buy Stuart Pearce but Cloughie would not answer the phone. It was the faithful Ronnie Fenton who passed the word that Pearce was not for sale. When later I developed an interest in the Forest midfield player Neil Webb, Clough once more made dealing with him an impossibility and, as a matter of principle, I abandoned all efforts to do so. As far as Webb was concerned, all I had to do was wait until he was out of contract in the following year. We duly signed him for £1.5 million in July 1989, glad to have acquired a creative footballer who was two-footed and had goalscoring figures that were healthy for a midfielder. His chances of making a major impact with United were, sadly, dealt a savage blow when he ruptured an Achilles tendon while playing for England in Sweden just a couple of months after joining us. That is one of the worst injuries a player can suffer and, although Webb recovered, I don't believe he was ever quite the same afterwards.

Three weeks before signing Webb, we had paid Norwich three-quarters of a million for Mike Phelan. Mike was a totally honest journeyman whose work was given extra value by the remarkable buzz of energy he took on to the field and his ability to fill a number of positions in defence and midfield. We bought him as a utility player and as such he served us well. We always had much higher ambitions for the twenty-one-year-old we added to our strength two months later, in September 1989. Les Kershaw, as chief scout, had long been raving about Paul Ince of West Ham and I, too, liked what I saw in him. He had two good feet, was quick, useful in the air, could tackle to serious effect and had a winner's drive. There was a question mark about his stamina but I was sure that could be sorted out. I was very friendly with John Lyall, West Ham's long-serving manager, so I decided the best way to initiate discussions about Ince was to pay John a visit at his home in Essex. The weather was flawless on the day I called and our meeting was made all the more pleasant by the beauty of his garden. Knowing what I do about the pressures on a club manager's time, I could only assume that John's wife, Yvonne, had played a big part in creating the most delightful setting I have ever had for talk about a transfer. Such talk seemed destined to be short once Lyall heard of my intention to take Ince north.

'No chance,' he declared. 'The boy's like a son to me.'

'Yes, but even sons leave home eventually,' I said. I had been trying unsuccessfully for an hour to argue him into some flexibility when the appearance of Yvonne with tea and sandwiches reminded me of his background. His father was a Scot and it was obvious that John and his wife had adopted the national tradition of serving sandwiches that are as substantial as a three-course meal. But if he was prepared to feed me, he was not ready to nourish my hopes of signing Ince. As I left, I resolved that, regardless of my respect for John Lyall, I was going to make a formal bid for the player. Only the amount and the timing of the offer had to be decided. Before they could be, just a matter of days later, football was hit with the bombshell announcement that John had been sacked by West Ham. When you have been in the game as long as I have, you get used to shock dismissals but this was the daddy of them all and I don't think anyone outside that club's boardroom could believe or understand it. It was the kind of decision that makes you wonder why directors are allowed to run football bodies such as the FA and the League. I phoned John to commiserate with him and I could sense his feeling of injustice. West Ham had treated him unforgivably after all the years he had given them, the countless hours he had worked and endless travelling he had done on their behalf. Quite often, while I was managing in Scotland, he would phone me when he was coming up on a scouting mission and I would go and meet him and Eddie Bailey, his assistant, and drive them to a game. I had looked forward to those nights and I worried that this blow might mark the end of a good man's management career.

Lyall's ugly removal relieved me of any trace of guilt about pursuing a deal over Ince and I did that with relish. Once it became generally known that we had tabled a bid, John gave us a lot of helpful information about Paul and his background and stressed the importance of showing him affection, of always being ready to put an arm round him. That advice would not be forgotten in the years ahead. The transfer itself was so complex that all involved were exhausted by the time it was completed. Paul did not smooth our path when he paraded himself in a United shirt before we had even spoken to him, a gesture that was not likely to amuse the new manager at Upton Park, Lou Macari, or the West Ham fans. A more serious concern developed as a result of his medical examination. When we made a minor inquiry about an earlier injury, Paul volunteered that sometimes he was in great pain. I attributed that to worry more than anything else but it did place our orthopaedic specialist, Jonathan Noble, in a difficult position and the transfer was put on hold. Paul was devastated and only the efforts of Claire, his girlfriend then and later his wife, pulled him round. Much as the rest of us tried to console him, it was Claire alone who was able to get through to him. I kept assuring him that it was not the end of the story and West Ham proved me right by proposing a compromise that took account of any future physical problems. They agreed to accept the £1.5 million fee in instalments. I believe the arrangement was £500,000 down and then £250,000 for every fifteen games he played. For Manchester United it was a nice deal at the time. Within a few years, it had turned out to be superb business.

My enthusiasm for Ince, who was a month short of his twenty-second birthday when he came to us, reflected my determination to replace the ageing squad I had found at United with an emphasis on youth. I accepted that a good leavening of experience was essential to success but I wanted plenty of young players who were hungry to learn and undaunted by challenges. Lee Sharpe had broken into the first team almost immediately after signing for us from Torquay on his seventeenth birthday in May 1988. Lee's arrival was an example of how people who are well disposed towards a club can render valuable service as unofficial scouts. Such a man was Len Noad, a former journalist from the Manchester area who had retired to Torquay. On one of his routine visits to see the local team play he had heard about a member of their youth team who was causing excitement. The lad was Lee Sharpe. I was advised that Len was a sound judge and that it would be wise to heed any tip from him, so we monitored Lee's progress. Our interest strengthened to the point where Archie Knox, Tony Collins (still our chief scout at that stage) and I went down to Torquay to watch him play. What I saw left me in no doubt that I wanted his signature on a contract without delay. He was quick enough to catch pigeons and his good physical lines made it plain that he was going to develop into a splendid athlete. An excellent crosser of the ball, he was brave enough to take advantage of that and his other assets. He showed no notable cleverness in beating his man, but we had to give him the benefit of the doubt on that score, since he was opposed on the night by a seasoned pro. The positives far outnumbered the negatives and it was time for decisive action. Cyril Knowles, the former Tottenham Hotspur full-back, was the Torquay manager and there was an obvious risk that he would alert the London club to Sharpe's potential. A deal had to be done that night. Len Noad had teamed up with our Manchester United raiding party and now he went off to fetch Cyril. While he was away I said to Archie, 'I'm not letting Cyril out of this car until we agree terms.' That is exactly what happened. We gave the beleaguered Torquay manager no respite until he surrendered to our wishes. The down payment was £60,000 and, if Sharpe made the first team, there were to be others up to £180,000. Lee made sure that his old employers had to wait only until September of that year to start collecting the extra cash.

Buying a player as young as Sharpe is highly unusual. If you want teenagers of the class to perform in the upper echelons of professional football, you nearly always have to produce them from within your own organisation. From the moment I became manager of United, I was committed to the creation of a youth policy that would be the envy of every other club in Britain. The first imperative was to find the raw talent and when I took over I was appalled by the shortcomings of our scouting network. I called for maps of Manchester and Greater Manchester and on them I marked out which scouts were responsible for which areas. The situation was that Joe Brown was in charge of youth scouting and development; to assist him in covering the City of Manchester and a huge and densely populated surrounding area, he had only five scouts. When I was managing Aberdeen, I had seventeen scouts covering Scotland which has a population of slightly under five million. Greater Manchester has at least as many inhabitants and every square mile of it is a breeding ground for footballers, so trying to take care of it with about a third of the scouts I had at Aberdeen was ludicrous. I tackled that deficiency and arranged a meeting at which I made a declaration of my priorities to the men who were scouting for me.

'I am not interested in the best boy in your street,' I told them. 'I want the best boy in your area. Don't bring bad players out of enthusiasm. I am happy to wait until you bring a good one. After all, it is no pleasure for me to have tell a lad that he is not up to standard.' They were an honest bunch and I believe they simply needed encouragement and reassurance that they had a vital role and that I had respect for the difficulty of their jobs. Everybody at United was becoming aware that my management philosophy was based on dedication to building an entire football club, not just a first team. I could feel a new determination spreading through the place and nowhere was it stronger than in the nurturing of the talented schoolboys we were unearthing.

For those working on a youth programme in football, the ultimate satisfaction and incentive is the emergence of a player with dazzling possibilities and just such a boy came our way. Many have claimed responsibility for bringing Ryan Giggs and Manchester United together but as far as I am concerned the name at the top of the credit list is that of Harold Wood. Harold was one of our ground stewards and when he came to see me at the Cliff one day in 1987 he had something interesting to say.

'There is this young lad who plays for Dean Sports and he is Manchester United daft but he is training with Manchester City,' Harold told me. 'It's absolutely ridiculous.' Possibly one or two scouts had taken note of Ryan Wilson, as he was called before he decided to drop his father's name and use his mother's. But nothing was done until I was given that unequivocal recommendation by Harold Wood. I instructed Joe Brown to watch the boy and, if impressed, to bring him in to see me. The reports were good and it was arranged that Ryan would take part in a trial at the Cliff. When he did, he gave me one of those rare and priceless moments that make all the sweat and frustration and misery of management worthwhile. A gold miner who has searched every part of the river or mountain and then suddenly finds himself staring at a nugget could not feel more exhilaration than I did watching Giggs that day. I shall always remember my first sight of him, floating over the pitch at the Cliff so effortlessly that you would have sworn his feet weren't touching the ground. He carried his head high and he looked as relaxed and natural on the park as a dog chasing a piece of silver paper in the wind. From that moment on we protected Ryan like the treasure he was and Archie, Joe Brown and I were regular visitors to the family home. We enrolled him in our School of Excellence and then, on his fourteenth birthday in November 1987, we signed him on a schoolboy form. Looking back now, I feel I can say honestly that whatever United have paid me in my thirteen years at Old Trafford was justified at a stroke by securing Ryan.

After such a demonstration of the rewards that could come from scouring the schoolboy ranks, it made sense to intensify our efforts and in 1988 I appointed Brian Kidd our Youth Development Officer. His mandate was to make sure we were aware of all the best boys in our own area. Brian, who had been a tremendous player in the United team that won the European Cup in 1968 and had recently been distinguishing himself in community work, attacked his duties with zest. He recruited seventeen new scouts for Manchester and the surrounding districts, all of them United supporters. From that platform, Archie and I set about making the School of Excellence fully worthy of its name. It claimed long hours from us but we enjoyed the involvement. Our scouting had improved and there was a rise in the standard of player attending our regular coaching weeks. At those seminars, we stressed our respect for our scouts' opinions by having them in on the final day, when assessments were made. They were able to enlighten us about any problem that might be preventing young lads from expressing themselves in the way that had caused them to be invited in the first place. We found this very useful, as nervousness can often totally obscure the truth about a young footballer's abilities.

Nervousness was not a condition anybody would have been inclined to associate with the unlikely figure who suddenly invaded the life of Manchester United in the summer of 1989. Michael Knighton seemed to have self-confidence to burn. My first inkling of the strange events that had brought him on the scene came at the end of the 1988–89 season when Martin Edwards phoned to ask me to go and see him in his office. The news he unloaded there left me speechless. Admittedly, during that summer nothing that occurred in the politics of football, or even on the field, was likely to appear truly significant. On 15 April 1989, the Hillsborough disaster had claimed the lives of ninety-five Liverpool fans who had gone to Sheffield to see their team play Nottingham Forest in an FA Cup semi-final. That calamity, and the great tide of grief it evoked, inevitably forced all of us in the game to recognise that issues we have become accustomed to regarding as momentous are really fairly trivial. There can never be an end to the mourning for the victims of Hillsborough. Yet football is such

a vital concern in the lives of so many people, and nowhere is
that more true than in Liverpool itself, that the petty dramas of
the game slowly reasserted themselves. There is no doubt that,
in purely football terms, Martin Edwards's words were calculated
to shake me.

'I'm going to sell the club,' he said. 'If you know anyone who
would be prepared to buy my shares for ten million pounds, with
a guarantee that he will spend another ten million on renewing
the Stretford End, then he can have it.'

I asked him why he wanted to sell and it was plain that he felt
he couldn't win over the fans and that he had no other way out.
I was sorry for him. We had a good relationship and I appreciated
the patience he had shown over the two and a half years I had
been in charge. I suggested he should take a year off away from
it all but he was convinced he should sell and our meeting finished
with me assuring him I would put out some feelers in Scotland.
I did but when I returned from holiday it was to learn, after
another visit to Martin's office, that the club had been sold. Some
days later, Martin invited me to meet the new owner of Manchester United, informing me beforehand that Knighton had
played for Coventry City at one time and assuring me that there
would be no changes in any department. There was little in Knighton's appearance – portly and dapper, with an RAF officer's mous-
tache – to remind you of his playing days. But I must confess
there was something charismatic about him and both the man
and what he said about his ambitions for the club made an impression on me. I had no doubt in my mind that this was a done deal
and I had been speaking to the new proprietor.

On the opening day of the season, Old Trafford was awash with
optimism. We had a new regime in the boardroom and new players
in the team to face the champions, Arsenal, on a baking-hot afternoon. My custom never changes on match days. I have my pre-
match talk at 1.30–2.00 p.m. and then I let the players get on
with it. I think if I am continually around them before the game,
talking to them or reminding them of this or that, I am suggesting
a lack of trust in them. Once you have made your tactical points

and let your men know what is expected of them, you must show confidence that they can handle the job. On that remarkable day, I kept to my routine and went off to my office for a cup of tea. Sometimes the opposing manager joins me and this is a good time to have a chat. After the game, both of you are liable to be more tense and, in any case, you may have to deal with the media for an hour before you can sit down and unwind. On this occasion I was joined by George Graham in a little office I had at the time, just along the corridor from the dressing-room. I get on well with George and when we are together there is plenty of lively banter. We were enjoying ourselves until my door opened and big Norman Davies, our kit man and a stalwart helper to me, came in to say that our new chairman was asking for a first-team strip to wear. George and I laughed and I told Norman to give Michael Knighton the kit but to tell him that the team had been picked. I was still wondering what the chairman had in mind when Norman burst into the room.

'You won't believe this but he's out on the pitch, juggling the ball.' I gasped and put on the TV monitor which shows the pitch and there was the bold Michael juggling the ball in front of the Stretford End. The supporters were loving it but I have to admit that I was starting to have a terrible gut feeling about my new chairman. It did not go unnoticed by George Graham.

'Isn't life wonderful?' he said with a chuckle. I was a bit subdued until the game began but, fortunately, it cheered me up. We trounced Arsenal 4–1.

At our next match, away to Derby, the Knighton phenomenon reached fever pitch and the start was delayed to allow our fans into the ground. Even then, many were left out. The police were understandably worried and came to our dressing-room with the word that it would be dangerous to kick off with the crowd in such a frenzy. Enter Michael Knighton, who had heard about the problem and suggested to the police that he should go out and try to bring some order. I had to admire his bravado, but, if anything, he made things worse. As Michael paraded round the track, asking for calm, all he got was a mad rush to the boundary barriers to shake his hand. He revelled in it. In contrast with the warmth between Knighton and the fans, there were icy feelings among the United directors as his ability to finance the takeover was called into question. Our match against Portsmouth was almost incidental to the off-field drama but it did give little Danny Wallace his debut in attack in a 3–2 victory and provided our followers with an excuse to talk about something else. The Michael Knighton affair eventually dwindled away and he retired disconsolate but definitely unbowed, as his much later activities at Carlisle would prove. When he was under fire at tense Old Trafford board meetings, I felt a little sorry for him. It appeared that he had no allies at all and yet, out of all the turmoil, the club made the controversial decision to become a public limited company. I believe the vote was unanimous. I didn't feel comfortable with our entry into the corporate world but the reality of the Stock Exchange flotation was still some way off. In the meantime, I had enough practical everyday worries to keep me occupied.

By late September our form was inconsistent and we chose the worst possible day to reach rock bottom. In a local derby with Manchester City at Maine Road we were slaughtered 5–1 in the most embarrassing defeat of my management career. After the game I went straight home, got into bed, and put the pillow over my head. I remained that way until Cathy came home. She didn't know the result and asked me what was wrong. A sense of guilt had engulfed me and I knew I was going to have to dig deep into my resources. Injuries had taken a toll of United but that could not be the whole explanation. Was I doing something wrong? I was convinced the training was fine and the players' general fitness was good. Analysing my team selections, my preparation for matches and my tactics, I couldn't see a major fault. I had worked hard at making sure my worry was not manifesting itself in the dressing-room and I felt my demeanour was good. But we weren't winning enough games, particularly in the spell from late November through to the end of December in which we did not have a single victory. There was speculation that I was about to be fired, some of it going as far as to link Howard Kendall with my job. Sir

Bobby Charlton has since said that the directors never considered sacking me, that they knew I was the right man to revive United. That is good to know but I admit that in those grim days ten years ago I was, for the first time, feeling uncomfortable about my position.

During November we went to Perth to play St Johnstone in the match that inaugurated their new stadium and, seeking to boost team spirit, I took the players to Dunblane for a few days of golf and relaxation. I also invited Sir Matt and Bobby Charlton on the trip, knowing both were always ready to give advice and ready to listen. The break went well but the game was a further monstrous embarrassment, a really stinking performance by us and the fact that it was only a friendly did not ease the pain. I was left subdued and withdrawn and did not stay around long in the lounge of the hotel, preferring to retire to my bed with my own thoughts. I was tending to do that all the time and found retreating into a cocoon of self-examination seemed to help me. Later in the night, Archie Knox came to my room and said I was not sharing enough of my problems with him. I could not challenge the truth of that statement but there was nothing I could do about it. My nature had taken me down a certain road and there was no turning back. During that bleak period, Archie would keep trying to encourage me to go out with him and Brian Kidd, but I couldn't. Away from work, I was a recluse. I wanted to find answers and going out would not help me. There had to be a way forward for Manchester United and, no matter how much support was available from my staff, I was the one who had to put the club on the right path. It was hard to believe that doing so would be made easier by the tie we were given when the draw for the third round of the FA Cup was made in December 1989. We were asked to take on Nottingham Forest, one of the most feared Cup teams of that era, on their own ground. But that fixture was to launch United, and me, towards happier times.

═ 16 ═
CUP COLLECTORS

OBITUARIES of my regime at Old Trafford were plentiful in the sports pages as we approached the third-round Cup-tie with Forest at the City Ground on 7 January 1990. Our struggles in the League had persuaded many of the pundits that my doom was imminent and most gave me little chance of saving myself with a good run in the Cup. On BBC television, Jimmy Hill suggested before the kick-off in Nottingham that even our warm-up was not impressive. Some years later when I had an outburst against Jimmy Hill, calling him a prat, he attempted to cool matters down and wrote that he had always got on well with me.

Unlike Hill, I strongly fancied us to beat Forest. My optimism probably had more to do with instinct than logic, since half our first-choice team missed the game because of injury. Webb, Robson, Ince, Donaghy, Wallace and Sharpe were all sitting in the stands and so was the useful full-back, Colin Gibson, who had joined United in 1985 from Aston Villa. Yet something told me we could win and then go on to do damage in later rounds of the competition. On the morning of our meeting with Forest, Danny McGregor, the commercial manager at Old Trafford, had placed a bet for both of us on United at 16–1 to win the Cup. I had never made such a wager previously but my gut feeling was too strong to resist. Our 1–0 victory is remembered, quite under-standably, for young Mark Robins's decisive goal but what I shall never forget is the defiant enthusiasm of our supporters. In spite of all that they had been suffering, they were buoyant and their incessant chanting definitely inspired the team, injecting zest and confidence. The game was always in our control but we were noticeably less creative in the second half and I often wonder if Brian Clough contributed indirectly to our win. Brian had been giving one of his midfielders stick for losing the ball and his annoyance led to a substitution. Almost as soon as it was made, a Mark Hughes pass set Robins up for the goal that settled the match.

Now the unique anticipation generated by a Cup success gripped our supporters again. The dream of travelling all the way to Wembley excited me, too, but mingled with my pleasure was an uneasiness about how Manchester United had come to rely overmuch on the short, sharp lifts provided by the knockout tournament. They had won the Cup three times over the past dozen years or so and there was a tendency to regard a trip to that old stadium on the northern outskirts of London as the only taste of triumph they were entitled to expect. For me, a Cup run merely heightened awareness of the true objectives of the club.

Obviously I did not underestimate its value as a means of buying me time and I was duly thankful that we survived by a single goal on a pudding of a pitch at Hereford in the fourth round. We owed a lot to the tremendous work in midfield of Mike Duxbury, a good, honest professional who was mainly a full-back but had the versatility to do a job in other positions. He was coming to the end of his time with us but he contributed notably to our Cup achievements that season. Our next test was at Newcastle and that was bedlam, as fortunes seesawed in a classic tie before we scraped through 3–2. The quarter-final at Bramall Lane against Sheffield United was won more easily than the 1–0 scoreline indicates and suddenly we were only two hurdles away from a trophy.

As we headed into the semi-final with Oldham Athletic, there was a major worry about the form of Jim Leighton. He had lost confidence and his decision-making had become suspect. I was questioning whether I should play him in the semi-final but Archie

Knox argued strongly for his retention, stressing that being dropped would have a brutal effect on Jim. Archie had been my second-in-command for nearly ten years and had been a good servant, so I took anything he said seriously and, against my own judgement, I yielded to his reasoning about Leighton. The collision with Oldham was even more thrilling than the match at Newcastle but much of the excitement was produced by the mistakes from both teams that riddled the play. Amid the nerve-racking action, I had cause to be glad that I had chosen to bring back Bryan Robson, Neil Webb and Colin Gibson after their long-term injuries. Bryan hadn't played in any league games prior to the semi-final but he was a giant on the day, at his demanding, snarling best as he bullied and cajoled his team-mates to meet every challenge. He, Webb and Wallace scored for us in a punishing marathon that ended 3–3 after extra time. Once again, Jim Leighton betrayed nervousness and, although he did not commit any spectacular blunders, he might have done more to prevent two of Oldham's goals. The replay was another frantic, nervy occasion but we managed to progress 2–1, with Mark Robins scoring the winner. Jim had done better in that match but my doubts were fed by his display in a league game at Forest, where he picked the ball out of the net four times in the first half.

My assessment of our Cup final opponents, Crystal Palace, was that they had been fashioned as an aggressive, hard-working team. They were good athletes and good workers but did not have a lot of class. Nobody can make assumptions about a final but I was sure we were equipped to win this one. In those days team coaches were allowed to use Wembley Way and as ours swung into the famous approach to the twin towers there was an unforgettable moment when we were swamped by the noise and colour of our supporters. It was a sweltering afternoon and out on the park the players would be obliged to heed my constant preachings about jealously guarding possession of the ball. One of the strengths of Palace's game was their excellent exploitation of set-pieces and we had taken pains during the week of preparation to rehearse counter-measures. Leighton's role was, of course, crucial and we decided that on free kicks in particular he should not come for the ball unless he was absolutely certain of taking it. That was the script but the reality was rather different. Palace's first goal came from a free kick that was struck wickedly into the six-yard box to be met by their big centre-half, Gary O'Reilly, with Jim in no-man's-land. We responded well to that setback and Robson's wonderful knack of timing his runs into the box might have produced much more than the equaliser he gave us. We were well in control when Mark Hughes hit one of his specials to put us 2–1 ahead and from that point I could not see us losing. I was entering the phase of the action that is always most electric for me in important matches. It is that time when I feel my men have done enough to win, the score is as I want it and I keep glancing at my watch and willing the referee to complete my satisfaction with the last blast on his whistle. In such circumstances that sound is the sweetest climax in football but it was denied to me that day at Wembley. Ian Wright, having come on as a substitute, saved Palace with a late goal to take the match into extra time.

In the first period of extra time, Palace put us firmly on the back foot when they went 3–2 up through another Ian Wright goal and all of a sudden we were struggling and the Wembley pitch and the heat were taking their toll. Paul Ince, who had been playing marvellously, was in such dire trouble that he had to be moved to right-back to ease the strain on legs tortured by cramp. He was not alone in having that problem. Lee Martin, the young full-back who had moved up through the ranks impressively at United and was now established in the first team, had already left the stage in similar difficulties. With time draining away, I had a horrible suspicion that disappointment was looming for us. Then Mark Hughes, whose big-match temperament always made him capable of being a one-man rescue squad, reacted characteristically to a cute pass from Danny Wallace and earned us a replay. When the whistle blew for time-up there was no reason for either side to complain. A draw was a fair conclusion to a pulsating game that left even the spectators exhausted.

In the dressing-room afterwards I noticed Jim Leighton with his head in his hands, completely shattered. I went over and gave him a pat but received no response. He looked to me like a beaten man and I told Archie to keep an eye on him. Jim knew he had given another poor performance and I think he felt helpless. At the reception after the game I kept glancing over at him, hoping he would brighten up, but he remained morose for most of the night. I felt for him but a decision that was bound to hurt him further was forming in my mind. I knew it would be controversial but, more importantly, I knew it was right. Les Sealey, who was brought in on loan from Luton Town at the end of 1989 as cover when injuries left us dangerously short of goalkeepers, had played in place of the rested Leighton a couple of times on the run-in to the final. Now I saw the East Londoner as a better bet than the Scot to supply goalkeeping reliability in the replay. Les was cocky and at times downright arrogant, so I did not foresee a failure of his nerve at Wembley. Was he a better goalkeeper than Jim? No, but he thought he was, and that can sometimes be important in a Cup final. He was a better organiser, but not as brave as Leighton. So there were pluses and minuses to be considered in both cases but I kept returning to the image of Jim Leighton in the dressing-room after the first game. I thought if I sent him out in the replay and he made another bad mistake it would destroy him and cost us the Cup. He might be equally devastated if I didn't play him, but if he had the courage to overcome the blow it was possible that he would come through the ordeal all right. In any case, there was really only one question to be answered: would Manchester United have a better chance of winning the Cup with or without Jim Leighton? The evidence against Jim was overwhelming. I was convinced that he was not in the right mental state to withstand another severe examination at Wembley.

Knowing how much of a fuss would be created by dropping him, I kept my cards close to my chest in the build-up to the second game. Only Archie Knox was privy to my thoughts. Archie disagreed with me. An assistant is often in closer touch with the chat in the dressing-room than a manager can be and from what

Archie said I gathered that Sealey was not the most popular person among the other players. I could understand Archie's concern but I always remember Jock Stein saying that his best team was not at all limited to players he liked: 'I wouldn't go out for dinner with half of them but they have won games for me.' I agree with Jock that you cannot allow players' personalities to sway your judgement when picking a team. My regard for Jim as a person did not come into it. I worked for Manchester United and my respect for the club and supporters required me to make a decision which would benefit Manchester United. I loved the club and wanted to stay there and enjoy it and quite clearly that meant winning the Cup. I had no illusions about that. Prior to dinner on the eve of the replay, I broke the news of Jim's omission to him and he took it very badly. I felt so sorry for him. Quite naturally, he was not really interested in listening to my best efforts to explain the choice of Sealey. At least our exchange happened in private, not in front of the other members of the team.

We won the replay 1–0 with a Lee Martin goal in a game marred by the extreme physical aggression of the Palace team. They tore into us with one bad tackle after another. The referee, Ally Gunn, had handled the Saturday match admirably but appeared to be caught off-guard by the sudden change in Palace. In fact, they helped us to win the Cup. If they had concentrated on their own strengths, they would have posed us more problems. Other than an Andy Gray free kick, they never made a proper chance and we won with a fair degree of comfort. The atmosphere at the end of the game was wonderful and I felt satisfied that all the pain and hard work had been rewarded. It was great to see Manchester United players celebrating at the finish. It was to justify such scenes that I had come to the club. My son Jason somehow managed to get on to the pitch and was chased by several stewards and policemen until I let them know who he was. His two brothers had been flabbergasted when he left them standing on the terraces and leapt over the boundary wall.

The dressing-room at Wembley is a fine place to be when you are a winner. This was my first experience of competing at the stadium and I found myself thinking that a little more of the same over the next few seasons wouldn't go amiss. At the press conference the main thrust of the questions related to Leighton. I expected that and wasn't uncomfortable about being grilled. I was made to feel much more uneasy when we met up with our wives and families at Wembley station. As I went forward to speak to Jim Leighton's wife, Linda, she gave me the two fingers and turned her back on me. That stung. The headlines next morning were varied, with the most severe accusing me of betraying Leighton. That allegation has hung in the air over the years and, in a way, Leighton has been glorified. My view of the affair is very different. I have something to ask those who see Jim as a victim and me as a villain: if we had lost the Cup final and I had lost my job, would Jim Leighton have felt guilty? Would he have apologised? I think the answer in both instances is no. To put it bluntly, I believe Jim was selfish. As far as I am aware, not once did he hold his hands up and take any blame. No, it was all Alex Ferguson's fault. It is all part of the self-protecting mentality common to goalkeepers. Everybody in the game recognises that theirs is a specialist position, where the slightest error can be disastrous, and that gives them the right to defend their interests aggressively. But it does not make them immune to judgement when their form falters. We are all open to criticism but Jim has not behaved as if he accepts that. I profoundly regret that our relationship deteriorated but I have no remorse. During the World Cup of 1990 I did my best to reconnect with Jim by phoning him at the Scotland base in Italy and trying to coax him out of the gloom that had settled on him after he was criticised for a goal lost to Brazil. There was no feedback from him. The gulf between us widened at Old Trafford when I chose to stay with Les Sealey as my goalkeeper in the following season. Jim went on loan to Sheffied United and Arsenal before being transferred to Dundee for a small fee. His career was becalmed for a while but eventually he restored momentum to it and played so convincingly that he represented Scotland at the 1998 World Cup in France just a month short of his fortieth birthday. I am happy that any damage done to him by the 1990 Wembley Cup final was not permanent.

That final did not effect a transformation in Manchester United but it did sow the seeds of one. My worries about the dangers of developing the mentality of a Cup team were swiftly eased by the clear evidence that this time the lifting of a trophy would have long-term benefits. I could see in new players like Pallister and Ince a sharpening of the appetite for winning that promised to carry them, and the club, on to a higher level of achievement. People were now recognising the qualities of Mike Phelan, not least his versatility, and there was reason to hope that the Wembley success would help with the confidence problem which was the one cloud over the prospects of Danny Wallace. He was a lovely lad, with plenty of talent, but there was always a doubt about whether the peculiar strains of playing for a club as big as United would be too much for his fragile self-belief. There was more tangible cause to be concerned about Neil Webb. Since returning after his dreadful Achilles injury, he had not been able to restore the edge to his game. I comforted myself with the thought that rigorous pre-season training might make a difference. On the whole, I was pleased with the progress of the mature players we had acquired and it was impossible not to be excited by what we were seeing from some of the younger lads on the staff. I was certain that Lee Martin was on the verge of proving that he was of international calibre and Lee Sharpe, having put his hernia troubles of the previous season behind him, was ready again to bring his tremendous pace to the left side of our attack. My son Darren, who had signed for us as a schoolboy, was coming along well and had earned the right to train with the first-team squad.

All my three boys had shown ability as footballers but Darren was the most talented. The eldest, Mark, a centre-forward with good technique, had played for Aberdeen reserves. Darren's twin, Jason, was also a centre-forward but more of the terrier type, with something of his father's capacity for causing ructions on the field. He was honoured by Scotland in the Boys' Club grade and later had a season with the Manchester United youth team. But both he and Mark realised that they could have more of a future outside football. Jason is building a career in television and Mark is highly rated as a financial analyst in the City. Darren's skills – he had wonderful composure on the ball and passed it with accuracy and imagination – more than justified sticking with football, and as an eighteen-year-old in the summer of 1990 he was giving strong indications that he would make the first team. If he didn't, his mother's opinion of my judgement as a manager was liable to be harsh.

Whereas most of the promising young footballers at Old Trafford evoked a restrained optimism, there was a less guarded enthusiasm for a slip of a lad who had just started life as an apprentice. The only honest reaction to Ryan Giggs was feverish excitement. He had made the transition from schoolboy to senior football with absolute ease and by the end of October he was lighting up the place. Leading players at the club raved about him as much as I did after I fielded him for the reserves against the first team at the Cliff one morning. Ryan was directly opposed to that ebullient character Viv Anderson and when they lined up Viv suggested that the skinny little boy standing forlornly on the wing would be better employed going off for some breakfast. The comment was soon regretted. As Ryan flew past him effortlessly and hit a screamer of a shot, big Viv was squealing like a pig. 'Who is that?' was what he was demanding to know, but in his discomfort he put the question rather less politely. From that day on, the members of the first team were constantly asking me when young Giggs would be joining them.

There was definitely a current of positive change running through Old Trafford and, with Denis Irwin signed from Oldham to further strengthen our defence, I felt we were entitled to expect a really good season. Whether we could match the consistency of Arsenal and Liverpool was another matter. Defeat at Sunderland in only our third game of the season, and then a 4–0 humiliation at Anfield, reminded us of how far our standards still had to be raised. But we were cheered by a smooth journey into the quarter-finals of the European Cup Winners' Cup, with eight goals scored and none lost in disposing of Pecsi Munkas of Hungary and Wrexham.

The League Cup, too, was a source of pleasure. In the third round we had a convincing 3–1 win over Liverpool on our ground and in the fourth we produced a result that ranks as the most amazing in my thirteen years at United when we walloped Arsenal 6–2 at Highbury. That Arsenal game involved extra pressure for both teams, since it came soon after the league meeting at Old Trafford in mid-October when the two sets of players decided they would rather fight than play football. The fracas began, improbably, with an exchange between Anders Limpar and Denis Irwin. Nigel Winterburn became involved and then Brian McClair waded in, perhaps venting anger that had been simmering since the penalty incident at Highbury a couple of years earlier. Soon there was a mass confrontation, a mêlée in which it was hard to distinguish the individual scraps from the efforts of the more sensible players to calm matters down. Afterwards both clubs were fined. In addition, Arsenal, whose previous bad behaviour was taken into account, were docked two points and we had one taken away. Such a background did not create the ideal climate for the League Cup-tie in London but the teams ensured there was no repeat of the nonsense. It was a straightforward football match and on the night we were superb. Danny Wallace gave his finest display in the United colours but the star of the game was Lee Sharpe, who was just about irresistible and scored a hat-trick.

Another hat-trick carried us through the next round. In fact, the two-legged tie with Southampton was a personal triumph for Mark Hughes, who kept us alive with a late equaliser in the 1–1 draw at the Dell and then hit all of our goals at home when we won the replay 3–2. Running Mark close for the honours in that tie was a young Alan Shearer, who scored once in Southampton and twice at Old Trafford. The calm with which Shearer took a penalty in the second game identified him as a player with great confidence in himself and also marked him down as someone we would be watching very carefully over the next season. Of more immediate concern was our League Cup semi-final against Leeds United, the second leg of which would take us to Elland Road, where the crowd invariably give us the impression that lynching would be too good for us. It often seems to me that the intimidating atmosphere created by their supporters inhibits the Leeds players more than it does ours and that was apparently the case as we set out to build on the 2–1 advantage gained in the first game. Leeds hardly threatened us and we did not really need the last-minute goal that brought the tie to a sour and controversial end. At the time, Lee Sharpe appeared to be in an offside position when he scored but TV proved that, by beginning his run from his own half, he had made the goal valid. Naturally, such niceties escaped the partisan spectators and there were one or two minor crowd invasions around the trackside. Eric Harrison, our youth coach, was on the bench for the game and was attacked by some fans from the main stand. Eric happens to be a Yorkshireman but that did not save him from the consequences of bearing a certain physical resemblance to me. I think he was drawing fire that was meant for his manager. Well done, Eric! Such self-sacrifice does not go unnoticed. In the worst of the other distasteful incidents that were reported, some of our directors and their wives had tea and other drinks thrown over them. Nice place, Leeds.

As our Cup challenges developed on two fronts, our league form was patchy. We had two consistent spells – one when we went ten games undefeated and the other when we were unbeaten through seven – but we were nowhere near championship standard and when we eventually finished sixth in the table it was a fair reflection of how erratically we had performed. I could, however, see signs that we were consolidating and approaching the stage of improvement when we might be a force in the championship contest. Success in the knockout competitions was making it easier to be patient about the rate of progress. With a League Cup final against Sheffield Wednesday up ahead, we prepared with relish for our Cup Winners' Cup quarter-final collision with Montpellier. When we have European engagements, if at all possible I watch our opponents in advance and, with the help of other reports from our chief scout, Les Kershaw, I acquaint myself thoroughly with their strengths and weaknesses. Leaving England in March to head for the south of France was no hardship and the trip to Montpellier became even more enjoyable after I booked into a nice little hotel called La Maison Blanche. It was owned by an interesting man named Jean Phillippe Casalta, who initiated me into the varied delights of French wines, implanting an interest that has since brought me much pleasure. Jean Phillippe's hospitality did not distract me from the purpose of my visit and it was reassuring to conclude that Montpellier were no more than a good team with one or two eye-catching individuals. The most spectacular of those was the Colombian midfield player Valderrama, he of the colourful hairstyle, but I reckoned him to be more of a luxury than a major strength and went away quite hopeful.

The first leg of the quarter-final started perfectly for us. Before a minute had been played, Lee Sharpe produced one of his electrifying bursts of speed and cut the ball back for Brian McClair to put us in front. For a while it looked as if we were going to swamp the French opposition but, in keeping with United's habit of turning comfortable positions into melodramas, we pressed the self-destruct button and let them back into the game. I must admit Lee Martin was terribly unlucky in presenting Montpellier with their equaliser. There seemed to be no danger when he freakishly sliced the ball past Les Sealey. Lee was not the most confident of people and that blunder was the last thing he needed in a season already blighted by injury. All the promise of the previous season, when he scored the goal that settled the Cup final at Wembley, had ground to a halt. There were hints that much the same might happen to United's bid for the Cup Winners' Cup. As we grappled to bring some semblance of order to our play, the tactical and technical superiority of our opponents underlined the cost to us of being out of European football too long. No amount of preparation or advice from me could be a substitute for the experience of playing. One of the most baffling problems for English teams that are not familiar with the continental game is the suddenness with which opponents can change their pace. Our players may be going along nicely, with the game seemingly under control, then in an instant the other team have gone up through the gears and are wreaking havoc. I drum into my men the necessity of maintaining total concentration as a safeguard against such sudden upping of the tempo but I know that now and again they will still be caught out. Having been shaken by that draw at Old Trafford, which had left Montpellier with the substantial advantage of an away goal, United were plainly facing a severe examination in southern France. It was going to be essential for us to exercise patience and jealously protect our possession of the ball. Of course, a little luck would also be welcome – and we were about to be given some.

Our good fortune came after the bad break of losing Paul Ince to injury early in the second match. I moved Clayton Blackmore into midfield from left-back and brought Lee Martin on as substitute to take over from Clayton. Almost as soon as Clayton had adapted himself to his new position, the ball fell so nicely for him about thirty yards out that he was never going to think twice about using his formidable shooting power. The shot was powerful but luck intervened for us when the French goalkeeper, Barabe, let the ball spill through his hands and into the net. Montpellier looked shattered as they came in at half-time and there could be only one theme for my team-talk: 'Don't give the ball away.' Even I am fed up listening to that edict but players cannot be reminded often enough of its importance. Our lads didn't let themselves down. They cruised through the second half, with a goal from Steve Bruce giving us a comfortable 2–0 scoreline on the night. In the dressing-room afterwards there was the special glow that comes from European success in the other team's country. The sense of achievement lifts everybody, from coach to player to kit man. That feeling was enhanced when the great Michel Platini came in to congratulate us on our performance.

When the draw was made for the semi-finals, we wanted to avoid Barcelona and Juventus. Our prayers were answered when we were paired with Legia Warsaw and, in preparation for the first leg in Poland, Archie Knox and Les Kershaw undertook the scouting duties. Archie always seemed to be unlucky in the allocation of these expeditions, although he accused me of taking the nice trips and sending him to football's bleaker outposts. He certainly didn't have a pleasant jaunt to Warsaw, where Polish security men stayed close to him throughout his stay and shared his bedroom for two nights. Archie says he slept with his back to the wall. There could be no assumptions of succeeding against Legia, since time has shown that visitors rarely have easy games in Poland. But we had reasons to be confident. Our form had improved, young Sharpe was flying and the big, wide pitch would be right up his street. As might be expected of an Iron Curtain team, Legia were quite rigid but had one or two gifted individuals who were relied upon to exert a major influence. Our task was to deny those players encouragement and we set about it quite aggressively, managing to worry our opponents with our emphasis on playing the ball forward to Sharpe. We made a few chances but missed them and that was a concern as the first half wore on. Then, as is liable to happen away from home, Legia counter-attacked and scored. Once again, fears about our ability to cope with the demands of Europe came flooding back and I wondered how we might be penalised for being without the experience and leadership of Bryan Robson, who had failed a fitness test before the match. Instant reassurance was provided when we went surging upfield from the kick-off and equalised through Brian McClair. It was an untidy goal but wonderful nonetheless. A few minutes later Legia had a man sent off for bringing down Sharpe when he was racing through with a good chance of scoring. That dismissal flattened them and goals from Hughes and Bruce gave us a healthy lead to take back to Old Trafford.

The second leg of the Cup Winners' Cup semi-final was played three days after we met Sheffield Wednesday in the Rumbelows Cup final at Wembley. Given how much a match on the famous turf can take out of players, that was obviously a problem. But first we had to deal with the League Cup final itself and, with Ron Atkinson as the Wednesday manager, I knew they would be pumped up for the occasion. I believe I picked the wrong team for the game. I am not certain that a different line-up would have altered the result but it would have enabled us to perform better. My selection was based on the midfield three of Webb, Ince and Robson, simply because the combination had never figured in a losing team during the couple of years those three players had been together at the club. That seemed adequate justification for leaving Mike Phelan on the bench. But on the day we lacked penetration on the right side of midfield and, with Sharpe on our left wing controlled by the experienced Roland Nilsson, we were far below our best. Having fallen behind to a goal scored by John Sheridan, a Manchester lad and United fan, we laid siege to the Wednesday goal but our former goalkeeper, Chris Turner, refused to be beaten. Losing 1–0 was a serious disappointment but I couldn't allow the gloom to settle on us and affect our performance on the following Wednesday night. Paul Ince had to miss the European assignment because of injury but neither his absence nor Wembley's draining effect on the others was likely to count for as much as the two-goal lead we had over Legia. There was never any doubt about the outcome once Lee Sharpe put us ahead in the first half. The Poles' late equaliser meant little and we qualified smoothly for a final showdown with Barcelona in Rotterdam.

So many old friends had turned up for that semi-final (including the usual contingent from Scotland) that we had to go to the dressing-room to continue our celebrations. It was a night of deep satisfaction for Archie Knox and me. We had been through a lot together since our days at Aberdeen and now we could really feel that our work at Old Trafford was lifting Manchester United back to where the club belonged. Yet I noticed that Archie, usually the life and soul of the party, was rather subdued. I was slightly puzzled, but not worried. We all have quiet moments when private preoccupations make us withdraw from what is happening around us. The next day the cause of Archie's quietness became crystal clear when I received bad news in a call from Walter Smith, who had just been appointed manager of Rangers. He told me that Archie had accepted his offer of the assistant manager's job at

Ibrox. I consider Walter a good friend and it was difficult to fall out with him over the approach he had made. 'I have to do what will be best for Rangers and will give me the maximum chance of being successful,' Walter said, and I couldn't argue with that. When I spoke to Archie it was obvious that the financial package at Ibrox was well above what we were paying him but I wasn't prepared to give up, so I spoke to our chairman about an improved contract. Over the next twenty-four hours I did my utmost to keep Archie and in my several discussions with him I stressed the attractions of being part of a European final against Barcelona.

'You may never be involved in such a match again,' I said. I thought that argument would persuade him to stay at least until after the final in Rotterdam, but he was set on going quickly.

Many people have drawn fanciful conclusions about our subsequent relationship and some have suggested that Archie and I haven't spoken to each other since the parting. That is absolute nonsense. It is true that I was disappointed. We had come through difficult times at Old Trafford and I felt he should have stayed with me to see our efforts reach fruition. What must also be said is that for some time before he left we had not been as close socially as we were at Aberdeen, when we went out together every weekend. Away from work, we seemed to drift apart as his friendship with Brian Kidd developed. But I believe our own friendship was still strong. The disappointment, however, did linger with me for a while and I found it hard to come to terms with his departure. People may imagine that a manager in my position has the skin of a rhinoceros and can shrug off any setback effortlessly, but nobody is unbreakable. Archie's decision to go did make me feel vulnerable for a while but there was never any bitterness in my reaction. I have no time for that. My priority was to ensure that his leaving did not affect the strong team spirit within the club.

A couple of weeks before we were due to face Barcelona in Rotterdam, I had an interesting phone call from Steve Archibald, who had been such an outstanding striker for me at Aberdeen. Steve had played for Barcelona and was still living in the city and his call gave me a chance to arrange for us to meet when I went to Spain to watch our opponents in a league game. I had studied both legs of their semi-final against Juventus on video but there is no substitute for watching football live. That Spanish league match produced a problem for them and a bonus for me as Hristo Stoichkov, their talented Bulgarian forward, damaged a hamstring so badly that he pulled up as if he had been shot. It was plain that he would not be in the Cup Winners' Cup final. Their renowned goalkeeper, Andoni Zubizarreta, was suspended, so by the time I arrived in the restaurant for a meal with Steve and his wife I was in a chirpy mood and ready to bombard him with all sorts of questions about the Barcelona players who would be on the field. Who were the team's key influences, on and off the park? Who were the nervous individuals whose temperaments might be exploited? His answers were extremely helpful. Steve then surprised me by saying that Johan Cruyff had been inquiring about me and particularly about how effective I was likely to be tactically. I asked Steve what kind of report he had delivered and his reply was that he had given Cruyff his honest opinion, that I would not be found wanting on tactics. I suggested it might have been more of a help if he had told the Barcelona coach I was hopeless but, obviously, I knew that anything said beforehand wouldn't matter much once the action started. My thoroughly pleasant evening with the Archibalds, during which I gave him plenty of ribbing about how much his career owed to my influence, did nothing to reduce the feeling of optimism that had been building in me as the biggest occasion of my first four and a half years with Manchester United drew near. I felt the passage to the final had been fairly comfortable. There was no certainty that it had made us ready for a crack at opposition like Barcelona, but I have always thought that once you are in a final you have every right to fancy your chances of winning.

What was vital was to make sure that the players were handling the off-field pressures. I had to keep them in a frame of mind to be stimulated by the challenge and not weighed down by it. A good friend of mine in Holland, Ton van Dalen, gave invaluable assistance with our preparation when he arranged for us to take over an entire hotel on the outskirts of Rotterdam. The treatment we received from the hotel staff was unbelievable. They could not do enough for us. For collective relaxation, a huge lounge had been set out with pool tables, darts, quiz games and a big TV screen with a good selection of sports and movie videos. I have often been accused of being a fiend for quizzes and I cannot claim that I remained aloof when disputes were raging about the validity of answers. Nobody did more to relax the players than Jimmy Steel, whose work as masseur with Celtic and Scotland over many years had proved his gift for having a healthy effect on the bodies and the morale of footballers. Jimmy was already well into his seventies but I never had a moment's doubt about the wisdom of inviting him to be a member of our party. For our training ground activities, we used the facilities of a small amateur team in the village beside the hotel and there, too, we were looked after splendidly. One of the drawbacks about finals of such magnitude is that, once you are at the location, it is very difficult to do any functional work relating to the game and how you will deal with your opponents, as there are so many press people and other outsiders floating around. So the specifics of the game plan have to be in shape before you arrive.

There was no lack of confidence in my pre-match tactics talks. I identified two key requirements in coping with Barcelona. In all their games their main objective was to create the extra man in midfield, either by having Ronald Koeman break out from the back or Michael Laudrup drop off from the front into the hole behind the other team's midfield. My instructions to Steve Bruce and Gary Pallister were that they must not be drawn in among the midfielders but, at the same time, make sure that they were defending high so that there was no substantial space in which Laudrup could hurt us. To offset Koeman's threat, I told Brian McClair to play in behind Mark Hughes and be ready to choke Koeman's space if he broke from the back, thus reducing the Dutchman's scope for his exceptional passing. Naturally, Brian was not to confine himself to a negative role. When we gained possession he was to use his running ability and good positional sense to give Barcelona trouble.

As our coach made its way to the stadium through streets brightened by the colours of the rival fans, the sight that warmed me most was the smiling face of Sir Matt Busby. He was glowing with pride. When the coach drew up outside the main entrance, our supporters were in a frenzy, battering the windows and sides of the bus, urging us with clenched fists and screaming out affection for the team. But as the door swung open and Sir Matt led us out, the clamour ceased instantly and in its place there was polite clapping, which he acknowledged with a dignified wave. There could hardly have been more reverence for the Pope in St Peter's Square. It was a moment I knew I would remember forever. I just followed on behind Sir Matt. 'I'm with him,' my body language was saying. Inside the stadium, my principle of staying away from the players in the period immediately before kick-off was difficult to maintain because there was nowhere obvious for me to go. As I flitted about the corridors, I bumped into Johan Cruyff and followed the example of Gothenburg by presenting Johan with a bottle of single-malt Scotch, just as I had done to Alfredo Di Stefano before Aberdeen beat Real Madrid in an earlier staging of this same final. I hoped the outcome of the evening would be as satisfying as the one in Sweden eight years before. With the teams ready to take the field, there was an unexpected hitch that delayed the start. It meant that our lads had to sit down again in the dressing-room. I noticed Paul Ince was really nervous and motioned to Eric Harrison, our youth coach, to have a quiet word with him. Then, in our moment of need, the bold Jimmy Steel started to sing and dance around the floor. 'Come to the ball, music and splendour for all' was not a line our young lads were likely to be familiar with, but their looks of amazement gave way to amusement and they relaxed. Even Incey managed a half-smile.

The first half was played cautiously by both teams, although I thought we shaded it, our only problem being that young Sharpe was positioning himself too predictably as an out and out winger. That simplified the task of Barcelona's right-back, Miguel Angel

Nadal, whose pace was a match for Lee's on the night. The lad had enjoyed a great season and there was clearly a possibility that it had taken its toll but I knew he could do a much better job for us if he reacted more quickly when our attacks broke down, tucking in closer to Ince and Robson and preventing us from being outnumbered in midfield. Barcelona were relying heavily on Laudrup to give them the extra man in that area, having found that Koeman's attempts to come out from the back were ineffective. I also felt that Sharpe would have more success if he began his runs well infield from the touchline, nearer to an old-fashioned inside-left position. I was pleased from the outset with McClair's contribution, pleased but not surprised. No matter what role he was given, he had a wonderful ability to adapt easily. On this occasion he was doing more than simply closing the door on Koeman. His running off the ball in the first half caused the opposition a lot of anxiety.

In the second half we picked up our game well and now Lee Sharpe was applying the advice to make his runs from those infield positions and Nadal was no longer sure about how to handle him. The greater variety in Lee's thrusts gave us much more penetration. There was no doubt that we were the more positive team but when reward came it was from a rather unexpected source. The awarding of a free kick to us thirty-five yards out was, as usual, a signal for our two centre-backs, Bruce and Pallister, to make a foray into our opponents' penalty box. The angle and distance did not suggest a goal opportunity, more a chance to put them under pressure. When Bryan Robson shaped to take the kick, I noticed that their goalkeeper had advanced slightly from his line and thought, 'Keep it away from him.' Robson's delivery was a tempter for the goalkeeper, not too far away but just far enough to give Bruce an invitation to compete for the ball. In that situation you knew one thing – Brucie wouldn't pull out. He has had his nose broken too often to allow any questions about his courage. He was first to Robson's cross, with the goalkeeper left in the wilderness. I was sure it was Steve's goal but replays on TV proved Mark Hughes had touched it before it crossed the line. What a moment that was for Sparky against the club that got rid of him. A bit of justice there, I thought.

Our second goal may have been a fraction offside but neutrals will remember it for Mark Hughes's brilliant finishing. When he took the ball wide on the right it appeared that the severity of the angle would rule out scoring. But Sparky was never discouraged by a hint of the impossible and, with the air of a man doing something simple, he drove his shot unerringly into the empty net, with the goalkeeper once again off picking daisies somewhere. Two goals up with fifteen minutes left, surely the Cup was ours. But it doesn't seem to be in the character of Manchester United to do things the easy way. Ten minutes from the end, a Koeman free kick put Barcelona back in the game with a vengeance. My main worry was the fitness of our goalkeeper, Les Sealey, who was starting to show signs of wear and tear from an injury suffered in the League Cup final three weeks before. I had Gary Walsh warming up vigorously with the intention of bringing him on if the match went into extra time, but obviously hoped that wouldn't be necessary. Hoping was my main activity as Barcelona made their push to equalise and, after looking so comfortable earlier, we were reduced to hanging on. It was at that point that Clayton Blackmore had his finest moment in the red jersey. Brought up in the club, the Welshman was possessed of huge ability but he lacked the yard of pace needed to make him truly outstanding in his natural midfield position. However, settled in at left-back for that season, he had made it his best ever and crowned it by kicking a shot from Laudrup off the line with only a few minutes left to be played. As long as there is a Manchester United, that rescue act will be remembered.

What do you do when the last blast of the referee's whistle clinches victory in a European final? I don't think anybody was surprised at my joyful cavortings or how they were matched by the rest of the staff and the players. I impersonated an orchestra conductor as the fans sang their new-found anthem: 'Always look on the bright side of life'. For everybody associated with United, it was a time to treasure. The celebration at the hotel was out of this world and to this day we still talk about it. The buffet alone would have made it unforgettable. There would be other nights for sleeping. This one was for a party, and it stretched on and on.

On the day after the final, I was in an optimistic fervour as I laid out my plans for the next season. 'We are going to win the League,' I proudly informed the gathering hordes. It was a risky declaration but an honest statement of how I felt. I had decided it was time I took the gloves off and challenged this team of mine. David Meek, who had been chronicling the fortunes of United on behalf of the *Manchester Evening News* for so long that he was part of the fabric of Old Trafford, had understandable reservations about my confidence.

'You were a bit over-bullish there, Mr Ferguson, don't you think?' he said to me. He had seen many false dawns in the past and was concerned that I might be storing up trouble for myself.

'David, if Manchester United can win a European trophy, why can't we win the League?' I said. 'It is about time I raised the stakes at this club.'

A deluge of rain did not prevent Manchester from giving us a magnificent and moving welcome home. All of us who had been in Holland were still flying on adrenaline and at the end of the long victory parade we were ready to do another circuit. A chance to savour my happiest summer since arriving at United came when Cathy and I treated ourselves to a month's holiday in America to mark the twenty-fifth anniversary of our wedding. I could look back and see the progress United had made in the year between taking the FA Cup and capturing the Cup Winners' Cup. Winning trophies had given me more authority in the handling of my job and the control of the players. As I have said before and will no doubt say again, only through success can a manager gain the control that is indispensable to him. Making good the promise I had delivered about the League would not be easy but my prospects would be improved by two summer signings. In completing those transfers I had my first serious dealings with international football agents. My experience of their strange world is a story that deserves to stand on its own.

— 17 —
AMONG THE AGENTS

'DON'T you remember me?' The speaker was a young, blond-haired man who was visiting Old Trafford in 1991 with a group from a Norwegian advertising agency interested in taking space on the perimeter boards at televised matches. I couldn't place him and he had to tell me his name. It was one that few people associated with British football in the Nineties are ever likely to forget: Rune Hauge. So I was acquainted with the most notorious agent in football even before he was an agent, or at least before he was operating officially in that capacity. Rune Hauge was, of course, the man found to have handed over £425,500 to George Graham in the 'bung' scandal that caused George to be sacked by Arsenal in February 1995 after managing the club with remarkable success since 1986. George returned all the money to Arsenal, plus £40,000 interest, but his job was gone and he was banned from football for a year. Now flourishing again with Tottenham, he must look back ruefully on his dealings with Rune. I was so upset by the implications in a story that appeared in the *Daily Mail* in 1997 under the headline 'Bizarre Tale of a Reviled Football Agent . . . and a Friend Called Fergie' that Manchester United's barrister, Tom Shields, was consulted. He advised me against going to court.

'They are not saying you are crooked,' I was told. 'They are saying you are a friend of a disgraced agent and that makes a libel action a dubious proposition. Nobody at Manchester United thinks anything other than that you are completely honest, and you should just forget this.' That was not the advice I was hoping to hear. I wanted to go all the way, as I always would with anybody who cast a slur on my reputation. But no doubt Tom Shields was steering me on the right and practical course. As he said, nobody in the game has any grounds for doubting my integrity.

The truth is that I am not on terms of close friendship with Rune, but I have never had any hesitation in dealing with him, since he is a brilliant judge of a player and a real professional when it comes to finding the best talent. There cannot be many chairmen or managers in the Premier League who have not availed themselves of Hauge's skills at one time or another. Only once did he mention money to me, in a roundabout way, and I cut him short. I remember exactly what I said to him.

'Look, Rune, don't talk money to me. You talk to the chairman about that.' He never again raised the subject.

I am sure only a small percentage of agents are involved with 'bungs'. The possibility of financial inducements being connected with a transfer has been put to me only two or three times, and the kind of response I gave Hauge has killed the conversation before it could develop. On one occasion, an Italian agent was desperate to take Ryan Giggs to Italy and, when informed that Ryan was not for sale at any price, he insisted there must be a way of doing business. I repeated that Giggs would not be leaving United in any circumstances. The agent then inquired how many children I had.

'I have three sons,' I told him, and asked why he wanted to know.

'Mr Ferguson, if you sell me Ryan Giggs, we will look after you and your sons,' he said. 'They won't have to work again.' This was an aspect of football so alien to me that I could hardly absorb the fact that he was serious. He certainly knew I was serious when I told him what he could do with his offer, and he never uttered another word about money.

Back in 1991 at Old Trafford, Rune Hauge was justified in asking if I remembered him. We had met fleetingly in 1984 when Aberdeen went to play Nuremberg in a pre-season friendly. Rune was youth development coach with Nuremberg at the time. Although there were clear indications seven years later that he was working in advertising, he seemed to be doing the groundwork for a career as an agent, for he asked me if I was in need of any players. I admitted that I was urgently on the look-out for a wide right player and he mentioned a young Russian, Andrei Kanchelskis, and said he would send a video of the winger playing for his national team against Italy. When I studied the video I was immediately impressed and phoned Hauge to find out how I could advance my interest in Kanchelskis. I soon learned that to do so I would have to enter the strange realm of the international football agent. Our target, it turned out, had three agents – a Russian (Grigory Essaoulenko), a German and a Swiss. We were beginning to think we were in a John Le Carré novel. But the price quoted was attractive and after Martin Edwards and I had watched Kanchelskis play for Russia against Germany in Frankfurt, I knew we were looking at a bargain. He showed exceptional pace and stamina that night. As I assured the chairman, for £600,000 we were getting a young player who was fast and athletic and had a great physique. If sold on, he would bring our money back at the least. We couldn't lose. After the match we returned to the hotel to tie up the deal with the agents. They had authority from Kanchelskis's club, Shakhtyor Donetsk, to conclude the transaction, and that was done quite quickly. The £600,000 fee would be almost doubled if the player made a certain number of appearances but the figure specified was high, and if he played all those games he would be well worth the extra payment. Negotiating the personal financial arrangements of Kanchelskis was more complicated, since everything had to be calculated in net sums. Most foreign players insist on talking net. To avoid any suspicion of illegality, it has always been the practice of Manchester United simply to add on the tax in such deals. They pay more that way, but it keeps everything above board. With all the money questions answered, and a work permit for Andrei secured, we were able to field our new recruit in our last match of the 1990–91 season and his power and pace made us optimistic that he could provide the penetration on the right side which had been conspicuously missing.

Rune Hauge had become involved, if only as a peripheral presence, in the later stages of the Kanchelskis signing in Frankfurt. I suppose he was around because he had brought United to the table. He was more centrally concerned in the other major transfer we completed on the Continent in the summer of 1991. Representing Peter Schmeichel over his move from Brondby in Denmark to us was, I think, what launched Rune as a football agent. My enthusiasm for Schmeichel dated from a time when I took our players to Spain for a break and found that we were staying at the same hotel as Brondby. We shared local training facilities, making sure our workout hours did not clash. I had heard of the big goalkeeper but had no plans to have him watched until I saw him on that Spanish training ground. Instantly I knew I was seeing somebody very much out of the ordinary. I sent Alan Hodgkinson, our goalkeeping coach in those days, to watch Schmeichel in several matches. Each time Alan spoke highly of him, stressing that he would have no problem adjusting to English football, which can be difficult for goalkeepers coming into our game from abroad. Soon it was common knowledge in Scandinavia that we were keen on the Dane and quite a few agents phoned or faxed me, claiming to represent him. Such claims are basic to one of the oldest tricks of the agency trade. The routine might start with agent X phoning me, letting me know that he is speaking on behalf of a player and asking if I would be interested in buying him. If the footballer involved is of high quality, I am liable to say I am interested. Agent X then goes to the player he has claimed to represent, but probably doesn't, and says he has authority from Alex Ferguson and Manchester United to set up a deal. It is neat, but nowadays most managers are alert to such machinations and will play along only if the end result suits their own agenda for their clubs. The agents who tried to work their way into our negotiations over Schmeichel had little chance. Our approaches to Brondby were simplified by the knowledge that Peter's contract was due to expire the following November. In the summer of

1990, Brondby had been demanding much more than we were prepared to pay. The signing, when it took place in August of 1991, was for a fee of £505,000, which made it one of the bargains of the century in football. During most of his time with us, a golden spell in our history that was to finish perfectly with the European Cup triumph in Barcelona, Peter Schmeichel was the best goalkeeper in the world.

Perhaps I should have guessed that my most disturbing experiences with an agent would involve Grigory Essaoulenko, the Russian member of Andrei Kanchelskis's advisory group. Grigory always conveyed a sense that he might be familiar with a shadowy world more dangerous than the boardrooms and hotel suites in which transfer business is usually conducted. Just how unorthodox he could be as a negotiator had not become clear in 1994 when Kanchelskis agreed a new four-year contract which put him on a par with all the top earners at Old Trafford. What I did not know about the contract then was that it included a clause that would entitle the player to a third of the fee in any future transfer. Had I been aware of that clause, I would have understood more readily the intolerable situation that developed in Kanchelskis's relationship with Manchester United in the ensuing months. But long before that trouble manifested itself I was to be shaken by something that happened between Grigory and me. The 1994–95 season was barely under way when we had our first televised match against Nottingham Forest at the City Ground on a Monday evening. We drew 1–1, with our goal coming from a fine volley by Kanchelskis. It was a fair result and we travelled back to Manchester in the coach quite contented. We arrived at Old Trafford about one o'clock in the morning and all started scurrying for our cars to hurry home. I had promised Maurice Watkins a lift to the Four Seasons Hotel, which was near the airport and pretty much on the way to my house. As I was about to leave the car park, Grigory Essaoulenko stopped me and I opened my window to find out what he wanted. He said that we needed to speak and that he had a gift for me. I told him I would collect it in the morning but he said he was leaving very early and would phone me shortly. Almost as soon as I had dropped Maurice off, my mobile rang and it was the Russian.

'I have to give you this gift tonight,' he said. I told him that wasn't convenient, that I was nearly home. 'I am at the Excelsior at the airport – it will only take a couple of minutes,' he insisted.

The detour was indeed minor, and I headed for his hotel. When I pulled up at the front entrance, Grigory was standing waiting for me, holding a handsomely wrapped box. He got into the car and handed me the parcel.

'This is a gift for you and your wife,' he said. 'I hope you like it.' Then he wished me good night and left the car.

I threw the parcel into the back seat and made off home. When I got in, Cathy was waiting up for me as usual, although it was now about 1.30 a.m. As is our habit, I unpacked and Cathy took my dirty gear through to the utility room. I began to open the parcel, assuming it contained a samovar or some other typically Russian present. I was in for a shock. What the box contained was money, bundles of the stuff. I shouted for Cathy and, when she rushed through, we stood staring at the piles of cash. After a while we counted it and in all there was £40,000. At first I didn't know what to do but Cathy said I should return the money to Essaoulenko immediately and that seemed sensible. Then alarming thoughts began to jump into my head. What if my meeting with Grigory had been filmed? I needed a witness to this madness. So we decided that I should take the box of cash to the club offices early in the morning. We hardly slept a wink that night and by nine o'clock I was at Old Trafford with the parcel, which could scarcely have made me more uncomfortable if it had been a bomb. I carried it to the office of the club secretary, Ken Merrett, and emptied it in front of him. When he had recovered from seeing all those thousands scattered across his desk, and from hearing the story I had to tell, we phoned Maurice Watkins for his advice. He instructed us to lodge the money in the club safe and document what we had done with the club solicitors and my own solicitor, Les Dalgarno of Paull and Williamson in Aberdeen. Les, like the rest of us, found the whole episode incredible. I was left wondering why Essaoulenko wanted to give me money. After all, I had never done anything out of the ordinary to help him. I wasn't even in on his negotiations with the chairman about Andrei's contract. If I had been able to foresee the dramas that were still to be enacted in the Kanchelskis saga, I might have wondered if the cash was meant to be not so much a thank-you for past assistance as an encouragement towards co-operation in the future. The £40,000 stayed in the Manchester United safe for nearly a year until Grigory turned up again at Old Trafford. While it lay unreturned, it made me uneasy, in spite of all the documentary evidence that established my innocence. There are hazards for managers out there among the agents, and not all of them can be traced to Rune Hauge. But the honest man has little to fear, so long as he takes pains to ensure that he is seen to be honest.

— 18 —
NEARLY BUT NOT QUITE

THERE were many reasons for our failure to fulfil my promise to win the last championship of the old First Division in 1992 and I don't hesitate to admit that the most important of them was the excellent campaign waged by Howard Wilkinson's Leeds United, who persevered resolutely and held their nerve well on the run-in. My congratulations to them when they finished four points ahead of us in the table were entirely sincere and, given that the disappointment endured then was the darkness before a pretty glorious dawn for Manchester United, I am hardly likely to turn sour about that season now. But there is a big difference between hiding behind excuses for a setback and trying to identify the reasons for it. Honest analysis of what went wrong enabled me to use 1991–92 as a springboard instead of allowing it to weigh on our spirits as an opportunity missed. Our supporters, having watched United complete a quarter of a century without a league title, found difficulty in seeing the late disintegration of our challenge as anything other than a disaster and many in the media felt my mistakes had contributed to the misery. I happen to believe that I was indeed culpable, but not in the ways that my critics suggested.

My main regret is not about something I did but about something I held back from doing. I think that with one decisive intervention I could have gained for us an advantage in the championship race that would have seen us over the line as winners. Quite simply, I should have gone ahead and signed Mick Harford from Luton when it was in my mind to do so. Mick probably did not strike many people as an ideal Manchester United player, especially when he was in his thirties. But, leaving aside the fact that the hard directness of his centre-forward play was underpinned by surprisingly good control, the quality of his aerial threat alone was sufficient to persuade me that he could be valuable to us. I am even more convinced now that his heading power could have helped us to cope with one of the three external factors that crucially handicapped our efforts to finish in front of Leeds. The three were the cabbage patch of a pitch at Old Trafford, the lunatic congestion of fixtures at the end of the season and a brutal accumulation of injuries that made it impossible for us to withstand a programme which at one point forced us to play four matches in seven days.

Our playing surface was the first problem to undermine us. It was terrible when I arrived in 1986 but, after I sought the assistance of an expert from Scotland, it improved and was fine from 1988 through most of 1991. But in the December of 1991 it just broke up and became a mess. To say it must have been just as much of a hardship for our opponents as for us is stupidly simplistic. Not many of them were as committed to the rhythm and flow of a passing game as we were. For players brought up with a dedication to control and to moving the ball smoothly on the ground, that pitch was a nightmare. We were rampant early in the season, collecting twenty-six of the first thirty points available to us and entering the Christmas and New Year period with only one defeat (away to Sheffield Wednesday) against our names. In spite of an horrendous home performance on New Year's Day against Queens Park Rangers, who beat us 4–1, our form did not come apart as dramatically as the pitch. But its dire influence was unmistakable as we ran up a series of draws against opponents we should have beaten and I had already recognised that relying on our passing game might be costly. It would obviously make sense to add an alternative attacking approach involving more crosses and a tall, brave centre-forward who could do damage in the air. Mick Harford struck me as the man who could give us aerial deadliness and I spoke to David Pleat, the Luton manager, about him. Sadly, I did not show enough resolve to push the deal through. If I had acted as purposefully as I should have done, we would have won the League.

As it was, we were at the top of the table when we went to Wembley to face Nottingham Forest in the Rumbelows Cup final on 12 April 1992, and when we beat Forest more comfortably than the 1–0 scoreline indicated there seemed every likelihood that the season's happy memories would far outweigh the other kind. We had already won the Super Cup by beating the holders of the European Cup, Red Star Belgrade, at Old Trafford. Anybody who was at that game must still be wondering how we managed to win it. I know I am. In the first half the Yugoslavs' star player, Dejan Savicevic, was absolutely sensational and it was a miracle that we came in level at half-time. I had to make a tactical move and once again it was to Mr Reliable, Brian McClair, that I turned. I told him to withdraw into the midfield to squeeze the space that Red Star had been exploiting. He did that to such good effect that we gained some decent possession and a measure of control. Then he scored the only goal of the match to claim a fairly outrageous victory. It was a bonus that I was able to bring on Ryan Giggs to give him a taste of the European atmosphere. Our good results in domestic competitions early in the season, and the high scoring rate we were maintaining, had a lot to do with the penetration we were achieving along the flanks. If young Ryan was flying on the left wing, so was our Ukrainian import, Andrei Kanchelskis, out on the right. With Peter Schmeichel steadily asserting himself as a remarkable goalkeeper and Paul Parker proving to be the strong, quick and disciplined defender I was sure we were buying when we paid QPR £2 million for him, I had ample reason to be satisfied with the previous summer's transfer business.

Winning the Super Cup scarcely compensated for the early collapse of our defence of the European Cup Winners' Cup. We had started satisfactorily by disposing of Panathinaikos of Greece but in the second round the loss of two goals in the last couple of minutes to Atletico Madrid in Spain left us carrying a 3–0 deficit to Old Trafford, and a 1–1 draw there meant we were well and truly dumped.

In the FA Cup, too, we had a painful exit. We drew 0–0 in a fourth-round tie at Southampton and then, after drawing 2–2 at the end of extra time in the replay at Old Trafford, we had the dubious distinction of becoming the first Division One team to be eliminated from the tournament in a penalty shoot-out. The blow was all the harder to take because our hopes had been raised by a 1–0 victory over Leeds at Elland Road in the previous round. That match, on 15 January, was our third meeting with Leeds on their ground within an eighteen-day period. By freakish coincidence, the League Cup draw had sent us into the same hostile territory for a quarter-final on 8 January and our league fixture had begun the sadistic sequence. We won two and drew the other and, of course, the draw had to occur on 29 December, with points at stake. Just three days later, we had that calamity against QPR on our own turf, or what was masquerading as turf. Their centre-forward, Dennis Bailey, thanked God after the game for the good fortune of his hat-trick. I don't blame him. Hat-tricks by opposing players are rare enough at Old Trafford to invite suspicion of the supernatural. Bailey did push his luck a little when he bounced into our dressing-room, full of the joys, wanting our players to sign the match ball. Much gossip surrounded that game and all of it was malicious rubbish. There was a popular rumour that our players were less than they should have been because they had spent New Year's Eve celebrating with me to mark my fiftieth birthday. We were certainly in the Midland Hotel together but I can assure anybody who is interested that the players were in bed early. Cathy had organised a surprise party for me and a lot of my friends from Aberdeen came down. There was, however, never the slightest danger that the celebrations would interfere with my preparation for the next day's match, let alone that of the players. The real explanation of our feebleness against QPR was simple. Several of our players were suffering from flu.

When I reflect on that middle period of the 1991–92 season, and specifically on our three-match series with Leeds, I find it intriguing that the Elland Road encounter which almost certainly did most to hurt our championship chances was not the drawn

League game but the FA Cup tie we won 1–0. In the course of it, Lee Chapman broke a wrist. Howard Wilkinson, realising that his tall striker could be on the sidelines for some time, went out and recruited a certain Frenchman on loan. I am sure that Eric Cantona would not have been signed by Leeds if Chapman had not been injured. So as a result of misfortune they acquired the player who was to prove their talisman in the winning of the title. That piece of business was bad news for us in February 1992. Though we could not possibly guess it then, before long we would be the true beneficiaries of the coming of Cantona.

Amid the ups and downs of that season, I had the reassuring feeling that we were making solid progress towards the standards I had set in my mind for United. The promotion of Brian Kidd in August 1991 into the assistant manager's job vacated by Archie Knox was an instant success, and we soon forged the strong alliance that was to prove so fruitful over the next seven years. Unfortunately, Brian's move upwards had regrettable long-term repercussions for one of his team-mates from the club's European Cup-winning era, Nobby Stiles. I had appointed Nobby youth team coach and he had been doing the work well but when Kiddo ceased to be Youth Development Officer I felt that Nobby, a local boy with hero status, would be the ideal replacement. However, it turned out that the job did not suit him and, since by that time the youth coaching post had been filled, the wee man was parted from the club he loves. I made a mistake in asking him to switch positions. He is a terrific person, Nobby, a belter, and I am truly sorry for any pain my wrong decision caused him.

With six league matches left to be played, I felt that even the horrors of a schedule that included four games within a week might not prevent us from preserving the lead we had held for most of the season. At that point our casualty count seemed manageable. We had allowed Mark Robins to have a cartilage operation and Bryan Robson was out with a troublesome calf injury but otherwise we were in reasonable shape. Then players started going down as if machine-gunned. In the first of those four congested fixtures, a 1–0 victory at Southampton, Paul Ince was injured. Next we went to Luton and, in the midst of a dis-appointing performance that turned the cruising comfort of a one-goal lead into a struggling draw, Paul Parker was hurt so badly that he was ruled out of the remaining four games. Lee Martin found an old injury flaring up again and Danny Wallace was another victim, so that in no time at all we had lost four players to add to the original pair of absentees, Robson and Robins. Two days after the costly trip to Luton, we faced Nottingham Forest at Old Trafford and, in addition to the shortage of fit men, I had a major worry about the form of Mark Hughes. He had gone fourteen games without scoring and I knew that, as a player to whom confidence was everything, he had difficulty hoisting him-self out of bad spells. His form did tend to dip towards the end of the season and for the crunch game with Forest on Easter Monday I decided to leave him out, opting for the front-line partnership of McClair and Giggs. I considered the football we played in that match to be the best we had produced for many weeks but we came up against an inspired goalkeeper in Mark Crossley (one save from a McClair volley in the second half was incredible) and we finished 2–1 losers.

There was deep depression in our ranks afterwards and I did my best to lift it. In those days many of my critics said that I lost my temper too often in the dressing-room, spreading anxiety among the players. That was nonsense. Of course, there were times when I was displeased with performances and let them know about it, but that is my style. I have always felt that if I have something to say I should get it off my chest, tell the players the facts as I see them. Then tomorrow is another day and I can start to prepare for the next game. I am not one for allowing two or three days of a cooling period before I voice my feelings. I am in too big a hurry to get on with life. After that defeat by Forest, I praised the players. They had done themselves proud. What I did impress upon them was the need for rest and I particularly stressed to Lee Sharpe that he was to put his feet up. His off-the-field behaviour had been worrying me for some time, but I was sure he would take my orders to heart at this important stage of the season.

By the time we went to West Ham on the Wednesday night for our fourth match in seven days, we were a tired team and my problems were certainly not eased by the signals coming from Neil Webb. His play had gone off and I was convinced that, after being substituted against Forest, he had gone into a huff. Only the fully committed would be wanted in the battle with West Ham, so I dropped Webb. The players I fielded did their best to overcome the effects of their exhausting schedule and some weird decisions from the referee and linesmen. One ruling in the first half probably cost us the game. It came when Lee Sharpe played a one-two in our half of the pitch and sprinted through to score. He was adjudged offside and that was a bitter blow. As the match entered its final phase, we had dredged up energy from I know not where and were exerting real pressure on the West Ham goal. A Mark Hughes overhead kick was brilliantly saved by Ludek Miklosko, the West Ham goalkeeper, and from the corner his save gave us they broke upfield and scored the luckiest goal imaginable. The cross that was put into our box was reasonable but it went straight to Gary Pallister. He booted the ball firmly out of the box but it hit West Ham's Kenny Brown flush on the knee and flew back past Schmeichel from eighteen yards. You could see the hope draining out of us, though we increased the pressure on the opposition right until the end. I brought my son Darren on and he made a noticeable difference, introducing an accuracy of passing that was pleasing to see. In the last minutes of the match a well-dressed man with a trilby called out to me, 'Alex, Alex!' I turned to look at him and he shouted, 'Fuck you,' and put two fingers up to me. It tells you something about men with hats.

The realisation that our chance of the title had almost certainly gone made our dressing-room like a funeral parlour. The players did not deserve to be suffering as they were and I told them so. They were the best team in the country, as they had demonstrated with early-season form that was never matched by any of their rivals. Bobby Charlton went round the room, thanking each player individually. It was the kind of gesture I had come to expect from Bobby and one that was much appreciated. Now we had to go

back up that motorway – four hours by coach. As we left Upton
Park, I saw a disconsolate United fan sitting on the kerb at the
side of the road, crying his eyes out. He looked up, spreading
his hands in despair as if asking, 'What happened?' It was Andy
Gregory, who is one of the most acclaimed heroes in rugby league
as a result of his brilliant and lion-hearted play at stand-off for
Wigan and Great Britain. I was feeling pretty sorry myself, but
when I saw Andy Gregory in that state I could have cried for him.
Still, sorrow had to give way to action. I had to show leadership,
let people know I was not down but determined. Next morning I
was at the Cliff at my usual early hour, waiting for the troops to
arrive. After all, there was still a chance we could win the title, albeit
a slim one. We had to rely on either Sheffield United or Norwich to
beat Leeds in one of the Elland Road club's two remaining matches
and, in the meantime, I had to prepare my drained squad as best I
could for a meeting with Liverpool at Anfield.

It was a trying time and the last thing I needed was anybody
around me creating extra, unnecessary trouble. But, as they say,
when one door closes, another bangs you in the face. I had no
idea how hard I was about to be clattered when, on the evening
after our sickening loss at West Ham, I went off to Morecambe
to attend an English Schools Football Association function. I was
in no mood for such an engagement but I had given my word
that I would be at the dinner, so I turned up. During the meal,
a member of the Association who was commiserating with me
suddenly mentioned that he had seen Lee Sharpe and Ryan Giggs
in Blackpool on the Monday night.

'Impossible,' I said. 'We had a game on that afternoon and
were getting ready for another on Wednesday. They were at home
resting.' The schools official was adamant.

'No, Mr Ferguson, I definitely saw them. Lee Sharpe was in a
Range Rover.'

By the time he had spoken those words, smoke was coming out
of my ears and I couldn't get away from Morecambe fast enough. I
drove straight to Sharpe's house and had to park about thirty yards
up the street because of the number of cars outside his door. Music

was blasting out from the house. When the door was opened to me, I burst in with all guns blazing. There was a full-scale party going on and there must have been about twenty people in the place, including Giggs and three young apprentices. It was the presence of those boys that really detonated my temper and I went berserk. I ordered everybody out of the house and as each apprentice passed I gave him a cuff on the back of the head. Yes, I know the guardians of political correctness wouldn't approve but I think the lads' parents would have supported me. Sharpe was nowhere to be seen. Obviously he was upstairs in the bedroom. I was angry enough without going up there. Eventually Sharpe appeared and I took him and Giggs to the lounge and tore into the two of them.

My anger was directed more at Lee than Ryan because there had been other signs of waywardness in Lee's off-field behaviour. I may have contributed to such tendencies by allowing him to have his own house when he was far too young (at the time of the escapade he was still only twenty). I look back on my dealings with Lee Sharpe as a disappointing episode in my years at United. My experiences with him trouble me more than those with Paul McGrath. Here was a boy who had a chance of making it big. He possessed just about everything a wide attacking player needs to be successful in top-flight football other than the ability to beat a man by dribbling. His pace, crossing, goalscoring and passing were all of a high standard and so were his physique and stamina. His rise in the game was swift but I soon concluded that his lifestyle was accelerating even more spectacularly. Little titbits about his conduct had been fed back to me from different sources. When I challenged him he was quick with denials but they did not have much credibility once I had learned about the outing to Blackpool and then charged in on his party. I had tried to warn him about how fast living would slow him down. 'Sharpie, to make it to the top in football you need to sacrifice,' I told him. 'If you lose that great speed of yours, you will end up an ordinary player. It is your biggest asset and it is mainly responsible for your success. But please don't take it for granted.' Lee is with Bradford now and I hope their promotion to the Premiership helps him to revive his career. I found him a lovely lad, with a wonderful smile, and his failure to make the best of his immense potential while he was with us filled me with sadness. He should have developed into a footballer of real significance at Old Trafford, instead of rather losing his way with us before being transferred to Leeds for £4.5 million in 1996.

Cases like his make me want to exert an influence on young players that goes far beyond their football. I have no desire to run their private lives but I am keen to educate them about the dangers they encounter as their careers progress, especially about how damaging a freewheeling attitude to drink can be. I believe that some day soon we will be able to test them each morning and if they have been drinking they will simply be sent home. Future contracts may be constructed to counter the kind of behaviour that reduces a player's capacity to fulfil his obligations. There is too much money in football now for it to accommodate the laxity that prevailed in the past.

It wasn't too long before the other players heard about the jamboree in Blackpool and they weren't too impressed with the way Giggs and Sharpe had chosen to 'rest' between the Forest and West Ham games. They had let themselves and their team-mates down and, while their youth provided a partial excuse, they weren't unintelligent and knew well enough how irresponsible they had been. I have never had any bother from Ryan since that incident. He has developed into a fine young man and I have become very proud of him over the years. He is a credit to his mother, Lynn.

I wish I could skip the details of the Liverpool match on 26 April. The players worked unsparingly but once again could not translate their possession into goals. We lost 2–0, which officially confirmed Leeds as champions. I was philosophical by that time. I thanked the players and assured them that the next season's challenge would be successful. My words were sincere but I knew that, if we were to reach confidently for the title, I had to add another element, an extra dimension to the team. At least I had all summer to find the remarkable footballer I needed.

Shearer, I had contacted his manager at Southampton as early as January and I felt there was a clear understanding that I would be fully informed about Shearer's position when the 1991–92 season ended. The story in early summer was that Alan was going on tour with England and would make a decision on his future when he returned and that Southampton would then phone me. I wasn't entirely happy but had to accept the situation as it was. As insurance, I also made inquiries about the other striker who had stirred my enthusiasm, David Hirst of Sheffield Wednesday. To be truthful, at that stage I was even keener on Hirst than on Shearer. Both were dynamic goalscorers and it was strictly on the basis of experience that I had a slight preference for Hirst, who at twenty-four was nearly three years older than Shearer. Such details hardly mattered when I made an approach to Trevor Francis about Hirst, for the Sheffield Wednesday manager gave me short shrift. Then, soon after the England tour, a piece appeared in one of the tabloids saying that Shearer had been given permission to talk to Blackburn Rovers. I was angry at this, having held back from pursuing him because of what I had taken as a firm assurance that I would be alerted by Southampton the moment it was appropriate to make a move. When I spoke again to the manager at the Dell, Ian Branfoot, the response was a rather convoluted story. I felt I had to act quickly, since it could be assumed that the Blackburn chairman, Jack Walker, would be throwing money at Shearer. So Maurice Watkins set up a meeting with Alan's agent, who turned out to be our old friend from the Gascoigne saga, Mel Stein. As was to be expected, the financial demands were quite high but they were not insurmountable and the next stage was to talk directly to the player, who was apparently due to give Blackburn his final decision on their offer the following day. There was obviously no time for me to go down to South-ampton and meet Alan. I had to rely on a telephone conversation and that is never ideal. Our talk did not last long. I found him very hard work and quite surly. One of the first things he said to me was, 'Why haven't you been interested in me before now?' That must have seemed a fair question to him but I pointed out that I had been in touch with his club as early as January and had been assured that he was aware of our interest in him.

'Well, nobody told me that,' he said. The tenor of his conversation suggested he was definitely going to Blackburn and that he had probably given his word, or perhaps had already signed. 'Kenny Dalglish was phoning me regularly,' he told me. I explained to him that I wasn't into making frequent phone calls to players in such circumstances, adding that I had promised his manager I would leave Alan alone until an official approach was in order. I must say I had come to regret giving that guarantee. There was one other point I tried to make forcefully to Alan in the summer of '92.

'Would Kenny have signed for Blackburn when he was a player?' I asked him. 'I know what he'd have done if United and Blackburn had both come in for him.' In answer, he snapped at me.

'I'm not interested in what Kenny would have done,' he said. 'It's about what I want, not Kenny.' Case closed.

We did sign a goalscorer in that close season and the deal came about rather strangely. John Beck, the manager of Cambridge United, phoned to tell me that they were having to sell their best player, Dion Dublin, and to recommend that I should be the buyer. John gave Dion a glowing assessment and asked if I would be prepared to check out his opinion on a video he could send to me. I had no problem with that, although I had difficulty imagining that we were talking about a man who could make an impact with Manchester United. What I saw on the screen was a revelation. I have watched thousands of videos on teams and players and have rarely been more surprised and impressed than I was by this one. The immediate eye-opener was the variety of goals scored by Dublin but I was also startled by the overall quality of his play. Having pulled out all the reports we had on him, I noticed the interesting fact that many of them differed in their identification of his main assets. That indicated that he had a range of strengths. The only conspicuous negative was that he was not extra quick – only average. I decided that, at twenty-three and with an asking price of a million pounds, this big lad could be a real snip and quickly completed the transfer.

I spent quite a bit of time with Dion after his arrival to facilitate the transition to the level of demand we were making of him. Three matches into the season, I felt he was ready for his debut with us and the miserable return we had taken from those opening games did nothing to encourage delaying his introduction. They produced a 2–1 defeat by Sheffield United at Bramall Lane, a 3–0 loss at Old Trafford to Everton and a home draw with Ipswich, giving us one point from a possible nine and exactly the stumbling start we had dreaded. The fourth match was at Southampton and Dion did much to make it a minor turning point, showing great tenacity, leading the line well and linking effectively with Mark Hughes. It was a marvellous bonus when he met a Darren Ferguson free kick to give us the winning goal in the eighty-ninth minute. He followed that with another fine performance in our 2–0 away win over Nottingham Forest, strengthening my conviction that our million pounds had been well spent. His enthusiastic and conscientious attitude to his work persuaded me that the success he was enjoying would not be fleeting. The other players admired his commitment and he rapidly achieved general popularity at the club. All of that intensified the sorrow that was felt when, in just his third outing for us, Dion suffered an horrific leg fracture against Crystal Palace. It would be unfair to blame the Palace player involved. His was a clumsy tackle rather than a bad one but, as Dion collapsed and lay prone on the turf, it was instantly clear that the damage was extremely serious. His season had finished on the second day of September. If he had escaped that terrible injury, I believe he would have become an excellent team player at Old Trafford. I also think that just maybe we would have won the League with him in the side, as he brought something different to our attacking and so filled part of the need I had recognised in my midsummer analysis.

But Dion's most ardent admirer could not claim that he was capable of being a catalyst on the grand scale. It was impossible to know then that somebody with that capacity would soon be among us. My immediate reaction to the loss of Dublin was to try again for David Hirst. This time around Trevor Francis refused to answer my phone calls and I had no alternative but to fax him, which brought a public outburst from Trevor. I could have done without that, but at least it left me in no doubt about the futility of attempting to break down Wednesday's resistance. Sadly, within weeks Hirst was so badly injured that his entire career was blighted. I felt desperately sorry for the boy and could not help wondering how events might have been rearranged if he had been allowed to join us. Looking back, it does appear that whatever fates control the game were playing some pretty heavy cards.

Martin Edwards and I could never have foreseen the hand that was about to be dealt to us as we sat in his office on that drizzly Wednesday afternoon in November, pondering possible ways of effecting the improvement we knew was necessary if we were to lay hands at last on the title. The process was harshly simplified by ruling out players belonging to our main rivals. It was pointless focusing on anybody at Liverpool, Arsenal, Manchester City and Leeds and probably one or two other clubs were also no-go areas. One man who did interest me was Peter Beardsley, who was not figuring as prominently in the Everton team as might have been expected. The chairman and I were discussing Beardsley when Martin's private phone rang and he found himself talking to Bill Fotherby, the Leeds chief executive. Fotherby was on to ask about the chances of buying Denis Irwin. That was an absolute non-starter and once Fotherby had been told as much he and the chairman drifted into a little friendly chit-chat. It was then that an idea jumped into my head and rapidly assumed a strange urgency. 'Ask him about Eric Cantona' I scribbled on the chairman's writing pad. When Martin looked at me quizzically, I nodded vigorously and he did as I suggested. Bill's response was hesitant and then he blurted out an admission that perhaps some business could be done over Cantona. He said he would speak to Howard Wilkinson and promised to phone back within the hour. As soon as he put the receiver down, Martin asked me, 'Why Cantona, what made you think of him?'

'Well, when we played Leeds earlier in the season and beat them 2–0, Bruce and Pallister were raving about him in the bath after the game and last week I was talking to Gerard Houllier, who has a very high opinion of his abilities.' The next few minutes were spent talking about Cantona's reputation for being unorthodox and possibly disruptive. Obviously we had to consider the danger that he would be bringing too much awkward baggage with him. But, from what Houllier had said about him, it did not seem that he was the big bad wolf portrayed by the media, so I was prepared to bet on the Frenchman. The key issue now was whether Leeds were ready to sell, and at what price. We did not have to wait long to find out. Inside half an hour Bill Fotherby was back on the phone with the word that Howard was willing to sell Cantona. The inevitable haggling over the fee was not prolonged and Martin did a fantastic job, arguing Leeds down from their initial demand of £1.3 million to the clinching figure of £1 million. One of the most extraordinary periods in the history of Manchester United was about to begin.

Next day Martin Edwards and I met Eric and his agent, Jean Jacques Bertrand, in the Midland Hotel. The transaction went smoothly and, as Martin and Jean Jacques sat in one corner of the suite discussing the contract, Eric and I were across the room talking about his role in the team. Between the peculiarities of my pidgin French and the difficulties posed by my Scottish accent when I spoke English, communication was not easy but I made sure he understood perfectly how much I wanted him and how highly I rated him. That counted for a lot with Eric. He wants to be wanted and it was obvious that he was keen to join us. During such conversations, the manager is obliged to do most of the talking and the player has the advantage of being able to study him at leisure. But I have learned to talk at length while observing the player closely and I was certain from what I saw in Eric's eyes that he was desperate to come to us. I believe he already had a sense that Old Trafford was the right place for him to give expression to his talents. Once the deal had been concluded, I offered to take Jean Jacques to the airport. I wanted to learn as much as I could about my new player and Bertrand was a good source. He made it clear that Eric was a passionate man whose emotions could create problems for him. 'But he is honest,' Jean Jacques stressed, and that declaration made me more confident about my controversial acquisition.

The following two days were incredible, with an intensity of press interest which made it hard to remember that the Cantona fee was precisely the same as we had paid for Dion Dublin. Unfortunately, I couldn't push through Eric's registration in time for our match with Arsenal on the Saturday but he travelled to London with us to watch the game. On the Saturday morning about 9.30, Brian Kidd came to my bedroom to tell me that Eric wanted to train. My suspicious Scottish nature made me ask myself why, but I told Kiddo to let him get on with it. When the team assembled for pre-match lunch at midday, Eric and Brian were not back from the workout. They walked in at twenty past twelve and, when Eric went to sit with the players, I immediately quizzed Brian about how he had trained. Brian's verdict was that Eric had worked brilliantly and when he filled in the details I remembered something Gerard Houllier had said to me about Cantona: 'He likes to train and also he needs to train hard.' If that was the case, he had come to the right club. Back in Manchester after a fairly comfortable 1–0 victory over Arsenal, I was eager to see Eric's training for myself on the Monday and I wasn't disappointed. He applied himself flawlessly but it was at the end of our session that he really impressed me. As his team-mates were vanishing from the pitch at the Cliff, he approached me and asked if he could have the assistance of two players.

'What for?' I asked.

'To practise,' he replied. That took me aback. It was not exactly a standard request. I had always organised my training programme around a general session, which could change each day, depending on the aspects of the work I was seeking to emphasise. Normally, I would try to incorporate many basic elements of the game – passing, possession, crossing, finishing. In that way I maintained a flow of activity and avoided letting the players stand around and get cold, which is an important concern in our climate. There could be problems with this approach when I was coaching and there was a need to stop and make tactical points to the players. In the midst of all that there could often be insufficient stress on practice. I was naturally delighted to accede to Eric's wishes and quickly provided him with two players to deliver the ball from wide positions and a young goalkeeper so that he could spend half an hour practising volleys. Quite fantastic, I would say. Meanwhile, the players who had gone indoors at the Cliff were realising that Cantona had not come back and before long the tom-toms had told them why. At the end of training the next day, several of them hung around to join in the practice with Eric and it is now an integral part of our regime. Many people have justifiably acclaimed Cantona as a catalyst who had a crucial impact on our successes while he was with the club but nothing he did in matches meant more than the way he opened my eyes to the indispensability of practice. Practice makes players.

The derby game against Manchester City on 6 December 1992 heralded the Cantona era at Manchester United. Though he came on only as a substitute for Ryan Giggs, his presence illuminated Old Trafford. Tall and straight-backed, with the trademark upturned collar, he conveyed a regal authority and the place was in a frenzy every time he touched the ball. I was struck at once by his insistence on making the easy pass whenever possible, a characteristic that showed itself as a great strength of his game in his time with us. Nobody had more imagination when it came to spotting the opportunity for an improbable and devastating pass, or more technical dexterity in threading the ball through crowding defenders. But, like all truly exceptional creative players, Cantona did something extravagant only when it was necessary. His precious ability to score vital goals at important times was first demonstrated in our colours when he secured us a draw at Chelsea in late December. We were an inspired and transformed team and I knew that when I had found myself longing in the previous summer for someone who would lift our already formidable qualities on to another plane I had been imagining a footballer very much like Eric Cantona. I knew, too, that some pretty spectacular performances were on the way.

We did manage to cut back the points lead held by Norwich and Aston Villa and, although the memory of how our challenge had crumbled in 1992 invited many to question our capacity to go all the way this time, I was confident that it was our destiny to take the championship. There were blips, of course, like a 2–1 defeat at Ipswich at the end of January and our struggle at home against a gutsy Sheffield United a week later, when it took a late Cantona goal to give us victory. I was praying that he would do something similar in our next game at Elland Road but Eric's first return to his former club was an ordeal. The hostility towards him and Manchester United that day had to be seen to be believed. He was booked for a trifling incident with Jon Newsome, the big Leeds centre-half, and I think the Frenchman was just glad to put the match behind him. In the circumstances, I was happy with a goalless draw.

A true test of any championship team is to go to a fortress such as Anfield and win, and on 6 March we duly beat Liverpool 2–1 at their own ground. That should have convinced everybody, ourselves included, that we were closing on the title but three days later we were beaten by a single goal at Oldham. We were under strain but I kept telling the players that the other teams would also be feeling the pressure. I said that if they trusted themselves and their ability they would be all right.

The collision billed as the game of the season came on 14 March when Aston Villa faced us at Old Trafford. We still trailed a couple of points behind Villa but were showing marginally better form than they were. We worked hard on our tactics all week, emphasising penetration from Giggs, who was operating on the right wing and would be expected to cut in profitably on to his favoured left side. We were also looking for a lot from Lee Sharpe, although he was against a sound defender in Earl Barrett. Our strategy was devised to put attackers in behind Paul McGrath and Shaun Teale. They were excellent defenders but did not like turning towards their own goal. United's performance was first-class and we would not have been flattered if we had won by a hatful but some glaring misses and good goalkeeping by Mark Bosnich kept us out until the match reached boiling point eight minutes into the second half when Villa took the lead with a stunning goal from Steve Staunton – a shot of such power that it made me gasp. At that moment the cameras caught Ron Atkinson in one of his wonderful poses, picking his teeth, not showing the slightest emotion. His demeanour was, to me, almost condescending, as if it was all merely another day at the office for Big Ron. Four minutes later he had more to chew over when we gained our just rewards with an equaliser. Mark Hughes headed it in after Cantona had knocked a header back across the goal and from then on neither side could break the deadlock.

In my post-match press conference, I voiced my conviction that we were the better team on the day. I was talking to our rivals in the League rather than the reporters when I made much of how strong we had looked and floated the notion that we were the team likely to play best in the decisive phase of the season. Deep down, I was sure we had a lot to come but at that stage of the campaign you hope you are not running out of time. We were dropping points here and there but that was equally true of the league leaders, Villa, and of Norwich, who were still seriously in contention. Norwich helped our position as well as their own when they beat Aston Villa on 24 March and the benefits we drew from that result were happily compounded on 5 April at Carrow Road as we trounced Norwich 3–1 with the most thrilling performance we had given in weeks.

Leagues can be won and lost in Easter week. It is a minefield in which many a team's ambitions have been blown away. You never seem to have an easy game at that time. We had to face an experienced Sheffield Wednesday side at Old Trafford while Villa had their derby against Coventry. Statistics indicated that Coventry had no chance and I fully expected Villa to be still top of the table on Saturday night. What was vital was that we should remain in the slipstream by winning our home game. In the first half we should have buried Wednesday but scoring seemed beyond us and as the match entered the second half there was a clear danger that we would pay for missing so many chances. In a game of continual attacking you are liable to leave the door open and we did, letting our opponents in to earn a penalty awarded for a rash tackle by Paul Ince on Chris Waddle. John Sheridan scored with the kick and, with frequent stoppages killing the flow of play, I began to think this was a game we were not going to win. The physios from both teams were certainly earning their corn. Several players had to be treated and then the referee, Michael Peck, went down and had to be replaced by the stand-side linesman, John Hilditch. Hilditch had been on only four minutes when he gave Wednesday their penalty but there could be no protest. It was a blatant offence. The one advantage for us of the referee change was that between half-time and the substitution I had been complaining to Hilditch about time-wasting and the need to take account of the lengthy interruptions because of injuries. I am sure my lobbying had a bearing on the amount of time added on at the end, which was the cause of controversy afterwards.

With twenty minutes to go, I sent Captain Marvel, Bryan Robson, into the fray and his energy and determination made an instant difference. It was win or bust but the prize was worth it. We bombarded their goal and as the minutes ticked away we won yet another corner on the right-hand side at the Stretford end. I thought it might be our last throw of the dice and as Robbo made a typical surge towards goal my eyes and hopes were with him alone. Practically all the other players had had chances in the game and it had begun to seem that they wouldn't score if they stayed on the park until midnight. Then, reminding us how brave he was, Steve Bruce stuck his head in front of one of their defenders and glanced the ball high into the far corner, with Robson charging into Phil King, the Wednesday left-back, who was guarding the post. So it was 1–1 and I estimated we still had about seven minutes left, even though every other game in the country was finished. I had received the good news that there had been a goalless draw at Villa Park and I tried to convey a message to Bryan Robson to bring calm to our match. Above all, we had to ensure that we did not lose another goal. But I am afraid that when the volume is turned up at Old Trafford on those special occasions, the players would have to be lip-readers to absorb instructions. From the moment we equalised, I stood on the touchline directing operations, cajoling the lads, encouraging them, praising any of them who might possibly be able to hear me. Trevor Francis, the Wednesday manager, was signalling to the referee that it was time-up when we won a free kick near the by-line wide on the left. Ryan Giggs took the kick and the ball seemed to take a touch from one of their defenders before ending up out on the other side of the pitch. Gary Pallister raced out to regain possession and, without looking up, hit a really good cross into the penalty box. A slight deflection off Wednesday's Nigel Worthington sent it directly into Brucie's path. The big Geordie was just the man to seize the moment. I was right in the line of the ball as it arrowed its way into the corner of the net, with Chris Woods diving in vain. Bedlam is the best description of the scenes thereafter. Everyone who was there will remember the Brian Kidd celebration. Now we were in the driving seat, one point in front with five games left.

After the match, Trevor Francis complained about the time added on, although while in my office he did so jokingly. 'You scored your winning goal in the second leg,' he said. The truth is that the extra minutes were totally legitimate. That night I watched the video of the second half and used my stopwatch to time all the stoppages for injuries and substitutions and there should, in fact, have been twelve additional minutes.

It suited us that we had no lull in which to reflect on being top of the League. Within two days, on the Monday, we were consolidating our position with a 1–0 win over Coventry at High-field Road. Aston Villa kept the heat on by beating Arsenal on the same day at Highbury but our confidence soared when what had appeared to be a troublesome home fixture with Chelsea, who were something of a bogey team for us, turned out to be a stroll in the sun, with a 3–0 scoreline. Our next opponents were Crystal Palace, who were battling to save themselves from relegation, and their understandably negative tactics made the match a non-event until the interval. The news I was able to give our players at half-time was like a shot of adrenaline. Blackburn were beating Villa 3–0. With the tension lifted, we flowed over Palace. A typical Mark Hughes volley sent us in front in the sixty-fourth minute and the French genius produced a magnificent pass to set up a goal for Paul Ince right at the end. When the final whistle sounded, our travelling fans went crazy. They knew that if we won our last home game against Blackburn Rovers the championship would come to Old Trafford for the first time in twenty-six years.

With television lapping up this climax to a memorable season, it was decided to show the Aston Villa–Oldham match on Sunday 2 May and our game on the following evening. I knew it would be a difficult game for Villa, as every point was life or death for Oldham as far as staying in the Premiership was concerned. I made up my mind that I would not put myself through the mill by watching the match. Instead, I went off to the golf course at Mottram Hall, near my home in Cheshire, with my eldest son, Mark. For the first few holes my concentration was terrible. Knowing my thoughts were on Villa Park, Mark said, 'Forget about it. Even if they win, you will still take the title if you win tomorrow. And if you can't win a game at Old Trafford, you don't deserve to be champions.' In an effort to make me concentrate on the golf, Mark appealed to my competitiveness and said he would give me a shot a hole for a five-pound bet. From then on we really did enjoy ourselves. At the fourteenth hole you can look over a large stretch of Cheshire and it is the best view on the golf course. I was gazing across the hills, waiting for four Japanese players ahead of us to take their shots, when Mark said, 'I think Villa have won. Someone would have told us if they had lost.' I thought he was right but I was perfectly relaxed, having reassured myself with Mark's point about how we could settle our own fate on the following evening. We were coming to a crucial stage in our wagering, as all I needed to do was halve the seventeenth and my money was safe, so when I pitched up to within twenty feet of the hole I was in family mood and teasing Mark relentlessly.

Suddenly I heard a car screeching to a halt and footsteps coming up the gravel path by the green and a chap appeared with a huge smile on his face.

'Mr Ferguson?' he called, and when I turned to him he shouted, 'Manchester United have won the League.' Mark and I hugged each other, joined by the bearer of this great news. God, what a feeling. The next shot was abandoned and as we made our way down the eighteenth fairway my thoughts went back to 1962 when Arnold Palmer won the Open at Troon. I'll never forget the sight of him marching between the massed ranks of his fans towards the last green. That's how I felt, like a real champion, as I strode up that fairway. Passing the Japanese group, I noticed that one of them had the name of our sponsor, Sharp, on his golf cap. He must be a United fan, I told myself, and informed him with great pride, 'United have won the League.'

'Ah . . . what you mean?' I was left feeling a little stupid.

'That went down well,' said Mark. Who cared? I picked up my mobile phone to call Cathy. It is at such moments that you realise who is the most important person in your life. She had endured a lot and done a great deal of worrying on my behalf over the years. Now she could savour the moment.

When I got back to the house there was a throng of photographers outside and for once I didn't mind the intrusion at all. After they had taken their pictures and gone, the marathon celebrations began and at Old Trafford they carried on throughout the night and all of the next day. Our 3–1 win over Blackburn was more of a party than a football match. Nobody was happier than Sir Matt. He was so proud to see his club win the League again. Bryan Robson had an article in one of the tabloids saying that he thought the difference between savage disappointment and triumph in consecutive seasons was to be found in me. He felt that I was more relaxed in 1993. I was not particularly conscious of that, but I do know I devoted more attention to my observation of players in the winning season. Watching certain individuals carefully during pressure periods, recognising those who needed reassuring, enabled me to handle the preparation for each game

Norman Whiteside possessed prodigious ability, but injuries and his drinking habits prevented him from fulfilling his potential.

Paul McGrath needed a change of scene to snap out of a drink-fuelled self-destructive spiral at Old Trafford.

Bryan Robson had everything: skill, stamina, bravery, a fierce competitive streak and outstanding leadership qualities.

Michael Knighton's pre-match posturing was more successful than his attempt to juggle the finances in his takeover bid.

'Sparky' Hughes (*left*) and Lee Sharpe were key figures in our successes during the early 1990s.

On his day, Jim Leighton's goalkeeping was second to none, but sometimes loss of confidence let him down.

Mark Hughes specialised in stunning goals, such as this one against Palace in the 3–3 draw at Wembley in 1990.

Brian McClair celebrates his first-minute goal against Montpellier as we move towards the Cup Winners' Cup final of 1991.

Steve Bruce's nose for goals put us on our way in the 1991 Cup Winners' Cup final, even if Mark Hughes got the last touch.

Four of our youth team of '92 graduated to treble honours – Gary Neville (*back row, second left*), Nicky Butt (*back, second right*), David Beckham (*front, second left*) and Paul Scholes (*front, second right*).

My son Darren is an astute midfielder but eventually made his career away from Old Trafford and the old man.

My son Jason scoring the first of his two goals in a match against Stockport County 'B' at Park Road, Cheadle.

I found meeting Nelson Mandela humbling and inspiring; courage, integrity and leadership born of adversity.

Soweto United: a team picture with a difference on the club's summer tour of South Africa in 1993.

Peter Schmeichel, pictured against Arsenal in the 1993 Charity Shield, combined huge presence and superb technique.

Andrei Kanchelskis (*left*) and Ryan Giggs gave us the penetration on the flanks which all the best United sides have.

With Cathy at Buckingham Palace in 1995 after I received the CBE from the Prince of Wales.

Wembley low: the body language says it all as Ryan Giggs and myself contemplate FA Cup defeat by Everton in 1995.

Ole Gunnar Solskjaer and Andy Cole scored regularly for me in the 1997–98 campaign but Arsenal took the double.

The man our fans called 'Dieu' takes pole position after scoring against Liverpool on his return from suspension in 1995.

Eric Cantona scores from the spot at Maine Road in 1996, taking us closer to the title and pushing City towards relegation.

Queensland Star, the horse I part-own and which is named after a ship my dad worked on, wins at Chester in 1998.

Golf, like racing, helps me unwind from the pressures of management. Here, I'm playing with my son Mark.

more effectively. It is only when you focus on one or two players at a time that you get a real insight into them. My management methods were evolving. For years I did everything on the training field myself. I did the coaching, the organising of the training programmes, the pre-season schedules, the warm-ups, the lot. But now I realised that, as my sense of the job's priorities developed, the art of observation had to play a bigger part.

If, as Bryan Robson suggested, United's rise to championship standard reflected the development in me, no one should have any doubt about the massive contribution made by Eric Cantona. He brought priceless presence and style to the team. I had resolved when he arrived that I would ignore all past attempts to present him as an *enfant terrible*. I would judge him on what he was like in his dealings with me, making it my aim to communicate with him regularly and to try to understand him. He was not, I soon discovered, the overwhelmingly confident person many perceived him to be. He needed nourishing. Like most players, he liked to be told he was special. What could not be denied was that he deserved his success and not simply because of his talent. He gave a great deal of himself to the game. I never tired of watching him train. Once, after studying him closely throughout a session and marvelling yet again at his level of concentration, I mentioned that quality to him.

'All the great players have good concentration,' he said. 'And imagination.' Whether playing or talking, Eric never gave anybody reason to question the richness of his imagination.

— 20 —
THE FIRST DOUBLE

How could it be right to pay the man in charge of Manchester United less than several other managers in the new Premiership were earning? It seemed a fair question to me at the beginning of the 1993–94 season and it still strikes me as reasonable six years on, but my arguments carried little weight with the chairman of the club. For the first time, but not the last, I had a disagreement with Martin Edwards over my contract. Even if United had not just ended a twenty-six-year championship drought, I would have been left bewildered by his insistence that the offer he had made to me was non-negotiable. I saw it as wrong that the club regarded as the biggest in Britain, and one of the two or three biggest in the world, should be prepared to lag behind leading rivals in England in the matter of paying the manager's wages. I knew that to be the case because George Graham had provided me with details of his contract with Arsenal. There are not many secrets in football and George and I did get on very well but it was still extremely generous of him to give me all that private information. The figures showed that I was being paid less than half as much as George. My accountant, Alan Baines, presented the facts to Martin but he found difficulty in accepting that what we told him about George Graham's contract was accurate. He said he would speak to David Dein, the Executive Director of Arsenal, to check the exact terms.

I was unhappy with that reaction. Even if we left George out of the equation, there was one of our players, Eric Cantona, who was earning three times as much as I was, and to my mind that was neither fair nor rational. It wasn't as if I had been continually complaining about my contract over the years. In fact, I was too timid when it came to fighting for my worth. Now, at the age of fifty-one, I had come to realise that I had very little in the way of financial security. I had served over seven years at Old Trafford, so there was scarcely a need to prove my loyalty, and the achievements of the previous two or three seasons made it hard to argue that my work wasn't satisfactory. Nevertheless, the chairman refused to budge an inch and I had to accept what was an improved contract but one that left me at a pay level far below that of either Graham or Cantona. My one reason for signing it was that I loved being manager of Manchester United. I was building something that was meant to last and I could not contemplate abandoning the foundations I had laid. I was, I suppose, a captive of my own passion for the club and the job I was doing there.

That passion could only intensify over a season that brought United the double of the championship and the FA Cup for the first time in their history. We had signalled our determination to keep our standards rising by adding Roy Keane to our midfield strength in July 1993. The twenty-one-year-old Cork man was a player I had long been desperate to sign and, with relegation forcing Nottingham Forest to acknowledge that they could not hold on to him, it was time to move in. One Saturday morning during the close season, I read a story in one of the tabloids that said Roy had met Kenny Dalglish and was ready to join Blackburn Rovers. Straightaway I phoned Frank Clark, the Forest manager, at his home to verify this report. Frank was raging over the story, pointing out that nobody had been given permission to speak to Roy and that if the story was accurate Kenny was in breach of the rules.

'I can't afford to lose this player, Frank,' I said. 'You know how much I have wanted him for ages but I kept my promise to you that I wouldn't interfere until you were ready to sell.' He was very helpful and I shall always be grateful for that. Once I had permission to talk to Keane, I alerted the chairman and Maurice

Watkins and left it to them to get his agent and solicitor, Michael Kennedy, up to Manchester immediately. I contacted Roy and arranged for him to come over to my house on the quiet the next day. When he did, I made it clear how vital I felt his role could be in the successful years I was sure lay ahead of Manchester United. If anything had passed between Keane and Kenny Dalglish, I was determined to avoid a repeat of what had happened with Alan Shearer. My overwhelming advantage this time was that I was dealing with a player who was set on playing for the best team in the business. There was an impressive resolve about the young Irishman and I knew he would not be deflected by the blandishments of Jack Walker. With Keane secured, I was optimistic that we were entering a period of dominance in English football.

Liberated from the pressures that a quarter of a century without a title had imposed, our players brought a new authority to their game and began to justify being rated as one of the very best teams ever to wear the United colours. Given the heights of quality achieved more than once in the Busby era, claims that the class of '94 were *the* greatest Reds could be severely questioned but I have no doubt they would stand up well to any comparison. Even after the dazzling treble triumph of 1999, I cannot say categorically that the brilliant crop of players who thrilled me all the way to the Nou Camp in Barcelona are superior to their predecessors of five years ago. I had said that the current squad would deserve to be set alongside the 1994 vintage once they had proved they possessed the mental strength and mature competitiveness of that earlier group. In the year of the treble they did that, with demonstrations of unbreakable spirit and technical resilience against Arsenal in the FA Cup and Juventus and Bayern Munich in the European Cup that were quite incredible. So now the teams of 1994 and 1999 are bracketed together as the best I have ever managed, though I expect the marvels of the Nou Camp to go on rising to new peaks. One obvious difference between the two teams is that the first double winners presented me with far more problems as a result of outbreaks of indiscipline on the field. We have our share of fiery characters around today (Roy Keane and

Paul Scholes missed the European Cup final because of suspension) but the overall chemistry in 1994 was much more volatile. If the composition of that remarkable team is analysed, it reveals that certain fundamental qualities were common to many of the players. In addition to outstanding skills, most of them had physical strength, courage, toughness of mind, speed, power and determination. They were winners and in quite a number of cases the other side of that coin was that they were bad losers. There were more than enough quick tempers to make them collectively combustible. Of course, there were some cool natures. Pallister, Parker, Irwin and McClair were out and out winners but reasonably calm players for whom discipline problems were rare. But that other bunch – Bruce, Ince, Robson, Keane, Hughes, Cantona and Schmeichel – were capable of causing a row in an empty house. They had the combative drive that I cherish and it made each of them, in my eyes, a true United player. When they were massed together the aggressive tendencies could get out of hand and in the 1993–94 season our disciplinary record lurched towards the unacceptable. There came a time when I had to call all the offenders into my office for a stern warning. 'No more,' I warned them. 'That's it finished – OK?' Laying down the law to that lot as they sat before me, presenting an array of powerful physiques and resolute faces, made me think afterwards that I must have been either the bravest or the daftest manager in the world.

Obviously, there were not too many lows in a season of such historic success but our European Cup experience took us about as far into the depths of depression as it was possible to go. The first round was smoothly negotiated with home and away victories over Honved of Hungary, but being paired with Galatasaray of Turkey in the second round let us in for a nightmare. Our sufferings were self-inflicted at Old Trafford, where we were two up and coasting after quarter of an hour but then, exhibiting our familiar gift for self-destruction, we replaced controlled aggression with self-indulgence. Players started to run with the ball and to make a habit of losing it. All momentum and rhythm went out of our game and Galatasaray were permitted such a sustained comeback that they went into a 3–2 lead and we needed a late strike from Eric Cantona to salvage a draw. The return leg in Istanbul exposed us to as much harassment and hostility as I have ever known on a football expedition. From the moment we were greeted by jeering crowds and aggressive banners at the airport, we were surrounded by the atmosphere of a bearpit. It reached a peak of intensity at the stadium, where the police were even more frightening than the fans, and perhaps we shouldn't have been surprised when the Swiss referee seemed to offer the Turkish team every assistance. At time-up Cantona incurred the official's anger by making gestures indicating what he thought of the refereeing! The Frenchman was given a red card after the final whistle and was to draw a suspension that proved costly for us when challenging again in the European Cup the following season. The goalless draw killed our 1994 hopes (Galatasaray's three away goals in Manchester swept them through to the next stage) and Eric's misery was completed as we left the field when a savage swing of a policeman's baton left a sizeable cut on his head.

There were, it must be said, times in the ensuing months when Cantona was not at all the innocent party. He was prominent in the creation of our team's lamentable disciplinary record over the second half of the 1993–94 season. One of his worst fouls was in our fourth-round FA Cup victory over Norwich at Carrow Road when his tackle on their midfield player, Jeremy Goss, was not only horrendous but inexplicable, since Goss wouldn't have harmed a fly. It was an even more serious offence when he stamped on Swindon's skilful midfielder, John Moncur, and that was the first time I lost my temper with him. There was no way I could condone what he had done. I did have plenty of sympathy the following week when he was ridiculously ordered off after a challenge for the ball with Tony Adams. I was undoubtedly right to side with Eric in that case but when I took a lenient view of Mark Hughes's behaviour after he was sent off in our third-round Cup tie with Sheffield United I was shown to be defending the indefensible. The big Sheffield defender, David Tuttle, had been kicking lumps out of Hughes all day and when Sparky was sent to the dressing-room for retaliation I thought he had been hard done by. To be honest, I had not had a good view of the incident and was probably a bit rash to speak out on Mark's behalf at the post-match press conference. When I viewed the game on video late that night I couldn't believe what I was seeing. Hughes had almost dislodged Tuttle's testicles. Can anyone wonder that I found it necessary to tell the more warlike of my players that I had seen enough red cards and it was time to draw a line under the wild behaviour.

In the main, of course, that astonishing 1994 team applied their tremendous talents and combative spirit legitimately and the League Cup, too, might have fallen to them. They battled through to the final but went down disappointingly by 3–1 to Aston Villa, managed by Ron Atkinson, my predecessor at Old Trafford. We were not helped on that Wembley occasion by another red card, but even neutrals could agree that the decision that sent Andrei Kanchelskis on his way for hand-ball was a harsh one. If we had to have a disappointment in our domestic endeavours, it was best that it should come in the League Cup. The FA Cup brought us plenty of nervous moments but our triumphant run will be remembered for some glittering demonstrations of the true quality of a team who, sadly, would be together and in their prime for only a single season. Nobody who was present will ever forget the heights they reached in thrashing the warriors of Wimbledon 3–0 on their own turf. A defining passage of that game came when Vinnie Jones made a ferocious tackle on Cantona and then watched helplessly as Eric almost immediately delivered a stunning volleyed goal. It was a reminder to Vinnie that it is pointless to try to intimidate a king. The third of the three goals has been replayed on TV many times. I think there were twenty-seven passes in the move that was expertly finished by Denis Irwin. We looked just about invincible that day but Peter Schmeichel contrived to make us vulnerable in the quarter-final when he was sent off for bringing down a Charlton player forty yards from his posts. Mark Hughes did more than anyone to steady the ship and ease us through with a 3–1 scoreline and he was a hero again in our semi-final with a dogged Oldham team when his last gasp equaliser kept us alive at Wembley. In the replay at Maine Road we overwhelmed Oldham 4–1.

Now the Cup final against Chelsea could be put on the back-burner while we went about sealing our second championship in a row. As in the previous season, there were many thrilling victories and a few shock defeats just to keep me and our supporters on our toes. All my United teams have treated me with a touch of sadism. Among the results that counted most were a 1–0 win over Arsenal gained by a thundering free kick from Cantona, and a 3–2 win in our derby fixture with City after being 2–0 down at half-time, with the maestro from France scoring twice and giving a display that should have been recorded as a coaching film. A wonderful 5–0 victory over Sheffield Wednesday in March let everyone know we were flying in a vital phase of the season and later we beat Liverpool 1–0, Manchester City 2–0 and, most impressively of all, Leeds 2–0 at Elland Road. The championship was tied up with a 2–1 defeat of Ipswich at Portman Road on 1 May and the weekend became one long celebration for our family when Tania, my son Jason's wife, presented Cathy and me with our first grandchild, Jake.

Parading the FA Cup around Wembley after a resounding 4–0 win over Chelsea was the perfect conclusion to our unforgettable season. Two penalties converted by Cantona and goals by Hughes and McClair made the match something of a procession. The only jarring note was finding myself having to leave Bryan Robson with no part in the final. Many people felt it was callous to deprive such a great servant of even a place on the bench but I had good reasons on the day for naming McClair and Sharpe as my substitutes. Sharpe was an automatic choice, as he could give me cover on the left side of the team. I had to choose between Robson and McClair to fill the other vacancy. Neither man had ever let me down but Robbo was leaving us to join Middlesbrough as player-manager while McClair was remaining in the ranks. I felt at the time that I made the right professional decision but I confess that I believe now I should have allowed sentiment to sway me.

Manchester United had won the FA Youth Cup in 1992 and we had an extraordinarily exciting group of young players ready to press for inclusion in the first team. The future of the club could not have looked healthier but, however exceptional the new crop became, they would have difficulty surpassing the wonderful collection of footballers who served me in 1994. Sadly, the Chelsea final was the last we were to see of that great team.

— 21 —
A LEAP INTO MISERY

IN all my managerial career I have never been so positive about
a group of young footballers as I was about those who were
coming through as teenagers at Old Trafford at the beginning of
the 1994–95 season. Their promise, as much as the achievement
of the double by their seniors, put the club in its strongest position
since my arrival. I could see nothing but blue skies ahead. In fact
a deluge of misery was waiting for us but even in retrospect I
think the optimism engendered by our emerging talents was justified. Their rapid development was adding so dramatically to our
reservoir of quality that any setbacks we suffered were likely to be
temporary. A season bare of trophies and awash with controversy
would still prove hard to endure but even when our spirits were
at their lowest, early in the New Year, I could take comfort from
the solidity of the foundations I had laid.

As early as January 1993, I had given eight of my teenaged
prodigies professional contracts. Their appearance in the final of
the FA Youth Cup in successive years had provided justification
of my faith. But what was really exciting was the way the best of
them had progressed to the point where they were competing for
places in the first team. Several were suggesting they could make
the transition almost as smoothly as Ryan Giggs had earlier. That
was certainly true of Nicky Butt, Paul Scholes and Gary Neville.
Keith Gillespie, Gary Neville's younger brother, Phil, and David
Beckham were also forcing themselves into consideration. I relied
mainly on graduates from the youth team (reinforced by the

experience of Irwin, Keane, May and McClair) for a first-round
League Cup tie against Port Vale on their ground and was
rewarded with a 2–1 victory, with Paul Scholes scoring both goals.
I introduced two more juniors, Chris Casper and John O'Kane,
for the second leg and this time we had a 2–0 win. In the next
round they played Newcastle United at St James' Park and were
absolutely brilliant, only losing out in the last ten minutes because
of fatigue. It was clear now that I had youngsters equipped to
play at the highest level. They would have to be monitored closely
to ensure that the demands on them were not excessive. All young
players of exceptional ability fly on gossamer wings but they can
fall to earth with a thud if their enthusiasm tempts their manager
to over-expose them. I was alert to that danger as a result of
bringing on groups of talented boys at St Mirren and Aberdeen.
Some of those lads in Scotland were notably gifted, and quite a few
of them had fulfilling careers, but a number suffered premature
burn-out and watching what happened to them had taught me a
lesson that would never be forgotten.

When the challenge of the European Cup loomed again in the
autumn of 1994 it was complicated for that one season by a ruling
from UEFA that limited the number of foreign players a club could
field to five. My first reaction was that the quota would not bother
us, since it would easily accommodate Cantona, Schmeichel and
Kanchelskis. The truth was, of course, that any non-English player
on our books was defined as a foreigner and that did create a
massive headache. Most of my first-choice squad were non-
English, with Keane, Irwin and Gillespie from Ireland, Hughes
and Giggs from Wales and McClair from Scotland. It was not
easy to reconcile the attempt to field our strongest team with the
restrictions of the new arrangement and it eventually contributed
to our failure in the tournament we most wanted to win. The
competition also had a new format. The introduction of the
Champions League involved four groups of four clubs, with the
top two in each going through to the quarter-finals. If the inclusion
in our group of Barcelona gave us a tingle, the presence of Galatasaray of Turkey made us shudder. IFK Gothenburg completed the

section and we made a bright start to the latest European adventure by beating the Swedish team 4–2 at Old Trafford. The visit to Istanbul was not nearly as hellish as it had been the year before and a goalless draw was acceptable.

By the time Barcelona came to Manchester, we were a point ahead of the Spanish giants. My adversary from the Cup Winners' Cup final of 1991 in Rotterdam, Johan Cruyff, played his normal attacking line-up. He had two wingers right on the touchline and Romario, his lightning-quick centre-forward, operating through the middle by himself. It was the cobra swiftness of the Brazilian that worried me and I had to concentrate hard on coping with him while remaining positive about winning the match. With the quality I had at my disposal in forward positions, I was confident we could beat Barcelona but only if we were sound and disciplined in defence. The decision to leave out my trusty captain and centre-back, Steve Bruce, was a surprise to most people but there were good tactical reasons for doing so. I had no doubt that Paul Parker was the right man to attend to Romario. Small, tenacious and extremely quick, Parker had been used to playing man-against-man in his Queens Park Rangers days and he was the one United player who stood out as having the single-mindedness to handle such a role. It was a match we should have won convincingly and I think we would have done so but for two instances of loss of concentration and discipline. We so dominated the opening twenty-five minutes that we were worth more than the one goal Mark Hughes headed in for us but we went to sleep in centre-midfield when Jose Maria Bakero lost Paul Ince and stole in behind him to play a through ball between Pallister and Irwin for Romario to break clear and score. That goal angered me as my instruction had been for Parker to stay with Romario throughout. Our trouble had arisen because of the British custom of defending zones and our habit of passing the responsibility for dealing with an opposing attacker on from one defender to another as the man enters a different area of the pitch. Big Gary Pallister had told Parker that he was ready to take care of Romario and then found that the Brazilian was leaving him stranded. What infuriated me was that we had spent three days adjusting our zonal defending method to incorporate man-for-man marking of Romario. I wouldn't have taken such pains if I didn't think the change was necessary. I keep harping on to our lads about how imperative total concentration is in European games. Disciplined adherence to a game-plan is the most important advantage continental teams tend to have over us. We undersell ourselves when we attribute our failures against them to inferior ability.

That home match with Barcelona finished 2–2 and we were left regretting that we had thrown away a golden opportunity to turn an electrifying night at Old Trafford into a triumph. In the aftermath, I reflected on how much we were missing Eric Cantona. The suspension meted out to him for his verbal attack on the referee in our game with Galatasaray the previous season was still in force and it would not be lifted in time to let him play in Barcelona. That would be a big loss. Eric has been widely criticised for failing to assert himself significantly on major European occasions but, although it is true that he never approached the heights that were commonplace for him in English competitions, I think that was at least partly explained by general shortcomings in the performances of the team. I believe he would have been a considerable asset to us at the Nou Camp.

The reasoning of a manager, whether about selection, tactics, substitutions or anything else, is seldom regarded as valid unless he wins the match. After we were battered 4–0 in Barcelona, practically everything I had done was bound to be seen as wrong. The condemnation started with my decision to leave out Schmeichel and play young Gary Walsh in goal. I had decided, quite simply, that I could gain more from my permitted quota of foreign players in outfield positions. Walsh wasn't responsible for any of the goals we lost and, indeed, did his job well but few of the critics allowed themselves to be inhibited by that fact. We were swamped because Barcelona were far cuter than we were and more patient in the application of their tactics and my anger in the dressing-room at half-time was a response to the naivety we had shown in midfield. There were three priorities in my tactical preparation for the match. The first was based on my observation when Barcelona visited Old Trafford that their full-backs, Albert Ferrer and Sergi, dealt fairly easily with the efforts of our wide attackers to dribble past them but were deeply uncomfortable when they had to turn and chase players who were running into threatening positions without the ball. I told Kanchelskis and Giggs that whenever possible they should pass infield and run behind the full-backs. My second requirement was that Nicky Butt should squeeze the area in which Josep Guardiola liked to operate, in front of his back four, combining and dovetailing with Ronald Koeman. To help to smother Koeman's influence, Mark Hughes would drop in against him. Then there was the third and vital need for Paul Ince to make sure he was always checking the forward runs of either Bakero or Guillermo Amor, leaving Roy Keane to play against the other one. The way Paul was responding to such instructions had been causing me concern. I sensed that he no longer wanted to be the anchorman in midfield, where there was none better at the job. It was clear to me that he now saw himself as an attacking midfield player, which was a hopeless misreading of his strengths. Players who can continually make energy-sapping runs from penalty box to penalty box are rare gems. I had brought Roy Keane to Manchester United because he was one of them, a man whose reserves of stamina put him in the Bryan Robson category. Paul did not have anything like the physical endurance of those two. But set him in around your back four and there was no quicker or more telling tackler in the game, nobody who could retrieve the ball more effectively when the opposition thought they had made a scoring chance. His strong suit was defending but he refused to embrace that reality. The refusal manifested itself markedly on that unhappy night in Barcelona and, while it would be grossly unfair to apportion overmuch of the blame to Paul, his blurred interpretation of his function did contribute appreciably to our nightmare.

We were now under pressure to win our next Champions League game in Gothenburg on a very difficult pitch and again our lack of patience and discipline let us down. Although not

playing well, nonetheless we battled back to level the score at
1–1 with a Mark Hughes goal, only to go completely gung-ho
and lose two goals to counter-attacks. Our disappointment was
compounded when Paul Ince was sent off by the Italian referee
for dissent. The stupid part about our bravado at 1–1 was that a
draw would have taken us through to the quarter-finals.

Failure of this kind can either leave you in the depths of gloom
or sharpen your appetite for trying again and most of us were
desperate to have another crack at winning the greatest prize in
club football. It added to our burning desire to retain the championship. That was never going to be easy, for the Blackburn team
assembled by Kenny Dalglish were stubborn contenders. I was
happy with my squad but had taken notice of how teams were
changing their tactics against us, particularly at Old Trafford.
Most of them were declining to come out to play, which was very
naughty of them but hardly unexpected. The threat of our two
fliers on the wings, Kanchelskis and Giggs, and the capacity of
Cantona to thread a pass behind defenders, had encouraged the
opposition to stay deep and defend their penalty box. I decided
that to solve this problem we would need either a striker who was
so quick that he could create space in the tighter areas of the box
or one who could play with his back to goal but also turn and
beat opponents to make openings. Acquiring a forward of the
right quality would involve a dramatic transfer fee but actually we
should have spent big before the season started. It is a good
principle to strengthen the squad by buying while you are successful and, as double-winners, we should have taken measures to
stay ahead of the competition, to apply what I call my 'repel all
boarders' philosophy. Apart from thinking about a striker who
could extend our range of options at the front, we should probably
have been improving our defensive cover. Paul Parker's knee problems were worsening and would soon bring his career to an end,
leaving a gap that would be difficult to fill. Buying a couple of
players in the summer would have had the huge advantage of
enabling us to give them a pre-season introduction to our
methods. As it was, we had passed New Year before turning really

serious in the search for a striker. The fact that we did so was no reflection on Mark Hughes but Mark was thirty-one and I had to think about the future. As far as I was concerned, however, he was in no danger of becoming redundant.

The two strikers who impressed me as likely to boost the potency of our attacking were men with conspicuously different attributes – Andy Cole of Newcastle United and Stan Collymore of Nottingham Forest. Andy had the speed and movement that could exploit the short passes from Cantona, and Collymore had the ability to turn and run at opponents. After initial inquiries about Cole were discouraged by Kevin Keegan, I made quite strenuous efforts to do business with Frank Clark, the Forest manager, over Collymore. It so happened that on the day I phoned with the intention of making a big offer for Collymore, Frank did not return my call, having apparently gone home with flu. I went back to probing Kevin about Cole and this time, after a little sparring on the phone, he said he would part with Andy for £6 million plus Keith Gillespie. I asked for an hour to weigh his proposal but I could have given him an answer there and then. There was no way I was going to let the deal founder on the Gillespie issue. I admired young Keith as a player but didn't honestly feel he was top-drawer. In any case, Andrei Kanchelskis had recently signed a new contract, so the Irishman had the status of an understudy. Had I known what was going to happen with Kanchelskis in the next few months, I wouldn't have parted with Keith and would have found another way of completing the transfer of Cole, which Kevin was clearly keen to conclude. In all of this, I took care to reassure Keith's mother that I wasn't railroading her boy. I knew from my contacts with Mrs Gillespie over the years that she trusted me and I could not risk letting her down. So I made certain the lad was well looked after by Kevin. By coincidence, the Cole transfer was immediately followed by the meeting of Newcastle and Manchester United at St James' Park and there was inevitable media speculation about how Cole and Gillespie would figure in the match. Sensibly, I think, both Kevin and I decided that the players should be spared such a fraught baptism. A week later, Cole had a quiet debut for us against Blackburn Rovers at Old Trafford in a match dominated by a spellbinding performance from Eric Cantona, who scored a late winner to reduce Blackburn's points lead over us at the top of the table. The next day Eric's agent, Jean Jacques Bertrand, met the chairman to discuss a new contract. Everything in the garden was lovely. Eric was happy at United and we were happy that he wanted to stay for the rest of his career. Nobody could have foreseen the horrors that were about to descend on us.

As a proud Scot, I have always regarded the anniversary of Robert Burns's birth, 25 January, as a special day but the date was made memorable in 1995 by events that had nothing to do with our national bard. Even Burns would have found it hard to be lyrical about what happened on that Wednesday night at Selhurst Park in South London. The build-up to our match with Crystal Palace could not have been more normal and we looked forward to another chance to cut Blackburn's lead. We expected the challenge from Palace to have a physical emphasis but that did not worry us unduly. Our currency is skill but if opponents are rough we rely on Manchester United players to stand up for themselves and refuse to be intimidated. I want them to show their courage by always taking the ball, even when the boots are swinging, and so long as the referee is good enough and strong enough I am happy. If he is not, there is an obvious danger of anarchy, not to mention the risk of a serious injury that could harm the long-term ambitions of an individual or the team. Unfortunately, on this occasion we had an official I would have to categorise as weak. I don't know Alan Wilkie and I am sure he is a decent man but to my mind he is a poor referee. His inability to stamp out the disgraceful tackles from Crystal Palace's two central defenders, Richard Shaw and Chris Coleman, made subsequent trouble unavoidable. I don't believe Shaw is by nature any dirtier than the next player but he does pull jerseys with unbelievable frequency and that is an offence that frustrates and infuriates creative attackers. On this night he added to his repertoire and shared out three horrendous tackles between Cole and

Cantona. Coleman, not to be outdone, inflicted a terrible tackle on Cole at the halfway line. All went unpunished by Mr Wilkie. I know that if I had been subjected to such treatment as a player, I would have done something about it myself, but as a manager my view of the game is entirely different and I recognise revenge as an unacceptable option. I tell my players that the answer is to make their opponents suffer by outplaying them and at the interval at Selhurst Park I made the point strongly to Eric Cantona about Shaw. 'Don't get involved with him,' I said. 'That is exactly what he wants. Keep the ball away from him. Pass it around him. He thinks he is having a good game if he is tackling.'

On the way out for the second half, I approached the referee and complained about the tackling in the first forty-five minutes. Mr Wilkie looked at me as if I had horns on my head. He did not seem to have appreciated the seriousness of what had been going on. The second half was only four minutes old when Cantona's decision to exact some retribution produced a blatant kick at Shaw and suddenly Mr Wilkie was a disciplinarian as he raced forward to flourish the red card. I was in a rage over Eric's stupidity. Not for the first time, his explosive temperament had embarrassed him and the club and tarnished his brilliance as a footballer. This was his fifth dismissal in United's colours and, in spite of all the provocation directed at him, it was a lamentable act of folly. His worst offences were not premeditated or in any way calculated but came from an instant loss of control. They nearly always happened when he felt that he was being wronged and that the referee was doing nothing about it. His attempts to administer his own version of justice were invariably so clumsily conspicuous that they were immediately self-destructive. On that evening nobody could possibly have envisaged how strange and horrifying the repercussions of his sending-off would be. As he started to leave the field, I told Norman Davies, our kit man, to accompany him on the seventy-yard walk to the tunnel, which was located at the far end of the pitch. I was preoccupied with the need to reshape our team to compensate for being reduced to ten men and, as I continued to watch the game, I missed the beginning of the violent drama that developed in front of the main stand. Much later I was to learn that Eric had reacted to the abusive taunts of a Palace fan by lunging high, studs first, across the boundary wall to land on his tormentor's chest. By the time I became aware of the scene, the Frenchman was throwing a punch and it took some minutes to restore order. The match had become almost incidental and it is easy to forget that, David May having put us ahead, a late equaliser held us to a 1–1 draw. Afterwards I ripped into Cantona with a fury I had vented only once before in our association – when he had trampled on John Moncur of Swindon in the previous season. Eric just sat there, not saying a word. I was, amazingly, unaware of the gravity of the incident with the fan. When a police superintendent called me out to tell me that there would be a full investigation I still did not grasp the scale of the storm that was brewing. I remained unenlightened as I sat sunk in my thoughts on the plane back to Manchester. People will doubt that I could have stayed uninformed for so long. 'He must have been told,' they will say. They are wrong.

I was still enclosed in my other world, as Cathy calls it, when I arrived home and not even the presence of my son Jason could lighten my mood.

'Have you seen it on TV?' he asked me.

'No,' I replied and headed upstairs to my bedroom, with Jason following.

'It is absolutely terrible,' he said.

'Jason, I don't want to hear about it,' I told him curtly. 'I'll see plenty in the morning.' And I went straight to bed.

Usually I am off to sleep in minutes but this night, not surprisingly, was one of the rare exceptions. By 4.00 a.m. I was up and watching the video of the game. What it showed was pretty appalling. Over the years since then I have never been able to elicit an explanation of the episode from Eric but my own feeling is that anger at himself over the ordering-off and resentment of the referee's earlier inaction combined to take him over the brink. There have been times in my own life when I have had deep regrets about explosions of temper and loss of control. Later in the morning, the Cliff training ground was besieged by TV crews and pressmen. There was no hiding place outside the main door of the building. My day was saturated with meetings and phone calls but the most important gathering was at the Alderley Edge Hotel in the evening, when Martin Edwards, Professor Sir Roland Smith, chairman of the plc board, Maurice Watkins and myself met to consider what action the club should take. We were unanimous that our response had to be powerful enough to protect Manchester United's reputation and we agreed that we should impose a four-month suspension on Eric, which would declare him out for the rest of the season.

During our discussion there had been telephone calls from the FA and the substance of them was that the ban we had applied would be accepted by them as sufficient punishment. Within days, however, they were summoning Eric before them for bringing the game into disrepute. The disciplinary hearing was held at a hotel in St Albans and its inclination towards farce was typified by a question from Ian Stott, the Oldham director who chaired the proceedings.

'Isn't it a fact that you are a kung-fu expert?' he asked Eric. Naturally, Eric was confused by the question and when Maurice and I had stopped chuckling we answered for him.

'No, he is not a kung-fu expert.'

When the verdict was announced it was a shock. The FA added a further four months' suspension to the four we had given Eric. I felt the sentence was definitely excessive and I believe the PFA, who preen themselves over protecting their members, should have done something to contest it. There was more trouble for Cantona when he had to appear at Croydon Crown Court to face criminal charges and another media frenzy. Ned Kelly, Manchester United's security officer, had his work cut out shielding Eric from the baying pack but coped very well. The court handed down a two-week jail sentence but, on appeal, that was replaced by 120 hours of community service.

Cantona gave proof of his determination and strength of character in his handling of his prolonged ordeal. Doing the community service put him under far more strain than it should have done. It was supposed to consist of controlled coaching sessions for schoolchildren, which he probably would have enjoyed. But with the mixture of ages and sexes presented to him, proper coaching was impossible. The sessions were apparently just an excuse for a lot of people to meet him. I began to change my mind about his chances of surviving in the English game.

As I struggled to prevent the 1994–95 season from becoming a sequence of disasters, I felt like the little Dutch boy trying to plug holes in the dyke with his fingers. What drenched me was more like sewage than water when Andrei Kanchelskis delivered an attack in the tabloids. His basis for the outburst was that he was not getting enough games. It was true that he wasn't playing regularly but my reason for leaving him out of the team was that he was carrying an abdominal injury and I thought I should spare him the rigours of constant action. When Kanchelskis first complained about his abdomen our physio, Dave Fevre, could detect nothing untoward and consultation with specialists had the same result. The reports of the injury had coincided with a dramatic change in the player's attitude. Where was that lovely smile and graciousness and gratitude he had brought to Old Trafford? This was not the boy we had lifted out of the Ukraine, where, I understand, his weekly wage was £6. This was a scowling, discontented young man. No manager likes to read criticism from his players in the newspapers, especially when there is no real justification for it, and I fined Kanchelskis a week's wages for the breach of club rules. He was still complaining of an injury and, although medical examinations again found no source, the fact is he subsequently needed a hernia operation. A transfer request was submitted and promptly turned down and the relationship between us soured rapidly. His behaviour was bemusing. After all, he had just signed a new three-year contract. Maybe if I had known at that time of the clause in his contract which entitled him to one-third of any future transfer fee, his conduct would have been less incomprehensible to me.

The proliferation of agents in modern football has caused many headaches and heartaches but those wheeler-dealers do have their uses when it comes to keeping abreast of what is happening on the transfer merry-go-round. So I was interested when my contact in Holland phoned to ask, 'Is it true you are selling Kanchelskis and Ince?' I told him there was no chance of that. The rumour about Kanchelskis had not originated in anything I had said or even thought. I was having trouble with him but was not intending to sell. However, the Ince story intrigued me.

'Where has that come from?' I asked and was told that Paul's representative had been talking to some Italian clubs, saying that he wanted to move. There was no way of telling how true that was but the mere mention of it persuaded me that I should prepare myself for any changes in Paul's behaviour. I was already bothered by his attitude around the dressing-room. He had attached a rather silly title to himself. 'Don't call me Incey, call me the Guvnor,' he was saying, and that did not go down well. There had been a cockiness about him from the moment he came to Old Trafford but I reckoned it was his way of masking insecurity. Deep down he worries and I was happy to give him some licence while he was young and immature. In our youth we all drift in and out of a make-believe world. One day I would be dreaming I was Willie Waddell, the next Stanley Matthews, and quite a lot of the time I imagined I was Denis Law, my hero. But you do grow up. Paul Ince had reached an age of maturity and this guvnor nonsense should have been left in his toy-box. On the field he had already worried me with an altered approach to his game. He was spending more and more time going forward but not coming back quickly enough and it was quite apparent that he was completely carried away.

Trying to maintain our challenge for the championship was difficult after the removal of Cantona. But there were encouraging signs of nerves in the Blackburn camp and, it goes without saying, I did nothing to ease the strain on our rivals. It is my habit to pay attention to post-match interviews with the managers of teams who are in close competition with us. The words a man utters don't interest me much. It is the face that I search and I thought

I discerned quite a change in Kenny Dalglish from earlier in the season. Kenny was singing all the right songs but he didn't seem to be enjoying them, so I felt that a few comments wouldn't go amiss. My line was that Blackburn were so much in command that now they could only throw the championship away. I drew an analogy with Devon Loch, the Queen Mother's steeplechaser that collapsed on the Grand National run-in with the great race at its mercy. It may have been a pretty corny psychological tactic but it was worth a try. The contest between Blackburn and ourselves came down to the final day of the season. I would have been delighted if we had been in direct confrontation but instead both clubs had awkward away matches – Blackburn against Liverpool and Manchester United against West Ham. There was foolish talk about the favours Kenny, as the most admired player in Liverpool's history, could expect at Anfield. I dismissed that as rubbish. I have always respected Liverpool for their traditions, their pride and their professionalism and there was no doubt that Blackburn would have a tough time on Merseyside. I knew that and so did Kenny.

For our match at Upton Park, I possibly made a tactical error by leaving Mark Hughes on the bench. I didn't want their clever midfield players to grab hold of the game and decided to play three against them in that area of the park. I was convinced that our opponents would eventually tire, allowing me to bring Sparky on to do his damage. I sat him down to explain this and, although disappointed, he understood my reasoning. Tactics are all very well if they are successful. On that day they were not. The first half was made peculiar by West Ham's insistence on just sitting in tight and relying on counter-attacks and we had only an Andy Cole shot against a post to show for all our possession. Then, out of the blue, they took the lead through Michael Hughes. After the interval I drafted in Mark Hughes and from then on we battered West Ham but our overwhelming domination yielded only one goal from Brian McClair. We were desperately unlucky. When news filtered through from Anfield that Liverpool had equalised (in the end they won 2–1) we knew all we had to do to be champions again was score one measly goal and the excitement became unbearable. We were denied a clear-cut penalty for hand-ball but I have to admit that we had sufficient chances to win a dozen games. I think every United player had a scoring opportunity of some sort in the last fifteen minutes but the ball just wouldn't go in. In the dressing-room afterwards our players were utterly drained and dejected but I was proud of them. They had given their all. Bobby Charlton's passionate speech on behalf of the club was warmly appreciated. Of course, we could not afford to wallow in sadness. In spite of the trials and tribulations of the past few months, we had marched steadily towards another FA Cup final and now we were just a week away from a showdown with Everton at Wembley.

Our Cup campaign had begun in January with two ties on either side of the Cantona drama at Selhurst Park and by a strange twist our opponents at the semi-final stage were Crystal Palace. The background meant the match at Villa Park carried a definite risk of crowd trouble and the Palace manager, Alan Smith, and I made speeches appealing for calm. Two hours of football failed to separate the teams but the 2–2 scoreline mattered less than the post-match report that a Palace supporter had been killed in a confrontation with United fans. In the replay, we won fairly comfortably by virtue of two goals from Bruce and Pallister but our day was marred by the deserved dismissal of Roy Keane, who responded to a dangerous tackle by stamping on Gareth Southgate. The suggestion that Keane found this one bad tackle too many from Palace did not provide a trace of an excuse for what he did. His Irish fire was fundamental to his immense value as a footballer but his tendency to go beyond the bounds of accept-ability would have to be curbed.

When we are in a Cup final, the board meeting on the preceding Tuesday is generally light-hearted. The directors are looking forward to another trip to Wembley and there is a good deal of banter in the air. But the tone of the gathering four days before our collision with Everton in 1995 changed abruptly when, under the heading of Any Other Business at the end of the meeting, I announced that I wanted to sell Paul Ince. The most common reactions were shock and dismay but I explained that I had observed Paul closely over the past five months and had decided that his attitude and his performances had altered to a degree that I could not tolerate. This was not a spur of the moment decision. It weighed heavily on my mind but I needed to be in control of my team. I felt Paul was no longer playing to the discipline I demanded. He was not a bad person at all and had very generous traits but if footballers think they are above the manager's control there is only one word to be said to them – goodbye. I was sure I would never regret the decision to sell him and the Cup final hardened that conviction. The goal with which Everton won the Cup proved once again that Paul took little account of my pre-match instructions. He had gone on a surge forward with the ball and left half a pitch of space behind him. As I prayed that he would knock a pass out wide to Irwin, he chose to try to beat Dave Watson, Everton's big, tough-tackling centre-half. Watson won the ball cleanly and dispatched it to Anders Limpar, our opponents' Swedish winger, who had acres of room. I could feel the threat as Limpar attacked our two central defenders, with Paul not remotely in touch or looking like getting back, and it was no surprise that the ball was ultimately headed into our net by Paul Rideout.

To lose any final is painful but to lose to a team as ordinary as Everton is just not acceptable. To say so is not to detract from the credit due to their manager, Joe Royle, who had performed miracles in getting them to Wembley. He deserved his day of glory and received nothing but praise from me. Everton's goalkeeper, Neville Southall, also earned the warmest tributes. He was inspired. While there was joy in the winners' dressing-room, in ours I did not mince my words in condemning our display. If some players had let their team-mates down, on or off the field, they would not be around Old Trafford much longer.

— 22 —
PUBLIC ENEMY NUMBER ONE

The decision to sell Paul Ince was mine alone and nobody at Old Trafford was inclined to let me forget the fact. There was nothing splendid about my isolation as our supporters reacted angrily to the jettisoning of a player they saw as a vital contributor to our recent successes. I agreed wholeheartedly with that assessment but felt I had to act on my conviction that the fundamental change in Paul's attitude, his insistence on trying to assume a role in the team for which he was not equipped, had diminished his usefulness to us to the point where a transfer made absolute sense. As the negotiations between Inter Milan and United gathered pace, the president of the Italian club, Massimo Moratti, arrived at Old Trafford with his entourage. They agreed to pay a fee of £6 million and guaranteed further profit for United through the playing of four matches between the two clubs over two years. The next stage was to bring Ince to the table and it was left to me to get in touch with him at Mottram Hall, where he was having a game of golf. I don't think he was surprised to see me waiting for him when he came off the course. I explained the latest position and told him that Moratti was in the chairman's office and waiting for a call. When I got through to Martin Edwards he said the Italians wanted to speak to Paul, so I handed the phone over to him. I was struck by what seemed to me to be a tone of familiarity in the ensuing conversation. Paul had been giving the impression to our supporters that United were forcing him out. Such a version of events was nonsense. Yes, I wanted rid of him but if he had been determined to stay it would not have been possible to push the transfer through. There is no way you could force Paul Ince to do anything against his will. I believe that he and his agent had been in contact with people in Italian football over a period of months. I was told that at our reception after defeat by Everton in the 1995 Cup final, Paul was heard declaring that he was on his way to Italy. Yet, in spite of all that, I was being branded as Public Enemy Number One for driving him away. I was out on my own, with no hint of support from the corridors of Old Trafford, and the people who keep queueing up for jobs as managers of football clubs should consider the vulnerability I felt then.

Once again I found the private world of my own thoughts the best place to be. My holiday with Cathy could not have come at a better time. We escaped to the United States, where I always enjoy sinking into the restful comfort of anonymity. But the Ince issue pursued me across the Atlantic. I thought it necessary to keep in touch with the club almost on a daily basis and during one of my calls I realised that I was talking to an extremely worried chairman. Martin Edwards back in Manchester was feeling the sharp edge of the criticism over the sale of Ince and he urged me to reconsider the deal. He also made the point that Brian Kidd thought we shouldn't sell Paul. That was a surprise. Brian had never voiced such an opinion to me.

'Could you have a word with Ince?' the chairman asked. 'You can persuade him to change his mind about going.' It was a request that obliged me to do some soul-searching. Had I read the Ince situation too harshly? I know I can be a bit too single-minded at times and there was no virtue in being dogmatic about this case. A cool, objective appraisal was needed in response to the emotion generated in Manchester, which was so intense that it easily communicated itself to me on another continent. But the more I analysed the matter, the more convinced I was that my original decision was the right one. 'Why should I be getting such hassle at this stage of my management career?' I kept asking myself. Success had given me the degree of control over the structure and playing methods of my team that I have always sought in management. I was not prepared to surrender that. I did promise the chairman that I would phone Ince from America. What I had decided to say to him, however, might seem to many outsiders a less than persuasive argument for remaining with United: 'Paul, what are you thinking about? You are not suited to Italian football. You are only suited to the game in England.' Whether that slightly provocative assertion hardened his resolve to go to Inter I can't be sure. I certainly did want him to sign, despite all the panic at home, and I was pleased when it was confirmed that he was heading for Milan.

My chances of relaxing on holiday were not improved when Martin Edwards phoned to tell me that Mark Hughes had signed for Chelsea. The news was a real shock.

'How did that come about?' I asked Martin.

Apparently there had been a problem over Mark's pension arrangements and he had held back from putting his signature to a new contract with us. Since he had not committed himself, the freedom of contract conditions that now apply had enabled him to leave. Contrary to popular opinion, his departure was not something I wanted. I could, of course, understand Mark's point of view. He must have worried about my acquisition of Andy Cole but, without question, I would have preferred the Welshman to stay. After hearing that he had gone, I was beginning to feel that the whole world was against me. Then, as can happen, my football worries were suddenly put into perspective. Cathy and I were roused in the middle of the night by a call from Ken Merrett at Manchester United. He informed us that our nephew, Stephen, had been killed in an accident at the age of nineteen. Word of that horrifying tragedy ended our stay in the States and we left immediately for Glasgow to comfort Cathy's sister Bridget and her husband John.

At Old Trafford, the madness that had characterised our summer took a more sinister turn with some of the happenings surrounding the transfer of Andrei Kanchelskis to Everton at the beginning of the 1995–96 season. The amazing clauses in his contract stipulating that he was entitled to a third of any fee involved, and that a further substantial share had to go to his former club in Russia, Shakhtyor Donetsk, caused our dealings with Everton to become a protracted and rather acrimonious saga. There was much toing and froing, including a trip by Maurice Watkins to Russia, before a settlement of all the various demands could be negotiated and we were able to collect a payment of £5 million. But the part of the affair that remains most vivid in my mind is the meeting with the player and his representatives at which it was made clear to Manchester United that a refusal to release him would have dire consequences. At first I was glad that Kanchelskis's agent, Grigory Essaoulenko, had turned up again because his visit gave me the opportunity to return his unwanted gift of £40,000. If I was delighted to have that money out of the club safe and passed back to him, he was reluctant to take it.

'Please, Alex, it is for you,' he said. 'It is a thank-you for all you have done for me.' I had done nothing for him other than showing the basic courtesies due to anybody with whom I was conducting business. He kept insisting that I should have the cash and eventually I had to call in the chairman. Martin handled the difficulty very well.

'Look, Grigory, Alex cannot accept this gift. It would reflect badly on his reputation if he did.' Although I was relieved that the episode had been brought to an end, I was still bemused about why the money had been presented to me in the first place. I had an inkling of an explanation once Martin, Maurice Watkins and I convened in the chairman's office with Grigory, Andrei and the player's local adviser, George Scanlon, who was Head of Modern Languages at Liverpool Polytechnic. Before long tempers were lost as Grigory demanded that Andrei be transferred. The angry exchanges came to a chilling climax when Grigory screamed at the chairman, 'If you don't transfer him now, you will not be around much longer.' There was no doubting the seriousness of the threat. The meeting ended shortly afterwards, much to our relief. We needed time to consider the implications of that alarming encounter. Obviously, Martin had most to think about, given the menacing words he had just heard.

'What are we going to do, Maurice?' he asked our learned friend.

'Sell him,' was Maurice's terse reply and by now I couldn't have agreed more. I was fully aware that the removal of Kanchelskis, so soon after Keith Gillespie's move to Newcastle, would leave us short in the wide right position but his attitude was so bad that there was nothing to be gained from trying to keep him. The formalising of Kanchelskis's change of club was delayed by the complex dispute over Shakhtyor Donetsk's claim for £1 million but finally he was able to make his debut for Everton on 26 August. His pace and strength on the wing had been huge assets for us while he was showing real enthusiasm for our cause but, given the transformation that had occurred in his behaviour, Merseyside was welcome to him.

With three big-name players departing in quick succession, the press felt free to give me a hard time. The *Manchester Evening News* ran a poll on whether or not I should be sacked. It was a nice way to thank me for all the assistance I had given the paper. Over the years, I had frequently compromised my position with the dailies by ensuring that David Meek, who covered United for the *News*, had the inside track on every story associated with the club. David was entirely trustworthy, and his experience made him a good judge of what material should and should not be used in his pieces, but I was surprised by the willingness of his colleagues to stir up a little extra trouble for me. It seemed that, compared to me, Gary Cooper in 'High Noon' was well off for backers. I had ample reason to be worried about the strength of my position at United and I was given another jolt when I approached Martin Edwards about a new contract. My timing may have been ill-conceived but I still felt seriously aggrieved over having been lumbered with a pay deal that left me trailing so far behind George Graham. Conversations with Martin Edwards are usually straightforward and pleasant until you ask him for more money. Then you have a problem. The difference this time was that it was obvious from the start that we were never going to agree and he suggested I should speak with Professor Sir Roland Smith and Maurice Watkins. I was encouraged by the prospect of more fruitful negotiations over my contract than I had achieved with Martin in the past. A meeting was set up by my accountant, Alan Baines, and both of us went to Sir Roland's house in the Isle of Man, ostensibly to thrash out the revised terms. Maurice Watkins also joined us on a lovely day and Lady Joan, Professor Smith's wife, made us welcome with cold drinks and sandwiches on the patio. It was, I thought, a perfect setting but my enjoyment of it did not last long. Sir Roland kicked off the discussion by asking what I had in mind as far as salary and length of contract were concerned. I explained that, at fifty-four, I felt I had six good years I could give the club and in essence I was looking for Manchester United to give me a contract that would cover the period until I was sixty. As for pay, I felt I should be on the same level as the highest paid manager in the League. Until his recent dismissal that distinction had belonged to George Graham and, having left Arsenal, George had kindly supplied me with a copy of his contract, which I produced at the Isle of Man meeting and duly handed over to Maurice. That certainly added a bit of spice to the proceedings. After all, when I had brought up this comparison during my last round of salary negotiations in 1993, the club had conferred with David Dein of the Arsenal board and later indicated that what he told them reinforced their scepticism about George's claims concerning his earnings. Now the proof was being laid before them. I let it be known that I would be happy to accept exactly what George had been paid at Arsenal, no more, no less. I did not think that was remotely unreasonable but the tenor of our meeting changed completely when Sir Roland put a direct and rather disconcerting question to me.

'Do you think you have taken your eye off the ball?' he said. I asked him what he meant. 'Well, some people at Old Trafford think you are not as focused as you have been.' I told him I simply did not understand how such a suggestion could be made.

'Neither the chairman nor anyone else has ever questioned my devotion to my job and you would have thought that if there was a problem Martin would have mentioned it to me.'

The raising of this unexpected subject diverted the discussion away from its original objective and the topic of my contract was put aside as I quizzed Sir Roland on the background to the question he had thrown at me. I could not extract any more information from him about the source of misgivings that were completely unfounded. My assessment at the time was that the decision to sell Paul Ince had not gone down at all well and now doubts were forming about the soundness of my thinking. The upshot of the meeting was that the club could not offer me a new contract. That would have to wait until the following June when the Remuneration Committee would formulate an offer. My request for a six-year contract was refused outright. No manager, they pointed out, had ever been on more than four years. Fair enough. It was also made plain to me that having any role in the club after I retired as manager was totally out of the question. They said they did not want a repetition of the Sir Matt Busby syndrome. I found that attitude perplexing. Was it sensible to decree that all my experience of managing Manchester United would be cut off from the club at a stroke instead of being put at the disposal of my successor, to be tapped if and when he had a use for it? Whereas I had hoped to go home boosted by the promise of a new financial agreement with United, I returned from the Isle of Man flattened, confused and worried. My mind was working overtime, sifting through the debris of that shambles of a meeting, searching for fragments of hope that could motivate me to get on with my job. The very next day a close friend at Old Trafford made a cautionary remark to me: 'You know what this place is like – they all listen to tittle-tattle. Even heroes are not immune to it.' I was reminded of a point made to me more than once by Sir Roland, who is Manchester-born. 'Mancunians are only happy when they are bringing people down. They enjoy that. They don't like to see people being too successful.'

One obvious way of appeasing our disgruntled supporters would have been to plunge into the transfer market and seek to replace the departed trio of Ince, Hughes and Kanchelskis and I did give serious consideration to that option, particularly in relation to the wide right position vacated by Kanchelskis. But there was not a suitable player who could be bought. Darren Anderton of Tottenham Hotspur was a player I liked a lot but he had just signed a new contract at White Hart Lane. Elsewhere, I could see nobody capable of meeting our needs on the right wing. I was confident that centre midfield would be filled by Nicky Butt and I was reassured by the promise of David Beckham. He was a late developer but was coming into the reckoning and, although I wasn't sure whether he would be operating wide on the right or in central midfield, he was certain to be an increasingly important member of the squad. There was also Paul Scholes, who could attack from deep positions as Cantona did or function as a front player in the manner of Hughes. Clearly Scholes did not have anything like the power or experience of either of those two but he was an excellent footballer with a strong combative streak and if he could continue to overcome the problems created by his asthmatic condition he was bound to have a bright future with us.

When we began the 1995–96 season by losing 3–1 at Aston Villa, a flood of negative comment in the media had to be expected. Alan Hansen delivered his now famous quote: 'You can never win anything with kids.' Actually there was not a lot wrong with his statement. Teams mainly composed of young and inexperienced players rarely succeed in the toughest competitions. But at Old Trafford the Busby Babes had already proved that there can be exceptions to the rule and we were about to see another group of remarkable young footballers step beyond the norms of the game. We did not have to wait long for an opportunity to answer the absurdly sweeping criticisms that followed the loss at Villa Park. On the following Wednesday, goals by Scholes and Keane brought a 2–1 home victory over West Ham and four more consecutive wins had the pundits doing somersaults. Now my youthful team were wonders and even our supporters, who have learned to be on the lookout for false dawns, were convinced they were indeed seeing a throwback to the Busby Babes as we carried on into November before suffering our second defeat. For the first time in months I was enjoying my work. Yet, though the strain of the summer ordeals was fading, I felt then (and I have no reason to think now that it was an inaccurate feeling) that my job was under more threat than in any other period of my stewardship at Old Trafford. I had no hard evidence, so perhaps I was being slightly paranoid, but I had the feeling that the chairman was listening to too many people. There is never any shortage of characters who want to ingratiate themselves with the chairman of the club and Martin's accessibility exposes him to a great deal of petty gossip. I am sure that the bulk of what was said was best ignored. So what if some were not in agreement with the selling of Ince and Kanchelskis. Did they honestly believe I would make a decision if I did not deem it to be in the best interests of Manchester United? The idea is absurd.

The success of my young team was giving me immense pleasure, not merely by justifying my belief in their talent but with the honesty and maturity of their approach to the game. Giggs, Butt, Beckham and the Neville brothers would all take part in a majority of the league matches we played that season and Scholes was not too far behind their tally of appearances. They were receiving plenty of praise and all of it was thoroughly deserved. Just when everything was going along smoothly we were hit by another problem and once again it centred on our favourite Frenchman. Under the terms of the ban applied to Eric Cantona after his offences at Selhurst Park in the previous January, he was not allowed to play in any type of organised matches, whether they were friendlies, for charity or whatever they were. But he could participate in games within the context of training. Given these parameters, we scheduled a series of games at the Cliff training ground against local teams – Oldham, Rochdale, Bury and others. I told Eric about the programme in order to keep his spirits up and let him know that we would be arranging such outings weekly until he made his return to competitive action at the beginning of October. After the very first of these training games the press got hold of the story and soon we were being censured in a letter from

Lancaster Gate for playing Cantona in what the FA chose to define as a friendly match. This was the final straw for the deeply frustrated Cantona and he informed the club that he was moving back to France. The moment I learned of his intentions, I rushed to his hotel in Worsley, where I found him alone in his room with an empty food tray at his bedside.

'Don't you eat in the restaurant?' I inquired.

'No, I don't get any peace in there. I prefer just staying in my room.' I could understand now how badly the suspension was affecting him and could sympathise with his reaction to the latest kick in the teeth from the FA. I started to agree with his decision to head back home. That night in bed I sat talking with Cathy about Eric's predicament and she remarked how surprised she was that I had yielded so readily to the idea of losing Cantona.

'It's not like you to give up so easily, particularly against the establishment,' she said.

Her words gave me so much to consider that I had one of those rare nights when sleeping was difficult. The next morning I contacted Eric's adviser, Jean Jacques Bertrand, and told him I was ready to fly to Paris. I said it was imperative that he met me and listened to some points I had to make. Cathy had kick-started my determination and there was no longer any thought of tamely accepting Eric's plan to leave us.

The night before my flight to Paris, I was in London for a book launch and representatives from several newspapers also attended the dinner. It was a relaxed evening and amid the enjoyment of good food and wine guards were lowered sufficiently for me to let slip that I was off to Paris the next day to meet Eric. This stirred a response and Fleet Street had the hounds out at Heathrow and on the plane, with reinforcements waiting for me when I landed in Paris. I made quite an impressive dash past the reporters and off into the city. Almost as soon as I was settled in the Georges V Hotel I was contacted by Cantona's lawyer, also named Jean Jacques. He said he would be collecting me at 7.30 p.m., adding that the porter would come to my room for me. When I opened the door to a knock at precisely half-past seven, the porter instructed me, 'Follow, Monsieur Ferguson.' I trailed after him along corridors, down stairways and out through the kitchen to the back door of the hotel, where Jean Jacques stood holding two helmets. He handed me one of them. 'Quick, put this on,' he said and off we went on his Harley Davidson through side streets to our destination. It was a restaurant in which Eric was waiting for us with Jean Jacques Bertrand and a secretary. There was no one else in the place and the owner had put the *fermé* sign on the door. It struck me that he must have thought a lot of Eric to be giving up a night's earnings for him. We had a wonderful time. Eric was delighted to see me and to hear what I had to say. I told him of my conversation with my wife and of how it had galvanised me and brought me to Paris to make sure that he wasn't going to give in to the pressures assailing him. We would find a way of easing his troubles, I assured him, further encouraging him with the news that Maurice Watkins was on the case and that sympathy for him was growing rapidly. I believe he wanted me to put an arm round him and convince him that everything would be all right, and in a sense that was what I was doing. The other point I made to him was that he had to get out of that hotel and into a house and that I had already done some groundwork on that front. He readily agreed that such a change was essential and the rest of the evening was spent pleasantly in reminiscing about great football matches of the past. I pride myself on having an excellent recollection of teams, goalscorers and dates and it impressed me that he was in the same league when it came to remembering outstanding occasions back in the Fifties and Sixties. Those hours spent in Eric's company in that largely deserted restaurant added up to one of the more worthwhile acts I have performed in this stupid job of mine.

Cantona's reappearance for Manchester United against Liverpool on 1 October 1995 was always bound to be overloaded with hype and Roy Evans, the Liverpool manager, rightly appealed to the public to remember that his team were involved too. But Eric erased any tiny possibility that somebody else would dominate the headlines when his first real impact on the game resulted in a goal for us. Drifting out wide to find acres of space, he controlled the ball, looked up and placed a glorious pass into the path of Nicky Butt, who flipped it up over Phil Babb, the Liverpool defender, and squeezed it beyond their goalkeeper, David James. Who could have written such a script? Liverpool did live up to their manager's vow that they would be much more than bit-players in the show and midway through the second half of a typically engrossing duel with our formidable rivals they were 2–1 up. Eric, however, had the last word, scoring with a penalty to give us a 2–2 draw after Giggs was brought down.

The season eventually shaped itself into an incredible triumph for Manchester United and the form Eric reached in his comeback may have represented his greatest feat in our colours. From 22 January until the clinching of the League championship, we won seven of our matches 1–0 and in five of them Cantona scored the goal. His contribution was truly extraordinary but in any successful season it is the team performance that is paramount and all the players did magnificently. Our young bucks had continued to take the country by storm and behind them Peter Schmeichel had consistently provided the kind of displays that have persuaded me that he is the best goalkeeper I have ever seen. Many of those 1–0 victories would have been impossible without his brilliance between the posts. Appropriately, he reserved his most inspired resistance for our main challengers in the championship battle, Newcastle United.

Newcastle had been flying high all season but there had been a hiccup or two on the way to our meeting at St James' Park. In contrast, we had won our previous five matches and in the game immediately before our visit to the north-east we had thrashed Bolton Wanderers 6–0 at Burnden Park. We had to fancy our chances but we might well have been blown away in the first half. It was almost a miracle that we emerged unscathed from the opening twenty minutes. Peter was unbelievable as he thwarted Newcastle time and again. Our first concerted attack did not come until just before the interval. It was a relief for the players and me to gather in the dressing-room and take stock of our position.

They say managers earn their wages in the ten or fifteen minutes they spend with their men at half-time. It is a wild over-simplification but there was some truth in it on this occasion. Motivation is never merely a matter of gung-ho ranting. Naturally, footballers cannot all be stirred by the same means. Some are self-motivated but sometimes even they have to be reminded of their own standards. That was the case in this match and so my words carried a general message for everyone in the room. In essence, I was asking if we could be happy with our standards in the first half and could we claim, on the basis of how we had performed in those forty-five minutes, that we wanted to win the title as much as Newcastle did? We were transformed after the interval and at last began to express ourselves effectively. Our improvement soon earned us a goal when Eric met a Phil Neville cross and volleyed the ball back into the opposite corner of the net. That blow drained the confidence out of our opponents. They had been showing signs of nerves in their games (the cavalier performances that had been deservedly acclaimed early in the campaign were extremely rare now) and I knew that losing to us would accelerate that tendency. Championship winners often find themselves grinding out 1–0 wins in the critical months of March and April. They are not necessarily playing the best football or creating good entertainment but they are demonstrating character and determination in surviving pressure to gain the results they need. We were certainly doing that.

On the run-in there can be as much strain on managers as on players and a psychological struggle can develop between the men in charge of the leading contenders. I have often been accused of playing mind games with my rivals and I must admit that at times there has been substance in the suggestion. But the widespread assumption that remarks I made after our home match with Leeds United on 17 April 1996 were designed to upset Kevin Keegan, the manager of Newcastle United, was quite wrong. I was confident that on a level playing field we would overcome New-castle. We were showing no traces of stumbling, whereas they were threatening to go into freefall. What concerned me was the question of whether Leeds would be as ferociously competitive when they entertained Newcastle at Elland Road on 29 April as they were against us at Old Trafford. On the morning prior to that game on our ground I received a call from David Walker of the *Daily Mail*. He mentioned the beleaguered manager of Leeds, Howard Wilkinson, with whom I got on very well, and asked if I would offer a few words of encouragement. David Walker and I discussed Leeds's recent results and their miserable position in the league table and we agreed that Howard's players seemed to be showing less than a do-or-die commitment on his behalf. I decided that anything I had to say would be best said after our match with Leeds was over to avoid any impression that I was trying to patronise Howard. The tremendous effort our opponents put in that day made a stark contrast with how they had been performing over the past few months. They appeared to draw a new determination from the opportunity to reduce Manchester United's chances of gaining more glory. I still think I was right to comment on the probability that their club would have been much better placed in the Premiership if that attitude had been in evidence throughout the season and to express the hope that they would fight as resolutely against Newcastle twelve days later. They did compete wholeheartedly at Elland Road, going down 1–0 to Newcastle as they had done to us in Manchester, but I am inclined to think I helped to stiffen their resolve by focusing so much attention on them. My remarks on 17 April were never meant to have anything to do with Kevin Keegan; they were aimed entirely at Howard Wilkinson's players. But Kevin took them personally and exploded in front of the cameras after his team's victory over Leeds. One would have thought he would have felt more secure, since so many of the emotional cards were stacked in his favour, with just about everybody outside Old Trafford rooting for him. I have a feeling that our 5–0 hammering of Nottingham Forest on the day before the Leeds–Newcastle game had pushed Kevin to the limit. It was an exercise in devastation at a crucial stage of the season and perhaps it made him realise that the championship was within our grasp.

On 29 April, I had been out for lunch with Roy Evans, the Liverpool manager, and Bob Cass and Joe Melling of the *Mail on Sunday* in connection with an article the newspaper was going to publish about United's imminent meeting with Roy's team in the FA Cup final. As often happens when Cass and Melling are out to play, lunch stretched into the evening and when I arrived home to face Cathy's wrath the game at Elland Road was just finishing, so I sat in my favourite seat to watch the closing minutes, hoping that Leeds would snatch an equaliser. After the final whistle, I started to attempt an explanation of why I was so late and was stopped dead in my tracks by Kevin's outburst. God, I felt for him. Looking at replays later, I was better able to digest what he said and at first it made me feel a bit guilty. Then I thought to myself that I had done nothing wrong. I had said something that related to the honesty of the game, which I had a right to do. And I stress again that my words were not directed at Newcastle or Kevin but at the Leeds players. I had always got on well with Kevin and had given him some advice in his early days at Newcastle. Although I was a little disappointed when he attacked me, I just put it down to pressure. There was plenty of that still around as the league season entered its last day. We required at least a draw at Middlesbrough to be certain of our third championship in four years. After some early frights from our opponents we won comfortably by 3–0. It had been a personal triumph for Eric Cantona to come back from an eight-month suspension and captain a title-winning team. Now he could make the month of May even more magical by lifting the FA Cup at Wembley the following weekend – or was a second double a dream too far?

Our early progress in the knockout competition had not been at all leisurely. We needed a replay to edge past Sunderland in the third round and, if the fourth-round dismissal of Reading was comfortable, the next assignment against Manchester City was made tense when they went ahead and we had to be grateful for the dubious penalty that drew us level. Having stepped up the tempo of our game in the second half, we won deservedly in the end with a Lee Sharpe goal. Our sixth-round opponents,

Southampton, were seen off 2–0 at Old Trafford and – in spite of being deprived by injury of our two stalwart centre-backs, Bruce and Pallister – we overcame the shock of falling behind in the first half of our semi-final with Chelsea to a Ruud Gullit goal. Andy Cole and David Beckham scored to put us through to the final, but the picture of Eric Cantona chasing back to clear a shot off our goalline with his head will linger long in the memory.

Cup finals at Wembley are glorious occasions but only if you win. Losing is a brutal experience, as we had found when we went down 1–0 to Everton the previous year. Set to face the more powerful of Merseyside's representatives in 1996, we were not willing to contemplate defeat. Having Liverpool coming out of the other corner brought an additional sharpness to our preparation. I confess that I was slightly worried by their system of playing three centre-backs, with wing-backs pushing forward and Stan Collymore floating from up front to deeper positions and Steve McManaman releasing himself from midfield. I was considering matching their system to ensure that they didn't have an advantage in possession on such a tiring pitch, and on the Thursday before the match I had a meeting with Schmeichel, our back four, Eric Cantona and Roy Keane. I am not in the habit of discussing my thoughts with groups of players in that way but I wanted to gauge their reaction to the idea of changing our formation. Just as I feared, they were not happy. Peter felt that although Liverpool had enjoyed a lot of the ball in our recent meetings they had not troubled him overmuch. I didn't see it quite like that. They had drawn 2–2 at Old Trafford and beaten us 2–0 at Anfield but in fairness the loss of those goals had little to do with the systems the teams favoured. Robbie Fowler had scored all four of them and a predator as deadly as he is will give the opposition problems regardless of their formation. I was satisfied that their wing-backs would not cause us major trouble but was concerned that our midfield should not become spread out so that Liverpool could find Collymore, Fowler and McManaman easily with the ball. Eric suggested that Roy Keane should sit in front of the back four, with a three-man midfield ahead of him, which would alleviate the worry of Collymore dropping off our centre-backs. That was a good idea and we set about practising this way of playing. There was no doubt who was the man of the match at Wembley. Roy Keane was incredible but he and all the rest of our players would acknowledge that they were given a boost before a ball was kicked when our opponents turned up looking like a squad of bakers in cream-coloured suits. The sight gave our lads a great lift. I noticed the embarrassment on Roy Evans's face and it was significant that he and his staff wore dark suits.

That final was not, by any stretch of the imagination, a good game. At half-time I kept on about the need to up the tempo of our play. We couldn't allow it to be pedestrian which would suit their two central midfield players, Jamie Redknapp and John Barnes, but there was not a lot of difference after the interval. The match was heading for the trash bin until fortune took a hand. I don't believe that what occurred was unfair to Liverpool, who were no better or worse than we were, but it was poetic justice for Eric Cantona. David Beckham is probably the best striker of a dead ball I have ever come across but even he seemed to be smitten by the poor standards of this game and was hitting all his corners into the hands of the big Liverpool goalkeeper, David James. As Beckham shaped to take another corner at the end of the ninety minutes, I said to Brian Kidd at my side, 'If he hits this into James's hands again he is coming off – he won't be around for extra time.' Unbelievably, over went the ball into goalkeeper territory once more but as James went for it so did David May. His aggressive presence prevented James from taking the ball cleanly and he could only knock it out to the edge of the box, where Cantona was lurking. Then we saw a dramatic demonstration of the value of all Eric's devotion to practice. The ball came to him at quite an awkward height and he needed good foot movement and perfect body position to execute a scoring shot. He produced the immaculate volleying technique I had seen from him countless times on the training ground. What a way to win a final! There was no way back for Liverpool and soon we were celebrating the double again. Roy and his staff were understandably sick but handled their disappointment with exceptional grace.

Our party in the evening was one of the best occasions of its kind I have known, a much happier experience for me than the previous night, when I had a furious row on the phone with Maurice Watkins over the club's offer of a new contract. I was absolutely disgusted. It was annoying that they had insisted on leaving the business until the end of the season in the first place and now their words, 'We'll look after you,' seemed utterly hollow. The following week my accountant, Alan Baines, met the Remuneration Committee while I stayed at home awaiting details of the terms suggested. The arguing over the figures I had requested went on all day. To be honest, it was pathetic. There is no other word to describe it and in a way what was happening was my own fault. The directors were armed with the knowledge that I didn't want to leave. I had put so much into the rebuilding of Manchester United and it was agony to think of walking away from that. But this time around it got to the point where I was not prepared to be ridiculed and felt that on a matter of principle I might have to resign. I was not going to accept a repeat of the previous nonsense over the contract. The meeting lasted about six hours before a compromise was reached. I was not given what I believed I was worth but, nonetheless, I had made huge strides in relation to my existing agreement.

Emerging from the most challenging season in my twenty-two years in management, I was especially satisfied with the vindication of the hard decisions I had taken a year before. In football very few managers achieve a position of comprehensive control over their teams and those who do must strive to retain it. Paul Ince had threatened my control. I never felt any smugness but I hoped that people inside Old Trafford and beyond would now accept my judgement. Nobody devotes more time than I do to analysing how we can remain successful. Our main aspiration now was to improve in Europe and our exciting young team had the potential to do that. A truly memorable season was ultimately blemished by only one sadness and that was the departure of the old warhorse, Steve Bruce, to Birmingham. Steve had exercised an arrangement he had with the chairman that allowed him to go on a free transfer. I was on holiday in France when I received the news. Real sorrow overtook me at the thought of being parted from such an admirable man and one who had been such a wonderful servant to Manchester United.

— 23 —
DEPARTURE OF THE TALISMAN

THERE were two successive days in the spring of 1997 that hit me like a punch in the stomach and a follow-up hook to the head. On the evening of 23 April we were bundled out of the European Cup at the semi-final stage by Borussia Dortmund, and next morning Eric Cantona told me he had decided to quit football. Even the convincing signs that we were about to win our fourth Premiership title in five years provided inadequate consolation for such a double dose of misery. As soon as Eric came to see me on that Thursday, I knew intuitively the message he was going to deliver. But it was not one I was ready to accept without a struggle.

For some time I had been worried by changes I discerned in Cantona. He was subdued and did not seem to be enjoying his football. Although never extrovert around the other players, he had always been a vibrant presence, quietly conveying authority and an intense commitment. Now somehow the spark had gone. It was almost as if part of him was already somewhere else. All of this was particularly noticeable after he returned from playing in a charity match in Barcelona early in the year. The game did not interfere with our fixtures, so I had agreed that he could travel to play in it along with Jordi Cruyff (the Dutchman and Karl Poborsky, of the Czech Republic, had been our main summer signings in 1996, after impressing us during the European Championship held in England). Cantona and Cruyff came back from Spain as inseparable friends and I am inclined to think now that

Eric's first thoughts of living in Barcelona, where he later settled, occurred to him on that trip. My concern about his mood, and about form that was moderate by his standards, deepened as I observed subtle differences in his body shape. He was a big man with the kind of physique that demanded constant and rigorous training, and now there were hints that, at the age of thirty, the thickening process had begun. The worries were serious enough to persuade me to call Eric in for a chat, just to find out if there was anything troubling him. In the past our meetings had invariably been positive and fruitful, whether we talked about European football in general, on which his knowledge was ency-clopaedic, or discussed how his own game was going. This time there was not the same liveliness in his responses. Yet he voiced no specific problems and, after I had stressed how vital the next few weeks would be for United, especially in the European Cup, I had hopes that the air had been cleared and that there might be a recharging of the great Frenchman's energies.

The way our season was poised should certainly have appealed to the romantic in him, and to his justified belief that he had a talent which belonged on the big stage. Our fortunes had fluctu-ated wildly at times but by the beginning of April we were con-fronting dramatic opportunities. In our Champions League group in the previous autumn, we had surrendered Manchester United's proud, forty-year-old record of never having been beaten in a European tie at Old Trafford. Fenerbahce of Turkey beat us 1–0 at the end of October to put a blot on my career that I had always dreaded, and Juventus shovelled salt into the wound by repeating the scoreline on our ground in mid-November. To be included among the last eight survivors in the tournament, we required a win over Rapid Vienna in Austria and on a bitterly cold night everybody rose to the challenge, none more remarkably than Peter Schmeichel, who produced a lunging, one-handed save in the first half that was comparable to Gordon Banks's miraculous reaction to a Pele header in the 1970 World Cup. Goals by Giggs and Cantona gave us the necessary victory but my other sharp memory of the occasion is less pleasant. It is of

Martin Edwards, Chairman of
Manchester United.

Time for concern during a hard-fought
game, chasing the 1999 title.

Ryan Giggs scores one of the truly great individual goals to beat Arsenal in the
FA Cup semi-final of 1999.

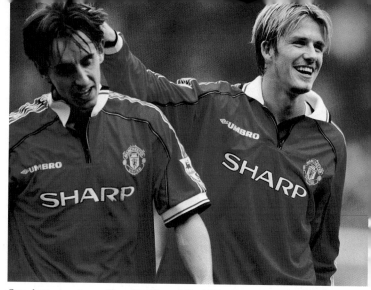

One down, two to go: Gary Neville and David Beckham after we reclaim the title *en route* to the treble.

Andy Cole shows subtlety to finish off Spurs and seal Manchester United's fifth championship under my management.

Teddy Sheringham scores our first against Newcastle at Wembley, just as he would do against Bayern.

Paul Scholes hits the clinching goal at Wembley but he had to sit out our European triumph because of suspension.

Now for Bayern . . . the FA Cup final defeat of Newcastle completes our third domestic double in six years.

With my grandson Jake, collar upturned à la Cantona or Yorke, before the 1999 FA Cup final at Wembley.

Two wings and a prayer as we board Concorde at Heathrow for the flight to the European Cup final in Barcelona.

I'm about to send on Teddy Sheringham against Bayern, scarcely imagining he would have quite such an impact.

Teddy Sheringham (*right*) wheels away after equalising against Bayern and still has another trick up his sleeve.

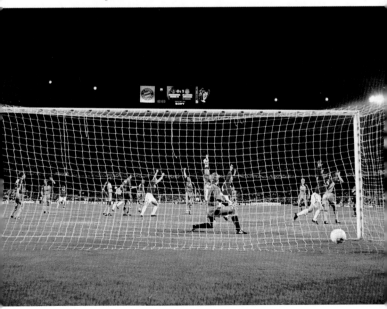

Seconds from glory: Ole Gunnar Solskjaer (*left*) waits as Teddy Sheringham heads on David Beckham's corner.

Ole Gunnar thrusts out his right leg to divert the ball past Oliver Khan and thirty-one years of hurt are over for United.

The magnitude of what he has done hits Ole Gunnar, who for a moment could no more believe it than could Bayern's defenders.

Peter Schmeichel, whose charge into Bayern's area helped to turn the final on its head, celebrates appropriately.

Waving not frowning: the incredulous smile that says United are European champions after that incredible finale.

How could we disappoint support like that? Sharing the moment with our marvellous fans in Barcelona.

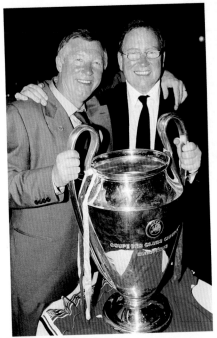

A cuddle for Ole Gunnar, our man of destiny, as the champagne flows in the dressing-room after beating Bayern.

Oh, brother! From Neptune Street to the Nou Camp Stadium, Martin has been there to support me.

Treble decker: we show our three trophies to the hundreds of thousands who welcomed us home from Barcelona.

Roy Keane's knee being ripped open to the bone by an opponent's studs. I am quite squeamish about such things and could hardly look when our doctor set about patching up the gaping wound in the dressing-room. Astonishingly, Roy was out of action for only a few weeks.

The three months between qualification at the group stage and the playing of the quarter-finals of the European Cup is a time to relish. There is the luxury of prolonged anticipation in the continental competition, and the uplifting effect of that often has a healthy impact on league form. We needed that kind of boost after having our capacity to defend the championship called into question in October 1996 when, within a week, we were slaughtered 5–0 at Newcastle and 6–3 at Southampton. We followed those disasters by losing 2–1 at home to Chelsea and the pundits were queueing up to act as gravediggers. But I did not believe for a second that the double-winners of the previous season had suddenly turned into punchbags. Others might feel that our commitment to Beckham, Butt, Scholes, Giggs and the Neville brothers represented an excessive faith in youth, but I knew that those young players had character as well as talent. They soon proved as much. Having lost three in a row, with an aggregate score against them of 13–4, they made a win over Arsenal the start of a sixteen-match unbeaten run that transformed the title race.

By late 1996 I had completed ten years at Old Trafford and the milestone invited some reflection on how my job had changed in that decade. From Cathy's standpoint, the most annoying development was the steady reduction of the time I was able to spend at home as I undertook more and more of the social engagements I regarded as part of my duties as United manager. Being an ambassador can be exhausting but it is unavoidable. Taking a broader view of my experiences since 1986, I identified the seeds of pain and frustration for future managers in ever-increasing player-power, the difficulties created by agents and the insatiable demands of the media. If there is one job I would hate above all others it is that of a football journalist, particularly that of a reporter on the tabloids, where the pressure to get a story at all costs seems to be relentless. What a life! The anniversary did make me consider when I should call it a day in my own job, but the internal debate did not last long. The very idea of waking up one morning and knowing I wouldn't be going to the training ground filled me with fear. The notion of a retirement age is anathema to me. There should be a law against it. The calendar can't decide how alert or vigorous a person is. I felt good at fifty-five and I was fed up being pestered about when I was going to retire.

To celebrate my ten years, I took Cathy to London for a couple of days during a quiet period at the club caused by an England international. We desperately wanted to see 'Art', a play in the West End in which Albert Finney, Tom Courtney and Ken Stott had been earning rave reviews. Finney was born in Salford, the heart of Manchester United territory, and Stott is Scottish, so I suppose I had more than simple cultural reasons for being keen to see the show. We had nightmare problems finding tickets but eventually a Greek friend of mine, Sotirios Hassiakos, succeeded in laying hands on a pair by paying well over the odds. When Cathy and I turned up at the theatre, we were surprised to be met by the manager and told that Albert Finney's girlfriend, Penny, would like us to join her for a drink. How could she possibly know we were coming? Penny's explanation was amusing. That morning Albert had answered the doorbell at his apartment and found himself facing his newsagent, a big United fan. The man was extremely agitated because he had picked up word that Alex Ferguson had been trying unsuccessfully to locate tickets for the play. 'You must get them for him,' he told the actor. Albert was as helpless as I have often been when landed with a similar request but the newsagent's intervention brought Cathy and me the bonus of being asked round to the star's dressing-room at the end of the evening. Finney had always been one of my favourite actors and, although I had never met him until then, I had heard enough about him from his close friend Harold Riley, the Salford artist, to know that being in his company was likely to be a pleasure. It was indeed. Cathy and I both enjoyed 'Art' but, to be honest, that little gathering in the dressing-room was the highlight of our stay in London. Albert opened a bottle of Dom Perignon to toast my ten years with United. We were joined by Tom Courtney and Ken Stott and a surprise guest was Joan Plowright, who looked fantastic. What impressed me about all of them was how easily they dispelled the popular impression that people in their profession are forever calling one another love and darling and generally indulging in over-the-top behaviour. They were just down to earth.

That was where I had to be as Manchester United's season accelerated towards its decisive phase. The draw for the quarter-finals of the European Cup spared us another collision with Juventus but threw us against the only other team who had remained undefeated in the group matches – Porto. The Portuguese champions had a strong contingent of Brazilian players in their squad and there was apprehension in the press and among our fans about our ability to cope with them in the first leg at Old Trafford on 5 March. Tactics were bound to be important. I was sure that Ryan Giggs could have a vital influence on the game if I did not use him in his normal position wide on the left but gave him a slightly different role. I believed, too, that I could increase the anxiety Porto were obviously feeling about Giggs and Cantona if I played three men up, with Eric dropping into a deeper position to feed them. My instructions were simple: get the ball into Cantona and let Giggs search the spaces left by our two strikers, Cole and Solskjaer. Our performance on the night was stunning, even allowing for the contribution made by the opposition goalkeeper to a 4–0 annihilation. The goals poured in by May, Cantona, Giggs and Cole meant that a semi-final place was assured if we dealt with the second leg sensibly, which we duly did, playing with impressive composure in Portugal to secure a goalless draw.

That swaggering display at Old Trafford was a peak of excellence and everyone on our staff was thrilled to be part of something so remarkable, but there was an immediate cost. The players, having been drained physically and mentally by their achievement, let their celebrations go too far and the effects were plain on the following Saturday when our long run without defeat in the Premiership came to an end. They sat in the dressing-room with their heads lowered after losing 2–1 at Sunderland. Nobody had to tell them that they had let themselves down. There was understandable criticism of my efforts to freshen up the team by taking risks with selection. I didn't mind that. It is always better for me to take the flak, rather than the players.

Our championship challenge was soon back on track and we could afford to concentrate on our overriding ambition – to capture the European Cup for the first time since the Manchester United of Best, Charlton and Law had done so in 1968. Even the FA Cup had shrunk in significance for us and our removal from it by Wimbledon, after a fourth-round replay, had been a minor blow. What happened against Borussia Dortmund in our two-legged semi-final of Europe's greatest club competition was an earthquake of disappointment. Being just one step away from a final at the Olympic Stadium in Munich, a name that reverberates poignantly in the history of United, gave me a tingle of anticipation I had never known before. Failing to complete that last step was agony. In those two games we suffered a bombardment of ill-luck that was typified by losing Peter Schmeichel and David May at our last training session on the eve of the match in Dortmund. Although both Raimond Van der Gouw in goal and Ronny Johnsen in central defence performed admirably, the late changes to the team spread an uneasiness through our ranks in the first half that prevented us from exploiting our clear superiority. However, any explanation of our failure must begin and end with a simple reality. In the supreme contests of football, you must take a respectable percentage of your chances. In that semi-final, we missed too many. We were undeniably the better team in both games but were twice 1–0 losers.

Eric Cantona was so low-key and marginal in Dortmund that I was left searching my mind for the reason. I questioned myself about whether there had been any alteration in my method of dealing with him. It had always been my practice to speak with him on a regular basis, particularly in his early days with the club and in the dark period of his eight-month suspension. He had responded well to personal contact and as we came away from Germany I was wondering if lately I had been talking to him less than I should. There was no gulf between us but, as he had emerged as a highly influential figure in the course of our recent triumphs, I had thought it best to let him handle his growing responsibility in the team as he saw fit. After Dortmund, I was puzzled. Why had he been so subdued? Of course, there were critics who argued that he just did not come through and deliver big performances on the major European nights. I could not go along with that entirely. There were such occasions when Eric played marvellously for us. But I do admit that there was something, perhaps some kind of mental block, that stopped him from being the best player in the world. I am sure he had the ability to achieve that status but there was an element in his nature that seemed to prevent him from realising the full potential of his incredible gifts.

In the second leg of the semi-final at Old Trafford, Borussia Dortmund could not believe their good fortune as we scorned scoring opportunities by the barrowload. No fewer than fifteen times we had only their goalkeeper to beat, and still we could not put the ball in the net. Some sinister magic appeared to be at work. But at a more practical level, I was again disappointed by the form of Cantona. It was characteristic of his evening when he reacted to the invitation of an open goal with a sluggishness that would have been unthinkable just a few months earlier. Conspiracy theorists were telling us that the loss of his edge was related to feelings of mutual dislike between Andy Cole and him. I can shed no light on that allegation but it is true that they were the main culprits in the squandering spree in front of goal. It is possible that they were just not a good partnership, full stop. Perhaps Andy, who had not yet fully settled in at United, did have a touch of nervousness about playing with the Frenchman. Maybe the chemistry between them was wrong. Both are quiet thinkers who respond to being trusted. At first, I found Andy hard to get to know but it was always clear that he was a man of integrity. His game thrives when he has confidence and to have that he must be sure that people like myself have faith in him. I don't believe for a moment that either he or Eric Cantona would have sacrificed the team's interests because of personal animosity. When Eric came to see me on the day after our European hopes were crushed for another year, I asked him why he felt he should give up football at the age of thirty. His answer was vague, amounting to little more than the suggestion that he had done as much as he could in the game and wished to take his life in another direction. I said he should think seriously about the consequences of what he was doing and advised him to talk to his father, to whom he was very close. There was still a chance, perhaps, that his father could talk him out of quitting.

Arsenal, Liverpool and Newcastle (under their new manager, Kenny Dalglish) were all pressing us in the final weeks of the Premiership season. But we had created a little cushion for ourselves and we were never really under strain on the run-in. We finished with 75 points, while our three main rivals were bracketed together on 68. Taking a fourth title in five years was pleasing and so was the knowledge that the 1997 team were relatively young and had plenty of improvement in them. I was confident that the rising graph of their development would, before long, embrace the winning of the European Cup. There was much less optimism in my thinking about Eric Cantona. As the season came to a close, he continued to have the air of a man for whom football had lost its appeal. Seeing the dullness in his eyes, and the changing outline of his physique, I had to acknowledge that perhaps he was right to terminate his career before blatant decline became an insult to the fierce pride that burned in him. But I clung to the hope that his problems had some underlying cause and that once it was tackled he might rediscover the standards that had made him a legend in a foreign country. I feared the worst, however, when my secretary, Lynn, phoned me on the morning after our last league match to say that Eric wanted to meet me two days later at Mottram Hall. Once we were sitting opposite each other in a private office at the hotel, there was a hesitancy on both sides about how to start the conversation. But I was struck instantly by the look of resignation on Eric's face. He was totally straightforward with me. He did want to finish, he had been considering it for some time and now the decision was irrevocable. When I asked him again why he felt that way, he was not as vague as he had been previously and specified two recent trends at Old Trafford that had left him disillusioned. He said he felt he had become a pawn of Manchester United's merchandising department and that he was not going to accept such treatment any longer. His second complaint was that United were not ambitious enough in the purchase of players. I had a lot of sympathy with him on both counts.

As I reconciled myself to losing Cantona – as talented, exciting and productive a footballer as I have ever managed – I pondered what he had said about the boardroom attitudes that limit my prospects of recruiting the biggest names in football. I have been severely handicapped by the club's insistence on a wage ceiling at Old Trafford. I understand that there has to be a rational approach to salary arrangements and that the club must consider the pay structure as a whole. But talent is not democratic and I believe strongly that if there are two or three exceptional players who can lift the team to higher levels than can be reached without them, those individuals should be on a special scale of remuneration. I am sure the team-mates who were paid less would accept the discrepancy if the presence of those outstanding footballers was crucial to making Manchester United the number one club in the game. Everybody benefits from being at the top. In recent years, I have been keen to sign Ronaldo, Gabriel Batistuta and Marcel Desailly but my hands were tied because Manchester United's policy on salaries gave me no chance of providing the financial packages required to secure those great players' contracts. I think the restrictions applied to wages prevented us from being the power in European football that we could have been in the Nineties. Becoming a public limited company has, naturally, affected all areas of the club's life and wherever money is involved certain procedures have to be followed and strict limitations are in force. The world of the PLC can be very frustrating for me. I understand that the interests of shareholders have to be carefully considered, especially those of the institutions that have invested heavily in the club. But what about the 55,000 supporters who turn out at every home match? They invest emotion and loyalty and some of them spend all their spare cash following us all over the globe. They expect no return other than the pleasure of seeing a successful team. Without a successful team the stadium may not be filled automatically and the revenues from merchandising and the restaurants may take a dive. In any case, I think the financial investors have had plenty from the gravy train. There is only one way forward for Manchester United and that is to be firmly established as the leading club in Europe. That, however, costs money and the club will come to realise that we cannot soar to where we should be if we are trapped under the salary ceiling.

In the meantime, I have to operate within the parameters set out by the PLC and it can be a wearying struggle. I would have thought I might have been given more leeway on the basis of my excellent buying-and-selling record since coming to Old Trafford. When, before the 1996–97 season, I sold Lee Sharpe to Leeds for £4.5 million, the deal meant that (with Hughes, Ince and Kanchelskis already gone) transfer fees totalling £19 million had come into the club in under two years. I had been nearly ten years in the job and my overall deficit in transfer business over the period stood at about £4 million, which was extraordinary considering how much had been spent by other clubs who had not achieved a fraction of our success. Nothing encouraged me more than our capacity to survive the departure of important players without any reduction of our effectiveness on the field. Over three seasons we had lost Parker, Bruce, Ince, Robson, Hughes, Kanchelskis and Sharpe and had remained the best team in the country. But would we be able to look back and say the same about Eric Cantona? Now we were losing not just a player but a talisman.

— 24 —
ARSENAL AT THE GALLOP

WHEN I woo a player on behalf of Manchester United, I do it wholeheartedly, but rejection doesn't leave me broken-hearted. I know that there may be a more fruitful relationship around the corner. There was a brief sense of having been jilted when Paul Gascoigne abruptly switched his affections from us to Tottenham Hotspur in the summer of 1988 but soon afterwards Paul Ince came along to be a significant element of one of the best teams in our club's history (and, at the risk of seeming mercenary, we made a £5.5 million profit when we sold him to Inter Milan). A year after the Gascoigne rebuff, we were given the run-around by Glenn Hysen, the Swedish defender we pursued all the way to Italy. While Hysen proved less than a roaring success with Liverpool, failing to get him strengthened our determination to sign Gary Pallister from Middlesbrough – and what a magnificent servant Pally turned out to be. Everybody at United was upset and slightly baffled when Alan Shearer chose Blackburn Rovers instead of us but that, too, was a good break in disguise. Had we secured Shearer, it is highly improbable that we would have gone for Eric Cantona. Could Shearer have illuminated Old Trafford as the great Frenchman did? I think not. All of those experiences, and many others, have convinced me that rejection is an overrated hardship in football. So when Patrick Kluivert, the gifted young Dutch centre-forward, was so unimpressed by our approaches in 1998 that he wouldn't even do us the courtesy of talking to us, I had no trouble believing that he was likely to be a bigger loser than we were. As I write, there is a growing mountain of persuasive evidence that the Dutchman's indifference indirectly did us a huge favour. It ensured that I would allow no obstacle to stand in the way of my long-standing ambition to sign Dwight Yorke from Aston Villa. I would have preferred to have both Kluivert and Yorke but, once one of them was ruled out, I simply refused to contemplate the possibility that we would not capture the other. We achieved only half of our objective, but it was the better half. In a single season with us, Dwight has already emerged as one of the most skilful and potent front players in Europe.

That there were obstacles put between me and the securing of Yorke was predictable. Nobody could expect John Gregory, the Villa manager, to be willing to let such a player go. What took me aback was that some of the difficulties I had to overcome were created in my own camp. While I was combining a family holiday in the south of France with scouting at the 1998 World Cup and a little broadcasting and journalistic work on the tournament, I made a call back to my chairman in England to inquire about progress in the rather complicated and often frustrating negotiations over Yorke. My straightforward question on the subject produced a degree of hesitancy at the other end of the line. When Martin Edwards eventually answered, I was shocked by his words.

'Well, we are not sure he is the right man,' he said.

'What do you mean, *we* don't think he is the right man?' I demanded. 'Who are *we*?'

'One or two of the directors and Brian Kidd,' was the reply.

'Brian Kidd?' I snapped. 'Who's the bloody manager?' Brian, Martin said, did not think Yorke was as good at beating men as I thought he was. 'Brian Kidd has never said that to me, ever, so why is he telling you and not me?' I wanted to know. The chairman said that Brian had not actually told him but had made the point to someone else at the club. When I asked who that someone was, Martin said he could not tell me and added that my assistant had 'been doing a bit of moaning about last season'. Pressed for the specifics of the moan, Martin said that Brian apparently felt the team had not trained hard enough. I suggested that, since Brian had a major share of responsibility for the team's training, that was a peculiar complaint. Then Martin threw in a bombshell.

'I think you have a problem with Brian and you should speak to him. He came to see me this morning, asking for permission to talk to Everton.' It was strange to be sitting in a rented villa on a clifftop in Cap Ferrat, looking out on the Mediterranean, and hearing of such dramatic and unsettling developments in Manchester.

'There is no way Brian will go to Everton,' I told the chairman. 'I am surprised at this. He has never said to me that he wanted to try management but, leaving that aside for the moment, I can't understand this stuff about Dwight Yorke and the training.' Martin's view was that Brian had a natural inclination to complain.

'I think you should have a chat with him unless you want to let him go,' he said. I stressed that my main concern was to reassure myself that my assistant was totally committed to me and happy in his job. Then I returned to another part of the conversation that was bothering me. In the context of Brian's reservations about Yorke, I wondered if he had expressed enthusiasm for any other forward we might go after.

'Well, he fancies John Hartson of West Ham,' Martin told me.

'Hartson – are you serious?' I shouted. 'Chairman, are you serious? Do you think of John Hartson as a Manchester United player?' Martin admitted that the mention of the name had surprised him.

I had to consider my next step carefully and I tried to analyse Brian's behaviour and to work out what was going on in his mind. Was he complaining to other people at Old Trafford and, if so, who were they and what should I do about it? Before I passed any judgement, it was imperative to hear Brian's side of the story. When I reached him by phone and put to him what Martin Edwards had said, he chuntered on for ages in a manner that had become familiar to me, so I repeated my question.

'Who have you been talking to?'

He answered, 'No one.' I asked him if it was true that he did not favour buying Dwight Yorke.

'I don't think he is the dribbler that you think he is,' he said. I questioned whether he could name one player in Britain who was better at it. Why, in any case, had he not brought the matter up earlier? We agreed that, whether or not we had Yorke, Patrick Kluivert would have provided the physical presence that our attack had recently been lacking. Brian was admirably open about his reasons for seeking permission to speak to Everton. 'Why should I work for Manchester United and get a third of what Everton are prepared to pay me?' was his understandable attitude.

'If it's about money, why don't you come to me? Do you want me to ask for more money for you?' He said he would appreciate my intervention on the pay issue.

My calls to the chairman and to Brian had kept me on the phone for more than an hour. At the end of the talk marathon I had several reactions, one of which was anger at myself for having allowed Brian too much say about the Manchester United training. The problem had arisen because of all the extra responsibilities that had accumulated around my job. My mornings were often crowded with so many meetings and phone calls that I had been separated from the habit of determining the details of what the players did every day. A few years before, any hint that my assistant was grumbling to others at the club would have brought a much stronger response from me. Age does mellow you and it makes you more understanding. I saw Brian Kidd as a complex person, often quite insecure, particularly about his health. He also worried about how good he was at coaching, and concerns over whether I still wanted him as my assistant and what would happen to him if I retired were common themes on his regular doubting days. Time and again I would have to encourage him and tell him not to worry about anything. I wasn't going to retire, I thought he was great at the training sessions and, of course, I wanted him as my assistant – of that there was no doubt. In the circumstances that had now developed, I was anxious to give Brian the benefit of the doubt. He had been at my side for seven years and our partnership had been productive and, to be honest, I didn't want to make changes in personnel again. That was further evidence of the ageing process, I suppose.

The next call to the chairman to give him the gist of my exchanges with Brian concluded with a request from him that I should fly to London a couple of days later to clear the air about Kidd and about our interest in Yorke. I knew Cathy would rage at the interference with our holiday and my own heart wasn't exactly singing at the prospect of heading to London for a day. I had been having a wonderful time on the Riviera, where Cathy and I delighted in the happiness of our grandchildren as they romped around the pool with their parents and uncles and aunts. But the happenings at the club were important and on the Friday of that week I duly flew to Heathrow, where I was picked up and driven to the Hong Kong & Shanghai Bank. There, Professor Sir Roland Smith, the chairman of Manchester United plc, had arranged a room in which he, Martin and I could meet. I was under the impression that the purpose of our gathering was to discuss Brian Kidd and Dwight Yorke but Martin Edwards began with a long speech about me. He praised my capacities as a manager but said that my success at Old Trafford had made me a celebrity and that I was not focusing on the job as much as I had done. My new-found interest in owning racehorses had obviously not gone down well. I could hardly believe what I was hearing but let Martin and Sir Roland make their points before asking, 'Do you want to call it a day?'

'No, no,' they both said quickly, adding further tributes to my management and insisting that they were only trying to give me advice. I had a question for them.

'Have you any idea how difficult it has been to manage this club for eleven and a half years? Don't you realise that the only way I can survive is to have a release away from football?' I reminded Martin that he had frequently pleaded with me to take one day a week off. He acknowledged that he had done so but said that he had meant I should take a rest, whereas I was always on the go. 'But maybe that's how I relax, by immersing myself in another interest like racing,' I said.

There was never going to be any agreement on the subject of my relaxation, so we moved on to talk about Yorke and I let them know in no uncertain terms that I believed there was nobody associated with Manchester United who was better equipped to assess footballers than I was. I trotted out a pretty impressive catalogue of the purchases made since my arrival, a collection of outstanding players who, along with our home-produced talent, had built United into the dominant force of English football in the Nineties. Anywhere they looked on the list they could find remarkable figures, such as Hughes, McClair, Bruce, Pallister, Irwin, Schmeichel, Sharpe, Ince, Kanchelskis, Keane and Cantona. They had to remember, too, that prior to the summer of 1998 (which had already seen the acquisition of the marvellous Dutch centre-back, Jaap Stam, at a record fee for a defender), the sums received by United for the sale of players over my years in charge had balanced my financial outlay. 'If you don't recognise that I am the best person to judge which players should be bought by the club, I may as well leave now,' I told Martin and Sir Roland. That seemed to settle the Yorke debate, but I could not feel happy about the situation in which I had been placed. Once again I reflected that, if all this had happened some years earlier, my pride and my temper wouldn't have allowed me to tolerate such a farce.

Brian Kidd's position was the next item on the agenda at our meeting and by now Brian was outside, waiting to be called in, and I thought it right to ask Martin Edwards directly if he thought my assistant was undermining me.

'I think Brian is basically insecure and likes to moan,' the club chairman said. 'But he will have to stop going round the offices at Old Trafford and dropping his little complaints.' Martin then sought my assessment.

'I am aware of his continual moans and complaints about other members of staff but I am disappointed that he didn't speak to me about Dwight Yorke,' I replied. Martin left it to me to decide whether Brian stayed or went.

'It is entirely up to you, but if you want to get rid of him, say so now and let's not go into new contracts.' I explained to him how I felt about the whole saga, saying that the last thing I wanted was to start looking for a new number two. The players liked Brian and our work together had yielded good results, so there was clearly no need for a change on that basis. It was my opinion that the way events involving him had escalated to the present level of seriousness might have given Brian enough of a jolt to settle him down. We discussed what to offer him and I made a suggestion, which was accepted. When Brian came in, I felt obliged to put it to him in front of Sir Roland and Martin that neither Manchester United nor I could afford to have the slightest trace of disloyalty in the assistant manager. Brian's answer was vehement.

'I am surprised you are even asking me about that,' he said. 'I have always been loyal to you.' There could be only one reaction to such a declaration.

'As long as you mean that, let's get on with the business,' I said.

Soon afterwards, I left the three of them to iron out the details of his revised contract and made my way back to France. On the journey, it occurred to me that Brian found much less difficulty than I did in gaining improved terms of employment. He had been given a new four-year deal in March and just three months later another agreement was being prepared. In the previous January, Sir Roland had promised that the club would look after me at the end of the 1997–98 season. But we had been top of the Premiership then, and flying. Arsenal had stormed past us on the run-in and gone on to take the double of championship and FA Cup and now I was being told that the redrawing of my contract was still under consideration. I was sure that the delay, like the criticism I had received at the beginning of the London meeting, had quite a lot to do with the way the second half of our season had gone wrong. That was unfair. Splendid as Arsenal's late surge had been, there was no doubt that a glut of injuries had contributed substantially to our loss of momentum. After Martin's comments on my loss of focus, I had said to him, 'If we had won the championship, we would not be talking like this and if you are honest you will admit that the injuries were the main reason for losing the League.' It was the truth as I saw it.

We might have recognised a portent of how that 1997–98 season was to be shaped for us when our new captain, Roy Keane, suffered a terrible injury to his right knee in the ninth match of our league programme at Elland Road. In fact, we rode the long-term loss of our most influential player amazingly well and were commanding leaders of the Premiership until ravaged by further physical problems late in the campaign. But no team could avoid being diminished by the absence of such a driving force and the effects became particularly apparent at vital stages of a European Cup challenge that took us as far as the quarter-finals. It was immediately obvious that the damage to Roy's cruciate ligament was so serious that he would be out of action for the rest of the season and would require a prolonged and carefully monitored period of recuperation. At such times the main concern is for the player and his future. To recover fully, Roy would have to show a great deal of patience and that was not something the rest of us at the club naturally associated with our Irish warrior. Remarkably, however, he proved to be the perfect patient, not only adhering conscientiously to the regime laid down for him but providing an inspiring example for one of the younger members of the playing staff, Terry Cooke, who was the victim of the same type of injury. They were good company for each other on the hard road back to fitness.

Keane had been hurt in a 1–0 defeat by Leeds that ended the unbeaten run with which we launched our defence of the title. We started with a 2–0 victory at White Hart Lane, where our new signing from Tottenham, Teddy Sheringham, was accorded the kind of welcome to be expected on his former stamping ground. Judas was probably the nicest name he was called and his tormentors enjoyed themselves after he missed a penalty in the second half. They weren't so gleeful when we hit Spurs with two late goals. Sheringham, although over thirty, was a sensible addition to our strength. He was a good finisher, especially in the air, and had the tactical perception and passing skills to release other attackers into scoring positions. His arrival would help us with the daunting task of filling the gap left by Eric Cantona.

Roy Keane figured in only one of our European matches, the smooth 3–0 win over Kosice in Slovakia. That success set us up for an Old Trafford confrontation with our formidable Italian rivals of the previous season, Juventus, who were clearly the principal threat in a Champions League group that also included Feyenoord of Holland. It is a ritual for me to drum into my players the necessity of maintaining absolute concentration against the best of continental opposition. On 1 October 1997 they heeded my warning for all of forty seconds. To lose a goal so early, albeit to a masterly piece of play by Alessandro Del Piero, was a sickening blow and our plight worsened when Nicky Butt was overcome by a bout of migraine and had to leave the field. When Nicky first had such attacks they were so alarming that we feared he might be afflicted with something really grave and the diagnosis of migraine was almost a relief. But it is a condition that temporarily incapacitates the sufferer (blinding headaches and distorted vision are common symptoms) and there was no way he could carry on playing in that match. Fortunately, the players coped marvellously with the enforced rejigging of the team and, lifted by the atmosphere of another magical European night, they equalised through Teddy Sheringham and soon had their opponents struggling. Juventus's main inspiration, Zinedine Zidane, was being well handled by Ronny Johnsen and in the second half our performance soared, with goals from Paul Scholes and Ryan Giggs. Near the end, Zidane scored with a memorable free kick but the 3–2 victory was proof that we could flourish in the most elevated company.

Similar form gave us home and away wins over Feyenoord. Andy Cole scored a hat trick in Rotterdam, where the Dutch tackling throughout the night was a combination of desperation and brutality. There was always the likelihood that somebody would be badly hurt and there was dismay far beyond our club when it turned out to be Denis Irwin, who was viciously cut down by the flying studs of Paul Bosvelt. Nowhere in football is there a more popular player than the unassuming Irishman, who is the ultimate professional, one of those quiet, under-praised heroes who constitute the bedrock of all great teams. What Bosvelt did to him was a crime. Yet the experienced Hungarian referee, Sandor Puhl, did not even punish the Dutch midfielder with a yellow card. Not surprisingly, UEFA subsequently banned Puhl from the remainder of the competition. By the time our last group fixture was played in Turin, we had qualified for the quarter-finals and, with our domestic obligations in mind, I rested a couple of players against Juventus. There was much talk about the wisdom of trying to kill off the Italian giants but, quite frankly, the thought of meeting them again later in the tournament did not worry me. At the Stadio Delle Alpi, we did all right for an hour but Juventus took control in the last quarter of the game, scored and slipped almost furtively into the quarter-finals.

Reconciling the demands of the Champions League and the Premiership is never easy and the style in which our lads did it in the latter part of 1997 made me proud. Our achievements in Europe were parallelled by some scintillating and high-scoring displays on the home front. We hit seven goals against Barnsley, six against Sheffield Wednesday, five down at Wimbledon (not many take them by the handful there) and four against Blackburn Rovers. Entering 1998, we were well ahead of the posse and on too much of a charge to be discouraged by having a visit to Stamford Bridge as our introduction to that year's FA Cup. We swamped Chelsea and went 5–0 in front before easing up and letting them do a cosmetic job on the scoreline with three goals. When we returned to west London in the League on the last day of February, it looked as if Chelsea were our main challengers for the title. Arsenal were finding form but still had a lot of ground to make up and when the rare phenomenon of a Phil Neville goal earned us three points at the Bridge we were in a dominating position. But that victory came at a cost, for Gary Pallister's troublesome back gave out on him and suddenly it was becoming clear that injuries might derail our trophy aspirations. February was a cruel month. Until then we had few serious fitness problems, other than the early removal of Keane, which we had survived impressively. But just seven days before Pallister injured his back, guaranteeing that we would be without our most experienced defender for several weeks, Ryan Giggs had swung his leg back to reach for a cross from David Beckham during our league game with Derby, and clutched anxiously at his hamstring. It proved to be torn and he, too, would be a casualty for weeks. These were the first of a devastating series of injuries that immediately prejudiced our chances in the European Cup quarter-final against Monaco and would eventually harm us severely in the Premiership. Between then and the end of the season, our physios were working overtime. We were frequently deprived of key players and some of those I sent out, notably Paul Scholes and Gary Neville, were only on the field because of their gameness and high pain threshold.

With our reduced resources, we had to be satisfied with a goalless draw in Monaco on 4 March but the iron-hard surface of a pitch laid over a car park took its toll and Denis Irwin missed our away fixture with Sheffield Wednesday on the Saturday, which we lost 2–0. Four days before the second leg against Monaco, Arsenal came to Old Trafford for a match that everybody recognised as crucial to the destination of the championship. They were unbeaten since mid-December and had more games left than we had, so if they beat us the winning of the title would be in their own hands for the first time. When they did, with an Overmars goal near the end, we could not complain. They were the better team over the hour and a half. As if that wasn't misery enough, Peter Schmeichel, having rushed up into the Arsenal penalty box in an attempt to produce a last-gasp equaliser, stayed around to make a clumsy challenge and pulled a hamstring. So on the Wednesday we found ourselves battling to stay alive in Europe without Schmeichel, Giggs and Pallister and with Scholes and Gary Neville carrying injuries that would normally have ruled them out. Any hope that my juggling with selection and tactics would paper over our weaknesses was severely dented after only six minutes when we sloppily surrendered possession on the edge of our box and presented Monaco's young, gangly centre-forward, David Trezeguet, with an opportunity to hammer a breathtaking shot into the roof of the net. Ole Gunnar Solskjaer brought us level early in the second half but the team's efforts to go on and win the tie always lacked verve and conviction, which was no shock if we remembered how draining the run-up to the match had been. Andy Cole and Teddy Sheringham had played six games in seventeen days and it showed in their performances. I felt sorry for them and, for my own part, was glad that a ten-day break caused by an England international would give my staff and me a chance to examine the state of our season.

Could we buy somebody to provide an injection of freshness and vigour? One player I thought about was the Argentine Ariel Ortega, who was on the books of Valencia in Spain but was reported to have fallen out with the coach. It was made known to me that Valencia were prepared to enter into a loan arrangement until the following December but the deal was complicated, requiring us to put down £1 million straightaway and a further £6 million if we wanted him at the end of 1998. That did not appeal to the Manchester United board and the negotiations collapsed at a point where I was becoming attracted to the idea of introducing new talent to put our league challenge back on track. I was disappointed but had to buckle down to the task of trying to overhaul Arsenal, who were now leading the Premiership, with the squad at my disposal. At least Schmeichel, Pallister and Giggs were restored to fitness and we managed to rack up some good wins: 3–0 over both Leeds and Crystal Palace, 3–1 at Blackburn and 2–0 over Wimbledon and Barnsley. But two home draws with Liverpool and Newcastle made Arsenal uncatchable. There could be nothing but praise for the champions and for their manager, Arsene Wenger. In the home stretch, they had put together a sequence of ten straight victories and only a truly special team could have done that in a league as tough as ours. They had notable quality in every department and Arsene Wenger deserves immense credit for integrating his English and foreign players into such a cohesive, powerful and highly motivated unit. His fellow Frenchmen Patrick Vieira and Emmanuel Petit did wonders for him in midfield and at the back he was served by men who performed as if the only significance of age is that it gives you experience. The defining spirit of the team was Tony Adams, a classic English defender – brave, reliable and capable not only of fulfilling his own responsibilities superbly but of organising and inspiring those around him.

After a season as wearing as 1997–98, I was more than ready for my Riviera holiday but, as I related earlier, events back in Manchester intruded rather forcefully on my relaxation with the family. My visits to World Cup matches were less irksome but they didn't thrill me much. As had been the case with the two previous tournaments in the United States and Italy, France '98 suffered from a dearth of players who could light up your dreams. Is there too much pressure in the modern game to permit the emergence of the kind of mesmerising individual talents we once saw in the World Cup finals? Was Diego Maradona in Mexico in 1986 the last of them? Ronaldo was hailed as a natural heir to that tradition but what happened to the young Brazilian in France should frighten the wits out of all coaches and doctors in football and make the commercial moguls realise that they cannot keep on taking pound after pound of flesh. My brief to all the members of my staff who were at the finals was to find one player who was as yet uncelebrated but had the potential to be a star. There was not one who fired our enthusiasm, who made us feel we must have him, and I was left fearing for the future of the great competition.

The articles on the World Cup that I contributed to *The Sunday Times* stirred a fair amount of controversy, especially when I criticised Glenn Hoddle, the England manager, for his heavy-handed treatment of David Beckham. I could find no justification for Hoddle's insistence that David had to appear at a press conference while he was still reeling from the shock of being dropped from the team for England's opening match with Tunisia. It would have been more sensible, I suggested, to give the lad private encouragement to react positively to the biggest disappointment of his international career. Being questioned by a roomful of reporters was not my idea of the best means of focusing his mind on battling to regain his place. Glenn took up the cudgels and declared that it was unprofessional of me to criticise a fellow manager. The accusation was rubbish. There was no criticism from me of his football decisions. I began my newspaper piece by saying that if he thought Darren Anderton could do a better job than David Beckham, that was the end of the argument as far as the selection of the team was concerned. Hoddle's was the only opinion that counted on such an issue. But obliging an emotionally devastated twenty-three-year-old to face a mass interview, during which he was expected to go over the details of his disappointment, re-opening the wounds, was in a different category. It struck me as an example of bad human relations and I have no regrets about having my say on the matter.

Some elements of the media tried to generate a feud between Hoddle and me but there was never any real problem. My basic view of him as national team manager is that he did not have enough experience for such a massive job. I don't think for a minute that he lacked ability. Essentially, his ideas on the game were good and if he had been ten years older he might well have been a success with England. Unless a man has the volume of experience of a Bobby Robson or a Terry Venables, managing England is an impossible job. To my mind, Terry Venables handled all the varied demands and pressures effectively and with confidence. His approach to the conflict that arises when clubs resent having players called up for friendly internationals was typical of the shrewdness and practicality he brought to his work. He knew he wasn't going to get all the men he wanted, so he would phone beforehand and ask club managers which of their players they were most reluctant to release. The friendly trust he created ensured that no reasonable club manager would dream of letting him down when it mattered, which means, of course, when European Championships and World Cups are involved. Terry's experience, and not least the time he spent abroad, in charge of Barcelona, a huge club, gave him advantages that the younger

Glenn Hoddle did not have. I hope Glenn can recover from the trauma associated with his departure from the FA. I think the quoted remarks that brought his downfall conveyed an impression of him that is inaccurate. I wish him well.

While I was flying back to Manchester from Nice at the end of June, I learned of David Beckham's sending-off in England's World Cup second-round match with Argentina and I thought to myself, 'That just puts the tin lid on it.' He had succeeded in giving Glenn Hoddle proof of his true ability in the last group game against Colombia and as the tournament moved into its knockout stages, he was poised to become one of its most exciting figures. But a foolish and blatant flick of his boot at Diego Simeone, and the Argentine's ludicrously theatrical response, brought Beckham's dismissal in St Etienne. After the brave resistance of England's ten men failed to prevent defeat in yet another penalty shoot-out, the reaction to Beckham's folly, in the media and among some so-called football fans, made me wonder if attitudes to sport in our country had gone totally insane. He could hardly have been more vilified if he had committed murder or high treason. Much of the stuff that appeared in the papers seemed to be driven by something close to blood-lust. I found it nauseating and I worried about how David would cope with the vicious hounding that went on long after the World Cup was over. We all know now that he coped magnificently. I tried to be of as much help as I could and so did everybody else at Manchester United and there is no doubt that his family gave him wonderful support. But the credit for the way he has dealt with the personal and professional pressures of the past year belongs entirely to him. The courage and extraordinary stamina he displays on the field were matched by the resolution and staying power he showed in coming through the storm of unjustified abuse that raged around him for months. He is more securely established than ever as a key member of the England team, and many of those who were condemning him last summer as a betrayer of the nation, ranting on in print as if banishment to Devil's Island would be too good for him, now can't stop shovelling compliments in his direction.

The hypocrisy of those people merely points up the strength of character David revealed throughout his ordeal.

He would be the first to admit that after the fiasco in France he wasn't playing very well. But he never shirked the challenge. He always wanted the ball and that is a measure of a great player. I remember Brian Kidd telling a story of his own days in the United shirt, of how the team had a particularly tough away game at the end of the 1966–67 season, when they were trying to close in on the championship. Some of the players were nervous and one or two had just about bottled it. But before they went out, Bobby Charlton said, 'Give me the ball and we'll be all right.' Brian was convinced that Bobby won United the title that season. Anybody who has watched David Beckham play knows that he is always ready to shoulder responsibility. He may look as if butter wouldn't melt in his mouth but underneath the boyish appearance and all the trappings of trendiness there is a steely determination that has to be admired. Without it he could not have maintained such high standards in his football amid the turmoil that has invaded his life over the past couple of years.

Since the start of his romance with Victoria, who is now his wife, he has been caught up in a swirl of showbiz publicity while continuing to face the demands for a disciplined lifestyle that go with his career as an outstanding player. Soon after they met, it was obvious that he was madly in love and, naturally, his feelings tended to take precedence over everything else. On the team coach in Germany, on the way to our 1997 meeting with Borussia Dortmund in the semi-final of the European Cup, I had to order him to switch off his mobile phone. He was obviously missing his new girlfriend badly and was continually calling her in New York. I am sure the glamour of being romantically involved with a world-famous pop singer was a thrill initially, but I imagine that their joint celebrity became a bit of a nightmare as the glare of publicity intensified. It has definitely changed David. Gone is the fun-loving lad of a few years ago and in his place there is a seriously private person, with inner reaches that few can penetrate. There was a period when I was troubled by the amount of travelling he was doing in his private life and about whether he was getting enough rest. Two or three trips a week to Ireland to be with Victoria was not an ideal preparation for what was being asked of him on the park and I had to stress that he had obligations to his own talent and to his team-mates. Fortunately, that is no longer a concern. Now that Victoria and David have settled in Cheshire with their baby son Brooklyn, normal habits have been resumed.

Nobody should ever underestimate David Beckham. At times I have disagreed with decisions he has taken off the field but he has a stubbornness that can't be broken and he will make up his own mind, whatever Alex Ferguson may think. I do like to have control of my players as they grow up but it is impossible not to admire his resolve. It has served me well on many occasions. When the chips are down on the football field, you can bet your life that David Beckham won't be found wanting.

IMPOSSIBLE TREBLE

NOTHING a manager does can guarantee greatness for a football club. But backing off from doing what he knows is necessary can make failure certain. There is little hope for anybody in my line of work who tries to avoid taking action that will make his life uncomfortable, whether it is replacing a popular player who is no longer fulfilling the requirements of his team or challenging boardroom policies that are blocking the road to success. In the early summer of 1998 I decided that I had to assert myself on the need for Manchester United to spend money in the transfer market. For too long I had allowed the PLC to overwhelm me, accepting too readily all the Cityspeak about institutions and dividends and the harsh realities of the business world. It was time to argue with renewed vehemence my long-held belief that nobody invests more than the fans who pack our ground whenever we play there. They don't get a penny back and they are entitled to expect everybody at Old Trafford to demonstrate a desire to be the best. Ours was supposed to be the biggest club in the game and there was an obligation to act in keeping with that status. We had gone thirty years without winning the European Cup and the domestic trophies we had piled up lately could not compensate fully for that omission. The papers referred to the European prize as our holy grail and, considering how we felt about it, the exaggeration was forgivable. I was about to lead United into the greatest of club competitions for the fifth time since becoming manager in 1986 and I had endured more than enough disappointment.

Reaching the semi-finals and the quarter-finals in the past two years had sharpened my hunger to go all the way but in the season just finished we had yielded the position of dominance in English football to Arsenal, who had completed the double of Premiership title and FA Cup triumph that had set United apart in 1994 and 1996. Arsenal would step straight into the Champions League, whereas we would have to earn a place in one of the six groups by surviving a qualifying round. These were circumstances in which complacency would be fatal.

We had to thrust ahead of Arsenal again in England and we had to give ourselves the best possible chance of ending at last our frustrations in the European Cup. To achieve those aims, I had to strengthen my squad, and the PLC would have to be persuaded that providing the money made sense. At the end of the 1997–98 season I met with Martin Edwards and David Gill, our finance director. Martin and David told me the sum available for transfers was £14 million. We had already committed £10 million to buying Jaap Stam, the Dutch central defender I had been quietly pursuing since late in 1997, so our purchasing fund could not provide anywhere near the amount required to make Aston Villa part with Dwight Yorke. The striker was a man I was absolutely determined to have, regardless of how much my assessment of him might be at variance with other opinions at Old Trafford. We signed the Swedish wide player Jesper Blomqvist, another long-term target of mine, for £4 million in July 1998. A solution to the problem of paying for Yorke was found by finalising the £12.5 million deal just a couple of days before the transfer deadline in mid-August. It meant our budgeting arrangements could be adjusted to include the expenditure in the following financial year. Ideally, I would have liked to add a further striker of international calibre to my armoury but at least I had pushed through the improvements to the squad that I saw as being essential if we were to have a successful season. The treble was to be a seeming impossibility that became a reality but, looking back, I am sure that it would have remained just a plain impossibility had we not shaken off commercial caution and bought Stam, Yorke and Blomqvist.

While those players were on the way in, a man who was fundamental to United's successes over the previous nine years was leaving us. I think the world of Gary Pallister and there was sadness in our parting but he knew his place in the team would be increasingly under threat and that an offer of £2.5 million from Middlesbrough was too good to be turned down. For Pally, there was the consolation of going back to his home-town club.

Hints of the glory to come were hard to find when Arsenal brushed United aside in the pre-season Charity Shield match at Wembley. As we slid to a 3–0 defeat, the critics took particular pleasure in telling us that we had made fools of ourselves by paying so much for Jaap Stam. He had known some bad moments in the World Cup finals in France, where Holland's defensive formation did him no favours, and his form against Arsenal convinced many that he would be a liability in the Premiership. I knew that was a crazy judgement, having seen enough of the Dutchman to identify him as a defender of the highest class. Jaap is quick, decisive, formidably strong physically and has the technique to play the ball effectively out of defence. He is also blessed with a calm, well-balanced temperament and all of those assets would soon show themselves as he steadily emerged as probably the most impressive centre-back in the country. Such quality in his vital position is something managers are always seeking but rarely come upon. At £10 million, Stam was a bargain.

The Charity Shield beating did not worry me but losing to the reigning champions by the same scoreline in a league match at Highbury on 20 September was a lot less tolerable. It was one of three defeats we suffered in the Premiership in the first half of the season and since the third of those (a 3–2 loss to Middlesbrough on 19 December) was inflicted on our own ground, there is no denying that our bid to regain the title took a while to build momentum. Part of the explanation was the strain of other commitments and the occasional stumble in the domestic competition was a price I was willing to pay for the progress we had made in the Champions League. After comfortably dismissing our preliminary-round opponents, LKS Lodz of Poland, we had found ourselves in the so-called Group of Death with Barcelona, Bayern Munich and Peter Schmeichel's former club, Brondby of Denmark. We certainly acted as undertakers for Brondby, running up an 11–2 aggregate over the home and away meetings. We drew twice with Barcelona and twice with Bayern Munich but anybody who infers a general dullness from those results couldn't be more wrong. The last of the fixtures, against Bayern, *was* noticeably short of a riveting climax but that was understandable, since both teams knew long before the finish at Old Trafford that the 1–1 score already on the board would send both of us into the quarter-finals. Word coming in from other groups had told us as much, and just about the only person in the stadium who seemed to have been kept in the dark was Schmeichel. As everybody else on the park waltzed uncompetitively through the final ten minutes, Peter kept frantically urging our troops forward. He sees himself as an attacking goalkeeper.

The great Schmeichel had, of course, decided by then that he would be leaving Old Trafford at the end of the season. His announcement of the decision in November had been a blow to everybody at the club but we all had to respect his desire to spend the last part of his career in another country, where the physical demands of league football would be less punishing than those in the Premiership. When he joined Sporting Lisbon in the summer of 1999, he carried with him our warmest wishes and the knowledge that our debt to him would never be forgotten. I don't believe a better goalkeeper has ever played the game. He is a giant figure in the history of United and it was fitting that his eight years with us should climax perfectly with the treble.

Our scoring feats in the Champions League had excited Europe. The two 3–3 draws with Barcelona might not be cited in any coaching manual dealing with defensive play but their openness and positive spirit made for wonderful entertainment. I was thrilled by the drive and ebullience of our display at the Nou Camp, although our best performance was undoubtedly against Bayern in Munich, where only an uncharacteristic clanger by the Viking in the last minute of the game denied us a memorable victory. In Barcelona, Yorke and Cole proved what a deadly partnership they could be. From the moment he joined us, Dwight had justified my conviction that he was a front player with a remarkable range of exceptional abilities. He is effortlessly neat on the ball, can beat opponents with swift dribbles or imaginative passes and is an excellent finisher, he has the heart and bodily strength to thrive in tough company and his joyous appetite for the game shines through the smile which is nearly always on his face. There is no doubt that his arrival has hugely benefited Andy Cole. They are soulmates off the field and, on it, Dwight's alertness and subtlety provide opportunities for Andy to exploit his pace and his predator's instincts. Between them, they were to score fifty-three goals before the season was over.

At the beginning of December 1998, with our last European group match against Bayern looming, I was stunned by the news that Brian Kidd was thinking of leaving Old Trafford to take over as manager at Blackburn Rovers. I was informed in a roundabout way when Stuart Mathieson, of the *Manchester Evening News*, told me that Martin Edwards had refused Blackburn permission to talk to Brian. When I spoke to Brian, I had the impression he wanted to stay with us. Called off the training pitch to take an urgent call from the chairman, I was surprised to hear from Martin that Brian's agent, Michael Kennedy, the London solicitor who also represents Roy Keane, had already been on requesting that my assistant should be allowed to go ahead and talk to Blackburn. The chairman asked me for my reaction.

'With the Bayern game coming up, it's a bloody bad time to lose him,' I said. Martin mentioned that he had been having a conversation with Peter Kenyon, another of our directors. They shared the feeling that every time a job came up they would have to give Brian a new contract. That was, admittedly, how it looked but my concern was the disruption that would be caused by his departure. I hoped the chairman would be able to avoid such an outcome when he met with Brian and Michael Kennedy the following day in London, where we were due to play Tottenham Hotspur in a League Cup tie. In the middle of that next afternoon,

Brian phoned me to say the matter was not settled. He made it sound as if negotiation had become impossible.

'All they keep talking about is compensation for Manchester United,' he said. It was close to kick-off when Brian arrived at White Hart Lane and he said nothing other than what I had heard from him earlier. Some minutes later, the chairman came to the dressing-room and beckoned me outside.

'He wants to leave,' Martin told me. 'Michael Kennedy is phoning Blackburn tonight to arrange a meeting for tomorrow.' I asked if Brian had been offered any inducement to stay. 'Yes, we offered an extra year's salary up front but he wasn't interested and said he wanted to prove himself.' The reference to proving himself was unexpected. Brian had never voiced a desire to go into management. After the game, I drew him into a little room off the dressing-room corridor and suggested he should consider carefully the big step he was taking. We parted having agreed that we would speak again in the morning. I did talk to him next day as he was on his way to Blackburn, but his mind was made up.

Naturally, the first-team players were sorry to see him go. He had proved himself an outstanding coach who was meticulous in his preparation for training. I had always recognised, and made a point of acknowledging, the important role he played in getting the team ready for games. The seven years we spent working together was a golden time for Manchester United. His forte was training players and with us he revealed a gift for getting close to them. Each individual in the squad came to feel that Kiddo wanted him in the team. In fact, when I gave Brian his say about who should play, naturally he had his favourites. Not surprisingly, they were mainly lads he had brought to the club when he was Youth Development Officer. Just as his predecessor, Archie Knox, gave me splendid backing while I was laying the foundations in my first five years at Old Trafford, so Brian was an integral part of the success that came in a flood afterwards. Along with his achievements as a player, his excellent contribution as my assistant assured him of an honoured place in the history of the club. Clearly he took a risk when he abandoned the comfortable niche he had at United to expose himself to the pressures of managing Blackburn, who were even then likely candidates for relegation. I suppose, as he neared the age of fifty, he decided that if he meant to try going it alone there could be no further delay. I give him credit for responding to the urge before it was too late. My main reservations concern his expectations of his new job and Jack Walker's expectations of him. Jack is not a man known for endless patience and he may not take kindly to discovering just how unlikely he is to repeat Blackburn's Premiership title triumph of 1995.

My relationship with Brian was a good one and, though there were periods in the summers of 1995 and 1998 when his tendency to moan to other people around the club left me feeling slightly undermined, I don't believe he behaved that way outside the confines of Old Trafford. I preferred to see it as just a quirk of his nature. I hoped Brian would not be disloyal to me after what I did for him. When I plucked him away from community work in Manchester, he was earning about £10,000 a year and when he left United his pay bore no resemblance to that figure. He will find out over the next few years whether or not he is suited to management. Of course, managing Blackburn Rovers is very different from managing Manchester United, and deep down I would have had serious reservations about Brian ever taking charge of United. I suspect that the constant demand for hard, often unpopular, decisions would have put an intolerable strain on his temperament.

That Tottenham match at which I realised that Kiddo was odds-on to join Blackburn was the end of our interest in the League Cup. Spurs beat us 3–1 and went on to win the trophy. There was little grieving over that loss. We had used the League Cup mainly to give young players experience and it had served its purpose. On the brink of qualification for the quarter-finals of the European Cup, with the Premiership contest about to intensify and FA Cup battles imminent, we could do without any more crowding of our schedule. But we could hardly claim to be satisfied with our overall record in December. Of the eight matches we played in various competitions that month, we lost two, drew five and had only one victory – by 3–0 over Nottingham Forest.

Tiredness was evident, never more so than when we were thoroughly outplayed at home by a vibrant Chelsea team and were fortunate to escape with a 1–1 result. Our luck did not hold three days later, on 19 December, when Middlesbrough shook us by leaving Old Trafford with three points. I missed that game. On the previous evening, my brother's wife, Sandra, died of cancer and I immediately caught a flight to Glasgow to be with Martin and his daughter, Laura. It was another of those occasions when real heartbreak made me wonder why we take football so seriously.

Inevitably, once I was back at the Cliff training ground, I was as immersed as ever in the little dramas of the game, and watching a video of the Middlesbrough defeat stirred me to deliver some plain words to the players. I pointed out how lack of concentration, unforgivable sloppiness, had cost us 'joke' goals on the Saturday and I let them know that we would have to work on sorting ourselves out without delay. 'There is nothing wrong with the quality in your game or the effort you put into it,' I told them. 'So let's get the show on the road.' I think it could be said that their response was adequate. They never lost again during the rest of the season, stretching their unbeaten run through thirty-three matches, collecting three of football's greatest trophies and the scalps of Liverpool, Chelsea, Arsenal, Inter Milan, Juventus and Bayern Munich along the way.

Nobody could have predicted at the end of 1998 how our season was about to take off. But, having plunged myself back into working at close quarters with the players on a daily basis, I sensed that a surge was coming. It was sheer enjoyment for me to be at the heart of the training again. I don't know whether the lads welcomed my announcement that as soon as the New Year came in we would be embarking on a programme of endurance work, but they have learned to appreciate the benefits of rigorous conditioning. Stamina would be one of their most effective weapons on the way to the treble.

There was a clamour for me to install a replacement for Brian Kidd but I was in no hurry. Jim Ryan's experience, knowledge of the game and conscientiousness made him a marvellous stand-in.

In many ways it would have suited me to have somebody familiar, especially somebody as capable and loyal as Jim, taking over the job. But he is in his fifties and I felt the permanent assistant should be younger, with fresher legs. He understood, as I knew he would.

I was determined that the new man would find the team in good form when he arrived, so that he would be entering an upbeat environment. In January we made a good start towards realising that objective, winning all five of our matches and scoring sixteen goals in the process. It was pleasing to avenge our recent embarrassment in the League by knocking Middlesbrough out of the FA Cup in the third round but the first sign that we might be on a momentous roll came in the fourth round against Liverpool at Old Trafford. The match began for us in the worst possible way when Michael Owen headed Liverpool into the lead in the third minute. From then until half-time we chased the game with more enthusiasm than guile and in my analysis at the interval I stressed that the opposition were forcing us to play in to Yorke while deploying plenty of bodies to smother his threat. We had to spread our play and oblige Jamie Redknapp and Paul Ince to come out of the central areas. We had to forget about using our strikers until we got into the Liverpool penalty box. When we applied those tactics in the second half, their centre-midfield players had to do a lot of running and, with about fifteen minutes to go, Ince had to come off. He was either injured or exhausted. However, in spite of shuffling the team through substitutions and committing so wholeheartedly to attack that we were often left undermanned in defence, we could not answer the frenzy in the stadium with a breakthrough. Roy Keane hit wood twice and it began to look as if it was not our day. Then, in the eighty-eighth minute, one of David Beckham's flawlessly executed free kicks was headed delicately back across goal by Andy Cole for Yorke to tap in the equaliser. Amid the bedlam, most of our fans were gratefully envisaging a replay but two minutes into injury time, and with the Merseyside supporters convinced the final whistle was overdue, we completed the kind of fight-back that was to epitomise our season. A long ball from Jaap Stam was chased down by Paul Scholes, creating a glimpse of an opening for Ole Gunnar Solskjaer. The amazing quickness of the Norwegian's reactions did the rest, and Liverpool's Cup dreams were dead. We had witnessed a demonstration of the morale that was to be every bit as vital as rich skill in the five months that lay ahead of United.

When critics of our game parade their theories about the attributes that lift certain teams above others, I am always amused by their eagerness to concentrate almost exclusively on technical and tactical comparisons. Frequently they discuss football in abstract terms, overlooking the reality that it is played by creatures of flesh and blood and feeling. Tactics are important but they don't win football matches. Men win football matches. The best teams stand out because they *are* teams, because the individual members have been so truly integrated that the team functions with a single spirit. There is a constant flow of mutual support among the players, enabling them to feed off strengths and compensate for weaknesses. They depend on one another, trust one another. A manager should engender that sense of unity. He should create a bond among his players and between him and them that raises performance to heights that were unimaginable when they started out as disparate individuals. The Manchester United of 1999 had talent by the bundle but there was nothing about them that I admired or valued more than their team spirit.

In addition to the epic with Liverpool, January encouraged us with a 4–1 defeat of West Ham on our patch and a 6–2 hammering of Leicester on theirs. Leicester's sufferings owed much to Dwight Yorke's first hat trick for United. We ended the month rather more edgily, requiring a last-minute goal from Yorke to beat Charlton on a day when it was hard to foresee the relegation nightmare that lay in wait for the London team. I had warmed to the way their young manager, Alan Curbishley, went about his business. He deserved better than what happened at the end of the season.

There was a manager of my own vintage in the opposing dugout for our next match at the beginning of February, and Jim

Smith knew that I wanted more than points from Derby County. Jim's assistant, Steve McClaren, was my choice to succeed Brian Kidd. I had instructed Eric Harrison, our former youth coach, and Les Kershaw, Director of the Academy, to scour England for the best candidates in terms of coaching ability and work ethic. Their researches had kept coming back to Steve. When I assessed his credentials, I was sure he was the right man and Derby stood aside to let him advance his career. I had always intended to make an appointment just before our European campaign was reactivated and I was delighted by how swiftly Steve stamped his personality on the job. He has deeply impressed me and I expect him to go on to great things.

The players soon provided McClaren with close-up evidence of their abilities. His first match as a United man (immediately after we had beaten Derby 1–0) was a visit to the City Ground in Nottingham. It was devastation on the grand scale, with Solskjaer confirming to Forest that he is the substitute from hell. He put away four goals in the last ten minutes to take the score to 8–1. There was a jolting contrast, as I knew there would be, when the fifth round of the FA Cup brought Fulham to Manchester. Kevin Keegan's team were charging towards promotion to the First Division and their sustained liveliness caused enough discomfort to make us grateful to squeeze through with an Andy Cole goal. When we switched back to the Premiership, it was to face Arsenal at Old Trafford in a match that threatened to have a huge impact on the contest for the title. The equivalent fixture the previous season had certainly done so. After beating us 1–0 in that one, Arsenal had control of their own destiny in the championship and they never surrendered it. We were determined that this game would not have the same gloomy consequences for us. It turned out to be a credit to both sets of players. Helped by first-class refereeing from Gary Willard, who balanced common sense with firmness, they slugged out an enthralling 1–1 draw. We had the edge and should have won but once again Tony Adams had other ideas. I praise Adams so much that people must think we are related. I have never even worked with him but I feel I know him well because I recognise in him the levels of determination and driving competitiveness that were present in some of the most influential players I have managed. There is something of Willie Miller and Stuart Kennedy from my Aberdeen days, and of Bryan Robson, Roy Keane, Steve Bruce and Mark Hughes. No one can be surprised by Arsenal's success so long as they have Tony Adams at the heart of their team. I can't wait for him to retire.

We had been anxious to avoid Internazionale of Milan in the draw for the European Cup quarter-finals. San Siro may be just about the most testing arena in football. But, in a season when we seemed to be fated to have the toughest possible route to every trophy we went after, to be paired with the Italian giants was nothing out of the ordinary. The first leg was at Old Trafford, so we had a chance to make the journey to Milan less hazardous. A couple of Premiership wins over Coventry and Southampton on the way to the tie did our confidence no harm but dealing with those opponents was rather different from coping with Ronaldo and his friends. The young Brazilian had been on my mind for weeks. At his best, he could destroy any defenders in the world and I had to try to prevent our lads from becoming overawed by the thought of what he might do to them. I was spared the worry. Ronaldo wasn't fit enough to play at Old Trafford. I would guess that even our fans, who love to watch great footballers in action, were no more heartbroken than I was about his absence that night. Tactically, there were two points to be emphasised. The first was that Inter were seriously vulnerable to crosses and David Beckham in particular had to punish that weakness. Our second priority was a defensive one. Inter's game-plan was geared to counter-attacking through the middle of the opposition. That meant that our full-backs had to go and play in front of our central defenders, where the Italians operated with two attackers withdrawn into positions behind their main striker, Ivan Zamorano. The withdrawn players, Youri Djorkaeff and Roberto Baggio, had plenty of ability and experience and must not be given room to create openings for their talented midfielders, Javier Zanetti, Diego Simeone and Benoit Cauet. It was also important that, when our attacks broke down and we regrouped, we should surrender the wide areas and close off the centre-midfield, again denying them their favourite avenue of penetration. Aggressively and defensively, the team applied themselves well and when Yorke met a Beckham cross with a diving header to put us ahead after seven minutes, we were in good shape. The same combination brought a second goal just before half-time and 2–0 was the final score. As I said at the post-match press conference, scoring in Italy would put us through and I felt strongly that we would secure the away goal.

Chelsea were our opponents in the sixth round of the FA Cup, giving us further proof that if we were to win that prize we would have to do it the hard way. Chelsea's record at Old Trafford in my time there has pleased them a lot more than it has me, and surviving their visit would not be easy. Looking at the big picture, however, I was more concerned about our scheduled trip to Anfield for a Premiership meeting with Liverpool on the following Wednesday. Liverpool would be going into that game with ten days' rest behind them and, stung by our dramatic victory over them in the Cup, they were bound to come at us like demons. I wanted to be ready for them, which was why I left Cole and Yorke out of the team that took on Chelsea. Phil Neville was included in the line-up to man-mark Gianfranco Zola. I always think it is that little genius who is the main source of purpose and thrust in their attacking play and I believed that if Phil could keep him quiet Chelsea would be deprived of their normal flow and pattern. Most people thought I would be depressed when a goalless draw set up a replay in London but it meant the Liverpool game was postponed and, in fact, a Wednesday night at Stamford Bridge suited me better than travelling to Anfield to meet old rivals whose period of idleness had loaded the dice in their favour. We wheeled out the big guns for the Chelsea replay and an excellent game it was. Both sides performed impressively but an early goal from Yorke put mental pressure on Chelsea. Dwight was in peak form and he crushed the home crowd's hopes with a second strike that was one of the goals of the year. Few players anywhere could deliver a chip on the run with such fluency and precision.

Physically and psychologically, we were handling our hectic programme well and – after Andy Cole had pained his former admirers at St James' Park by claiming the two goals that beat Newcastle and kept us at the top of the Premiership – we flew to Milan without undue trepidation. I saw that expedition as having massive significance for us. In the electric atmosphere of San Siro, my players would learn much about themselves. It tests not only ability but self-belief and courage. Success there on the evening of 17 March would, I felt, represent the biggest step forward Manchester United had taken under my management. The news that Ronaldo was a starter dictated my tactics. I deployed Ronny Johnsen alongside Roy Keane in centre-midfield so that either one could choke the space in which the great Brazilian likes to operate. Knowing that neither Ronaldo nor Baggio would press for the ball or hunt it down, I urged on our full-backs, Gary Neville and Denis Irwin, the importance of profiting from the possession they would have. If we could stretch our play through Denis and Gary, I believed that it would be hard for Inter to win back the ball. So it proved and we had the superior volume of quality possession during the match.

Admittedly, we had an advantage before a ball was kicked. Ronaldo may have been in the blue-and-black stripes of Inter but not all of him was there. The area outside the dressing-rooms at San Siro is usually crowded with all sorts of people on match nights and by the time the two teams entered the hallway leading to the pitch there was a scene of clamorous tension. Both groups of players were psyching themselves up with what almost amounted to war-cries. Simeone, the aggressive Argentine, was screaming exhortations at his team-mates while directing a few glares towards our lads. At times like that, you are glad the big Viking is on your side. When Schmeichel raises his voice the walls shudder. In the midst of that fever of anticipation, I glanced across to the far corner of the hall and there stood Ronaldo, leaning back with a football pressed between him and the wall. He looked vacant, utterly uninterested in the happenings around him, as if he didn't want to be in that place at that time. I had a fatherly impulse to go over and say something to him. But I decided I was the wrong man to intrude on his solitude, and left him alone.

Predictably, Ronaldo was only a shadowy presence in the match and he might have been replaced long before he gave way to Nicola Ventola with an hour played. Our players maintained their composure admirably, refusing to be distracted by the tidal wave of hostile noise or the oranges and coins tossed on to the field. The French referee, Gilles Veissière, was equally unintimidated. In fact, it must be said that his bravery extended to turning down legitimate Inter claims for a penalty when Schmeichel threw his body in front of Zamorano. There were other twitchy moments when Zanetti hit a post in the first half and Ze Elias missed a sitter late in the second. But nobody comes through that kind of ordeal without a little luck and we were playing well enough to deserve our share. Even when Ventola scored just three or four minutes after coming on, I wasn't desperately worried. I suspected that they had spent most of their energy to cut our lead in half and that a game-saving effort was beyond them. And I had an ace to play in the shape of Paul Scholes. He took over from Johnsen, who had done a good job but was tiring. I am fortunate to have a lad as fearless as Scholes to call upon in such circumstances. He went into that cauldron as calmly as someone popping round the corner for a newspaper, and only those who don't know him could be surprised when, in the eighty-eighth minute, he slid in the goal that took us to the semi-finals. Having gained such a result, we feared nothing the European Cup could throw at us. Quietly, among ourselves, we all hoped to meet Juventus at the next stage. There was no complacency or disrespect implicit in that attitude. Only an idiot would lack respect for the Old Lady of Italian football. We felt as we did because we had confronted Juventus four times recently and were keen to prove that we had learned from the experience.

We were now leading the Premiership and were in the semi-finals of both the European Cup and the FA Cup, and press speculation about the treble had begun in earnest. Those who asked us to comment on our chances of completing it knew the answer in advance. How could we say anything other than that we would deal with one match at a time? It is better to be clichéd than crazy. Letting the mind skip over immediate assignments and on to future possibilities is a good way to wreck concentration. A rock climber who starts thinking about hand-holds twenty feet above him will take a short-cut to the ground. When I did think two or three games ahead, it was not to conjure up dreams of triumph but with the practical purpose of working out the team changes that might keep us fresh for the recurring challenges produced by pressing forward on several fronts. Nowadays, the demands on players are so intense and incessant that what I said earlier about team spirit has to apply to a squad rather than to eleven men. Achieving the right balance of fairness, freshness and a winning selection can be dreadfully difficult for a manager and he needs the understanding of the individuals who are being rotated. Good results are the best persuaders when it comes to justifying the teams that have been picked and a home win over Everton and a draw at Wimbledon, with David Beckham making a welcome return to the scoresheet, were quite satisfactory. Now it was time for the little matter of entertaining Juventus at Old Trafford.

Nothing contributes more to the greatness of Manchester United than the passion of our supporters. All of us employed by United feel a responsibility to the fans and sometimes that sense of obligation can be a trap for the players. The urgings of the crowd can encourage a cavalry charge when a more patient approach is needed. That was a major part of our problem on 7 April when Juventus repeatedly ripped us open in the first half. Our basic tactics were quite simple. We were meant to play with three in midfield at all times, with Beckham or Giggs out wide to give us prospects of penetrating the Juve back four and stretching their midfield. When one of the wide men was attacking, the other was supposed to tuck into the middle of the park and link up protectively with Roy Keane and Paul Scholes. But, intoxicated by the atmosphere of a classic European occasion at Old Trafford, Beckham and Giggs simultaneously pushed too far forward, leaving Roy and Paul to struggle against three of the most effective midfielders in the world: Didier Deschamps, Edgar Davids and Zinedine Zidane. In addition, instead of my full-backs fulfilling our plan to force their wide players, Antonio Conte and Angelo Di Livio, to retreat, the roles had been reversed and Gary Neville and Denis Irwin were being driven back. In those first forty-five minutes we might have lost three goals instead of the one scored by Conte.

A lot of sorting out was done at the interval. In the second half, Beckham played in tight, eliminating Juve's numerical advantage in midfield, and Giggs supplied the penetration we had expected of him. We took control and could have won the match but, remembering that it could have been all over at half-time, I could not be dissatisfied with the draw we earned through a late goal from Giggs. We deserved criticism after being thoroughly outplayed in the first half, but the critics who assumed our interest in the tournament was over obviously did not understand what they had seen after the interval. It was a different game then and I was genuinely optimistic about going to Turin. Zidane had seen the last of the wide open spaces he found early at Old Trafford.

As a relaxing diversion before we went to Italy, we had an FA Cup semi-final at Villa Park against our most consistent rivals of the Nineties, Arsenal. With our commitments, we wanted this tie to be settled (in our favour, of course) after ninety minutes, so naturally it went to extra time and then a replay. The contest lasted four hours and I have never been involved in a more engrossing semi-final. But it should not have gone beyond the first hour and a half. We were denied an entirely valid goal by an outrageous decision perpetrated by a linesman and endorsed by the referee, David Elleray. The offside ruling related to Yorke's position in Arsenal's box at a time when Giggs, far out on the left, was in the process of playing the ball past Lee Dixon and sprinting after it to cross from near the by-line. If Giggs was passing to anybody, it could only be himself. His action was the equivalent of a dribble and it was blatant nonsense to disallow the goal that his centre permitted Keane to blast into the Arsenal net. My anger at half-time was directed at the linesman but the real culprit was Elleray, who should have rescued his assistant from an horrendous mistake. Three and a half weeks later we would have even more serious cause to regret finding ourselves in the company of Mr Elleray. In the meantime, it was enough of a headache to have the replay cluttering our preparation for the showdown in Turin.

I resolved to freshen up the team for our second go at Arsenal, also at Villa Park. When I have to do that, Teddy Sheringham and Ole Gunnar Solskjaer are invaluable alternatives to Yorke and Cole and once again they excelled. Jesper Blomqvist penetrated effectively for us on the left and by the hour mark the game should have been over. Instead, we had only a goal gloriously struck from the edge of Arsenal's penalty area by David Beckham to show for our superiority, and missing chances invites trouble. Yet we were coping well with Arsenal's main threat, Dennis Bergkamp, until luck came to his aid midway through the second half. Receiving the ball in his familiar deep position, he delivered a shot that was going straight to Schmeichel until it hit Jaap Stam and was deflected several feet into the corner of our net. The goal revitalised our opponents and their confidence had a further lift minutes later when Roy Keane was sent off for a foul on Marc Overmars. It was the third time Roy had been dismissed by David Elleray. TV replays showed the decision to be harsh but my concern at the time was organising my ten men to resist the bombardment that was surely coming. Just when I thought we had withstood it, Arsenal were awarded a penalty for a Phil Neville foul on Ray Parlour. 'We don't deserve this,' I said to myself. From the moment Bergkamp's kick was brilliantly saved by big Peter to send the match into extra time, I believed we could at least take it to a penalty shoot-out.

The following thirty minutes exhausted me, and probably everyone else in the ground. If ever a tie could be described as epic it was this one. Something special would be required to decide it. What was provided by Ryan Giggs (who had come on as a substitute) was not just special. It was historic. When a misdirected pass by Patrick Vieira carried the ball to Ryan about fifteen yards inside our half of the field, our bench rose with a roar of encouragement. 'Go and attack Dixon,' was my thought, for I had detected signs of tiredness in the Arsenal full-back. Ryan attacked just about everybody in front of him who was wearing a red shirt. By the time he crowned a mesmerising sixty-yard run with a thunderous shot into the roof of Arsenal's net, his fierce surges of pace and dazzling two-footed control of the ball had contemptuously dismissed the challenges of four international players and left them trailing in abject pursuit. Given the importance of the game, the point it had reached and the pressure our ten men were under, that has to be one of the best goals ever scored in major football. Between the first drawn match with Arsenal and that replay, I had called Ryan in for a one-to-one chat with the express purpose of reminding him that all his commendable efforts to widen the scope of his game must not mislead him into neglecting his greatest asset, which is his capacity to terrorise defenders by running directly at them. Maybe I must take some blame for the blurring of his priorities. Over the past three years, at my insistence, he has been striving to improve his vision of the game, his awareness of space and of passing opportunities. I am delighted that he has worked so hard to be a more rounded footballer but the last thing I want him to do is lose sight of the qualities that put him among the tiny élite of the world's most penetrative front players. He is so richly endowed with speed, balance, touch and courage that, whether he is dribbling with the ball or sprinting past opponents to receive it in areas of maximum threat, he can leave the best defenders with twisted blood. His inner struggle to become the complete player has frequently inhibited the expression of the amazing talent that broke Arsenal on 14 April. The real Ryan Giggs should step forward more often.

Once we had seen out the eleven minutes that remained when that wonder goal went in, our dressing-room was a wild place. Even at celebrations, experience counts. Peter Schmeichel always removes his clothes to a safe haven. As we left Villa Park, he was probably the only man who didn't have champagne on him as well as in him.

Arsenal were quite bullish in the aftermath of that semi-final, arguing that being able to concentrate solely on the Premiership would help them to win the title. There was logic in their case but our players seemed to have the reserves to defy it. At home to Sheffield Wednesday on the following Saturday, Solskjaer, Scholes and Sheringham scored and we won 3–0. Morale could not have been higher for our trip to Turin and the match that could take us into the European Cup final for the first time in thirty-one years. I have developed an immense respect for Juventus. They are a class act from top to bottom and I hope United use the great Italian club as a benchmark. We went to the Stadio Delle Alpi knowing that the new coach, Carlo Ancelotti, an outstanding player in his day, had steadied the ship skilfully after the abrupt departure of Marcello Lippi. But I kept thinking what a godsend it was that Lippi was not in the Juve dug-out. Lippi is one impressive man. Looking into his eyes is enough to tell you that you are dealing with somebody who is in command of himself and of his professional domain. Those eyes are sometimes burning with seriousness, sometimes twinkling, sometimes warily assessing you – and always they are alive with intelligence. Nobody could make the mistake of taking Lippi lightly. On top of all his other advantages, he is such a good-looking bastard he makes most of us look like Bela Lugosi. I was certain Juventus would miss him, although I had heard nothing but good reports about Ancelotti.

Unfortunately, Ryan Giggs's reward for his miracle at Villa Park had been an ankle injury and he missed our unforgettable night in Turin, which was the greatest performance ever produced by a team under my management. All my life I have based my football creed on passing the ball, possession with rhythm and tempo. For thirty minutes of the first half against Juventus, my ideals were almost totally realised by United. That we had fallen two goals behind before we rose to that level of excellence only made the achievement all the more remarkable. I was disappointed and angry at losing the first goal after six minutes to a ploy engineered by our opponents at a corner. When the ball was steered back upfield to Zidane, wide on the left, he had ample time and room to calculate the trajectory of his angled centre to the far post, where Filippo Inzaghi was far more alert and decisive than our defenders. We should be above surrendering goals like that. When the second blow came from an Inzaghi shot deflected off Stam's boot, I was numb but I did not feel that the match was over. Only eleven minutes had been played but that was a blessing. I had always felt we would have to score two goals. Now that had been confirmed as our target, and at least we had plenty of time to reach it.

What was imperative was that we should keep our composure and express ourselves. Doing so was made more difficult when the referee harshly cautioned Roy Keane. The implications of that yellow card were drastic. If we qualified for the final in Barcelona, suspension would make Roy a spectator. I didn't think I could have a higher opinion of any footballer than I already had of the Irishman but he rose even further in my estimation at the Stadio Delle Alpi. The minute he was booked and out of the final, he seemed to redouble his efforts to get the team there. It was the most emphatic display of selflessness I have seen on a football field. Pounding over every blade of grass, competing as if he would rather die of exhaustion than lose, he inspired all around him. I felt it was an honour to be associated with such a player. When he leapt to meet a Beckham corner and headed in our first goal, it was if his will had given the ball no choice but to land in the net. Another marvellous header by Yorke brought an equaliser before half-time and at 2–2 the away-goals rule meant that we were halfway to Barcelona. I was thoroughly relaxed and couldn't envisage anything other than victory. There was the usual defending to do in the second half but it was far from desperate and our counter-attacking play was stretching Juventus towards breaking point. Then Yorke thrust through their straining central defenders, Paolo Montero and Ciro Ferrara, and you could sense that a goal was coming. Dwight was dragged down by the goal-keeper but the ball rolled to Andy Cole and he coolly completed as good a night's work as any team had ever done in Juventus's backyard. My one regret was that I had sent Paul Scholes on as a substitute in the second half. He was booked for what I thought was a fair tackle and, like Keane, was banned from the final. It was heartbreaking for Paul, who is not only an outstanding player but a wonderful lad. He and Roy would have to settle for the FA Cup final. It said something about our season that an appearance in the old showpiece at Wembley could be considered a mere consolation prize.

Before we faced Newcastle in north London on 22 May, however, our nerves would have to withstand an agonisingly close finish to the title race. Even the bookmakers could not make up their minds about whether United or Arsenal were the favourites and the betting odds fluctuated several times on the run-in. Chelsea had been serious contenders for much of the way but they wearied under the weight of injuries. There is little doubt that Gianluca Vialli will have them back challenging next season. I think he has done a splendid job at Stamford Bridge. Along with Arsene Wenger, he has demonstrated just how effective foreign coaches of high quality can be in the Premiership. I have enjoyed Gianluca's company after matches and have been impressed by how detailed and perceptive his observation of games invariably is. I expect him to put plenty of problems in Manchester United's way. The same can be said of David O'Leary at Leeds United. He has had the courage to commit himself to an exciting crop of young players and they haven't let him down. Furthermore, they seem to have fun playing football and that is refreshing to see. Their bubbly aggression soon posed a threat to our championship ambitions at Elland Road on 25 April. Achilles tendon trouble had caused the late withdrawal of Jaap Stam and, with our Norwegian players on international duty, I fielded a new defensive partnership of David May and Wes Brown. They took time to adjust to the sudden call-up and Leeds dominated the first half, fully justifying the 1–0 lead they held at the interval. Our character asserted itself in the second half. Andy Cole scored and we ground out a 1–1 draw. Against Aston Villa in our next match an improbable penalty miss by Denis Irwin, just about the most reliable professional on our books, made us more nervous than we should have been but the 2–1 win gave us three more points.

Above: Phil Neville (right) and Arsenal's Dennis Bergkamp hit the ground at Highbury in August but a 2–1 success proves our season is up and running.

Right: Massimo Taibi makes a commanding catch on his debut at Liverpool. My Italian recruit handled the pressure of being a United player less well.

Below: Roy Keane (left) turns to celebrate after his tap-in against Palmeiras in Tokyo puts United on top of the world, at least until January.

Myself, Martin Edwards (centre) and the FA's David Davies at the announcement that United will not defend the FA Cup, a mess not of our making.

Dwight Yorke explores a route to goal against Vasco da Gama in Rio but we were to pay for a lost toss and uncharacteristic errors by Gary Neville.

Teddy Sheringham contests possession with Vasco da Gama's Mauro Galvao in the sapping heat of Maracana, where we ended up being put in the shade.

David Beckham's dismissal against Necaxa and subsequent ban meant he had energy to spare in the win over South Melbourne (below) that completed our Rio obligations.

Dwight Yorke's header seals our 3–1 revenge victory over Fiorentina at Old Trafford as the quest to retain the European Cup gathers momentum.

Teddy Sheringham heads off any lingering doubts by scoring our second at home to Bordeaux, leaving a place in the quarter-finals within reach.

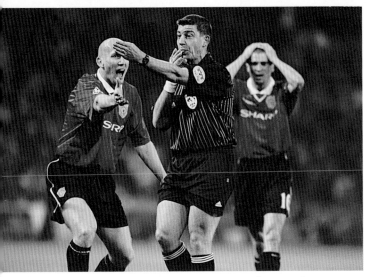

Jaap Stam (left) and Roy Keane during a rare moment of concern in our curiously anti-climactic 0–0 draw with Real Madrid in Spain.

Andy Cole takes on the Real defence at Bernabeu, where a scoreline most people saw as satisfactory filled me with foreboding.

Above: David Beckham sits out our vital win at Leeds after learning that even the most high-profile United players cannot flout club discipline.

Opposite top left: Match-winner Andy Cole has the beating of Leeds's Jonathan Woodgate at Elland Road as we begin to burn off our pursuers.

Below: Mark Bosnich endured a mixed season on his return to Old Trafford, shaking off weight problems to perform especially well in our Tokyo triumph.

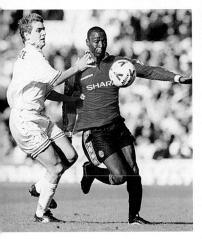

Right: After the setback over Ruud van Nistelrooy, the deal that brought Fabien Barthez's class and charisma from Monaco to Manchester was concluded with pleasing ease for all concerned.

Below: The freshly shorn David Beckham scores our second in the 3–1 defeat of Spurs and a championship that once looked like being a close race is won by 18 points.

Above: Sunshine and showers – of champagne – as we savour our sixth title in eight years. Ryan Giggs (sixth left) has medals from all of them at the grand old age of 26!

Left: The knighthood reminds me how far I have come in life; Cathy, who was initially reluctant to accept, makes sure I stay firmly rooted in the family Ferguson.

Now the rescheduled Premiership collision with Liverpool at Anfield was looming and I was confident that the heat of traditional rivalry would revive the form that had carried us to the top of the table. But my optimism was shaken when I learned that an injury to Paul Durkin, who was originally due to referee the match, had led to the appointment of David Elleray. The last official I wanted was the Harrow schoolmaster. For most of the hour and a half, it appeared that the identity of the referee wouldn't matter. We went in front early through an exciting goal that originated in good passing along our right flank. David Beckham whipped in the kind of perfectly flighted cross that is his speciality and Dwight Yorke responded with a fine header at the far post. Liverpool were playing quite well but could not create a noticeable chance and when, in the second half, Blomqvist was caught by a high kick from Jamie Carragher in our opponents' box, maximum points for us seemed guaranteed. It was a penalty and Denis Irwin, untroubled by the memory of his aberration against Villa, established a two-goal lead that looked unassailable. But we soon learned it wasn't. After Blomqvist slid in to sweep the ball cleanly away from the feet of Oyvind Leonhardsen, the referee awarded one of the least likely penalties even Anfield has seen. As Liverpool exploited their outrageous good fortune to reduce our lead, the anger of our players was understandable. But much worse was to come. Denis Irwin, who had been booked for a foul earlier, was chasing the ball along the touchline when it bobbled slightly out of play. Carried forward by the momentum of his run, Denis knocked a short pass inside to a team-mate. Television evidence later indicated that there had been only a fraction of a second between the sound of the referee's whistle and the pass but Elleray had no hesitation in flourishing a second yellow card at Irwin, apparently for the offence of kicking the ball away. Presumably, the reasoning behind the caution, which was automatically followed by a red card, was that our full-back had been guilty of a time-wasting tactic. Does anybody really believe that Denis had a sinister motive for what he did? The ordering-off was an affront to common sense. Its effects were dire. Apart from reducing us to ten men and putting our entire championship challenge under siege, it ruled one of the best-behaved and most respected pros in England out of the Cup final. Even Phil Thompson, who is the ultimate Liverpool fanatic, shook his head in disbelief and apologised to me. It was almost inevitable that all our players' hard work would now go to waste and, with one minute remaining, Paul Ince equalised. Paul once gave sterling service in the United shirt but he made a sour exit from Old Trafford after my opinion of his strengths on the field began to diverge dramatically from his own. It was no surprise that his celebration of his goal was gloatingly excessive. I hope he enjoyed it. Unless I am mistaken, his time in top-level football is dwindling fast. In a post-match interview on Sky TV, I made a vow with David Elleray in mind: 'We will not let this man deny us our title.'

Our prospects of making good the promise improved conspicuously within a week. On the next Sunday the team returned from Middlesbrough with a 1–0 win (another Dwight Yorke goal) that left Manchester United and Arsenal locked at the top of the Premiership, each with 75 points from 36 matches and dead-heating on goal difference too. But the number of goals scored might yet be the tie-breaker and if so we would be well ahead. We had amassed twenty more than Arsenal. That last figure reflected our adventurousness since the start of the season and did, in my view, give us marginally the better right to be champions. Of course, we wanted a more comfortable margin in our favour and it was presented to us by Leeds when they beat Arsenal 1–0 at Elland Road on Tuesday, 11 May. We arrived at Blackburn on the following night aware that a victory at Ewood Park would put us three points in front of the reigning champions and send us into our final fixture against Tottenham on our own ground requiring nothing more than a draw to be assured of the title. It was strange to have my first manager-to-manager confrontation with Brian Kidd in a match that had such contrasting implications for the two of us. If Blackburn failed to win, they would be relegated. I was astonished to find them playing with a lone striker, Ashley Ward, and deploying two wide players and three central midfielders in a formation that seemed designed to contain us rather than beat us. We had ninety per cent of the game but could not score and I was angry that we did not succeed in breaking them down. With Arsenal expected to defeat Aston Villa at Highbury on the Sunday, our simultaneous meeting with Spurs would have to be won if we were to be sure of regaining the championship. But if the goalless draw with Blackburn was awkward for us, it was fatal for them and I did not relish going into Brian's office afterwards. Fortunately, he was in tremendous spirits, happily trading banter with my staff and recalling the good times he had among us in the past. I could not help wondering if he regretted separating himself from all that.

As a good friend of mine and as manager of Tottenham Hotspur, the nearest neighbours and fiercest rivals Arsenal have in English football, George Graham was presumably hoping that Manchester United would emerge as winners of the long battle for the 1999 Premiership title. Too much has happened since his triumphant days at Highbury to make it likely that he still craves success for his former club. But George, like me, is addicted to winning and I knew he would bring Spurs to Old Trafford on Sunday, 16 May with only one thought in his head – to come out on top in a football match. I knew that Tottenham wouldn't hand out any favours. What I didn't know was that *we* would. We just had to put ourselves through the emotional wringer yet again by presenting a silly goal to Les Ferdinand. Equally typical was the thrilling response that blunder evoked. We battered the Spurs defence and created quite a few chances before David Beckham took a fine pass from Paul Scholes and powerfully drove the ball high inside Ian Walker's right-hand post. At half-time I replaced Teddy Sheringham with Andy Cole and Teddy was hardly overjoyed about the change. I didn't blame him but in studying the Spurs defence I had noticed hints that John Scales, who had missed a lot of football because of injury, was tiring and might be hurt by Andy's pace. Substitution can be a minefield for a manager. Sometimes it works, sometimes it doesn't. This time the justification was almost immediate as Andy controlled a long pass with remarkable finesse and lifted the ball over Walker to give us the lead. Although Spurs did not threaten us in the second half, our own wasteful finishing kept us on edge, especially after news came in from London that Arsenal had gone ahead. Minutes were like days until the referee, Graham Poll, made the championship a reality for us with the final blast on his whistle. A prize that we cherish had come back to us. Whatever the glamour of the FA Cup or the historical significance of the European Cup, there is only one stamp of supremacy in our country's football and that is the Premier League title. I was ecstatic at the end of that match and acknowledged to myself that we could indeed win the treble. But there would be no trumpeting from the United camp. Answering the bugle is more our style.

The next day Jim Ryan, Steve McClaren and I travelled down to St Albans for the League Managers' annual dinner, where I received the two main awards for the season. Honours from your peers always bring special pleasure. My break for socialising did not last long. By Thursday the team were in Windsor to prepare for the FA Cup final on the Saturday. We would stay in London on the Saturday night, then return to Windsor before flying out to Barcelona on the Monday. There was a healthy spirit among the troops but a few of their bodies were in a doubtful state. Different types of viruses seemed to be circulating, spreading a variety of worrying symptoms. The two Nevilles were heavily bunged up and Ronny Johnsen had a nasty throat infection but the worst case was Paul Scholes, who had a head cold and a chest problem. Those ailments were made worse by the asthmatic condition that is always with Paul, and strong dosages of medication were administered to him. After the disappointment of being banned from the European Cup final, the wee man would be given until the last second to prove himself fit for Wembley. My own affliction was the headache that came from trying to pick a team for our first cup final while keeping our second one in mind. There was an obvious danger that the sapping turf of Wembley would rob us of the energy and freshness needed in Spain. One player I didn't even consider fielding against Newcastle was

Nicky Butt. He understood when I told him that, because Keane and Scholes weren't available to face Bayern Munich, he was essential and therefore couldn't be risked on the Saturday. Stam and Yorke were two others who would be saved for Barcelona, although Stam's Achilles trouble had cleared up sufficiently to take him off the injured list. But when I asked Beckham if he wanted a rest, he looked appalled. 'No chance, boss,' he said. 'I want to play.' He always does.

By the morning of the Cup final, the bugs that had attacked the squad were in retreat and we had no invalids. We did have a major casualty almost as soon as the match was under way, which was not surprising in view of the aggressive recklessness of Newcastle's tackling in the early minutes. The scything lunge with which Gary Speed brought down Roy Keane was to force the Irishman to admit that 1999 was not his year for finals. He hobbled about the field for a while in the hope of playing through the hurt Speed had inflicted, but the ankle damage was too severe and in the eighth minute Roy had to come off. I considered sending on Jesper Blomqvist but he would have a lot of running to do in Barcelona, so I didn't want him involved in practically the whole match at Wembley. My decision was to take a gamble by drafting in Teddy Sheringham and moving Ole Gunnar Solskjaer from his starting position as a striker to wide on the right. Teddy had been on the park barely three minutes when he joined in an intricate exchange of passes that ended with Scholes releasing him cunningly into the Newcastle box. The Sheringham finish was cool and efficient and we had a lead that was never to be in serious jeopardy. In my fairly simple pre-match instructions I had emphasised the importance of maintaining a good tempo on a pitch where a tendency to be ponderous in possession is a common fault and I was pleased to see that Beckham, plainly relishing the centre-midfield role he had assumed, was ensuring that there was nothing sluggish about our build-up play. I was delighted, too, by the way Teddy had used his quick goal as the platform for a confident, influential performance. I had not enjoyed leaving him out of the team in the first place.

We were in control and the liveliness our opponents generated at the start of the second half, after the arrival of big Duncan Ferguson as a substitute, was brief. It was quelled by our second goal. Solskjaer won the ball from Nikos Dabizas and passed to Sheringham, who returned the favour Scholes had done him earlier by producing a delicate lay-off that encouraged the little red-head to score with a low shot from eighteen yards. Paul was certainly having better compensation for missing the European Cup final than Roy Keane had been allowed. Our superiority should have brought more goals but I was content to tell myself that we might be saving them for Bayern Munich. I used the latter part of the hour and a half to let Stam and Yorke have just long enough on the park to be sharpened but not tired. The entire day had gone well and winning our third double in six years was a cause for celebration. There was some, but hardly any alcohol was consumed and by 1.30 a.m. the players had decided, without any pressure from me, that it was time for bed. They didn't have to be told that history-makers shouldn't have hangovers.

On the Sunday we moved out of London to the quiet of the Buckinghamshire countryside and in the afternoon we had a training session at Bisham Abbey. The players looked astonishingly fresh, further proof of how splendidly they had coped with a crowded programme of fixtures in which virtually every match was momentous. After dinner that night, they were shown a video of our two Champions League games against Bayern Munich, with the most relevant passages condensed into a forty-minute edition. That was the only video they were going to see. A mass of film evidence, like a bombardment of tactical theory, can be more confusing than enlightening. My thoughts about the team we should field in Barcelona were clear but I had a dilemma concerning the deployment of Beckham and Giggs. Ever since the suspensions incurred against Juventus in Turin had made Keane and Scholes unavailable, I had been contemplating the use of Giggs in centre-midfield, where his speed and penetration would be a handful for the Germans. But opting for Ryan's surging style in that area would mean surrendering an essential part of our game – the kind of controlled, sustained possession that calls for a player adept at holding the ball and spreading calculated and accurate passes. Once both Keane and Scholes were out of the picture, Beckham was the best bet to meet those requirements and his tremendous showing in the FA Cup final left no doubt about his eagerness to shine in his favourite position. The downside of allocating it to him was that we would miss his devastating crosses from the right wing.

Positives and negatives were finely balanced in the debate on how to play Beckham and Giggs, but I was swayed by the recognition that a high standard of passing in central midfield was the core of United's football. I also felt that if I played Ryan on the right wing, his pace could give Michael Tarnat, Bayern's left-side defender, problems quite different from those he had been anticipating from David. With Beckham in midfield and Giggs on the right, I could play Blomqvist on the left. That would assure me of the width in our attacking which I saw as indispensable against opponents so afraid of that quality that they had lobbied successfully to have the Nou Camp pitch narrowed for the match.

The thoroughness of the preparation for Manchester United's biggest challenge in more than three decades was indicated by the staff we took to Spain. We tried to leave nothing to chance, even flying in our chef from Old Trafford, Jesper Jesperson, and our nutritionist, Trevor Lea. On the medical side, we had our doctor, Mike Stone, two of our main physios, David Fevre and Robert Swire, and Jimmy Curran for massages. There were two kit men, Albert Morgan and Alec Wylie, and two stalwarts from the club's administrative office. Club secretary Ken Merrett handled the organisational side of the trip and made sure that Steve McClaren, Jimmy Ryan and I were never distracted from our work with the squad. His assistant, Ken Ramsden, was there as usual to organise the media side of things. Our hotel, overlooking the sea at Sitges, was ideal. It had more amenities than we had the leisure to use, locked as we were in the private world of the travelling football team. The favoured gathering place, as always, was the physios' treatment room and when a bunch of us assembled there it seemed the atmosphere of our Cliff training complex at home had been shipped intact to Sitges. There was the familiar good-natured savaging of Albert Morgan, the only Manchester-born member of the backroom staff and a rabid fan who just happens to be an employee. He is a star at lightening the players' mood, and mine too if necessary. I was excited rather than apprehensive as the showdown drew near and I was glad when the quiet hours of playing the game through in my head gave way to the noisy, colourful reality at the Nou Camp. As I suggested at the beginning of this book, Bayern were pretty much as I expected them to be. They were strong and well organised and those attributes doubled in value once they had scored in the sixth minute.

When Mario Basler prepared to take a free kick and Markus Babbel set about blocking out Nicky Butt on the end of our defensive wall, I was itching to run on to the field and stop Nicky from falling for the ploy. But I was helpless as a gap was created and so was Peter Schmeichel when Basler swept his shot into our net. Edginess had something to do with our early vulnerability and with the fact that we never at any stage reached the heights of fluent, penetrative football that demoralised Juventus on their own ground in the semi-final. Our lads are used to important occasions but a European Cup final was another dimension for them, especially with the weight of their club's history and all the feverish speculation about the treble loaded on their shoulders. I thought Dwight Yorke, who may be as talented a front player as there is in the game today, looked more nervous than I had ever previously seen him. It did not help, of course, that he was opposed by a brilliant marker, Thomas Linke. The man marking Andy Cole, Samuel Kuffour, was even more impressive and to my mind Bayern's outstanding player in the final. The most prolific scoring partnership in the Premier League was subdued on the night and our superior possession went unrewarded for ninety minutes.

If, however, there was frustration in all that for us and for our admirers, it did not come close to justifying some of the critical interpretations of our performance that were printed afterwards.

The truth is that we were much the more convincing team for the bulk of the hour and a half, and we were infinitely the more ambitious. After their goal went in, Bayern settled for a negative policy of containment. Even when we over-committed ourselves in the search for an equaliser and left openings for counter-attacks that permitted them to hit our woodwork twice, they could not find the self-belief to come out and attempt to outplay us. We had to make every yard of the running. Bayern Munich tried to back into the winner's enclosure. Those observers who thought they were in smooth, sophisticated control were imagining things. Martin Edwards told me later that the great Franz Beckenbauer, the Bayern president, had watched the game in the agitated state of somebody who feared his team were going to lose. Beckenbauer said afterwards that we deserved to win. He wasn't wrong.

Unlike many reporters, I was happy with my decision to use Beckham in central midfield and Giggs on the right. Anybody who doesn't think Beckham was the most effective midfielder on the park was taking a strange view of the action. By comparison, Stefan Effenberg was anonymous. The suggestion that Giggs had little impact is hard to square with the frequent demands for back-up that Tarnat directed at his bench. The strain Ryan put on the opposition was one of the factors that steadily drained them in the second half. We had so much of the ball that their strategy of protecting their flimsy lead became an exhausting one and by the end several of them were almost out on their feet. Teddy Sheringham, who had replaced Blomqvist with twenty-three minutes to go, was giving them particular trouble with shrewd runs on our left. But, naturally, when ninety minutes had been played I had to start practising to be a good loser. I was out on the touchline when the fourth official displayed his electronic board signalling that there would be three minutes of stoppage time and I was still out there when we won a corner on the left. Then I caught a flash of the mad Dane hurtling upfield and into the Bayern box. 'What the hell is he doing?' I said to Steve McClaren, but I suppose you couldn't fault Peter. After all, there were only two minutes remaining in his last game for United –

he probably expected to score. He distracted the Bayern defenders as Beckham's corner came over and one of them let the ball glance off his head. It landed beyond the back post, from where Yorke headed it goalwards but only to Thorsten Fink, who had come on for Lothar Matthaus ten minutes earlier. Had Matthaus received that ball, he might have carried it calmly out of the area. Fink made a panicky effort at a clearance and mishit it straight to Giggs. Ryan, on the edge of the box, swung his right foot with more hope than accuracy. His shot screwed away towards the left-hand post but it was our next piece of good fortune that Teddy was lurking in its path. He spun as the ball came past him and deftly added to its momentum, tucking a skilful shot just inside the upright. As madness erupted around the stadium, I would have bet long odds-on that the Cup was ours. The Bayern players looked like people staggering away from a plane crash. Steve McClaren pounced on the practicalities.

'Now let's get ourselves organised for extra time,' he said. 'Go back to four-four-two.' Just as the words had left his mouth, the ball dropped to Denis Irwin in the middle of our half and I said, 'Steve, this game isn't finished.' Denis hit a long ball up towards the corner flag on the left and Ole Gunnar chased it down. When another corner was won, there was almost a feeling of inevitability about what we were seeing, as Bayern wearily tried to regroup. Beckham delivered one of his specials to the near post, where Sheringham was arriving, having made a late run. His header wasn't much more than a touch but it steered the ball into the heart of the six-yard box and there was Solskjaer's jutting leg to do the rest.

The celebrations begun by that goal will never really stop. Just thinking about it can put me in a party mood. At the time, all of us associated with the team were blissfully demented. Gary Newbon tried to interview me for television and, I am sure, got a flood of gibberish for his pains. I didn't mind sounding like an idiot. There was no happier idiot on the planet.

Ryan Giggs was the first player to rush towards me. We go back a long way, to that day when I first saw him as a thirteen-year-old, floating over the turf of our training ground with the unmistakable aura of a boy who was born to play football. Now, at twenty-five, he is the longest-serving player at Old Trafford, a reminder to me that I have spent half of my twenty-five years as a manager in the service of Manchester United. Martin Edwards is the only one of those currently prominent at the club who was there when I arrived.

The chairman and I have got on well much of the time but in recent years there have been serious strains in the relationship and always the disharmony has developed over money. There have been difficulties about what I thought should be spent to secure great players for United and about my own wages. I feel I should have received a better salary over my period at United than was forthcoming from Martin, who is extremely guarded with money. He kept out of the negotiations on my latest contract and I found that dealing with Professor Sir Roland Smith and Maurice Watkins was a quicker and less contentious process. Like Sir Bobby Charlton, Maurice and Sir Roland have done much to ease me through the occasional rough passage I have had at Old Trafford. I appreciate that life at United has changed drastically since the advent of the PLC and that Martin Edwards has a difficult job. The new set-up has sadly reduced communication between us. Gone are the days when we maintained a constant, healthy dialogue. No manager could have had better treatment than I have had from my chairman when it comes to running the playing side of the club. He has never interfered in the slightest with my decisions about the players. His support of my youth policy has been total. For that, and for his unceasing efforts to upgrade the stadium, the fans have reason to thank him.

Many, but by no means all, bitterly disapproved of the plans for a takeover of Manchester United by BSkyB but government intervention has killed the proposals, so the dispute is academic now. My own feeling is that the club is too important as a sporting institution, too much of a rarity, to be put up for sale. I think United should be pressing ahead to become the greatest power in world football. One change that must be accepted to make that possible is in the system for paying our footballers. Star players must be paid more than other players. All should be paid their worth but it is unrealistic to suggest that all should be paid the same.

Until my dying day, I shall be grateful to Manchester United for all that my association with the club has given me. For somebody who loves football as much as I do, there is no better place to be. When I learned during the summer that I was to receive a knighthood, I had to smile at the thought of how far football had brought me since the time in my Govan childhood when I had to wait for a neighbour to give me a pair of hand-me-down boots before I could turn out for the street team. I am thrilled about the knighthood but I hope it can be seen as honouring my family and my friends and everybody who ever worked with me. In particular, I hope it can be seen as honouring Manchester United and all the people, from great players to canteen ladies, who have helped me there over the years.

I relate to ambitious individuals but I appreciate that in millions of lives talk of ambition is an insulting irrelevance. Sometimes I joke about recognising people's natures in their choice of ideal holidays. Some want to go to Blackpool, others to Spain and some want to go to the moon. I tell myself I identify with that last group. Then I remember the people I was raised among. The great holiday adventure of my childhood was to go to Saltcoats on the Ayrshire coast for the Glasgow Fair fortnight. As I mentioned early in my story, some families in Govan couldn't afford even that and would go to the local Elder Park or Bellahouston Park in order to be surrounded by a little greenery. For the men, it was respite enough to be spared the noise and grime of the shipyards for a couple of weeks, to escape the hammer of the Clyde. Ambition had nothing to do with their lives. Survival was the essence. Yet there was an incredible warmth of fellow feeling among them, a loyalty that was deep as the marrow. I wish I could revisit, however briefly, the sense of community that existed in the Govan of my childhood. It could be a rough world but there were wonderful values at the heart of it. Loyalty has been the anchor of my life and it is something that I learned in Govan.

— 26 —
THE WORLD TO PLAY FOR

In the summer of 2000 there is nothing in my story to be changed but much to be added.

Before the last champagne bubble had popped at our Barcelona celebrations, some people were ready to point out that my competitive edge was sure to be terminally blunted by winning the treble. Now that the European Cup had at last been added to the list of trophies won, I would, according to a few sports page psychologists, find it impossible to drive myself and my teams quite as hard as I had done in the past. Nobody went as far as implying that I would settle for cruising towards retirement but there were suggestions that, at the age of fifty-seven and after such a rewarding season, I was bound to ease off the throttle.

Perhaps that thinking was not unreasonable but it was totally out of touch with how I was feeling in the aftermath of United's unforgettable night at the Nou Camp. Although I recognised the treble as a marvellous peak in my football life, a triumph to be deeply enjoyed at the time and cherished forever, I never for a moment saw it as the final summit. Maybe a couple of years on, when I have left the manager's chair at Old Trafford, I'll be obliged to look back on the spring and early summer of 1999 as the period of maximum achievement in my career, but it would be a contradiction of my nature to have that perspective now. The urge to compete and to win is not something I can switch on and off. It seems as natural to me as breathing, and I can't imagine that it will ever wane. Obviously, I am liable to be wrong about that. Age gets to everybody eventually. However, I honestly don't think it is showing any signs of getting to me so far. So I wasn't just making the noises I thought were expected of me when I said that the treble could be used as a platform to launch United to even greater heights. That's how I felt in my bones. Having won the European Cup, why shouldn't we win it again, and again? Having made ourselves club champions of our own continent, why shouldn't we set out to be champions of the world?

We were, of course, going to have an opportunity to fulfil the second of those ambitions. Our victory over Bayern Munich in Barcelona had qualified us to meet Palmeiras of São Paulo (who had just proved themselves South America's best) in the World Club Championship in Tokyo at the end of November. But the six months between the European Cup final and our date with the Brazilians in Japan would turn out to be eventful for me and for United. They brought me some wonderfully happy experiences but there was sadness, too, mainly produced by the serious injuries that afflicted a number of my players.

There was, naturally, no way of knowing the scale of the problems up ahead as I lay by a swimming pool in the south of France during my summer holiday, and I felt entitled to wallow in blissful relaxation. Admittedly, emptying my head of football was difficult. Whenever I closed my eyes I kept seeing Ole Gunnar Solskjaer scoring that goal. Reliving the moment at leisure in my mind was all the more pleasurable because I had been given so little time to savour the details of the incredible climax in Spain. I thought of how different it was for Fabio Capello when he was coach of the Milan team that overwhelmed Barcelona to take the European Cup in Athens in 1994. Imagine the well-earned pride and satisfaction he must have felt when they were leading 4–0 with thirty minutes left and he could stand there and let the glory of their magnificent performance wash over him. I had about thirty seconds to comprehend that we had actually won the prize we had been pursuing for so long. I would just love to win that trophy again and to be in a position to savour the joys of winning for the last ten minutes or so. Down on the Riviera, I was every inch the carefree holidaymaker but the old hunger was only on hold. Retirement before 2002 never struck me as an option worth considering.

It was while on holiday that I learned I had been chosen to receive a knighthood. The news caused me to do much thinking about how far I had travelled in life and to wonder if I deserved the honour. My wife, I must say, was not in favour of becoming Lady Cathy. She values her privacy and is always happiest when in the midst of her family and close friends. Involvement in the public dimension of my work has never appealed to her and she was worried about the extra burdens the knighthood might create for her. When important issues have to be debated in the Ferguson household, we make sure all members of the family take part and on this occasion Cathy was completely overruled by our three sons. Mark, Jason and Darren were adamant that I should accept the honour with gratitude.

One of the immediate implications was that I had to miss United's pre-season tour of Australia, Shanghai and Hong Kong. That was a landmark trip, the longest and most arduous the club had ever undertaken in preparation for the domestic programme. While the players and my senior staff were trying to decide whether the expedition was more exciting than it was exhausting, I was concentrating on my special appointment at Buckingham Palace. What a perfect day 14 July 1999 was for the Fergusons. After the thrill of the ceremony at the Palace – no, the Queen didn't offer any suggestions about players I should buy – we went to the Savoy Hotel for a family lunch in the famous Pinafore Room. In a setting often used over many years for gatherings of movers and shakers in the world of politics (a tradition initiated by Sir Winston Churchill), we were given regal treatment. That lunch was always certain to be exceptional, since it had been set up by my friend Mike Dillon of Ladbrokes, who is an organiser's organiser, and was flawlessly supervised by the Savoy's excellent general manager, Michael Shepherd. A nice little bonus was added to our enjoyment when a horse of mine, Ninety Degrees, won at Yarmouth. Throughout the rest of the day it would have been possible to detect hints of celebration in our suite at the hotel.

By the time work was back on the agenda and the new season was under way, Mark Bosnich had arrived from Aston Villa to replace Peter Schmeichel in United's goal. There were several reasons for believing that Mark was a good choice. He had grown up at our club as an apprentice and was therefore familiar with our ways. He had turned twenty-seven in the previous January, so was at just the right age to be assuming the huge responsibility of succeeding the great Schmeichel, who had joined us as a twenty-seven-year-old in 1991. Mark had the reassuring advantage of having played in the Premiership with Villa for a good number of years, which guaranteed that his proven talent was backed by the right level of experience. We were satisfied that we would continue to be well served between the posts. It was elsewhere that the signs were gloomy. Ronny Johnsen was about to have surgery that would keep him out of football for most of the season. That was a cruel blow for the Norwegian lad, who had proved to be a tremendous acquisition for the club and had established himself as the ideal partner for Jaap Stam.

Soon there were to be equally alarming developments concerning another of our Scandinavians, Jesper Blomqvist. The Swede's troubles shocked us out of the sense of well-being that existed in the squad at the end of the tour to Australia and the Far East. Pre-season activities have to be demanding if they are going to restore the players' fitness to the required level and there is inevitably anxiety over the danger that they will collect injuries in the process. For a few days after the completion of that particularly hard tour, we thought we had survived it without any ill-effects. Then Jesper reported to our physio, Rob Swires, complaining of pain in a knee. Internal examination indicated that the knee would have to be cleaned out. The diagnosis was disappointing and frustrating, since I was convinced that Jesper was going to be a significant player for us, one whose self-belief would be strengthened by having earned a European Cup-winner's medal. Barcelona, I felt, was just the boost this shy young man had needed. What he definitely didn't need was the next report on his condition. It was discovered that his problems were far too serious to yield to anything as straightforward as a cleaning-out procedure. He would be inactive for the entire season.

Before long the doctors were delivering further depressing bulletins, leaving a dent in our defensive resources. Wes Brown, our really promising centre-back, suffered a bad cruciate ligament injury that condemned him, too, to a season's absence. Then David May had to endure a painful series of mishaps. First, in a friendly against Wigan, he fell awkwardly and damaged his knee. No sooner was he on the mend than he injured a hamstring, and worse was to follow when he ruptured an Achilles tendon. It would be difficult to find an unluckier footballer than David. His misfortune was a reminder that however destructive injuries may be to the playing prospects of a club, their most devastating effects are on the individuals concerned. Reflecting on the sad predicament of those four lads, I found myself recalling that the last competitive match in which they had participated was the final in Barcelona. Ronny and Jesper played, of course, and David and Wes were substitutes. Nobody has to tell *them* that there is always a thin line separating the good times and the bad in football.

The worries plaguing our start to the 1999–2000 league campaign were increased by evidence that Mark Bosnich's fitness was not what it should be. It was put to him firmly that he would have to lose weight and, to be fair, he buckled down to give the necessary response. But I was not prepared to risk lacking cover for the goalkeeper position and our efforts to provide it were accelerated when Mark pulled a hamstring muscle. We believed we had found the answer in Massimo Taibi. Massimo had been watched a few times by my brother Martin and, although he wasn't in the absolutely top bracket of goalkeepers in Italy, Martin was confident he could do well for us. So a deal was quickly concluded with Venezia at our hotel in Monaco prior to United's Super Cup match against Lazio in late August.

Critics of our performance in that game may feel that we were more interested in the transfer than in the contest that pits the holders of the European Cup against the team successful in the Cup Winners' Cup. Our position, as I have stated repeatedly, is that we want to win every match we play. But crowded fixture lists force managers to identify priorities and, with a programme that was committing us to four games within nine days, I had no hesitation in facing Lazio with something less than our strongest team. Losing 1–0 to the Italians was a genuine disappointment but it was made more bearable by the fact that we won all three of the Premiership fixtures that were crammed into that hectic sequence. The first of them was a 2–1 victory at Highbury, which was a result that amounted to a declaration of intent in relation to our defence of the title.

What happened to Massimo Taibi while he was with us emphasised once again how dramatically a player's form can be affected by joining United. Some arrivals are instantly uplifted by the charged atmosphere that pervades the club. They are stimulated by the pressure that comes from a combination of past achievements and current expectations. But others seem from the outset to be doomed to fail in our ranks. Sometimes they are undermined by a spectacular blunder or two and find themselves on a downward spiral from which they cannot recover. That is how it was with Taibi. Yet the early indications were encouraging. He did make a bad mistake in his debut match at Anfield, getting caught under a deep cross and losing a soft goal, but I was impressed by how he shrugged off the error and went on to excel in the second half. Such a demonstration of resilience, from a man with a strong and engaging personality, justified hopes that he might ultimately be a success story at Old Trafford. Instead, his plight worsened rapidly. In a 3–3 draw with Southampton, he suffered a moment of embarrassment so extreme that it will figure for years to come in TV compilations of goalkeeping howlers. Letting the tamest of shots squirm first through his arms and then through his legs and on into the net was the kind of gaffe that was likely to breed self-doubt in his mind. Any chance he had of overcoming that uncertainty, and rediscovering his confidence sufficiently to show his true abilities in our colours, disappeared a week later at Stamford Bridge. Our Premiership game with Chelsea had hardly begun when he came flying wildly off his line and missed the ball completely, allowing Gus Poyet to head in a ludicrously simple goal that put our London opponents in the mood to give us a hiding. It was clear by then that our association with Massimo was not in the interests of either party and shortly afterwards he was back in Italy, seeking to rebuild his morale in familiar surroundings.

When we were on the wrong end of that 5–0 rout at the Bridge on the first Sunday of October 1999 we were maintaining our strange and (for me) rather disturbing habit of punctuating the generally impressive pattern of our results with occasional disasters. United don't go in for half-measures, whether winning or losing. A few of the batterings we have taken have been historic. As is mentioned earlier in this book, there was a single week of October 1996 that brought us a 5–0 defeat at Newcastle and a 6–3 drubbing at Southampton. And we followed those two beauties with a 2–1 loss to Chelsea at Old Trafford. We soon steadied ourselves, however, and went on to win the championship. So anybody who read far-reaching omens into that 5–0 beating by Chelsea should have had his head examined.

Of course, a lively reaction to the scoreline was inevitable, especially in the light of comments I offered when interviewed on Sky TV before the kick-off. I was asked what I thought of our main challengers in the title race: Leeds, Chelsea, Arsenal and Liverpool. The point I made about Chelsea was that they remained much the same team as they were when finishing behind us the previous season. They had added Chris Sutton to their squad but I couldn't see that changing them conspicuously. Sutton or Tore Andre Flo with Gianfranco Zola at the front – take your pick. Presumably, Chelsea people regarded my assessment of their championship prospects as unjust and, once United had been buried under five goals, it was probably natural that they should want to have a go at me. Gianluca Vialli, a young manager for whom I have the utmost respect, raised doubts about our capabilities but, not surprisingly, it was Ken Bates who decided that the day's result had given him limitless gloating rights. Has any chairman since Mao had more faith in his own opinions than

Ken has? If laying down the law were an Olympic sport, he would be staggering under the weight of gold medals. I don't suppose he'll ever change. Just about everybody in the game has had to take the sharp end of his tongue or had to put up with being a target for the aggression he pours into his writings in the club programme and his regular column in a Sunday tabloid. Any manager or player who said half as much would never be out of Lancaster Gate. The truth about that one-sided match at Stamford Bridge is that it did us more good than it did Chelsea. Whereas their Premier League challenge collapsed, we took the lesson well and wasted little time in putting our pursuit of another title back on course. My assertion last October that Chelsea were the same team as they had been the previous season was slightly inaccurate. In 1999 they finished third in the table. In 2000 they were fifth.

Our form early in the season was erratic. Three weeks after being hammered by Chelsea, we were beaten 3–1 by Tottenham at White Hart Lane. Yet what should have been our toughest assignment in London, the earlier trip to Arsenal, had produced a victory loaded with significance. It was no surprise that Highbury was bathed in August sunshine for the match. Every time we go there we seem to encounter a baking-hot day. Over the first twenty-five minutes we played very well and should have been in front but Arsenal were always likely to be encouraged by our failure to take our chances and they duly took control of the latter part of the first half. Now it was their turn to create openings and they were particularly dangerous when we gave away free kicks and permitted our concentration to lapse. We paid the price just before the interval when imaginative and skilful attacking play led to an excellent goal by Frederik Ljungberg. At half-time, I stressed the need to maintain concentration, especially at set-pieces, and urged my players to exploit the vulnerability I detected on the left side of Arsenal's defence, where they were weakened by the absence of the injured Tony Adams. I must admit that nothing I said had an immediate impact on the second half. Arsenal continued to dominate and they should have scored a second goal.

But the chance that followed a free kick fell to a young defender, Matthew Upson, and he missed the target with his header. We all recognise how a goal can transform a match and a perfect illustration of the old truth was provided at Highbury that day. In one of our better forays into the opposition's territory, Roy Keane reminded everybody that his wide range of talents includes the capacity to be a deadly finisher, and suddenly United had rid themselves of any thought of losing the game and were going for the throat. It was another forward surge by Keane that proved decisive. Again he worked a quick, penetrative one-two and again he put the ball away with brilliant economy. Unfortunately, the Irishman was prominent for other reasons before the afternoon was over. The closing minutes were marred by a squaring-up incident involving Keane and Patrick Vieira and both men had cause to be grateful for the common-sense reaction of the referee, Graham Poll. I think many people were surprised when Poll's superiors censured him for not being strict enough.

Passion is guaranteed when Liverpool and Manchester United collide and the noise alone might be sufficient to unnerve newcomers to the feverish atmosphere generated by the two northern giants of English football. So I was asking a lot of Massimo Taibi and Mikael Silvestre when I decided that their first appearances for United should be in the league match at Anfield on 11 September 1999. Young Mikael, who had joined us from Inter Milan, knew in advance that he would have an especially hot reception. His quickness and good touch on the ball had attracted an offer from Liverpool but the French defender had preferred to come to us, and the Scousers could be relied upon to let him know what they thought of that decision. I thought he coped with the strains of the occasion magnificently. Massimo, as I have already recorded, had a mixed game, but a string of fine saves in the second half ensured that he was well in credit by the end. For our outfield players, the first half was a golden period in which the fluency and inventiveness of our attacks repeatedly opened up Liverpool's defence. Strangely, we required the help of two own-goals (along with a scoring strike by Andy Cole) to give us the comfortable lead we deserved. In the second half, Liverpool changed their tactics, opting to play with three centre-backs and deploying their aggressive right-back, Rigobert Song, to mark Cole. Song implemented his instructions too literally for our man's taste and when Andy retaliated rather wildly he was ordered off. The remainder of the match was a real battle, with the tension mounting after our opponents tightened the scoreline to 3–2 in our favour, but the ten men held out stubbornly to secure a vital win.

My satisfaction with those away successes against Arsenal and Liverpool was tempered by the subsequent inconsistency in our form and, as our Tokyo confrontation with Palmeiras approached, I was determined to drive out the slackness that had been creeping into our performances. I viewed that clash of continental champions as one of the most important tests I had faced as a manager. Some English clubs who qualified to take part in the past were apparently disinclined to give the match one hundred per cent commitment but for years it had been one of my inner desires to have a team in the World Club Championship. To my mind, it was a valid test of our status in the global game and I intended to make sure that we took the opportunity to show our quality. At the same time, I couldn't afford to blind myself to the reality that our big effort in Japan had to be fitted into the relentless demands of our domestic season.

Travel arrangements had to be planned with immense care. The aim was not only to deliver the players on to the field in Tokyo on Tuesday 30 November with enough physical and mental freshness to do themselves justice but to give them the best possible chance of recovering their vigour for the Premiership meeting with Everton at Old Trafford on the following Saturday. Given that we had a Champions League fixture in Florence on 23 November, and would have to take the squad back to Manchester after that to check on injuries and ease tiredness with a little light training, the earliest we could leave for the Far East was the morning of Friday 26 November. The big question was whether it would be better to go then or to delay our departure until the last possible moment, which some saw as a means of minimising the effects of jet-lag. I was utterly against that second option and my opposition was reinforced when I heard that Stuart Webb, who organised the trip for Nottingham Forest when they lost 1–0 to Naçional of Uruguay in 1981, said that arriving late had been a disaster. Having sounded the opinions of Ottmar Hitzfeld, Marcello Lippi and Louis van Gaal, outstanding coaches with experience of the problem, I was convinced that we should head for Japan as soon as we could. The decision scarcely gave us an advantage. When we reached Tokyo, we learned that our opponents had already been there for ten days. It was plain that they were deadly serious about our meeting. That wasn't a shock. When did Brazilians ever have any other attitude to football? They are the standard-bearers for us all. The great names that are threaded through the history of the game in their country ring in the imagination of everybody who loves football. Their abbreviated form seems to increase the magic: Didi, Vava, Pele, Garrincha, Gerson, Rivelino – the list goes on and on, with the tradition of brilliance sustained in the present era by such as Ronaldo, Romario and Rivaldo.

The proof that Palmeiras were revving up for a real cup final put a further edge on my thoughts about the match. There would be no fudging the issues here. I wanted to win this, and we were going to have to apply maximum care to team selection and tactics. I was fascinated by the challenge and I think it is worth dwelling on the details of how we coped with opponents who were to present us with quite a conundrum on the pitch. Steve McClaren had brought along a few videos of the Brazilians' recent games and my staff and I studied these avidly. Once we had picked the match we felt would give the best idea of how Palmeiras would play against us, we showed it to the players.

In simple terms, they operated a 4-4-2 system, which is not unusual in Brazilian football. But their application of it was not at all orthodox. They did not ask their midfield to provide the team with width. In fact, their standard formation could be more accurately represented as 4-2-2-2, with one pair of central midfielders deep in front of the back four and another pair pushed up behind the two strikers. They relied for width on their attack-minded full-backs, Arce on the right and Roque Junior on the left, and when allowed to function freely their system was difficult to counter. We decided that we would play with one central striker and two wide attackers, David Beckham and Ryan Giggs, confident that by doing so we would confront their full-backs with a fundamental question: could they defend? I suspected that was not the strongest component of their game and, in any case, having Beckham and Giggs marauding in wide positions was an integral part of our most effective method of playing. I chose Solskjaer as the central striker because one of his greatest assets is his ability to play off the shoulder of a defender and I felt that with three central midfielders, Butt, Scholes and Keane, we would have plenty of support coming through for him. I believed, too, that there would be enough penetration in passing from Scholes and Keane in particular to give Ole Gunnar the ammunition he thrives on. But the essential element of our game-plan was the role of our wide players. Beckham and Giggs had to make sure they were forcing Arce and Roque Junior to defend. What we could not possibly foresee was that David and Ryan would have their task seriously complicated by a major deviation from the Palmeiras tactics we had seen on the videos.

All of the tapes indicated that our opponents' strikers concentrated their energies exclusively on creating a central threat. When the contest was under way, it was a jolt to say the least to find that they were frequently foraging out wide, almost on top of our full-backs, Gary Neville and Denis Irwin. Of course, good teams are always capable of varying their tactics but this was a pretty basic change and there is no denying that it caused us huge problems. With Neville and Irwin tied down by the strikers, Beckham and Giggs had to defend like extra full-backs as Arce and Roque Junior came storming along the flanks. Our pre-match script was in tatters and there wasn't a lot we could do about it until half-time. We tried to communicate instructions before then but were too far from the touchline to be heard. I was in torture during most of those first forty-five minutes as Palmeiras made a string of chances. Only a sterling display of goalkeeping by Mark Bosnich kept the match from swinging away from us.

However, as if to remind us that our original ideas on how to hurt the opposition had been valid, in one of our rare counter-attacks Giggs got behind their right-back and delivered a cross that tempted their goalkeeper to come for it. When Marcos could manage no more than a feeble, flapping attempt at interception, Keane was left with a tap-in and we emerged from the half with a lead that was distinctly flattering.

Drastic action had to be taken at the interval. In the first half we had looked for our three in midfield to give us control of that vital area but we had found that most of the possession was in our own half and, with our wide players so far back defending, Solskjaer had become isolated. My priority was to devise a way of achieving the original objective of exerting pressure on the Palmeiras full-backs and to that end I replaced Ole Gunnar with Dwight Yorke. Dwight has few peers when it comes to holding up the ball and acting as a forward link-man. His influence allowed Beckham and Giggs to move without the ball into advanced attacking positions and soon we were looking at a totally different match. Now Palmeiras were having to turn and defend. Our pass-ing up to Dwight was good. The support from midfield was undermining their system and Giggs especially was exploiting the weakness we had diagnosed before the kick-off. Ryan had an outstanding second half and helped us to establish some domi-nation of the game and to create a lot of chances. We finished strongly in a match that epitomised the positive beliefs central to two remarkable football traditions. I have always seen Manchester United as having an affinity with the Brazilian way of playing, with the emphasis on flair and the willingness to take risks. I cannot exaggerate how delighted I was to win in Tokyo. That result ranks with the most satisfying I have been able to accomplish.

The pleasure was completed by the agreeable exchanges I had after the final whistle with the Palmeiras coach, Luis Felipe

Scolari, who is known to English-speaking journalists in Brazil as Big Phil. I had read a lot of stuff about Scolari's wild-boy reputation and one or two papers had suggested that I was about to meet my Waterloo. The gist of the stories was that this guy doesn't mess about – he just thumps you and argues later, or sees you in court. I was sure that meeting such a passionate man would be memorable and so it was, but mainly because of his perfect manners. He was extremely gracious to me and I consoled him with a reminder that none of us in football can ever forget the part that luck plays in what we do. He nodded, smiling, and walked away to commiserate with players who had certainly not let him down.

The Brazilian pressmen who covered the event were surprised that we didn't celebrate as their countrymen would have done if the 1–0 scoreline had been reversed. They would have had a bit of a carnival, whereas we settled for a champagne reception for the troops and the directors back at our hotel. That was a quiet sort of occasion but it wasn't hard to sense the depth of contentment over a big job well done. My staff, led by Steve McClaren, had shared my assessment of the importance of the World Club Championship and were as proud as I was of what the players had achieved. Everybody, from our irrepressible kit-man Albert Morgan to the physio and medical staff, had made a valuable contribution but nobody was more entitled to a glow of delight than our senior coach, Tony Coton. Tony works very hard with all the goalkeepers and he rightly took enormous satisfaction in Mark Bosnich's performance. For me, a wonderful night was capped by the arrival of an old friend from Scotland, Eddie Thomson, who used to be coach with Australia and was by then working in Japan. It was marvellous to have Eddie and his wife joining in on our party, even if, like a true Scot, he mixed congratulations with a swing of the verbal boot. Eddie maintains I was the dirtiest player he ever met on the field. I merely point out that I had to defend myself against such a murderous thug.

In every way, Tokyo was a tremendous experience, and one that impressed on all of us who travelled out from England just how swiftly and dramatically football is changing. Who would have dreamt two or three decades back that the Japanese would take so passionately to the game? And they bring a lot to it, not least the gift for organisation that made everything about our visit run smoothly and enabled them to stage the match without a trace of bother. I'll be astonished if they don't make a notable success of their part in the World Cup finals of 2002. They have already demonstrated that they can promote mammoth events in other sports. The Olympics of 1964 proved that and so, year after year, does one of the jewels of international horse racing, the Japan Cup.

It's nothing but an ugly rumour that I arranged for the Palmeiras match to occur in the same week as the Japan Cup. But I admit that it was no hardship to take a Manchester United group to the track on the Sunday before the game to share with 150,000 others the excitement of one of the world's most glamorous races. My enjoyment was not diminished by the prospect of making a modest financial gain from the outing. I have a partnership in a horse called Chinatown with the famous Hong Kong trainer Ivan Allan and I was glad to be able to catch up with him in Tokyo and discuss our plans. Chinatown is trained at Newmarket by Sir Michael Stoute. Ivan treated me to an exquisite Japanese meal on the eve of the Cup race, and before we parted he insisted that I must back his horse, Indigenous, next day. 'It won't be out of the first three,' he assured me. I love that kind of confidence and went off to bed with a nice buzz of anticipation. When the United party reached the racecourse, we were lavishly received. We were bound to feel at home with so many people from Britain and Ireland around us. I hugely appreciated the hospitality of Michael and Doreen Tabor and of Sue Magnier and all the warmly welcoming Irish contingent. They do know how to have a good time, and how to spread the happiness around. As the big race neared, my loyalties were stretched. Michael Tabor owned the favourite, Montjeu, already a superb winner of the Prix de l'Arc de Triomphe, and he was undoubtedly the class horse of the field. But I couldn't neglect Ivan Allan's advice about Indigenous. I took the safest option by backing the two of them. It was a good decision. Ivan's horse ran second and paid 15–1 for a place. Unfortunately, Montjeu had travelled badly from France and he sweated up in the preliminaries and was slowly away from the starting gate. He was never moving with his usual fluency but his sheer quality and the assistance of the wizard on his back, Michael Kinane, enabled him to finish fourth, beaten little more than two lengths.

The many people who can't relate to racing would have difficulty appreciating what invaluable relaxation that day at the track provided for me amid the serious pressures of our trip to Japan. Those who raise their eyebrows at my interest in horses don't realise how much it has helped me to retain my drive in my football work. For twenty-two years I was utterly obsessed with the game and if I had continued to be as blinkered, my efficiency would definitely have been eroded. When you are in a job that makes severe daily demands on your nervous energy, you have to find a way of surviving the strains. During my worst days at United, in 1989, I developed the habit of slipping into a cocoon of private thoughts. That withdrawal technique was a godsend then, and I have used it ever since. I think it is now essential in management to cut yourself off from the hectic activity around you and create a quiet time for thinking, a period of isolation in which you can examine objectively all the facts that have to be considered and the decisions that have to be taken. Sometimes I retreat into myself while in discussion with my staff, and they have the impression that I am not listening to them, but part of my mind is recording what they are saying. If something important is said, I snap out of my reverie and make a response. But I know my habit of withdrawing to that private place can be disconcerting for those close to me. Cathy often says I am in another world, and I can't deny it.

In a completely different sense, racing takes me into another world. I get happily caught up in its excitements and dramas, and the involvement gives me precious release from the worries of my job. Every time I am at the course or on the gallops it is like a little holiday that restores my spirits and my vigour and makes me better able to deal with the problems my life in football throws at me. It would, however, have taken more than a few afternoons at the races to lift the gloom brought by the problem that was already assuming crisis proportions when we returned from Tokyo. Manchester United, the holders of the FA Cup, were not going to defend the trophy and a storm of protest and condemnation was gathering around Old Trafford. There were no prizes for guessing who would be the target for most of the criticism.

— 27 —
FLYING THE FLAG

The controversy over Manchester United's withdrawal from the FA Cup in 1999 was without question a catastrophe for the club, and it will be hard to repair the damage done to our reputation. But, on the basis of the facts as presented to me by our chairman, there was no realistic alternative to the action we took. The pressure applied to persuade us to compete in the international club tournament FIFA had decided to launch in Brazil during January 2000 was so intense that we were made to feel it was a patriotic duty to go to South America. Perhaps we should not have been surprised to find that the men from the Football Association and the Government who orchestrated that pressure somehow faded into the background and behaved like mere bystanders once the media fastened on to the issue and it became obvious that the absence of the trophy-holders from the oldest knock-out competition in football was being treated as a national scandal. All the quiet promises of official backing suddenly evaporated and we were left on our own as the convenient villains of the piece. None of those who had lobbied so relentlessly to put us on the plane for Rio did anything to dispel the impression fed to the public that we were defecting from the Cup to suit a private and selfish agenda. According to the popular interpretation of our motives, we were either acting out of greed (an accusation hardly justified by the financial facts of the transatlantic expedition) or we had simply become so arrogant that we felt free to trample on the traditions of the English game.

The truth is that I feel deeply about the FA Cup. The prospect of battling through a series of sudden-death showdowns to a climax at Wembley has always held a romantic appeal for me, and my attachment to the unique magic of the competition could only be increased after success in the 1990 final marked the turning point in my fortunes at Old Trafford. These days it pains me to witness a decline in the significance of the Cup and I would do everything in my power to arrest that process. The notion that I would willingly belittle the competition is crazy. I was desperately keen that United should figure as the defenders in 1999–2000. It was only after searching long and hard for a feasible compromise that I realised none was possible and accepted that we could not participate.

To the best of my knowledge, initially nobody at Manchester United was interested in going to Brazil. Then the chairman of the plc, Professor Sir Roland Smith, was invited to a meeting with the FA. The Minister for Sport at the time, Tony Banks, was also present and it was put to Sir Roland that if United did not take up the invitation to play in the Brazil tournament, Bayern Munich would be delighted to go in our place. He was left in no doubt that, with England and Germany pushing rival bids to secure host nation rights to the 2006 World Cup finals, the appearance of Bayern instead of us would have huge political implications. The so-called world club championship (a description more appropriate to our match with Palmeiras in Japan, considering that the contestants in Brazil included Necaxa from Mexico and South Melbourne from Australia) was a pioneering event that meant a lot to FIFA and the South Americans who were staging it. It was impressed upon United that seeming to snub the tournament could cost England enough votes to swing the World Cup issue in Germany's favour. That danger was emphasised to the club chairman, Martin Edwards, when he attended further meetings with the FA.

Co-operating with their grand strategy for 2006 was not a simple matter for us. We now knew that the fourth round of the FA Cup would occur while matches were being played in Brazil, and Martin Edwards left me to decide whether I was ready to contemplate facing such a domestic challenge with youth-team players. Under the ill-conceived revamping of the Cup schedule, the third round had been brought forward to 11 December and we could be reasonably optimistic about surviving that test, since we would still be three weeks away from departure for Rio and so able to field our strongest team. But would it be fair to ask young lads who were just learning the game to take over for the fourth round, when there was a major possibility of colliding with formidable opposition? After prolonged consultations with my staff, the conclusion was that the risk of causing long-term damage to those immature footballers was too serious. Suppose I had committed our youth team to fourth-round action and they had been drawn to meet Liverpool, Leeds, Arsenal or, maybe even worse, our neighbours Manchester City, away from home and had lost by a hatful of goals. Who can say what the consequences would have been for the lads who put that kind of humiliation into the history books, never to be erased?

While the controversy was gathering heat, the *Daily Mirror* was in the forefront of those fanning the flames and, in the hope of persuading the newspaper to adopt a more balanced attitude to our position, Martin Edwards agreed to meet with a senior representative of the organisation. The message Martin conveyed to me from that meeting was that if we played our youth team in the FA Cup the *Mirror* were prepared to change tack and campaign to get the country behind the lads. When my staff and I had looked at the problem from every angle, I told Martin I couldn't justify competing in the Cup with players who, in the vast majority of cases, didn't even have experience in the reserves. The chairman duly relayed that decision to the *Daily Mirror* editor, Piers Morgan. Whether it was because he felt it would be a sweetener or for some other reason, Martin opted to do a one-to-one interview for the paper. He came to regret his helpfulness when the *Mirror* subjected him to the worst kind of tabloid hounding during United's stay in Brazil. Immediately following the interview, however, Morgan and his men did switch their attention away from our chairman to make me the focus of their hostility. Now the whole mess was my fault. Their attacks were never likely to weaken my belief that I had arrived at the right decision. If we had gone the other way, what would the *Mirror*'s support have been worth? They might well have kept their word and backed our youth team, but how would the other tabloids have reacted to that? It would probably have made them more venomous than ever. In any case, I couldn't afford to be concerned with that stuff. I had to be governed solely by my assessment of what was best for the future of our young players. We have a heavy responsibility in relation to them and I think we discharged it honestly.

I have to say that I was disappointed by how the FA and the Government reacted, or failed to react, to the trouble their intervention stirred up around our heads. When the flak was flying, nothing was heard from the people who had done all that urgent lobbying. How could they distance themselves like that? They should have acknowledged their role in our withdrawal from the Cup. They should have owned up when we were under fire. I was enjoying my bloody holiday until they came on the scene with their master plan for promoting England's World Cup bid.

The Brazil trip itself was a mixed experience for us. As respite from the English winter, the couple of weeks in Rio had obvious benefits for the players and none of them could fail to be thrilled by the opportunity to perform at Maracana. But weather conditions in matches were extremely taxing and, off the field, Manchester United were criticised for being less accessible than the media would have liked. Naturally, the papers back home enjoyed telling their readers how the papers out there were giving us a hard time. The public relations difficulties we had, which were certainly not eased by the inexperience of the liaison officer appointed to work with us (there were days when I was expecting to give a press conference but found that no arrangements had been made), were supposed to be causing displeasure at the FA, FIFA and even the British Embassy. I think if any complaints had been conveyed to our party they would have been communicated to me, and I never heard a word. Clearly the press, British and local, weren't happy with us. Maybe there is nothing new in that but in this instance I must say that the lack of contact with me that annoyed them was largely due to inadequate organisation. Had I known that a daily press conference was expected of me, I would have complied.

In the midst of all this fuss, some journalists questioned my sincerity when I said that I loved being in Rio. But I meant what I said. I really enjoyed the place and would relish going back there. Not much of my enjoyment, I must admit, came from the action on the pitch, where United's contribution was disappointing. The tournament had very much the atmosphere of an inaugural event. A motley group of competitors had been assembled by invitation and there was little of the buzz and crackle of a major championship, nothing to equate with the stimulating tension I had felt when we confronted the South American champions, Palmeiras, in Japan. But I am not trying to use any of that as an excuse for our poor showing. We entered to win, not to make up the numbers, and our early dismissal was a blow to our pride.

We had the worst possible start when David Beckham was ordered off in our first match against Necaxa. Playing in a temperature of around 100 degrees Fahrenheit, and facing into the angled glare of the sun, we had gone a goal down to our Mexican opponents but were gradually taking their measure until Beckham's lunge at Jose Milian brought him a red card. Initially I thought David had been disorientated by finding the ball coming over his shoulder and had put his foot up to protect himself. But television pictures proved that he had made a bad challenge and deserved to be sent off. Our ten men fought well in the second half and Dwight Yorke, having missed a penalty, eventually produced an equaliser for us.

If being absent from our next game, against Vasco da Gama, was misery for the suspended Beckham, being involved in the game was absolute torture for poor Gary Neville. It was painful for me, too, as I watched Gary, a model professional and usually the most reliable of defenders, give the opposition's strikers a windfall midway through the first half with two misguided attempts to pass the ball back to Mark Bosnich in our goal. One error allowed Edmundo to pounce, draw Bosnich and then square the ball to let Romario put the Brazilians ahead, and two minutes later Gary chested the ball down into Romario's path and presented him with a second goal that was no more complicated than his first. A third, memorably brilliant goal by Edmundo shortly before half-time put the match hopelessly beyond our reach. To our credit, we battled against the inevitable after the interval and the scoreline was made marginally more respectable when Nicky Butt scored ten minutes from the end.

It may seem pointless, in the context of such an outcome, to mention the importance of losing the toss. But it was undoubtedly a massive advantage for Vasco to be defending the shadowed part of the field in the first half, when the blinding sun beating down on our area of the pitch was much more of a menace than it would be later. Necaxa had won the toss, too, and I have never known that simple bit of luck mean more in football matches than it did in the conditions at Maracana. Our defenders had a first half in the shade when it mattered least, in the match with South Melbourne that completed our Rio obligations. Having cruised to an academic victory, we headed back to Manchester and the familiar sound of Premiership rivals telling us that our defence of the title was being aided by preferential treatment.

From the moment it was announced that we wouldn't be participating in the FA Cup, there had been complaining noises from other clubs. To be fair, most of the grousing was short-lived. Only Arsenal complained repeatedly and vehemently throughout the season. The rest got on with their business once the decision was irrevocable, but not Arsenal or their manager, Arsene Wenger. The essence of their gripe was that the reduction in our domestic fixtures, and the restorative effects of two or three weeks in the sun, would give our players an unfair edge. I don't know where anybody dug up the idea that being spared FA Cup ties was such a big issue for us. Playing every round of the competition the previous season hadn't done us much harm. And let's just remind everyone that by the end of the 1999–2000 season the only Premier League team who had played more matches than United were Chelsea. Any implication that we were indulged and pampered as far as our fixture list was concerned is ludicrous. Ask anybody in football about the demands of flying halfway round the world to meet South America's best team in Tokyo on a Tuesday, then flying back next day to face a Premiership match on the Saturday. You can bet all our challengers were rubbing their hands over the likelihood that we would drop points. Instead, on that Saturday, we beat Everton 5–1. Now I concede that being abroad for a couple of weeks in January worked out in our favour, that the period involved may even have had a decisive impact on the title race, but the other contenders for the championship have only themselves to blame for that. If I had been in their position, I would have been making a supreme effort to pile up points, trying to establish a lead and ensure that the absentees had ground to make up when they returned. Far from doing that, our rivals stalled while we were away and the chance they squandered would never come again. It is true that our players had some useful poolside rest in Brazil but the trip also entailed exhausting flights and matches played in 100 degrees of heat, so the trip shouldn't be confused with a visit to a health farm.

The claim that it set us up to win the League was pure fantasy, though no wilder than a contention by Arsene Wenger that, in competing with United, Arsenal were seriously handicapped by having to play so many derby matches against teams also based in London. When I read that, I had to think it was some kind of joke. Throughout the game it is accepted that every other club in the country sets such store by getting a result against Manchester United that there is a derby atmosphere every time we take the field. But even if we apply a stricter definition of the term, is he actually suggesting that it has taken the recent promotion of Manchester City to put a derby back on our programme? How does he define United–Liverpool or United–Leeds? Come to that, on any scale of intensity, I reckon United–Everton might just hold its own with Arsenal–Wimbledon.

Arsene disappoints me when he seems reluctant to give us credit for what we have achieved, and I don't think his carping has made a good impression on the other Premiership managers. Anyone who looks at the 18-point gap that separated our two clubs by mid May must wonder why he still appears to doubt our worthiness as champions. When Arsenal captured the Double in 1998, I held my hands up and praised them unreservedly for the storming finish to the season that had pushed us aside and given them the glory. I could have dwelt on the damage done to our chances by our horrendous toll of injuries but I knew the hour belonged to Arsenal and, as is recorded earlier in this book, I saluted an exceptional team and their exceptional manager. I suppose I'll just have to accept that between Old Trafford and Highbury appreciation is pretty much a one-way street.

As it happens, Arsene Wenger is somebody I would like to get to know better. People who do know him well tell me he is a good man. But I don't suppose I'll ever find that out for myself. He seems to pull down the shutters when you meet up with him and never has a drink with you after a game. I was brought up in football to believe that, no matter how fierce competition is between clubs, the opposing managers should have the grace, win or lose, to have a drink and a chat when the dust has settled. We all hate to lose but there is a bond connecting us and we all tend to feel for any one of our number who is going through a bad time.

There is no more bitter rivalry in England than that of Liverpool and Manchester United and yet the atmosphere between the camps after a match is marvellous. Yes, Kenny Dalglish and I did have a serious spat once but that was a one-off – a case of two argumentative Scots going over the top. The exchanges that used to occur between Ronnie Moran and me were more typical of how our staff and theirs treat one another. Some of the arguments I had with that baldy headed old bugger (that's what I called him when I was being polite) were enough to make the dug-out catch fire. Of the rich variety of descriptions he attached to me, the only printable part was big-head. I had to respect a man whose passion for his club was boundless. Even as a coach on the sidelines, he fought for every ball at Anfield. And argue? You've never heard anything like it. But after the ball had been put away, there were smiles and the banter was terrific. I have the highest regard for Ron and the people like him who have made Liverpool such a great club.

At Leeds I am always giving them stick about the quality of red wine they serve but I recognise that it is the quality of the people working for the club that has brought a new, exciting era to Elland Road. Down at West Ham, it is a delight to be with Harry Redknapp. He is one of the most colourful of our managers and nobody could offer warmer hospitality. Men like the legendary Jim Smith at Derby make our game worthwhile and to be in his company is one of the pleasures of my job. I could go on listing individuals, for it is a simple fact that I enjoy the company of all the managers. That sociable chat when the action is over is one of the most attractive elements of a matchday. It is then that you get a feel for the character of your colleagues. I know it can never be made mandatory, but I wish it could.

Somewhere in the middle of the protracted commotion over our absence from the FA Cup, the newspapers found another justification for working Manchester United into a few provocative headlines. They were based on criticisms of me attributed to Martin Edwards but this particular story was so lacking in credibility that it was petering out almost as soon as it was launched. It had originated in a book written by Mihir Bose which contained claims that Martin had described me as being useless with money. Bose is usually defined as an investigative journalist but I would have to question the quality of his investigations. Martin wrote to me categorically denying that he had ever spoken to the man about me. The remarks quoted amounted to such blatant nonsense that I had never for a moment believed the chairman could find himself capable of uttering them. For a start, Martin has no knowledge whatsoever of my personal finances, so in that area there could be no foundation for comments of any kind. Suggestions that my record with United had shown me to be useless with money would be rather difficult to sustain, considering that Martin's fortune has swollen by upwards of £120 million over the past ten years as a result of his shareholdings in the club. There was no substance to the story and I can only assume that Bose had been listening to a lot of the tittle-tattle which, as I have observed earlier, is always plentiful around a big organisation like ours.

Nobody can have any doubts about how determined we were to retain the European Cup we had won so dramatically in Barcelona, and we had grounds for optimism after we finished top of our groups in both league phases of the competition. At the first stage, we finished ahead of Olympique Marseille, Sturm Graz and Croatia Zagreb with a total of 13 points from six matches and then had an identical haul in the much more demanding company of Valencia, Fiorentina and Bordeaux. Our only defeat in the second phase came in Florence and we avenged that impressively at Old Trafford with one of our best performances of the season. Even a brilliant early goal by Gabriel Batistuta could not undermine our confidence that night. Playing with splendid pace and penetration, we tore Fiorentina apart to finish 3–1 winners, with our striking partnership of Cole and Yorke outstanding. Our 3–0 demolition of Valencia in Manchester had been equally pleasing. Bolstered by home and away victories over Bordeaux, we were in a comfortable frame of mind when we flew out to complete our group fixtures in Valencia, where we had little trouble holding our opponents to a goalless scoreline that left us at the top of the table.

A quarter-final draw that paired us with Real Madrid reminded our fans of momentous collisions between the clubs in the past. In 1957, when Matt Busby was developing one of the most exciting collections of young footballers ever assembled in this country, United performed creditably against Real but went down 5–3 over two legs to a team who were building the irresistible momentum that would carry them to five European Cup triumphs in a row. The Munich air disaster denied that United team any further opportunity to lay hands on European club football's biggest prize, but their great manager, having come close to death in the crash, went on to put together another remarkable squad of players. In 1968, his prodigious feat of rebuilding had its perfect reward. United knocked out Real 4–3 on aggregate in the semi-final of the European Cup before beating Benfica in the final. Now, more than thirty years on, the Spanish giants were blocking our club's path to a third success in the competition.

It was again time for me to pinch myself to make sure that all the experiences packed into the nine months since July 1999 were not happening in a dream. From the Nou Camp, by way of Tokyo and Maracana, to facing Real Madrid at Bernabeu – it had been a magical ride. Playing in the stadium where the team of Di Stefano, Puskas and Gento first set the standards that made the European Cup the most desirable of all club trophies was an exhilarating prospect. But the match turned out to be a strange anti-climax, with a 0–0 result that hardly anybody could have foreseen. A lot of people on our side of the fence thought it was a good result but I was disappointed and worried. Maybe I was a bit like the old farmer who can divine the weather in his bones, getting pains and funny feelings when the rain is coming. I could feel the rain coming.

The second leg at Old Trafford was one of those nights when just about everything that could possibly go wrong for us did so in spades, and we were left looking back on the match with the sense that Real were simply destined to progress into the semi-finals. That conviction is only strengthened by the memory of the formation they assumed immediately after the kick-off. They were playing to a system that did not deserve to be successful: three central defenders, two wing-backs, three men up front, Steve McManaman as a floating player (although mainly on the right) and one central midfielder in Fernando Redondo. 'Give us a break,' I thought to myself. 'That can't work.' But they defied logic and drew encouragement from the least likely source when given the lead through an own-goal turned in by Roy Keane. Some of our attacking play was superb. However, their eighteen-year-old goalkeeper, Iker Casillas, was inspired and as the spurned chances accumulated I began to think about changing my own system.

To our cost, I delayed too long. If I had altered the team early to a 4-3-3, playing two men wide and one central striker, I am sure we could have won handily. I know that, and could kick myself for delaying the change. With three central midfielders, we would have been able to get against Redondo as a priority and would also have handled Raul better when he dropped into midfield from his normal front position. Instead, we allowed our opponents to hit us with quick breaks and, helped by moments of poor defending on our part, they were 3–0 up soon after halftime. It was an inconceivable deficit at Old Trafford against opponents I still regard as being less formidable than we can be at our best. Tightening the score to 3–2 before the finish was poor consolation. Although Real went on to lift the European Cup for the eighth time in their history, I believe that if we played them in ten matches we could expect to win seven. But they did us in on that night in Manchester and that was what counted.

One of the forceful reminders delivered by that defeat was that consistent success in Europe would be more readily achieved if we improved our capacity to defend against the counter-attack. Whereas in the more open game in England there is a tendency to attack and defend as a team, on the Continent teams are adept at counter-attacking with only two or three players. They are liable to go all out for the jugular only a few times in a match, and the suddenness of those isolated thrusts can catch you off guard. The alertness and concentration needed to cope with the counter-attack are qualities without which no team can hope to be dominant in European football.

With the defence of our European championship painfully ended, we had to be doubly pleased that we had been doing a good job of protecting our domestic title. I had always felt that the lack of consistency which had troubled us at various stages of the season would cease to be a problem in March and April. My faith was justified during that crucial period with performances that were notable not only for the fluency and verve of our football but for the mental intensity of the players. Just as the away victories over Arsenal in August and Liverpool in September had been vital in helping to give our campaign early impetus, I saw the match against Leeds at Elland Road in late February as an opportunity to demonstrate that there would be no wobbling on the run-in.

That Sunday clash with David O'Leary's youthful and exuberant team was always going to attract a lot of media attention but it became a far bigger story when David Beckham failed to turn up for our training session on the Friday before the game and also failed to convince me that he had a satisfactory reason for being absent. The explanation, that young Brooklyn Beckham was unwell, would normally have made me totally sympathetic (I would expect a parent to put a child's welfare in front of everything else) but when it was well known that Victoria was out in London on that Friday I had to think that David wasn't being fair to his team-mates. Nicky Butt, Phil Neville and Ole Gunnar Solskjaer cannot count on being regulars in our first team but they are model pros who never miss training and I had to imagine how they would feel if David could adjust the schedule to suit himself. There was no way I could consider including Beckham in the team to meet Leeds. That much was crystal clear in my mind before David worsened the problems between us when we met up on the Saturday by making me lose my temper badly, something I hadn't done for years. At first he simply refused to accept that he had anything to answer for, and that made me blow up. I don't go out of my way to prove to people who is the manager. But from time to time somebody in my job is confronted with a situation which must be handled in a manner that signifies control. Because of all the hype that constantly surrounds David, my decision to leave him in the stands at Elland Road became a bit of a drama but it was quite straightforward for me. It doesn't matter to me how high a player's profile is. If he is in the wrong, he is disciplined. And David was definitely in the wrong. Some thought the importance of the Leeds fixture would save him from being dropped, but rules and principles don't mean much if they are bent the moment there is a practical disadvantage in applying them.

The after-effects of the episode were entirely positive. It brought home to David the seriousness of my attitude about how he should prepare for games. Living in the south of England was not fair to me, the club, his team-mates or the fans who have supported him so loyally. Nor, in football terms, was it fair to him and there is no doubt he benefited afterwards from recognising more clearly that his apartment in Cheshire must be his working base. I often think of his parents and of all the sacrifices they were glad to make in his interests. When he was a boy, they used to bring him along to every match we played in London and I had many conversations with them. They were concerned about his height, wondering if he was ever going to grow, and I used to reassure them that he would be a six-footer. David is a loving son who appreciates everything his mother and father did for him and I am certain he won't let them down. He will work at having the great career they always wanted him to have. The strongest guarantee is that the boy just loves playing football. He could never do without it.

Against Leeds, I decided to play Paul Scholes on the right side of midfield in David's place, with Nicky Butt alongside Roy Keane in centre-midfield. Nobody could be happy about losing the influence of a player like Beckham on the right but I was confident that the cleverness of Scholes would compensate significantly. As is the case in a lot of important games, it was obvious on that Sunday that the team who scored first would have gone a long way towards winning. When Andy Cole put us in front early in the second half, I was sure that at least we wouldn't lose. For the first time in a while, I felt that our players' concentration was back to its best and they stayed ahead of Leeds's gallant youngsters fairly comfortably. That result tightened our grip on the championship trophy and, after draws with Wimbledon and Liverpool, we launched into a record-breaking run of eleven consecutive league victories that sealed our sixth Premiership title in eight years.

We clinched the title at Southampton, when we still had four Premiership fixtures to play. That was an extraordinary degree of comfort to have in a League famous for being competitive, and our 18-point winning margin at the end astonished everybody. It merited a grand celebration with our supporters and the natural occasion for that was our final home match with Tottenham Hotspur on 6 May. But while arrangements for the party were being made, I was already working on more long-term preparations, trying to ensure that we would be an even stronger force in England and Europe in the seasons ahead.

For a long time we had been monitoring the progress of Ruud van Nistelrooy because his remarkable scoring feats with PSV Eindhoven identified him as a striker of the highest calibre. Now everything was in place to enable us to sign him and on Sunday, 23 April, the day before we were to meet Chelsea at Old Trafford, he flew to Manchester for what were assumed to be the formalities of completing the deal. That evening I had dinner with Ruud and his girlfriend Lillitanne, Steve McClaren, Jim Ryan, Jaap Stam and his wife Eilish, and Roger Linse, who is Van Nistelrooy's agent. There was a lovely warm atmosphere and it was easy to sense that Ruud was keen to join us. I was quite excited, for I could tell just by looking into his eyes that this was a young man of substance. At that dinner there was so little hint of any looming difficulties that Steve, Jim and I had a bit of fun by suggesting that our only problem would come from having to tolerate another Dutchman at the club. We should, we insisted, get gold medals for putting up with them. 'Four Dutchmen,' I kept muttering. 'How am I going to handle this?' Jaap corrected me. 'You can't count Jordi – he's Spanish.'

The relaxed mood was not clouded by undue concern over some trouble Van Nistelrooy had been having with his right knee. His description of the symptoms indicated to me that a medial ligament was involved and, recalling my own considerable experience of that sort of injury during my playing career, I was not terribly perturbed. Damage to one of the two cruciate ligaments in a knee, the anterior and the posterior, is infinitely more serious. It can be career-threatening, although the continuing advances in medical technology have vastly increased the likelihood of recovery. Roy Keane has returned unimpaired from such an injury and, still more remarkably, the great German player Lothar Matthaus also came back after rupturing a cruciate at the age of thirty-two. I was sure, however, that those examples wouldn't be relevant to the findings that would emerge from the stringent medical examination Ruud had to undergo before he could sign for us. My main concern at that stage was that PSV Eindhoven had given out news of the transfer. I don't think that is proper. The buying club, not the selling club, should control the public relations associated with a move.

PSV's announcement meant that next day the media treated our match with Chelsea as merely the backdrop to the story of Ruud's arrival. The game was a strange one, with neither team getting out of second gear. But, given our home record against the London team over the years, I was delighted with a 3–2 win. I believe it was only the fourth time we had beaten Chelsea at Old Trafford in my thirteen years as manager. At the press conference, a few mild questions about our performance soon gave way to the subject at the top of the journalists' agenda: why had I signed Van Nistelrooy? I explained that we were protecting our future position. We had looked at the Dutchman over quite a long period and had decided that, if we did not secure him now, two years on we might be lamenting a missed opportunity. All the members of our staff who had watched him play agreed that his potential was huge. The consensus was summed up by Jim Ryan, after seeing him star for Holland against Germany: 'He could be a world-class striker in two years' time.' I liked hearing that.

The reporters' next question was an obvious one: Who would be leaving United when Van Nistelrooy came in? 'Has anybody put for-sale signs up?' was my answer. I wanted to smother speculation regarding my strikers. We had built up a formidable squad and had no desire to weaken it. In fact, I did accept that there was a bit of pruning to be done and had told Martin Edwards I was scrutinising our playing personnel in that context. One worry I had was the uncertainty surrounding Teddy Sheringham. Teddy's agent had been in negotiation with the club but had not yet let us know what was likely to happen. The jungle drums were sending out the message that Teddy was leaving and that was a message I didn't welcome. I realise he is not happy about the limited number of games he plays for us but in my view our approach is almost perfect for him at this point of his career. Without doubt, used selectively, he makes a vital contribution for us and I was pleased to learn eventually (after the dramas around Van Nistelrooy had come to their sad conclusion) that he was committing himself to United for another year.

A simple decision I had taken weeks before Ruud's transfer had become an active issue caused me to be in Spain on the day of his medical. I had picked out the couple of days following the Chelsea match as giving me the best chance of a short break to recharge my energies for the climax of the season. Although I regretted not being on hand when Ruud was tested, I was optimistic about the outcome and in cheerful spirits as I headed for a brief stay at a friend's villa in Malaga, so much so that I even enjoyed a dirty trick played on me by my staff. There is a lot of superstition in football and I am not immune to it, which explains why a certain rather battered bag is my favourite piece of luggage on my European travels. Our kit man, Albert Morgan, refers to it as my painter and decorator's bag. My affection for it was a little strained on the journey to Spain because it seemed to be much heavier than usual, enough of a burden to make me check it in for the flight to Malaga. The extra weight ceased to be a mystery when I unpacked at the villa. My bag was loaded with paint brushes and paint-rollers.

In normal circumstances, my hours of sunbathing by the swimming pool next day would have been an opportunity to plot revenge on the evil-doers. But, of course, my mind was on the medical. At lunchtime I spoke with Steve McClaren and apparently everything was in order, so I switched my mobile phone off for the rest of the afternoon. By teatime I had gone into the villa and Sky News was covering events direct from Old Trafford, where a press conference was about to start. Just then my mobile rang and it was Steve with grim news. There was serious concern about Ruud's cruciate ligament. I talked immediately with Mike

Stone, the club doctor, and Jonathan Noble, our orthopaedic specialist, and they told me they were not prepared to pass the player on the evidence before them. It was shattering news and my thoughts went instantly to the lad himself. I kept wishing that I was there to offer personal support. It was imperative that I speak to him and when I did I tried to be as positive as possible, emphasising that we might yet find a way out of the nightmare. Our medical people suggested that he should have an arthroscopic examination to determine exactly what was wrong, and I don't think there was anything unreasonable about that proposal. Equally, I think Ruud was right to turn it down, on the grounds that he wanted to play in Euro 2000 and having the arthroscopic examination could have harmed his chances.

After both sides had discussed at length what the next step should be, it was decided that Ruud would return to Holland to continue remedial treatment. Soon we had the devastating word from over there that he had broken down and was facing the full horror of a seriously damaged cruciate. I felt I had to go across and see him at his home to let him know the depth of the sympathy I felt for him. Within a week or so, he had gone from being on top of the world, looking forward to great years with United, to being in the darkest place he had ever known as a footballer. The club's disappointment was severe but that mattered a lot less than the suffering Ruud was going through. That trip to Holland was one I had to make.

So, on the Tuesday before our celebratory match with Tottenham, I flew to Eindhoven. I was met by Roger Linse, and on the twenty-minute drive to Ruud's apartment Roger brought me up to date on how the lad was feeling and the options open to him in terms of where and when he was to have his operation. Our day together convinced me more than ever that Ruud has the strength of character to cope with his ordeal, that he will come back as the oustanding player who thrilled so many of us such a short time ago. I sought to encourage him with stories of the singlemindedness shown by Roy Keane while he was battling his way back to fitness and of the even more dramatic example provided by Lothar Matthaus. During the long process of rehabilitation that enabled him to re-establish himself in the German national team, Lothar had set his alarm clock for 4 a.m. each morning. He had punished himself with remedial exercises for two hours, then returned to bed for two hours' sleep before travelling to Bayern Munich's training ground to put in a full day's work on his recuperative routine. That little parable deeply impressed Ruud and I hope it helped to reinforce the drive he will need to resurrect his career. With all my heart, I wish him well.

The complications and mutual sadness of our experience with Ruud made a stark contrast with the swift, trouble-free bit of business that brought Fabien Barthez from Monaco to United a few weeks later. Signing the Frenchman was a decisive move to bring about the reinforcement of our goalkeeping strength that I had tried to achieve by acquiring Massimo Taibi. Fabien's winner's medal from the 1998 World Cup is in itself proof that he can perform at the highest level, and the quality of his play is not the only reason to be delighted about his arrival. He has a strong, bubbly personality that I'm sure will appeal to his team-mates in the dressing-room and our supporters in the stands. Barthez loves big stages, and they don't come much bigger than Old Trafford.

Our stadium has rarely presented a happier picture than it did on 6 May 2000, the Saturday that had been designated Championship Day. We were presented with the trophy at the end of the Tottenham match (we safeguarded the party mood by beating Spurs 3–1) and the warmth and happiness that swept through the stadium made all the sweat and strain of the previous months more than worthwhile. The occasion had an extra glow when the players' children were brought on for the lap of honour. Those scenes gave everyone a reminder of what a family club we are. Over the years some supporters have wondered about my willingness to let the players bring their kids to training during the school holidays. It seems natural enough to me. We are dealing with people, not commodities. Footballers are away from their homes so much in connection with their work, especially at weekends, and I'm glad to give them a chance to take the children out from under their wives' feet. The youngsters aren't a minute's bother. Give them a ball and they are as happy as Larry. Mind you, that is true of the fathers, too, although they are never really satisfied unless their exertions are bringing in a few trophies.

Half-a-dozen Premiership titles in eight years is quite an achievement, particularly for Ryan Giggs, who has all six medals and is still only twenty-six. I use Ryan as the challenge to the others (Denis Irwin has the same total, but Denis is thirty-four). Two years ago I was telling the squad, 'When you can boast four championship medals then you know you are a Manchester United player.' Last season I was able to up the figure to five, and now I can go to six. I like being able to make that kind of adjustment to the script. You can bet that I'll be trying hard to keep the habit.

CAREER RECORD

Senior playing career

1958–60 Queen's Park

1960–64 St Johnstone

1964–67 Dunfermline
Played for Scottish League (0) v. English League (3) at Hampden, 15 March 1967.
Scotland summer tour 13 May–15 June 1967: scored 10 goals in appearances against Israel, Hong Kong Select, Australia (three matches), Auckland Provincial XI, Vancouver All Stars.

1967–69 Rangers
Played for Scottish League (2) v. Irish League (0) in Belfast, 6 September 1967. Scored one of the goals.

1969–73 Falkirk

1973–74 Ayr United

Managerial career

July–October 1974 East Stirlingshire

October 1974–May 1978 St Mirren
Finished fourth in Division One in 1975–76; Division One champions 1976–77; finished eighth in Premier Division 1977–78.

1978–86 Aberdeen

1979	fourth in Premier Division
	Scottish Cup semi-finalists
	Scottish League Cup runners-up
1980	Premier Division champions
	Scottish Cup semi-finalists
	Scottish League Cup runners-up
1981	runners-up in Premier Division
	Drybrough Cup winners
1982	runners-up in Premier Division
	Scottish Cup winners
1983	third in Premier Division
	Scottish Cup winners
	European Cup Winners' Cup winners
1984	Premier Division champions
	Scottish Cup winners
	Scottish League Cup semi-finalists
	European Cup Winners' Cup semi-finalists
	European Super Cup winners
1985	Premier Division champions
	Scottish Cup semi-finalists
1986	fourth in Premier Division
	Scottish Cup winners
	Scottish League Cup winners
	European Cup quarter-finalists

Season 1978–79

	P	W	D	L	F	A	Pts
League	36	13	14	9	59	36	40
Scottish Cup	5	3	1	1	12	6	
League Cup	8	6	1	1	25	7	
European Cup Winners' Cup	4	2	0	2	7	6	
Friendlies	9	7	1	1	23	6	
Overall	62	31	17	14	126	61	

Highlights: international goalkeeper Bobby Clarke made his 600th first-team appearance for Aberdeen in a pre-season friendly. Three first-team players transferred or released.

Season 1979–80

	P	W	D	L	F	A	Pts
League	36	19	10	7	68	36	48
Scottish Cup	5	3	1	1	16	3	
League Cup	11	7	2	2	23	11	
UEFA Cup	2	0	1	1	1	2	
Drybrough Cup	1	0	0	1	0	1	
Friendlies	11	9	1	1	32	10	
Overall	66	38	15	13	140	63	

Highlights: three first-team players transferred to other Scottish clubs.

Season 1980–81

	P	W	D	L	F	A	Pts
League	36	19	11	6	61	26	49
Scottish Cup	2	1	0	1	2	2	
League Cup	6	3	1	2	15	4	
European Cup	4	1	1	2	1	5	
Drybrough Cup	3	3	0	0	10	4	
Friendlies	7	6	0	1	31	11	
Overall	58	33	13	12	120	52	

Highlights: Drybrough Cup won with a 2–1 victory over former club St Mirren in the final.

Season 1981–82

	P	W	D	L	F	A	Pts
League	36	23	7	6	71	29	53
Scottish Cup	6	5	1	0	14	6	
League Cup	10	7	1	2	21	4	
UEFA Cup	6	3	2	1	13	9	
Friendlies	8	5	2	1	18	6	
Overall	66	43	13	10	137	54	

Highlights: Willie Miller made his 500th first-team appearance for Aberdeen in a league game v. Morton on 17 April 1982.

Season 1982–83

	P	W	D	L	F	A	Pts
League	36	25	5	6	76	24	55
Scottish Cup	5	5	0	0	9	2	
League Cup	8	4	2	2	19	11	
European Cup Winners' Cup	11	8	2	1	25	6	
Friendlies	4	3	0	1	14	1	
Overall	64	45	9	10	143	44	

Highlights: ten days after winning the European Cup Winners' Cup with a 2–1 extra-time victory over Real Madrid in Gothenburg, Aberdeen won the Scottish Cup 1–0 – again after extra time – against Rangers at Hampden.

Season 1983–84

	P	W	D	L	F	A	Pts
League	36	25	7	4	78	21	57
Scottish Cup	7	5	2	0	11	3	
League Cup	10	7	2	1	23	3	
European Cup Winners' Cup	8	3	2	3	10	7	
European Super Cup	2	1	1	0	2	0	
Friendlies	12	4	3	5	19	17	
Overall	75	45	17	13	143	51	

Highlights: title-winning points tally of 57 set new Premier Division record. Billy Stark signed from St Mirren pre-season. Stewart McKimmie signed from Dundee for £90,000. Gordon Strachan's second goal against SK Beveren (Belgium) in second round of the European Cup Winners' Cup was Aberdeen's 100th goal in European competition. Mark McGhee scored Aberdeen's 100th League Cup goal. Peter Weir scored Aberdeen's 600th Scottish Cup goal.

Season 1984–85

	P	W	D	L	F	A	Pts
League	36	27	5	4	89	26	59
Scottish Cup	6	3	2	1	10	4	
League Cup	1	0	0	1	1	3	
European Cup	2	1	0	1	7	8	
Friendlies	9	5	2	2	14	9	
Overall	54	36	9	9	121	50	

Highlights: Aberdeen retain the Premier Division title with a new record points tally of 59. Jim Leighton missing from Aberdeen's goal v. Hibs on 5 January after 100 consecutive appearances. Willie Miller made his 50th Scottish Cup-tie appearance in the semi-final against Dundee United.

Season 1985–86

	P	W	D	L	F	A	Pts
League	36	16	12	8	62	31	44
Scottish Cup	6	5	1	0	15	4	
League Cup	6	6	0	0	13	0	
European Cup	6	3	3	0	10	4	
Friendlies	11	6	2	3	29	11	
Overall	65	36	18	11	129	50	

Highlights: won League Cup without conceding a goal in six games. European Cup quarter-finalists, losing on away goals rule. Losing 1–0 to Hearts on 18 January was first home defeat in 26 games, including 19 league games. Willie Miller passed the 700 mark in first-team appearances. Jim Bett signed after a spell in Iceland. Doug Bell transferred to Rangers for £115,000.

Season 1986–87 (August–1 November 1986)

	P	W	D	L	F	A
League	15	7	5	3	25	14
League Cup	3	2	0	1	8	2
European Cup Winners' Cup	2	1	0	1	2	4
Friendlies	6	2	3	1	11	6
Overall	26	12	8	6	46	26

Highlights: Davie Dodds signed from Neuchatel for £200,000. Frank McDougall retired from football on medical advice. Ian Angus transferred to Dundee in exchange for Robert Connor. Bryan Gunn transferred to Norwich for £100,000.

Summary

	P	W	D	L	F	A
League	303	174	76	53	589	243
Scottish Cup	42	30	8	4	89	30
League Cup	63	42	9	12	148	45
European competitions	47	23	12	12	78	51
Drybrough Cup	4	3	0	1	10	5
Friendlies	77	47	14	16	191	77
Overall	536	319	119	98	1105	451

Aberdeen's European campaigns during Alex Ferguson's managership

Season 1978–79 Cup Winners' Cup

Round 1 Marek Dimitrov (Bulgaria) (a) 2–3, (h) 3–0, Agg: 5–3
Round 2 Fortuna Dusseldorf (W. Germany) (a) 0–3, (h) 2–0, Agg: 2–3

P	W	D	L	F	A
4	2	0	2	7	6

Season 1979–80 UEFA Cup

Round 1 Eintracht Frankfurt (W. Germany) (h) 1–1, (a) 0–1, Agg: 1–2

P	W	D	L	F	A
2	0	1	1	1	2

Season 1980–81 European Cup

Round 1 Austria Memphis (Austria) (h) 1–0, (a) 0–0, Agg: 1–0
Round 2 Liverpool (England) (h) 0–1, (a) 0–4, Agg: 0–5

P	W	D	L	F	A
4	1	1	2	1	5

Season 1981–82 UEFA Cup

Round 1 Ipswich (England) (a) 1–1, (h) 3–1, Agg: 4–2
Round 2 Arges Pitesti (Romania) (h) 3–0, (a) 2–2, Agg: 5–2
Round 3 SV Hamburg (W. Germany) (h) 3–2, (a) 1–3, Agg: 4–5

P	W	D	L	F	A
6	3	2	1	13	9

Season 1982–83 Cup Winners' Cup
Preliminary round FC Sion (Switzerland) (h) 7–0, (a) 4–1, Agg: 11–1
Round 1 Dinamo Tirana (Albania) (h) 1–0, (a) 0–0, Agg: 1–0
Round 2 Lech Poznan (Poland) (h) 2–0, (a) 1–0, Agg: 3–0
Quarter-final Bayern Munich (W. Germany) (a) 0–0, (h) 3–2, Agg: 3–2
Semi-final Waterschei (Belgium) (h) 5–1, (a) 0–1, Agg: 5–2
Final (Gothenburg) Real Madrid (Spain) 2–1 (aet)

P	W	D	L	F	A
11	8	2	1	25	6

Season 1983–84 Super Cup
SV Hamburg (W. Germany) (a) 0–0, (h) 2–0, Agg: 2–0

Cup Winners' Cup
Round 1 Akranes (Iceland) (a) 2–1, (h) 1–1, Agg: 3–2
Round 2 SK Beveren (Belgium) (a) 0–0, (h) 4–1, Agg: 4–1
Quarter-final Ujpest Dozsa (Hungary) (a) 0–2, (h) 3–0 (aet), Agg: 3–2
Semi-final FC Porto (Portugal) (a) 0–1, (h) 0–1, Agg: 0–2

P	W	D	L	F	A
10	4	3	3	12	7

Season 1984–85 European Cup
Round 1 Dinamo Berlin (E. Germany) (h) 2–1, (a) 1–2, Agg: 3–3 (lost 4–5 on penalties)

P	W	D	L	F	A
2	1	0	1	7	8

Season 1985–86 European Cup
Round 1 Akranes (Iceland) (a) 3–1, (h) 4–1, Agg: 7–2
Round 2 Servette (Switzerland) (a) 0–0, (h) 1–0, Agg: 1–0
Quarter-final IFK Gothenburg (Sweden) (h) 2–2, (a) 0–0, Agg: 2–2 (lost on away goals rule)

P	W	D	L	F	A
6	3	3	0	10	4

Season 1986–87 Cup Winners' Cup

Round 1 FC Sion (Switzerland) (h) 2–1, (a) 0–3, Agg: 2–4

P	W	D	L	F	A
2	1	0	1	2	4

Overall

P	W	D	L	F	A
47	23	12	12	78	51

October 1985–June 1986 Scotland

Full Internationals

	P	W	D	L	F	A
Home	3	2	1	0	5	0
Away	7	1	3	3	3	5
Overall	10	3	4	3	8	5

Results

October 1985	East Germany (friendly, home) 0–0
November 1985	Australia (World Cup play-off, home) 2–0
December 1985	Australia (World Cup play-off, away) 0–0
January 1986	Israel (friendly, away) 1–0
March 1986	Romania (friendly, home) 3–0
April 1986	England (Rous Cup, away) 1–2
April 1986	Holland (friendly, away) 0–0
June 1986	Denmark (World Cup, Mexico City) 0–1
June 1986	West Germany (World Cup, Queretaro) 1–2
June 1986	Uruguay (World Cup, Mexico City) 0–0

1986– Manchester United

Season 1986–87
The Today League Division One
United's record up to Alex Ferguson's arrival

	P	W	D	L	F	A	Pts
Home	7	3	1	3	12	8	10
Away	6	0	3	3	4	8	3
Total	13	3	4	6	16	16	13

Littlewoods Cup: third round

United's record under Alex Ferguson

	P	W	D	L	F	A	Pts
Home	14	10	2	2	26	10	32
Away	15	1	8	6	10	19	11
Total	29	11	10	8	36	29	43
Overall total	42	14	14	14	52	45	56

Final position: 11th
FA Cup: fourth round

Season 1987–88
Barclays League Division One

	P	W	D	L	F	A	Pts
Home	20	14	5	1	41	17	47
Away	20	9	7	4	30	21	34
Total	40	23	12	5	71	38	81

Final position: runners-up
FA Cup: fifth round
Littlewoods Cup: fifth round

Season 1988–89
Barclays League Division One

	P	W	D	L	F	A	Pts
Home	19	10	5	4	27	13	35
Away	19	3	7	9	18	22	16
Total	38	13	12	13	45	35	51

Final position: 11th
FA Cup: sixth round
Littlewoods Cup: third round

Season 1989–90
Barclays League Division One

	P	W	D	L	F	A	Pts
Home	19	8	6	5	26	14	30
Away	19	5	3	11	20	33	18
Total	38	13	9	16	46	47	48

Final position: 13th
FA Cup: winners
Littlewoods Cup: third round

Season 1990–91
Barclays League Division One

	P	W	D	L	F	A	Pts
Home	19	11	4	4	34	17	37
Away	19	5	8	6	24	28	23
Total	38	16	12	10	58	45	59★

★One point deducted

Final position: 6th
FA Cup: fifth round
Rumbelows Cup: finalists
European Cup Winners' Cup: winners
FA Charity Shield: joint winners

Season 1991–92
Barclays League Division One

	P	W	D	L	F	A	Pts
Home	21	12	7	2	34	13	43
Away	21	9	8	4	29	20	35
Total	42	21	15	6	63	33	78

Final position: runners-up
FA Cup: fourth round
Rumbelows Cup: winners
European Cup Winners' Cup: second round
European Super Cup: winners

Season 1992–93
FA Premier League

	P	W	D	L	F	A	Pts
Home	21	14	5	2	39	14	47
Away	21	10	7	4	28	17	37
Total	42	24	12	6	67	31	84

Final position: champions
FA Cup: fifth round
Coca-Cola Cup: third round
UEFA Cup: first round

Season 1993–94
FA Carling Premiership

	P	W	D	L	F	A	Pts
Home	21	14	6	1	39	13	48
Away	21	13	5	3	41	25	44
Total	42	27	11	4	80	38	92

Final position: champions
FA Cup: winners
Coca-Cola Cup: finalists
European Champion Clubs' Cup: second round
FA Charity Shield: winners

Season 1994–95
FA Carling Premiership

	P	W	D	L	F	A	Pts
Home	21	16	4	1	42	4	52
Away	21	10	6	5	35	24	36
Total	42	26	10	6	77	28	88

Final position: runners-up
FA Cup: finalists
Coca-Cola Cup: third round
UEFA Champions League: Group A
FA Charity Shield: winners

Season 1995–96
FA Carling Premiership

	P	W	D	L	F	A	Pts
Home	19	15	4	0	36	9	49
Away	19	10	3	6	37	26	33
Total	38	25	7	6	73	35	82

Final position: champions
FA Cup: winners
Coca-Cola Cup: second round
UEFA Cup: first round

Season 1996–97
FA Carling Premiership

	P	W	D	L	F	A	Pts
Home	19	12	5	2	38	17	41
Away	19	9	7	3	38	27	34
Total	38	21	12	5	76	44	75

Final position: champions
FA Cup: fourth round
Coca-Cola Cup: fourth round
UEFA Champions League: semi-final
FA Charity Shield: winners

Season 1997–98
FA Carling Premiership

	P	W	D	L	F	A	Pts
Home	19	13	4	2	42	9	43
Away	19	10	4	5	31	17	34
Total	38	23	8	7	73	26	77

Final position: runners-up
FA Cup: fifth round
Coca-Cola Cup: third round
UEFA Champions League: quarter-final
FA Charity Shield: winners

Season 1998–99
FA Carling Premiership

	P	W	D	L	F	A	Pts
Home	19	14	4	1	45	18	46
Away	19	8	9	2	35	19	33
Total	38	22	13	3	80	37	79

Final position: champions
FA Cup: winners
Worthington Cup: fifth round
UEFA Champions League: winners

Season 1999–2000
FA Carling Premiership

	P	W	D	L	F	A	Pts
Home	19	15	4	0	59	16	49
Away	19	13	3	3	38	29	42
Total	38	28	7	3	97	45	91

Final position: champions
FA Cup: did not enter
Worthington Cup: third round
UEFA Champions League: quarter-final
World Club Championship: winners

Summary

Home	P	W	D	L	F	A	Pts
League	270	178	65	27	528	184	599
FA Cup	28	20	6	2	53	17	
Europe	35	19	12	4	70	31	
League Cup	24	20	2	2	53	20	
Super Cup	1	1	0	0	1	0	
Total	358	238	85	35	705	252	

Away	P	W	D	L	F	A	Pts
League	271	115	85	71	414	327	430
FA Cup	37	23	8	6	66	34	
Europe	37	16	13	8	48	34	
League Cup	28	13	4	11	38	36	
FIFA CWC	3	1	1	1	4	4	
WCC	1	1	0	0	1	0	
Super Cup	1	0	0	1	0	1	
Charity Shield	7	2	3	2	10	9	
Total	385	171	114	100	581	445	
Overall total	743	409	199	135	1286	697	

FIFA CWC – FIFA Club World Championship
WCC – World Club Championship
Super Cup – UEFA Super Cup

Honours

European Champion Clubs' Cup (UEFA Champions League)
Winners: 1999

European Cup Winners' Cup
Winners: 1991

FA Premier League
Champions: 1993, 1994, 1996, 1997, 1999, 2000
Runners-up: 1995, 1998

FA Cup
Winners: 1990, 1994, 1996, 1999
Finalists: 1995

Football League Cup
Winners: 1992
Finalists: 1991, 1994

World Club Championship
Winners: 1999

European Super Cup
Winners: 1991

FA Charity Shield
Winners: 1993, 1994, 1996, 1997
Joint winners (with Liverpool): 1990

Manchester United players, under Alex Ferguson

Listed here is the name of every player to appear in a senior competitive fixture for Manchester United during Alex Ferguson's time as manager, up to the end of season 1999–2000

Albiston, Arthur
Anderson, Viv
Appleton, Michael
Bailey, Gary
Barnes, Peter
Beardsmore, Russell
Beckham, David
Berg, Henning
Blackmore, Clayton
Blomqvist, Jesper
Bosnich, Mark
Brazil, Derek
Brown, Wesley
Bruce, Steve
Butt, Nicky
Cantona, Eric
Casper, Chris
Chadwick, Luke
Clegg, Michael
Cole, Andy
Cooke, Terry
Cruyff, Jordi
Culkin, Nick
Curtis, John
Davenport, Peter
Davies, Simon
Donaghy, Mal
Dublin, Dion
Duxbury, Mike
Ferguson, Darren
Fortune, Quinton
Garton, Billy
Gibson, Colin
Gibson, Terry
Giggs, Ryan
Gill, Tony
Gillespie, Keith
Van der Gouw, Raimond
Graham, Deiniol
Greening, Jonathan
Healy, David
Higginbotham, Danny
Hogg, Graeme
Hughes, Mark
Ince, Paul
Irwin, Denis
Johnsen, Ronny
Kanchelskis, Andrei
Keane, Roy
Leighton, Jim
McClair, Brian
McGibbon, Patrick

McGrath, Paul
McKee, Colin
Martin, Lee
Maiorana, Giuliano
May, David
Milne, Ralph
Moran, Kevin
Moses, Remi
Mulryne, Philip
Neville, Gary
Neville, Phil
Nevland, Erik
Notman, Alex
O'Brien, Liam
O'Kane, John
O'Shea, John
Olsen, Jesper
Pallister, Gary
Parker, Paul
Phelan, Mike
Pilkington, Kevin
Poborsky, Karel
Prunier, William
Rachubka, Paul
Robins, Mark
Robson, Bryan
Schmeichel, Peter
Scholes, Paul

Sealey, Les
Sharpe, Lee
Sheringham, Teddy
Silvestre, Mikael
Sivebaek, John
Solskjaer, Ole Gunnar
Stam, Jaap
Stapleton, Frank
Strachan, Gordon
Taibi, Massimo
Thornley, Ben
Tomlinson, Graeme
Turner, Chris
Twiss, Michael
Wallace, Danny
Wallwork, Ronnie
Walsh, Gary
Webb, Neil
Wellens, Richard
Whiteside, Norman
Whitworth, Neil
Wilkinson, Ian
Wilson, David
Wilson, Mark
Wood, Nicky
Wratten, Paul
Yorke, Dwight

Major transfers

In

Yorke, Dwight	£12,600,000 from Aston Villa	Aug 1998
Stam, Jaap	£10,600,000 from PSV Eindhoven	July 1998
Barthez, Fabien	£7,800,000 from AS Monaco	May 2000
Cole, Andy	£6,250,000 from Newcastle United	Jan 1995
Berg, Henning	£5,000,000 from Blackburn Rovers	Aug 1997
Blomqvist, Jesper	£4,400,000 from AC Parma	July 1998
Taibi, Massimo	£4,400,000 from Venezia	Aug 1999
Silvestre, Mikael	£4,000,000 from Internazionale	Sept 1999
Keane, Roy	£3,750,000 from Nottingham Forest	July 1993

Poborsky, Karel	£3,500,000 from Slavia Prague	July 1997
Sheringham, Teddy	£3,500,000 from Tottenham Hotspur	June 1997
Ince, Paul	£2,400,000 from West Ham United	Sept 1989
Pallister, Gary	£2,300,000 from Middlesbrough	Aug 1989
Hughes, Mark	£1,800,000 from Barcelona	July 1988
Parker, Paul	£1,700,000 from Queens Park Rangers	Aug 1991
Johnsen, Ronny	£1,500,000 from Besiktas	July 1996
Solskjaer, Ole Gunnar	£1,500,000 from Molde	July 1996
Webb, Neil	£1,500,000 from Nottingham Forest	July 1989
Fortune, Quinton	£1,500,000 from Atletico Madrid	Aug1999
Wallace, Danny	£1,300,000 from Southampton	Sept 1989
Cantona, Eric	£1,200,000 from Leeds United	Dec 1992
May, David	£1,200,000 from Blackburn Rovers	July 1994
Dublin, Dion	£1,000,000 from Cambridge United	Aug 1992
Kanchelskis, Andrei	£1,000,000 from Shakhytor Donetsk	May 1991
McClair, Brian	£850,000 from Celtic	July 1987
Bruce, Steve	£825,000 from Norwich City	Dec 1987
Phelan, Mike	£750,000 from Norwich City	July 1989
Donaghy, Mal	£650,000 from Luton Town	Oct 1988
Irwin, Denis	£625,000 from Oldham Athletic	June 1990
Schmeichel, Peter	£500,000 from Brondby	Aug 1991

Out

Ince, Paul	£6,000,000 to Internazionale	July 1995
Kanchelskis, Andrei	£5,000,000 to Everton	Aug 1995
Sharpe, Lee	£4,500,000 to Leeds United	Aug 1996
Poborsky, Karel	£3,000,000 to Benfica	Dec 1997
Pallister, Gary	£2,500,000 to Middlesbrough	July 1998
Dublin, Dion	£2,000,000 to Coventry City	Sept 1994
Hughes, Mark	£1,500,000 to Chelsea	July 1995
Curtis, John	£1,500,000 to Blackburn Rovers	May 2000
Robins, Mark	£800,000 to Norwich City	Aug 1992
Davenport, Peter	£750,000 to Middlesbrough	Nov 1988
Whiteside, Norman	£750,000 to Everton	July 1989
Cooke, Terry	£600,000 to Manchester City	Apr 1999
Appleton, Michael	£500,000 to Preston North End	Aug 1997
Mulryne, Philip	£500,000 to Norwich City	Mar 1999
Walsh, Gary	£500,000 to Middlesbrough	Aug 1995
McGrath, Paul	£450,000 to Aston Villa	Aug 1989

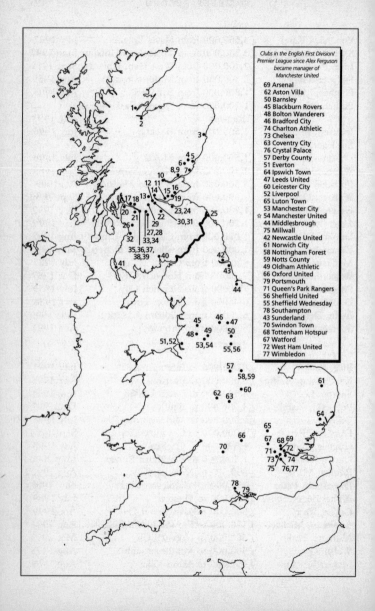

Clubs in the English First Division/
Premier League since Alex Ferguson
became manager of
Manchester United

69 Arsenal
62 Aston Villa
50 Barnsley
45 Blackburn Rovers
48 Bolton Wanderers
46 Bradford City
74 Charlton Athletic
73 Chelsea
63 Coventry City
76 Crystal Palace
57 Derby County
51 Everton
64 Ipswich Town
47 Leeds United
60 Leicester City
52 Liverpool
65 Luton Town
53 Manchester City
☆ 54 Manchester United
44 Middlesbrough
75 Millwall
42 Newcastle United
61 Norwich City
58 Nottingham Forest
59 Notts County
49 Oldham Athletic
66 Oxford United
79 Portsmouth
71 Queen's Park Rangers
56 Sheffield United
55 Sheffield Wednesday
78 Southampton
43 Sunderland
70 Swindon Town
68 Tottenham Hotspur
67 Watford
72 West Ham United
77 Wimbledon

Scottish League Clubs

by club

☆ 3 Aberdeen (Pittodrie)
34 Airdrieonians (Broomfield Park/ Shyberry Excelsior)
33 Albion Rovers (Cliftonhill)
14 Alloa (Recreation Park)
7 Arbroath (Gayfield Park)
★ 32 Ayr United (Somerset Park)
25 Berwick Rangers (Shielfield Park)
4 Brechin City (Glebe Park)
35 Celtic (Celtic Park)
29 Clyde (Broadwood)
18 Clydebank (Kilbowie Park, later shared Boghead)
15 Cowdenbeath (Central Park)
17 Dumbarton (Boghead)
8 Dundee (Dens Park)
9 Dundee United (Tannadice)
★ 11 Dunfermline Athletic (East End Park)
16 East Fife (Bayview)
☆ 31 East Stirlingshire (Firs Park)
★ 30 Falkirk (Brockville)
6 Forfar Athletic (Station Park)
20 Greenock Morton (Cappielow)
28 Hamilton Academical (Douglas Park, later shared Firhill)
23 Heart of Midlothian (Tynecastle)
24 Hibernian (Easter Road)
2 Inverness Caledonian Thistle (Caledonian Stadium)
26 Kilmarnock (Rugby Park)
22 Livingston (Almondvale Stadium)
5 Montrose (Links Park)
27 Motherwell (Fir Park)
36 Partick Thistle (Firhill)
40 Queen of the South (Palmerston Park)
★ 37 Queen's Park (Hampden Park)
19 Raith Rovers (Stark's Park)
★ 38 Rangers (Ibrox)
1 Ross County (Victoria Park)
★ 10 St Johnstone (Muirton Park/ McDiarmid Park)
☆ 21 St Mirren (Love Street)
12 Stenhousemuir (Ochilview Park)
13 Stirling Albion (Forthbank Stadium)
41 Stranraer (Stair Park)
39 Third Lanark (Cathkin Park) – now defunct

by ground

22 Almondvale Stadium (Livingston)
16 Bayview (East Fife)
17 Boghead (Dumbarton, Clydebank)
29 Broadwood (Clyde)
★ 30 Brockville (Falkirk)
34 Broomfield Park/Shyberry Excelsior (Airdrieonians)
2 Caledonian Stadium (Inverness Caledonian Thistle)
20 Cappielow (Greenock Morton)
39 Cathkin Park (Third Lanark) – now defunct
35 Celtic Park (Celtic)
15 Central Park (Cowdenbeath)
33 Cliftonhill (Albion Rovers)
8 Dens Park (Dundee)
28 Douglas Park (Hamilton Academical)
★ 11 East End Park (Dunfermline Athletic)
24 Easter Road (Hibernian)
36 Firhill (Partick Thistle, Hamilton Academical)
27 Fir Park (Motherwell)
☆ 31 Firs Park (East Stirlingshire)
13 Forthbank Stadium (Stirling Albion)
7 Gayfield Park (Arbroath)
4 Glebe Park (Brechin City)
★ 37 Hampden Park (Queen's Park)
★ 38 Ibrox (Rangers)
18 Kilbowie Park (Clydebank)
5 Links Park (Montrose)
☆ 21 Love Street (St Mirren)
★ 10 Muirton Park/McDiarmid Park (St Johnstone)
12 Ochilview Park (Stenhousemuir)
40 Palmerston Park (Queen of the South)
☆ 3 Pittodrie (Aberdeen)
14 Recreation Park (Alloa)
26 Rugby Park (Kilmarnock)
25 Shielfield Park (Berwick Rangers)
★ 32 Somerset Park (Ayr United)
41 Stair Park (Stranraer)
19 Stark's Park (Raith Rovers)
6 Station Park (Forfar Athletic)
9 Tannadice (Dundee United)
23 Tynecastle (Heart of Midlothian)
1 Victoria Park (Ross County)

★ clubs Alex Ferguson has played for
☆ clubs Alex Ferguson has managed

Stadium information as at the end of the 1998–99 season

INDEX

Photographic Acknowledgements

The author and publisher would like to thank the following for permission to reproduce photographs:

Aberdeen Football Club, Aberdeen Journals, Aerofilms, AllSport, Cliff Butler, Colorsport, Dunfermline Press Group, East Stirling Football Club, Empics, Express Newspapers, Falkirk Football Club, Glasgow City Archives, Ian Kirk, Mark Leech Sports Photography, *Manchester Daily Express/Science & Society*, *Manchester Evening News*, Mirror Syndication International, Doug Newlands, News Group Newspapers, P A News, *Paisley Daily Express*, Bert Paton, *Perthshire Advertiser*, John Peters, Popperfoto, Queen's Park Football Club, Reuters, St Johnstone Football Club, *Scottish Daily Express*, *Scottish Daily Record*, Scottish Football Association Museum Trust, Scottish Media Newspapers, SNS Group, Sporting Pictures, Elizabeth Thomson, University of Glasgow.

All other photographs are from private collections.

"I'm not Malcolm."

Harper didn't take her eyes from the man as she said, "I know."

He might look like her boss, but there was an intensity in every part of him—from his gaze to the way he held himself—that easygoing Malcolm had never had.

Then she remembered a little-discussed feature of Tate Armor Ltd.—it was jointly owned by Malcolm and his brother.

"You're twins," she whispered and he nodded.

All the pieces finally fit into place. She'd been confused about why she'd never been drawn to her boss before the night of the masked ball, and why he hadn't stirred a reaction in her since.

But she'd made love with *Nick* that night. Things between them had happened so fast that even though she'd thought she'd sensed something different about him, she hadn't had time to stop and question it. He'd kissed her and she'd melted and all coherent thought had ended.

And it was also why Malcolm had been able to act like nothing had happened when she saw him the next morning at work. Nothing *had* happened with him. Nick, on the other hand… Well, he'd rocked her world.

* * *

Tempted by the Wrong Twin
is part of the series Texas Cattleman's Club:
Blackmail—No secret—or heart—

is safe in Royal, Texas...